MULTIMEDIA STORY
FOR DIGITAL COMM
IN A MULTIPLATFORM WORLD

Multimedia Storytelling for Digital Communicators in a Multiplatform World is a unique guide for all students who need to master visual communication through multiple media and platforms. Every communication field now requires students to be fluent in visual storytelling skill sets, and as the present-day media adapt to a multiplatform world (with ever-increasing delivery systems from laptops to cell phones), students specializing in different forms of communication are discovering the power of merging new multimedia technology with very old and deep-rooted storytelling concepts.

Award-winning journalist and multimedia professor Seth Gitner provides students with the tools for successfully realizing this merger, from understanding conflict, characters, and plot development to conducting successful interviews, editing video in post-production, and even sourcing royalty-free music and sound effects. Incorporating how-to's on everything from website and social-media optimization to screenwriting, *Multimedia Storytelling* aims to be a resource for any student who needs to think and create visually in fields across broadcast and digital journalism, film, photography, advertising, and public relations.

The book also includes a range of supplemental material, including exercises for each chapter, interviews with seasoned professionals, key terms, and review questions.

Seth Gitner is a tenured Associate Professor of Newspaper and Online Journalism & Multimedia Photography and Design at the S.I. Newhouse School of Public Communications at Syracuse University, where he teaches multimedia storytelling, photography, and video journalism classes. He has served as head of the Visual Communication Division for the Association for Education in Journalism and Mass Communication (AEJMC), and serves as an elected member of the board of the National Press Photographers Association. Prior to entering academia, Gitner was an award-winning multimedia editor and photojournalist working for newspapers in Maryland and Virginia.

MULTIMEDIA STORYTELLING FOR DIGITAL COMMUNICATORS IN A MULTIPLATFORM WORLD

Seth Gitner
with a foreword by Thomas R. Kennedy

Routledge
Taylor & Francis Group

NEW YORK AND LONDON

First published 2016
by Routledge
711 Third Avenue, New York, NY 10017

and by Routledge
2 Park Square, Milton Park, Abingdon, Oxon OX14 4RN

Routledge is an imprint of the Taylor & Francis Group, an informa business

Library of Congress Cataloging-in-Publication Data
Gitner, Seth.
  Multimedia storytelling for digital communicators in a multiplatform
world / by Seth Gitner ; with a foreword by Thomas R. Kennedy.
    pages cm
  Includes bibliographical references and index.
  1. Mass media—Authorship.   2. Digital storytelling.   3. Broadcast
journalism.   4. Online journalism.   5. Interactive multimedia.
6. Reporters and reporting.   I. Title.
  P96.A86G58 2015
  070.4′3—dc23
  2014048781

ISBN: 978-1-138-85576-2 (hbk)
ISBN: 978-0-7656-4132-8 (pbk)
ISBN: 978-1-315-72010-4 (ebk)

Typeset in Classical Garamond
by Apex CoVantage, LLC

This book is dedicated to my wife, Angela, and to my daughter Sadye.

CONTENTS

FOREWORD

In this book, Seth Gitner, assistant professor of newspaper and online journalism and multimedia photography and design at the S.I. Newhouse School of Public Communications at Syracuse University, seeks to define the fundamental concepts of multimedia storytelling and help students to grasp the core craft practices necessary to produce it effectively. Methodically, chapter by chapter, he describes how different media can be employed to create valuable information in specific story elements necessary to communicate a full story to an audience. To be effective as storytellers in the new media landscape of the early twenty-first century, students will need to understand and master the use of these elements as tools. Craft practice will be essential to understanding and mastering the elements, and each chapter offers up valuable suggestions for skill-building activities designed to enable meaningful practice.

One true power of multimedia storytelling resides in its capacity to "shape shift" elements to showcase those most crucial to absorbing and acting on the story information being provided in the narrative. Individual stories can be told with unique structures, taking full advantage of the basic DNA of the platform devices being used to transmit them, as well as taking into account the motivations of the audience choosing to use a particular device in the moment to access the story.

Those are valuable opportunities to be understood and utilized by multimedia storytellers.

Multimedia storytelling permits the full engagement of the heart and mind in the audience. The intellect can be stimulated and emotions engaged so that the story message resonates and offers reasons for audiences to consider their own lives and actions. As you'll discover in subsequent chapters, this capacity is at the heart of the stories being told. Skilled practitioners know how to calibrate and adjust story structure for maximum impact, applying different kinds of narrative structure depending on the intention of the communication.

As the chapters of this book unfold, they offer full consideration of story structure and the capacity of multimedia stories to support various types of communication, ranging from persuasion through fictional entertainment to pure journalism. This is a crucial understanding that both unifies and clarifies why the transformations of the past twenty-five years have been so profound in the field of media and communications. We are now very much in a landscape where the multimedia story is the key language being used to reach an audience, whether it is to sell a product or service, encourage a new behavior, offer information that solves a problem in the moment, or offer meaningful information and insights that would transform a political or economic process. It is relevant whether one is seeking to use one's skills to entertain an audience or inform them with a piece of journalism.

A fundamental difference between multimedia storytelling and earlier forms of mass media lies in the potential for delivering interactive engagement with the audience. For the first time, media can be both highly customized and yet still reach great numbers simultaneously. Global audiences, with niche appetites and interests, can respond to stories by sharing them across social media platforms, and that information can be fed back to the storytellers, allowing them to build new kinds of relationships with the audience. Using this information, storytellers can use multiple platforms to tell different facets of a story, maintaining the attention of the audience. Also, story producers can use the reactions to fuel further creative efforts. The communication system provided by the Internet crackles with the energy of engagement. The authenticity of multimedia storytelling is part of the current that drives the energy flow. It differs from the highly processed and mediated content of the past, which was designed to fit within specific production processes and serve a more passive audience.

Further, by employing detailed observations as the basis of nonfiction multimedia storytelling in particular, and determining which media assets are most helpful to the story-shaping process, a storytelling team can better target and hold audience attention.

The chapters that describe specific areas of craft practice alternate with those devoted to explaining the premises behind specific kinds of storytelling, drawn from conversations with leading academics and industry practitioners. Gitner's range of interviews and the nature of his conversations deliver a wealth of solid information that provides deep insight into the opportunities and demands of this form of storytelling. These conversations are supplemented at the end of each chapter by lists of additional resources and key definitions. A set of review questions enables the reader to begin putting the material into practice.

As Gitner suggests at several points, multimedia storytelling builds on fusion, knitting together individual media forms and enabling formulas for storytelling best suited to a particular story, rather than demanding that stories all be filtered through a particular narrative prism. For media organizations currently involved with some form of multimedia storytelling, it means re-engineering their workflow and editorial processes. They need to move away from the "silos" that supported the mass production of a particular type of media programming and instead move to more open, fully collaborative forms of workflow. Multimedia storytelling is a collaborative art, requiring specialists working together for maximum effectiveness. Since its power lies in the capacity to fuse forms of media to tell a full story, it requires the expertise of multiple people, each with a particular kind of fluency. It also requires everyone involved to understand how each individual skill contributes to the larger effort.

In 1993, my own first true look at the future of multimedia storytelling began when I went to New York as part of an eclectic industrywide editorial team that was being brought together in the basement of the Time-Life building. A group of magazine editors had been invited to participate in a development effort led by John Papanek, then the director of new media for Time Inc. Dubbed the Open project, our task was to use all-digital tools and methods to create a magazine and CD-ROM in one week. While that may sound simple from today's vantage point, we were using tools at the cutting edge of technology at the time. Also, we were trying to simultaneously invent a workflow and production process for the execution of a weekly magazine, while also remaining true to the journalistic storytelling that typically propelled such products. This pilot effort would determine early feasibility of digital delivery of content for products that previously had existed only in print.

Meanwhile, nearly simultaneously, Marc Andreeson and a team at the National Center for Supercomputing Applications at the University of Illinois Urbana-Champaign were preparing a web browser program that would for the first time enable the display of images inline with text for something called the World Wide Web. This extension of earlier information transfer protocols, enabling computers to connect on networks known as the Internet, was about to unleash a revolution in communications first envisioned some three decades earlier in the mind and writings of Marshall McLuhan, the Canadian media critic.

McLuhan had described a media landscape where communications based on the visual and aural would exist side-by-side with text, and offer a worldview distinctly different than text could alone. As McLuhan described it, this would be the revival of "tribal" languages that offered a very different sensory impression of the world, and which were first used for communications at the dawn of modern human history. He saw the early storytelling as forms of communication that involved all our senses equally, and that were based primarily on "orality" and visual expressions of a new order, rather than the storytelling capacity supplied by text that conferred a different kind of literacy. He described his observations as "probes" designed to look at the impact of media, shaped by various technologies, on the audience. Rather than simply focusing on the content message of the information flowing through these media channels, McLuhan was trying to examine their consequences as mechanisms of information transmission.

He understood that the relationship between audience and message differed according to technology being deployed and that each media format carried a signature DNA that would shape the nature of the interaction in some profound way. While responding to the media of the moment, McLuhan was also looking ahead. From the vantage point of today's media landscape, he seems eerily prescient in some of his descriptions of what was coming.

Further, McLuhan's description of the emerging media landscape, as revisited by Paul Levinson in his book *Digital McLuhan: A Guide to the Information Millennium*, talks about how the digital landscape has altered the interplay between media elements. This point is crucial to understanding multimedia. As the elements are fused, those properties they borrow from older forms of media are altered and transformed. To fully exploit them, one needs to understand and grasp the story expressions native to the new fusions.

When participating in the Open project, I quickly became aware of how valuable sound could be as an extension of still photography. Instead of depending solely on captions to explicate the photograph, we could hear from the subjects themselves or listen to natural sound from the situation as it was being recorded. It also occurred to us that someday soon we could be mixing photography and audio with video to tell richer, more complete stories in the service of journalism.

Within five years, I was leaving my position as director of photography at *National Geographic* to accept an offer to build up "multimedia" for the *Washington Post*'s website, a separate company created to be Washingtonpost. Newsweek Interactive (WPNI). In joining the company, I was being asked to build up visual storytelling and make it valuable to our audiences as we began to shape a daily journalism product available to the digital audience encountering it on the World Wide Web. Thanks to new browsers, we could code and build pages that would showcase still photography telling stories, and present it either as a standalone effort or integrated with text on a web page.

I was determined to replicate the thorough story narrative I had learned working with photographers at *National Geographic*, and to extend it by mixing it with other media elements in a more seamless way. To extend the normal channels supplied to organize content, I proposed adding a channel for multimedia storytelling. While creating such an environment ran the risk of segregating and isolating the new form of multimedia in yet another silo, it seemed essential to create a "play space" in which the new forms of multimedia storytelling could be explored and experimented with. It would be difficult to bring various forms of media together within the confines of previously existing media platforms.

One challenge was transcending the limitation of "literalism," in which newspaper photographs merely confirm the facts of text stories rather than acting as story elements with their own distinctive power. Still photography could go further in conferring a sense of story narrative, particularly for major projects. At the same time, given that we were emerging as a companion to print-based journalism, it made sense to tap the conventions of film and broadcast media to shape the visual and aural representations we were beginning to offer. As a result, I spent a lot of time developing a documentary video unit that could co-exist and complement the visual journalism flowing naturally from the still photographers at the newspaper. Our efforts were integrated often on major projects with representations of visual data in the form of information graphics.

In the early part of the first decade of the twenty-first century, much effort went into continuing to fine-tune the processes we were using to produce stories, while also experimenting with the vocabulary and syntax being used to tell them. A crucial element of that experimentation was determining the right presentation to showcase the more complex multimedia packages. As an aside, much work needs to be done in this regard. While multimedia storytelling has matured in the past ten years, it is still in its early development as a communications format. To fully realize the potential of telling multimedia stories, we must continue to experiment with presentation. This is particularly true because the noise of the Internet and the limited time for consumption of media in increasingly busy lives makes time the new scarcity that drives the media diet. To grab and hold audience attention is more than an artistic conceit. It is a business imperative.

As I have pursued my own career interest in contributing to the evolution of digital multimedia storytelling and helping others develop their talents, I have had the pleasure of working with many professional colleagues, including this book's author. Seth Gitner and I first made contact and began a personal and professional friendship while I was working at WPNI and he was nearby in Virginia, at *The Roanoke Times*. We compared notes, shared information, met at professional conferences, and offered each other encouragement as we sought to enhance the value of multimedia storytelling to our respective organizations. More recently, I had the pleasure of being a fellow professor with Seth for two years in the S.I. Newhouse School of Public Communications. As kindred spirits, friends, and colleagues with a shared passion for this topic, we had many conversations about how best to contribute to its further evolution in and out of the classroom. Expanding on those conversations, we worked together one summer leading a group of students on reporting for the News21 project, along with fellow professors Aileen Gallagher and Jeff Passetti. Our efforts to report on the inflow of Latino immigrants to the Lehigh Valley of Pennsylvania was a multimedia story driven by initial examination of 2010 U.S. Census data.

Throughout our time at Syracuse, I was impressed by Seth's grasp of the possibilities for multimedia storytelling and his desire to transmit to students what he was observing and continuing to learn about its best practices. His heart, enthusiasm, and passion are in this book, and he has done an excellent job of producing a textbook that is both current and germane to the work of developing the next generation of multimedia journalists.

In organizing the book, he has addressed the nature of the craft practices necessary to support multimedia storytelling as well as the best structures for organizing stories. In doing so, he clearly spells out what should be borrowed and adopted from earlier forms of media used to present stories as entertainment and information. He has distilled the organization and framing of stories into core principles that can be applied to various forms of messaging, and effectively distinguishes among craft practice, story organization, and intentionality of messaging so a reader can be clear about their relationships. By asking his own questions and doing his own "probes," Gitner offers a clear blueprint for learning basics that can be very difficult to teach. It is then up to the reader to build skills to accomplish the kind of storytelling that will captivate audiences and even move them to action.

This book can also equip those studying communications with much of the literacy necessary to understand the contemporary media landscape—a landscape being rapidly changed by relentless technological evolution but also by audience demand. The need for media companies to harness social media to encourage conversation, sharing, and retransmission of their multimedia stories is one small example. At the same time, generational splits over the motives of corporations, governments, and other organizations using social media—particularly those concerns about privacy and the use of big data supplied by user interactions—are going to drive reconsiderations of how best to teach media.

Part of the challenge of multimedia storytelling is the time it takes to create content and the effort required to get it seen, heard, and responded to over the high noise level of the Internet. Filtration and curating mechanisms are inescapably part of the challenge to multimedia storytellers. It is important to stay current and recognize that no media form is truly static. Media are forever mutating, and wide-scale adoption by audiences may switch in an instant if a newer, better method comes along. Audiences are fickle, and they are always looking for the latest, newest technological shortcuts around barriers they encounter in the digital environment.

The mastery of multimedia story creation also requires a clear understanding of the tools involved and how they shape the responses of the observer. The power and capacity of these tools change along with technology, but it is valuable to get a fix on the most valuable tools at the moment. This book provides an inventory of the tools most prevalent in story creation, as well as great insights from professionals on how to use them effectively.

While the skills needed for quality multimedia storytelling can change as software evolves, certain fundamentals expressed in this book are likely to stay the same—namely, the importance of multimedia storytelling as a way to transmit valuable information that transports people beyond the boundaries of their own lives and puts them in direct contact with the larger forces that shape the human experience. At the same time, while social, political, economic, cultural, and technological forces are reshaping the world daily, there are certain aspects of being human that simply don't change, and never will. They are the stuff of great stories.

My hope is that readers of this book will be able to find that part of the multimedia landscape most amenable to them as a career opportunity, whether it is photography, audio recording and editing, video production, video editing, creation of still or motion graphics, digital platform presentation design, or even software development and the quest for new ways to shape and translate "big data" as the basis for narrative storytelling. These are but a few of the career paths integral to multimedia storytelling.

It is likely that as technology continues to evolve, the forces shaping the media landscape will continue to morph and twist in ways that McLuhan first described. To navigate the roiling waters of the current media environment, and to embrace the exhilarating nature of unfolding multimedia storytelling possibilities, read this book and learn to do it yourself.

Tom Kennedy is an internationally known visual journalist with extensive print and online journalism experience, including positions as managing editor for multimedia at washingtonpost.com, director of photography at the National Geographic Society and deputy graphics director at *The Philadelphia Inquirer.* He has created, directed, and edited visual journalism projects that have earned Pulitzer Prizes, as well as Emmy, Peabody, and Edward R. Murrow awards.

Kennedy is currently the executive director of the American Society of Media Photographers, and served previously as managing editor/digital for *PBS NewsHour.* Prior to that, for two years, he was on the faculty of the S.I. Newhouse School of Public Communications at Syracuse University as the endowed Alexia Foundation chair for documentary photography.

Kennedy serves on the board of directors of the Eddie Adams Photo Workshop, and has served on the board of visitors for journalism programs at the University of North Carolina–Chapel Hill, the University of Florida, and the Knight Center in the School of Communications at the University of Miami. He is currently an independent consultant on multimedia strategies for digital platforms, and teaches regularly at universities and multimedia conferences.

A cum laude graduate of the University of Florida, Kennedy worked early in his newspaper career as a photojournalist at *The Gainesville Sun* and the *Orlando Sentinel Star.*

Thomas R. Kennedy

PREFACE

Our Own Storytelling

Stories are a vital, inescapable part of our early learning and development. As children we listened to stories with our ears, watched them unfold with our eyes, and even drew our own stories from our imaginations. Our adventures with storytelling began before we even got to kindergarten. Our family members read stories to us before bed, from fairy tale adventures like *Peter Pan* to stories about princesses like *Sleeping Beauty*. Before we could read, the images in our books assisted us in learning how to understand the words.

Later, when we came home from school and our parents asked what had happened that day, our response was likely to take the form of a story: This happened, then this happened, and then this happened—a linear recitation of events.

The multimedia storytelling of today still involves words and pictures, but it also encompasses much more. You are about to begin a journey into its inner workings, exploring storytelling that brings together still images, moving images, color, sound, speech, music. You will learn to tell compelling stories for any platform.

What Is This Book About?

As present-day media adapt to a multiplatform world, many different forms of communication are becoming intertwined. This book is about how to tell stories using these different forms, stories that are to be distributed in the digital space.

From cave drawings all the way up to videos on a mobile device, some things have stayed constant. The media might have changed, sometimes drastically, but many concepts remain the same. Stories are about emotion; they track character transformations through time and life. They involve problems—commonly known as conflicts—and they leave the viewer content with a satisfying end.

You will grasp the principles, many of which you may already have learned and put to work in your own life, and they will help you tell stories going forward. From social media strategies through broadcast journalism, the ideas and principles of storytelling remain the same.

What Is Meant by Multimedia Storytelling?

The Merriam-Webster dictionary defines multimedia as "a technique (as the combining of sound, video, and text) for expressing ideas (as in communication, entertainment, or art) in which several media are employed; also: something (as software) using or facilitating such a technique" (Merriam-Webster Online). Not included in the definition but nonetheless essential are still pictures.

So multimedia is a form of communication that serves our ears, our eyes, and our minds simultaneously, or in quick succession. It's not just the medium of audio, or of video, or of the written word. It's a combination of these elements to maximum effect.

What This Book Does for You

Whether your stories will be viewed on a corporate website or on distribution networks such as YouTube, Vimeo, or social media services, this book will explore the ins and outs, steps, rules, equipment, and guiding principles of making a successful short multimedia story. Regardless of your chosen specialty, communicating in the digital age requires fluency in photography, film, and videography, among other skills, and the ability to combine these media into an effective story. This textbook will help to provide you with these basic skills.

Multimedia Is Storytelling, Not Technology

Technology allows anyone with access to it to engage in visual storytelling. Virtually anyone can now tell a story that is recorded and saved for all to see. It's this capability that gives this book its purpose.

We live in a multiplatform world, and we're hit with other people's messages everywhere: on television, in print, on the web, on social media. It is important to be able to pick the best tool in your tool box to tell the story you want to tell. With new technology constantly being introduced to the market, and as new platform services arise, the gathering of stills, audio, and video to tell a story is becoming the norm. This book blends multimedia technology and skills with visual storytelling concepts to create a resource for anyone in a communications field.

Becoming Conversant with Storytelling

From journalism to filmmaking to YouTube video advertising to flash mob videos posted virally for public relations campaigns, there is a growing need to be conversant with visual media tools and skills. In today's wildly expanding world of multimedia storytelling, where nearly everyone carries a video and still camera right in their phone, budding professionals need to acquire the skills to use the various types of gear effectively. It's not just having the gear that really matters. The gear is everywhere now. It's how one uses it.

With the capability of storytelling comes great power. We can craft stories to emotionally engage with viewers wherever they may be. But audiences have new expectations as well. For one thing, they expect multimedia content to communicate or tell a story across multiple platforms. This book is set up for you to learn core multimedia storytelling concepts for all forms of communications, without setting one form of multimedia or communication above the rest.

Whom This Book Is For

This book aims to make digital communicators into visual storytellers. It is for beginners, and not necessarily even those headed for the filmmaking profession.

Because beginners tend not to have access to professional camera, audio, or lighting gear, or to high-end editing software, we aim specifically at ways of producing professional-quality videos using the tools that are now more readily available. Your camera may be small, or even built into a mobile phone. You may have rudimentary audio recording equipment, and simple desk lamps and natural light. You may need to use open-source software that is essentially free.

None of that is a problem.

The emphasis here is on the intangibles of multimedia storytelling—the ideas and concepts that the gear helps you put into practice. Learning how to see, craft, and understand stories is a vital part of digital communication. This book is designed to provide a solid base in visual storytelling, enabling you to move forward into the more advanced realms of digital communications.

Sources

Merriam-Webster Online. Accessed September 5, 2014. http://www.merriam-webster.com/dictionary/citation.

ACKNOWLEDGMENTS

I am not sure where this book would be without the support of my wife, Angela, and my daughter Sadye. They stuck with me and encouraged me every step of the way. And this book would not have become a reality without the encouragement of my older brother, Dan Gitner. Whenever I thought all was lost, my brother was there to pick me up and tell me that it could be done. I have always looked up to him, and I appreciate all he has done for me. I'd also like to thank my father, Gerry, and my mother, Deanne, for their guidance throughout my life. I would never have gotten to where I am without their encouragement.

Prior to academia I worked for *The Roanoke Times* in Roanoke, VA. Upon leaving there and entering the academic world, I realized how many expert and creative colleagues I had worked with in my "previous life." Specifically, my former editor Mike Riley transitioned me from a photojournalist to the paper's multimedia editor. Carole Tarrant believed in and facilitated my ideas for innovation in storytelling. Throughout the writing process I was nudged, pushed, and guided by my friend Alec Rooney, whom I also met at the *Times* and who served as a freelance development and copy editor throughout the entire writing process. Artwork, graphics, and drawings were provided by Chris Obrion, another good friend and a former *Times* graphic artist.

I'd like to specifically thank my department heads at Syracuse University, Steve Davis and Bruce Strong, for their help in guiding me to this point in my career in academia. I'd also like to thank my mentor in teaching multimedia storytelling, Peter Moller, who guided me through my first semester teaching what is now contained in this textbook. Very special thanks are also due to the dean of the Newhouse School, Lorraine Branham, for bringing me from the newspaper world to the academy. Also deserving of sincere thanks are my research assistants, Geoff Campbell, Ethan Backer, Omnia Al Desoukie, and Dan Cheng, for their help in finding material for this book.

Many of my Newhouse colleagues were generous in sitting for interviews, passing me ideas, or opening up their Rolodexes. My thanks go to Evan Smith, Richard Breyer, Doug Quin, Larry Elin, Bill Ward, Michael Schoonmaker, Robert Kucharavy, Roy Gutterman, Maria Russell, Edward Russell, Brian Sheehan, Suzanne Lysak, Mike Davis, John Nicholson, Barbara Fought, Larry Mason, David Sutherland, Bob Lloyd, Melissa Chessher, Aileen Gallagher,

Sean Branagan, Jon Glass, Tula Goenka, Joe Blum, Jason Kohlbrenner, Amy Falkner, and Wendy Loughlin.

In addition, I'd like to thank all of the faculty, staff, and students at the S.I. Newhouse School of Public Communications at Syracuse University. This book is based in large part on my experiences in the classroom while teaching at this institution.

Also, a special thank-you goes to Juliet Giglio for assisting me with her knowledge of screenwriting, to Mike Mount from Canon USA Inc. for his technical expertise, and to my former colleague Tom Kennedy for writing the foreword. I spent a summer living with Tom and working on a class project for which he and I supervised the visual content. I learned a great deal from him, and I appreciate his efforts toward the success of this textbook.

I'd also like to thank all of my photographer friends who contributed their work for this book, and added so much real-world value to it. My longtime friends Toby Metcalf and Jim Harmon were not included in the book but gave me great advice. I'd also like to thank my editor at *News Photographer Magazine*, Donald Winslow, who first asked me to write a column about multimedia storytelling. The column keeps me centered in photojournalism, an industry that is ever-changing but that I know and love so much.

For the past several summers I have co-directed a Multimedia Storytelling Workshop for the National Press Photographers Association (NPPA). Many of the people interviewed in this book have been part of this project, including Will Sullivan, my friend and co-director, and much of my knowledge about multimedia storytelling comes directly from it. It is a real gift to have such a wonderful group of experts volunteer to teach what they know each summer.

I'd also like to thank my former acquisitions editor, Suzanne Phelps Chambers, for her hard work and guidance during the writing of this textbook. As a new author I found her expertise greatly helpful. She was instrumental in helping to find my book reviewers, Rich Beckman from the University of Miami, Curt Chandler from Penn State, and Susan Kirkman Zake from Kent State University. I appreciated their time, ideas, and input as they helped to shape and organize the final product.

Finally, I'd like to offer my sincere thanks to all of the professors at the Newhouse School who came before me. Many of the people interviewed in this book are graduates of Newhouse, and the professors helped make the graduates into the experts they are today.

Last but not least, a special acknowledgment is due to Michel du Cille, an acclaimed photojournalist and former assistant managing editor for photography at the *Washington Post*. Du Cille died December 11, 2014, of an apparent heart attack while covering the Ebola epidemic in Liberia for the *Post*, while this textbook was in production. His method of categorizing photographs is a vital component of visual journalism and is featured in Chapter 1. Du Cille will be greatly missed as a friend, colleague, and pioneering visual storyteller.

ABOUT THE AUTHOR

Seth Gitner is an assistant professor in both the Newspaper and Online Journalism and the Multimedia Photography and Design departments at the S.I. Newhouse School of Public Communications at Syracuse University. He is a former multimedia editor and multimedia photojournalist at *The Roanoke Times* and roanoke.com in Roanoke, VA. His work in multimedia journalism has won numerous awards, including Documentary of the Year from Pictures of the Year International and the Scripps Howard Foundation Web Reporting Award. A well-known volunteer for the National Press Photographers Association, he is a recipient of a President's Award, the Joseph Costa Award for outstanding initiative, leadership, and service, and the Robin F. Garland Award, which recognizes outstanding service as a photojournalism educator. He writes a monthly column on multimedia storytelling for the association's monthly publication, *News Photographer Magazine*.

1 VISUAL STORYTELLING

In What Ways Do We Think about Visual Storytelling Every Day?

In this chapter you will learn

- What is shaping the landscape of image-making today
- What is considered a "moment" in image-making
- Reasons for recording images
- Parts of an image that go beyond the ordinary
- Ideas on how to compose a photograph or frame a video
- What makes an image not just good, but great

Introduction

Anyone who is at least twenty-five years old has virtually grown up with a camera in hand—if not a professional camera, then at least a rubber-coated, Fisher-Price toy model that can be dropped or thrown by a two-year-old.

From nearly the moment of birth, or at least on the delivery-room scale, children are having their pictures taken. The dark, shiny eye of a camera lens might be the first thing many babies see in their lives, even though they can't know what it is or what it is doing. Children now have a variety of handheld games that involve taking pictures. My daughter, five years old as this is being written, has an iPod Touch that takes photos. Her mother calls her every morning from work, on FaceTime, to chat while she is getting ready for school. Image-making is part of our lives every day, and every image shot, be it video or a photo, can be shared instantly with friends and family, or anyone else. The recorded image has become ubiquitous. One reason for this is the technological marriage of photography with our means of communication. With virtually every mobile phone capable of shooting high-definition video and still photos, most people are never without a camera, charged and ready, in hand, with a huge storage capacity and the built-in means for worldwide distribution.

Yet there is a big difference between capturing daily life in a random way, and actually using visuals to communicate in the way that this book is all about:

to tell stories. True visual communication takes skill, practice, vision, and the mastery of certain concepts. While the random shooter may occasionally capture a picture or video that is interesting and conveys a deeper meaning, the professional visual communicator must be able to do it consistently and on-demand. This skill is not magical or inborn, even if some people take to it more quickly than others. It is learned.

The capture of visually interesting content is at the foundation of visual storytelling. Whether one is shooting video or taking a still picture, the ability to see and evaluate with a well-educated eye is vital. The best way to start acquiring this education is with still photography. Once the art of the still photograph is grasped—the delicate balance of subject, composition, "moment," light, and a handful of other factors—one can begin to understand how a story can be told through a picture, a series of pictures, and finally a moving picture. So while everyone and their brother is taking pictures and shooting video clips these days, careful study of how to create a still image will begin to separate you from the pack almost right away.

This is not to say that aspiring photographers need to lock themselves into rigid rules and practices. In the book *Photography Speaks* by Brooks Johnson, photojournalism master Henri Cartier-Bresson is quoted as saying, "I hope we will never see the day when photoshops sell little schema grills to clamp onto our viewfinders, and the Golden Rule will never be found etched on our ground glass" (148). Cartier-Bresson lived until 2004. When the iPhone came along in June of 2007, its camera app had a setting that allowed (and still allows) the user to overlay patterns onto the LCD screen that assist with photo composition. Makes you wonder what Cartier-Bresson might have had to say about it.

So you'd be hard-pressed these days to find anyone who doesn't have a camera, usually in a mobile phone and used on nearly a daily basis. Everyone is taking pictures, shooting video, and sharing it. Social networks have instituted the "like" button, which for some people means, "hey, good picture," and for others is just an acknowledgment that yes, they have seen it.

Evan Vucci, a staff photographer for the Associated Press covering the White House in Washington, D.C., sees people all the time using mobile phones at events to capture the president of the United States shaking hands. Before the camera phone, he and other members of the press corps were the only ones sending photos out into the world from historic and newsworthy events. Now, he says, he is actively competing with a slew of other people who are also trying to get "the shot." Vucci describes the scene:

> You know where the president is going to be, you know this epic thing is going to happen, and you worked really hard to get there . . . you've pushed through the crowd, you've gotten to your spot, and you're like, 'this is the spot,' and it is going to happen, and the next thing you know you put your camera up and—guess what happens—you have fourteen people with iPhones and iPads in front of you that are completely blocking your shot.

This proliferation of devices is a major challenge faced by the student starting out in visual communication, which these days is nearly always digital, or computer-based. Yet at the same time, now that visuals are a means of sharing messages more quickly and widely than ever, visuals such as information graphics, video, and photographs are more powerful than ever before.

The big challenge is to stand out from the crowd and leave others behind, while at the same time using the new power of the image carefully and responsibly. We'll begin by talking about the essential elements of still photography, with some references to video skills sprinkled in.

The Evolution of Visual Storytelling

Visual storytelling is evolving. It has progressed from images being formed on glass plates, to rolls of film, to digital images and video being taken with mobile phones, the technology of which will be discussed later. Photographs are no longer viewed only in printed or projected form; they are e-mailed and shared on Internet sites and social networks. Audiences that were once built through print media are now being reached on an even wider, faster scale via Facebook, Twitter, and Instagram, through both still images and motion.

"There are people out there who are not photographers, but everyone has something to share," said Melissa Farlow, a photographer who has worked extensively for *National Geographic* and was part of the Pulitzer Prize–winning team that documented desegregation of the Louisville, KY, public schools. As she explains:

> Going through someone's life and seeing their children or what their lives are about. It's just interesting to see what is important to them, what they decide to take a picture of and put up. It may not be fine photography, but it is interesting.

Of the current state of photography, Farlow said, "It's probably a more important time than ever for people who do have something to say or visually want to have an effect on communicating with images."

The need to share imagery using social networks is rapidly becoming ingrained in us as humans beings. What used to be an expensive, exclusive hobby (photography) has become a feature of everyday life. "What every five-year-old has on their iPod Touch is a capture device. It's a device that captures a visual or moving image and transmits it to the world. It's not really a camera," said Richard Koci Hernandez, an assistant professor of journalism at the University of California at Berkeley. "A camera traditionally was a dedicated device with lenses and shutters," he explained, but "all of these things are being increasingly stripped away. I think all of these things we see look like photography, and it feels like photography, but it's not photography."

In 1986, photographic historian and teacher Beaumont Newhall stated in his book *The History of Photography*:

> More and more people are turning to photography as a medium of expression as well as of communication . . . the direct use of the camera for what it can do best, and that is the revelation, interpretation, and discovery of the world of man and nature. The present challenge to the photographer is to express inner significance through outward form.
>
> (294)

From concert venues to ballparks to birthday parties, camera phones are taking over and becoming part of who we are and how we save—and savor—our memories, via stills or video. This is mostly because cameras are easier to use, more powerful, and more omnipresent than ever before. Pocket-sized consumer cameras with film cartridges and the old, plastic "flash cubes" have been around for decades, but when cameras were integrated with mobile phones the ability to have a camera available at all times really became the norm. Likewise, the makers of mobile phones are morphing into camera manufacturers. In a Twitter post on September 10, 2013, Philadelphia-area writer and blogger John Gruber (@gruber) wrote, "Apple has quietly become a leading camera company. Huge amount of demo time for 5S camera." He tweeted this during Apple's announcement of the iPhone 5S.

Today, in nearly every single moment and every situation that you might find yourself, someone will have the capability of pulling out a camera and capturing what is happening.

"We live in a world of what I call the ubiquitous nature of the camera; everybody has one, whether they want one or not, and you have generations being forced to participate in a visual conversation of still photography," said Kenny Irby, a senior faculty member in Visual Journalism and Diversity at The Poynter Institute in St. Petersburg, FL:

> For me the challenge is: How are these visual stories, what I call 'visual vignettes,' able to be interpreted and processed? [They are more than] just sources of information or more, deeper narrative. [They are an] informational source . . . that people will pay for and spend time with.

Smiley Pool, who won a Pulitzer Prize as a photographer at the *Dallas Morning News* for aerial images of Hurricane Katrina's aftermath in New Orleans, is now chief photographer at the *Houston Chronicle*. Pool wonders if the current upsurge in photography has a depth to match its breadth:

> As technology becomes ubiquitous, the question is going to be, Do people get past simply recording with these devices and then slapping a filter on it in Instagram, because it kind of looks cooler, and then calling it a day? Or do the masses start getting bored with that? One of my photo editors once challenged me to quit taking pretty pictures and start telling stories.

The Resurgence of Visual Image-Making

Being a good image maker requires practice, which often means shooting whatever scenes and subjects come up in the course of daily life, using whatever camera is on hand. If you are fortunate, a string of daily assignments for a publication will serve as your practice field. Whether just practicing or shooting on assignment, however, photographers' work is a reflection of how they see the world and assign importance to all its countless scenes. Whether the shooter is a first-day beginner or seasoned professional, their work represents their take on life. It is an art, a mode of creative expression, an example of the very human pursuit of capturing reality and seeking out larger truths behind it.

For many photographers, the now-omnipresent mobile phone camera is a way to get back to thinking about photography on a daily basis. "There are times that I see something in the light or the composition; something about it strikes me," said Melissa Farlow of *National Geographic*. "Most of the time I am on a mission or I am on an assignment, or I am working [and] there is something of a reason that I am there to photograph," she explained:

> Growing up as a journalist and approaching it that way, I am less of the free spirit—of responding to light. If anything, having the ability to do it with your phone frees you up to find that place again where you just were excited about the visual aspect of it.

The proliferation of cameras through the rise of digital technology and the mobile phone is driving a resurgence in photography and video. Instagram and other photo-sharing networks, which allow instant and unlimited sharing of images and video on the web, have become a huge part of what people do with their communication devices. Instagram even allows some off-the-shelf image manipulation with settings such as "inkwell," "toaster," "sutro," and "1977," among others. It also allows GPS tagging and captioning of images, further enhancing the communicative power of photography and video storytelling.

Socially Networked Image-Making

"Instagram is not about photography; it is about visual communication," said Richard Koci Hernandez, who has over 180,000 followers on Instagram. "If I walk down the street and see some graffiti and shoot that, it is visual communication." Once a photojournalist for the *San Jose Mercury News* who carried a camera every day out of necessity, Hernandez has come to see the mobile phone as a game-changer in how he expresses himself through photography. But rules still apply, he says. "Photojournalism has a deep, deep responsibility to represent situations as close as humanly [possible] . . . with as little filtration as possible. We filter by lens choice too." As a photographer, he said, you must stay "as true as you can to the color of the situation, not [go] overboard with saturation and contrast."

Hernandez's photographs on Instagram are beautiful; any photographer looking at his images would be impressed with his quality of vision. But at the same time, for Hernandez, the camera is just a tool, much like the professional DSLR he used when he was a newspaper photographer:

> I take pictures because I am trying to leave a visual record of my time here, with intent. I shoot a lot of pictures throughout the day. What I leave on social media or share is very edited and very specific—very much my statement that this is my day, and this is how I saw the situation. I see what I am doing as a visual journal.

National Public Radio has long been known for its impeccable and pristine audio storytelling. Now, with the move toward digital, more and more of its reporters are aware that their stories will have more shelf life and go farther in social media if they have visuals attached. Many of them now carry iPhones

Figure 1.01 Photography is an act of capturing life as we see it. Whether a photographer is carrying a film-based camera, a DSLR, or an iPhone, it's not the camera that chooses what will be captured; it's the photographer. (Photo by Lynn Johnson)

and have point-and-shoot cameras. One reporter, Ari Shapiro, has over 50,000 followers on his Instagram account. "We need our reporters— if they are doing unique stories and we don't have the resources to send a photographer—we need them to make images and make good images, and a lot of them do an exceptional job," said Kainaz Amaria, NPR's supervising producer for visuals. She added that once a reporter starts thinking visually for one story,

> they start thinking visually for every other that they do, and that is really exciting. . . . You've opened up a new way for them to think about their story. Radio *is* visual, setting up the scene; they are painting a picture for you.

But while technology has spread the camera far and wide, giving it vast new powers, it is not the key to taking viewers to that next level of seeing. *National Geographic* photographer Lynn Johnson describes this fact with a uniquely photographic image: "Technology does not really enable us to go deep. It is really about moving fast and staying on the surface. It's like being a water bug moving across the surface and not really going underneath and investigating." Chosen by her peers in 2013 to receive the *National Geographic* Photographer's Photographer Award, Johnson summed it up: "You have to have the courage of looking outward as well as inward."

What Is a Moment?

A moment is exactly what it sounds like: a very short bit of time. But it is a very important bit. It is the instant when an event is crystallized, when its significance is packed into a fleeting incident, expression, or gesture. A daughter heading a soccer ball while playing with her father on the front lawn, a baby opening his eyes for the first time, a girl's first kiss: They are all moments—sometimes sequences of moments—within a larger event that capture the pure essence of that event. Visual storytellers must look for moments with their cameras, whether they are shooting video or stills. Moments are crucial to arousing emotion and empathy in the viewer.

Video cameras on average capture a series of stills at anywhere from twenty-four to thirty frames per second. Video footage therefore yields a series of images, leading up to and following the moment. One is able to see the before and the after of the recorded moment, in a miniature story arc. A still camera, however, captures only a single moment, and requires a different kind of mental skill on the part of the photographer.

"A still moment is one frame in twenty-four; a sequence tells how that person got to that moment," says Mick Davie, an independent videographer who freelances for the National Geographic Channel. "Every sequence or scene has a beginning, middle, and end. Every scene should have that journey throughout the scene."

Capturing moments in still photography requires an almost instinctive situational awareness. The still photographer must be a keen and patient observer of the world and of life, watching and waiting and able to anticipate what will happen next—what must happen next.

In his book *Words and Pictures,* Wilson Hicks describes a moment: "The 'most meaningful moment,' or, as it is also referred to, the 'exact instant,' is a climax of, or a significant point in, action or emotion or both together" (122).

Bob Lynn, the author of *Vision, Courage and Heart,* a book about management principles in visual journalism, gave his own definition of the moment in still photography:

> A moment is where you feel something or you reveal something of the personalities of people or what that person is dealing with. It might not be with another person; it might just be a little moment of reflection, of the head down or something, that reveals something of that person. It could be good or bad.

To capture a real moment requires a special kind of trust between subject and photographer. The subject must be unconcerned about the presence of the photographer, maybe even unconscious of it. The photographer must be the proverbial fly on the wall, waiting and watching for the moment to occur. To shoot too much could be a major mistake. It could cause the photographer to stop being an observer, and to miss the moment as it happens.

"My video is collections of moments," said Davie:

> I tend to think of moments in video more as punctuation marks of a scene that build toward a climax. Once the climax happens, everything else comes together. Light is brilliant, the background is significant, it comes to a crescendo like a wave breaking.

Tips for Identifying Moments

- Be patient. Unguarded moments can happen at the most unexpected and awkward times.
- Arrive early and stay late—moments don't happen only when it is convenient for you. You need to be on the ball all of the time to be present at that perfect moment.
- Strive to read the facial expressions of your subject. You know what someone looks like when they are ready to cry. Look for signs of building emotion in people's features and don't shy away from them.
- Study human interactions; observe and interpret body language. Body language helps to tell a story.
- The moment can be the scene itself. Think about the sense of place, which is not always just an "establishing shot." Don't just shoot the front of a building. Wait for some kind of action to take place. Wait for a revealing moment.

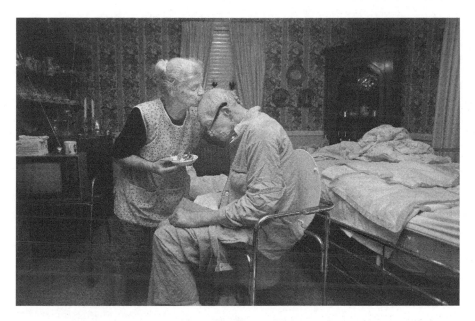

Figure 1.02 Capturing a real "moment" requires a special kind of trust between subject and photographer. The photographer must be the proverbial fly on the wall, waiting and watching for the moment to occur. By the time Emma and George were forced to face the terrible pain of Alzheimer's, "Oma" had spent her entire life giving herself to her family. She wasn't about to let hospital staff or anyone else care for her ailing husband. She knew that with help from her family she could give "Opa" better care and more love at home—and she was right. (Photo © 1991 Bruce Strong)

Exercise: Getting Familiar with Moments

Use this exercise as a way to practice and get familiar with the camera. Take a minimum of fifty different images over the course of seven days that reveal your life.

Show where you live, whom you live with, your daily interactions with friends and others, your activities. Shoot indoors and outdoors, at night and during the day, at all hours of the day, including rising and going to bed.

Take lots of images. Experiment. Get as familiar as possible with all of the camera's buttons and dials. While shooting, take notes about your experience with the camera for later discussion.

- If using a DSLR: Try out all of the camera's exposure modes. Take a variety of images, some in Program (P), some in Aperture Priority (A), and some in Manual (M). Try different lens lengths and different focus settings.
- If using a mobile phone: Try different apps; get familiar with the device as a camera and not merely as a phone. Think of it as a capture device only. Try different settings that might alter the image as it is viewed.

Being a Good Image Maker

Images are all around, from advertising at the bus or subway stop to the grocery aisles. They are a big part of our everyday media consumption. "The problem that we are dealing with today [is] that we are being visually bombarded with bulls—," said Jim Colton, a former photography editor at *Sports Illustrated* who has been acknowledged as one of the 100 most important people in photography by *American Photo Magazine*. As he explains,

> We are in sensory overload because everybody has a camera, or a camera phone, or smart phone. Everybody has the ability of creating an image, and they feel that there is a need to share it with the world. It comes down to being a good image maker and realizing what a good image is.

There is much, much more to capturing an image or video than aiming the camera and pushing a button. This kind of image-making leads to the overload and visual clutter that Colton describes. A true visual storyteller must think about what is in front of the camera and, possibly even more importantly, why it is there.

"Whether you are editing or you are shooting, I don't think it really matters. As long as you realize what you are shooting for," said Colton:

> That's a huge difference. It's a different mentality if you are out covering the Super Bowl for *Sports Illustrated*, knowing that the primary concern . . . is getting great images for the magazine, but also knowing that they are going to put stuff up on the website right away. You have to have sort of a different mentality.

Shooting Visual Imagery for a Reason

Despite the trends that have arisen from mobile-phone picture taking and image-sharing services, photography is not about taking random pictures, adding filters and color, or making images look like they were done in a darkroom in 1976. Photographs don't need fake light leaks or filters to look cool, any more than a dozen effects pedals make a good electric guitar solo.

If you have been shooting pictures or video like this, it is time to recalibrate what you know about image-making and to understand that what is in front of the camera matters and has significance, both before and after it is recorded. Carrying a camera comes with responsibility; captured images have the power to influence opinions and emotions, and even to shape history. Whether carrying a camera that shoots still photos or video or both, shoot imagery with a purpose. Make sure to always have a reason to capture the content in front of your lens.

"In this day and age where everybody has a camera of some sort—at the very least almost everybody has a camera phone . . . everybody thinks they know how to take pictures," said four-time Pulitzer Prize-winning photojournalist and editor William Snyder. When he was director of photography at *The Dallas Morning News,* the paper's photography staff was awarded the Pulitzer Prize for Spot News Photography for their coverage of Hurricane Katrina. Now a professor and chair of the photojournalism program at Rochester Institute of Technology in New York, Snyder says that when he was young, "Photography incorporated 'magic.' There were potions and darkrooms and all of that stuff. But now everybody can take pictures."

Part of capturing a good visual is being able to see the world from another perspective, breaking a scene down into levels of content, to the extent of mentally wireframing it and seeing with a new level of understanding. What is before your eyes at any given moment is more than just scenery, people, or objects. It all has a past and a future and a purpose, and is loaded with meaning. It is part of a greater storytelling experience.

In his book *Photography Speaks,* Brooks Johnson quotes Gordon Parks, the American photographer, musician, writer, and film director:

> I feel it is the heart, not the eye, that should determine the content of the photograph. What the eye sees is its own. What the heart can perceive is a very different matter. For me at least, the camera is a technical device, used as a writer uses his typewriter or as a painter uses his brush.
>
> (216)

Say you are outdoors at sunset, and someone remarks about how the light is golden. You might whip out the phone and take a shot of the sunset. Anybody can do that, but something will be missing. The shot will not say anything about the light itself—the light that moved you to try and capture an image. For a viewer to react emotionally to what you saw, what originally got you excited, takes reflection and consideration. Sometimes it even takes genius. To make the scene meaningful and memorable, look for an object that the light is hitting. Look for something that is being transformed by that light, just as the light transformed you. And don't just take a photo of the light hitting the object and call it a day. Continue to look for meaning and substance. Seek out what others might miss in the scene.

"To me, a good image, to be effective, has to be affective," Jim Colton said:

> What that means is . . . you have to be moved in some visceral way. You appreciate the image for its content, its beauty, its composition. It makes you feel something: mad, happy, laugh, cry. It makes you do something. That's what a good picture is, on all levels, whether it is sports, news, features—whatever it may be.

Maybe the light is glinting on the metal poles of a swing set in a backyard, calling to mind childhood and swinging on the jungle gym bars just before going in for dinner. Maybe it is streaming through the branches of a tree that will soon lose its leaves to winter. Maybe there are actually children in the tree, with the light shining around them. This level of thinking elevates that original idea of a sunset. It's no longer just a time of day, or a set of atmospheric conditions. There is storytelling to be done, and substance and meaning to be explored. There is a reason to take this particular image, which goes beyond taking pretty pictures. The image has an important reason to exist.

"Go past the surface, what we called eye-candy pretty pictures—pretty pictures that are colorful and well-designed but have either no emotion and/or news value," William Snyder said.

Whatever ends up on the film, the tape, or the memory card, a photograph or video should have a story—a visual reason to exist that can be grasped, told, felt. Even a photograph posted to a social network should have an element that engages the viewer, and keeps it from being a dull picture of a tree, a rock, a bunch of people. There must be an element that makes the viewer want to know more.

Tom Franklin, a photojournalist with the *Bergen Record* in New Jersey, photographed John F. Kennedy's grave for the fiftieth anniversary of his death. Franklin said he spent a day or two looking for the images that told the story best. "The grave plaque—where it is engraved, it is flat on the ground. It was difficult to get a strong picture of people looking at the grave, and for it to be obvious that it was Kennedy's grave," said Franklin, known best for his photograph of the American flag being raised in the wreckage of the World Trade Center after the Sept. 11, 2001, terrorist attacks. His iconic image was later made into a postage stamp. For the Kennedy assignment, Franklin said, he waited until late afternoon, when the light was just right. Deep shadows were crossing over the plaque's face, creating a shot that could resonate with readers:

> Because of the light and the shadow it created a little bit of mood. Anybody with an iPhone would have been able to make that picture if they knew how to properly expose their iPhone for the highlights, so that the shadows were properly exposed. But I don't know if people would have had the patience or the dedication to stick with it until the picture was just right.

"Make pictures that go beyond just showing stuff happening," said Mike Davis, a photography editor and educator who holds the Alexia Chair for Documentary Photography at the S.I. Newhouse School of Public Communications at Syracuse University.

The art of understanding what a photograph is, and how it can affect a viewer, is not limited to photographers. Sometimes the real meaning of an image is recognized and drawn out by a picture editor. Davis was a picture editor at both *National Geographic* and at the White House, and was twice named newspaper picture editor of the year. He brings to that task an understanding of all forms of imagery and how they relate to viewers and the world.

"The only thing that really counts is *why* you are making a picture, what are you trying to say about what you are dealing with. If there isn't clarity in that part of the process, you are simply executing a mechanical process," he said. Davis supports the view that the *how* and *why* of taking pictures should come before the details of how to use the device in your hands, which is a simple matter of reading instructions and pushing buttons. Five-year-olds can be taught how to take pictures with mobile phones, just as they can be taught to tie their shoes. Seeking out meaning is a weightier task.

"People typically start by photographing facts," Davis explains:

> That's another way of saying, photos are verbs or nouns—they simply show something happening or present it as a fact. Facts almost never make interesting photographs. Imagine if you read something that only contained verbs and nouns and the words you need to connect those two, how boring would that be.
>
> Traditionally, typically, you start teaching people how to make pictures by teaching them how to use the machinery and the software now. To me, that is completely ass-backwards. If you are not trying to develop people's minds, their sensitivity to nuance, their power to convey important messages, to understand complex subjects, to [strive] to say something about the world, then you are pointing them down a dead-end path. . . . What distinguishes us as professionals is the ability to say things that matter, things that connect with an audience.

Photographs can be evaluated according to different sets of criteria, but usually those criteria run along the following lines:

Color

Color plays a very large part in the mood and meaning of an image. A picture of a homeless man in a bright and colorful setting has a much different feel than one with a drab and monotone environment. Bright and vivid colors at a wedding send a different message than subtle, pastel hues. If the photograph is of a cake, there are colors that can, in a scene, make that cake appear more or less appetizing. Color can be lush, balanced, and pleasing, or it can be harsh and discordant. It can also be muted and pale, or warm, or cold. Black and white photography—the complete absence of color—has a feel and mood all its own. To a point, a photographer has control over color. Camera settings can affect it, and subjects can be moved into more or less colorful surroundings. Always be aware of what the color in an image will convey to a viewer.

Davis recommends asking questions about color. "If you remove all other aspects from a given scene and see only the color, how much of the scene is helping convey the quality that I want to convey, and how much is detracting from it?" he asked.

Figure 1.03 Color plays a very large part in the mood and meaning of an image. Camera settings can affect it, and subjects can be moved into more or less colorful surroundings. In this photo, which unfortunately had to be printed in black and white for this edition, a three-day-old yellow duckling peeks over a curbstone at Lake Spring Park in Salem, VA, trying to rejoin its siblings after their mother hopped into the water. The yellow duckling made it to the top of the "wall" after two failed attempts, and the ducklings joined their mother in the pond. (Photo by Josh Meltzer, *The Roanoke Times*)

Light

Learn to think about the light that falls upon a subject. It is, after all, the very thing that makes photography possible. Good light is vital to good exposure, and to effective image enhancement later on.

Is the light coming from above or from the side? Light from below has a very distinct effect. Are you outdoors and able to take advantage of natural colors, diffusions, and intensities of light? The light will also affect the angle at which to photograph a subject. Learn to seek out light and its opposite, shadow. It's one of the hardest things a photographer must learn—to see light in a creative way. To understand its role in photography is to harness a powerful force.

Learning about light will lead to thinking about it in new ways. Light can help to tell a story. If you are shooting a portrait of someone in an office setting, a nice glow from a window might make things look comfortable and pleasant. Maybe there are blinds in the room that can throw shadows on your subject, adding depth, texture, and meaning. The lonely, upward glow of a desk lamp could evoke long hours and hard work.

Not understanding light causes immediate problems. Photographing that wedding cake with the main light source behind it, say, silhouetted in front of

Figure 1.04 Light can help tell a story. Good light is vital to good exposure, and to effective image enhancement later on. UW-Whitewater cheerleaders' shadows are cast along the visitors' side of the Salem football stadium during the 2006 Stagg Bowl Division III national football championships in Salem, VA. (Photo by Josh Meltzer, *The Roanoke Times*)

a window, will yield a cake-shaped blob of darkness. Davis says it is important to recognize "at what angles or points of view should I not even try to make the photograph, because the light [is poor] or is contrary to what I think is important to convey what is happening."

Silhouette

A silhouette is produced when a foreground subject is exposed against a brighter background, making the subject darker than the background. It is a technique that should be used sparingly, and can often be seen as cliché. A silhouette can be used to add drama and emotion to a video—a dark subject contrasted with a sunny sky can say a lot. For example, if the story is about a factory closing in a town, a good storytelling image would be a shot of faceless workers silhouetted in a factory doorway. The shot would not center on one person, but be representative of the entire workforce and what they are experiencing.

Moment

As described earlier, a moment is that single point in time at which action may be stopped to tell the story in a single frame. It is the peak point of events, where images seem to make the most sense. The classic example of what a

Figure 1.05 A silhouette is produced when a foreground subject is exposed against a brighter background, making the subject darker than the background. A fisherman casts his net off of Playa de la Malvarrosa in Valencia, Spain, as the sun rises over the Mediterranean. (Photo by Luke Rafferty)

Figure 1.06 With a paddle tucked in his belt, Red Boiling Springs, TN, school principal Charles Biles reprimands two students for their conduct on a school bus. Biles chose to "just give them a scare," instead of using the paddle. (Photo by Stephen Cherry)

moment can be is a photograph of one boxer landing a hard punch on another. It would probably take a camera that shoots upwards of five or ten frames per second to capture this (what used to be called a motor-driven camera, before digital), but it would be the ultimate example of a captured moment that would otherwise pass too quickly to be really seen.

"More power comes from the coming together of multiple occurrences, the completion of the frame. This creates moment value," says Davis. "How successful, how *dimensional* is the moment's value, as opposed to just saying is there a moment? It's a piece of cake to get a moment, compared to having a high-value moment."

Composition

Take the boxing example, and imagine capturing that "high-value moment" of the boxer's glove striking the chin of the opponent. Thinking about the image on additional levels, there are multiple elements that could make it even better. For example, is one of the coaches visible in the corner, yelling or grimacing in reaction to the punch? Is a member of the crowd leaping up with hands in the air, mouth open in a shout? Such elements add greatly to the storytelling value of the image. It's not just the presence of these elements in the scene, but where they are placed within it that help an image to become great.

"Photographs have geometry—geometric planes that intersect and triangulations that intersect in different planes of the frame. They are three-dimensional,"

Figure 1.07 Each Armenian Christmas, on Jan. 6, nuns participate in a pageant held in Yerevan, Armenia, to mark the country's status as the first nation to adopt Christianity as its national religion. (Photo © 2010 Bruce Strong)

says Davis. "Successful photographs feel three-dimensional, and the reason that happens is because things that are in the foreground connect to things in the background in . . . triangulated ways."

Distance

Think about how far a subject is from the camera. When having a conversation with someone it is usually better to be close to them than far away—it creates a more intimate relationship. More information can be conveyed, body language and facial expressions read, mannerisms understood. The same idea holds true when photographing someone. Standing ten feet off, a photographer is going to have a different relationship with a subject than if the person is three feet away.

When making images using a camera, think about using the whole space within the frame, easily defined as the LCD screen on the back of your camera. Even when using a mobile phone, think about the edges of the frame and what is inside it.

"You tend to not think about 'how far away we are' as an aspect of conveying something about what we are photographing," says Davis, on how distance is a variable that tends to be overlooked. "It's usually, 'I need to stand this far away from something to show it.'"

Figure 1.08 Distance from the camera can affect the sense of intimacy with a subject. Rebecca Chupp, 6, rides in a horse-drawn Amish wagon with her father, Larry, while gathering dried hay in a pasture in rural Giles County, VA. (Photo by Josh Meltzer, *The Roanoke Times*)

Exercise: Getting Familiar with the Action of Photography

Go to the grocery store and pick up several types of fruit: apples, oranges, a pineapple. Back at home, put them in a bowl.

Using whatever kind of camera you have, photograph the bowl of fruit two or three times a day, in your living space, at different times: morning, afternoon, night. Do this for one week. As you take images, think about what has been discussed so far.

> **Color** – What color are the objects? What color is the bowl? What color is the background? How do these colors change over the space of a day, or a week?
>
> **Light** – Is the light coming from a window or from a lamp? Is it overhead light, or the glow from a computer screen?
>
> **Moment** – Stationary objects can have moments, too. Is there a time of day when a ray of sunshine peeps through the window, illuminating the scene?
>
> **Composition** – Are you shooting from above? From the side? Are you putting the entire bowl in the shot or just part of it? Are you seeing angles, lines, and shapes?
>
> **Distance** – How far is the camera from the bowl? What does the lens do to the bowl as you get close, or as you move farther away?

Make a habit of thinking about these elements every time you shoot. All of the resulting images should be different from each other. No two should be the same. At the end of one week you should have about twenty-one images.

MEET THE PRO

Evan Vucci, Staff Photographer, The Associated Press, Washington, D.C.

Based in Washington, D.C., Evan Vucci is a photojournalist and multimedia producer for the Associated Press. He has been recognized by Pictures of the Year International, NPPA's Best of Photojournalism Competition, the White House News Photographers Association, The Associated Press Managing Editors Association, and the national Edward R. Murrow awards. He ventured into multimedia journalism in 2007 and is committed to developing short- and long-form documentary storytelling at The Associated Press.

Figure 1.09 Evan Vucci, staff photographer for The Associated Press in Washington, D.C. (Photo by Jason Reed)

Evan Vucci loves photography, whether it be shooting for the AP wire or for his

(Continued . . .)

(. . . *continued*)

Instagram account, which has over 58,000 followers. Vucci loves visual image-making.

"I sort of look at Instagram and everything else as a celebration of photography. If you truly love photography, it is awesome to get on Instagram and see you have the world in your pocket," said Vucci, who says he has been intrigued by many of the people he has found on Instagram. "You start to talk to these people, and you are like, 'Holy cow, this guy is an accountant, but he is an incredible photographer.'"

Vucci said he sees Instagram as a visual journal for his everyday life. "As far as communicating what I am doing that day and what is going on, it's awesome. It's like my diary." Vucci said he often posts Instagram images to his personal account from his day job working for the AP, which can involve anything from shooting a congressional meeting at the Capitol, to covering a Washington Nationals baseball game, to photographing a speech that the president is giving in the Rose Garden of the White House.

It's not just a matter of getting to the sidelines at a game or to the front row at a press conference. Vucci knows that to do his job day in and day out, he has to be able to deliver photographs that will work in newspapers and on websites across the country:

> I am responsible to, sort of, get the bread and butter of things. So if there is a new commerce secretary that is being announced, I need to have a headshot for everyone's files. I need to have him or her shaking hands with the president of the United States.

Many of these photographs are admittedly nothing special—just informational, mechanical chores that Vucci needs to do because it is his job. Vucci tries hard to get those things out of the way early in a shoot, so that he can "really start looking for those different moments," he said.

On assignment covering the White House for The Associated Press in late 2013, Vucci was with the president of the United States at the memorial service for former South African president and anti-apartheid icon Nelson Mandela, held at FNB Stadium in Soweto, near Johannesburg, South Africa. He said, "You know you have a responsibility to document that and show the world what is happening . . . there is a responsibility to do your job and to be the eyes of everyone." Vucci said he traveled with the White House press corps for eighteen hours on Air Force One to South Africa, getting shots of President Barack Obama entering and leaving the plane, and for five minutes during his speech. "Some days you get the bull; some days you get the horns," said Vucci of the experience. He said he was most proud of one picture from that experience:

> There was one moment where the president was getting ready to walk out, and I got two frames off, of him just sort of waiting there. He took

(*Continued . . .*)

(. . . continued)

a quick moment to sort of gather his thoughts . . . it was just like he was sort of taking it all in [the passing of Nelson Mandela]. That's what it seemed like to me, and the picture sort of shows that . . . At the end of the day it is about heart and whether or not you are connecting with people.

For photojournalists, taking pictures is a job. With that job comes a great deal of responsibility to the eventual audience, whether the story at hand is a heated issue at a local town council, a Christmas parade, or an event at the White House.
"You are on the frontlines of history," Vucci said.

Figure 1.10 President Barack Obama waits to walk to the stage to speak to crowds attending the memorial service of former South African president Nelson Mandela in Soweto, near Johannesburg, South Africa, in December of 2013. (Photo by Evan Vucci, The Associated Press)

Framing the Image for Stills and Video

Elliott Erwitt, who works with the respected Magnum Photos cooperative and is well known for his photographic moments of dogs, says this about photography:

It's just seeing—at least the photography I care about. You either see or you don't see. The rest is academic . . . it's how you organize what you see into a picture . . . Photography, as I see it, is simply a function of noticing things, nothing more.

(quoted in Danziger and Conrad, 89)

Portrait photographer Arnold Newman was very much influenced by the Dutch painter Piet Mondrian, whom he used to watch paint. In the book *Interviews with Master Photographers,* Newman is quoted as saying,

> What is composition? It's the way the picture is pulled together, the way the picture works. There are no rules and regulations for perfect composition. . . . The more you show of a person's environment, the more you'll know about the person. Space is interlocked with vision.
>
> (Danziger and Conrad, 125)

Image makers need to make sure that everything in front of the lens is important and needed, but they also need to be alert to anything that might distract from or harm their image. Everyone has taken a picture of someone, then realized later on that a streetlight, tree, or sign seems to be protruding from the subject's head. Or how about shooting a photograph of a student sitting at a desk in a classroom, and then realizing that the head of a person sitting behind the subject seems to be sticking out of the subject's shoulder?

These problems are easy to remedy by moving up, down, or to the side, and changing the vantage point. Just because you are six-foot-one does not mean that every photograph needs to be shot from that height. But before they can be avoided, such problems need to be recognized, and this takes practice and awareness. A great feature of digital cameras is that the LCD displays a picture just as it will appear when captured, which gives even less reason to commit flaws in composition.

As Henri Cartier-Bresson wrote, "Composition must be one of our constant preoccupations, but at the moment of shooting, it can stem from our intuition, for we are out to capture the fugitive moment, and all the interrelationships involved are on the move" (34).

A Mantra for Seeing Within the Frame

For retired U.S. Air Force Master Sgt. Jeremy Lock, seven-time Military Photographer of the Year, thinking visually day in and day out was not just a passion, but a job. Flying from one hot spot to another all over the globe, Lock brought the Air Force's stories back home to the friends and families of personnel. He learned visual storytelling as a student in the Syracuse University Military Photojournalism program, where he first learned an important mantra: *Fill the frame, control the background, and wait for moments.*

"You literally say it out to loud to yourself every time you pull that camera to your face," said Lock, explaining that the first two parts of the mantra are now automatic. "It just seems like I don't do that anymore," he said. "I just look for the moment."

An experienced photojournalist, Lock has also seen his share of combat—all through the viewfinder of his camera, while also carrying a gun. But moments come in many forms, he said:

Once you start looking for it . . . It might not be that in-your-face moment. It now becomes that quiet, subtle touch, that mother tucking in the daughter to her bed, or that certain body language or expression that you wouldn't normally get.

Lock holds true to his roots as a visual storyteller, warning young people not to get caught up in the new tools and gadgets of the latest and greatest technology: "There's no meat and potatoes . . . learn how to tell a story through photographs first . . . before jumping into the gee-whiz kind of things," he said.

Fill the Frame

All standard cameras are equipped with a lens and a viewfinder, which nowadays consists of an electronic LCD screen offering a live view of whatever the camera can "see." In many ways, this makes it easier to think about what is in the frame. When framing a friend in a dorm room, are you going to put them smack dab in the middle of the frame?

That would be the natural tendency for a beginning photographer. The more seasoned shooter will be thinking in terms of story. What will this picture be trying to say? What other details in the room might convey the subject's personality, situation, likes, or dislikes? Are the subject's arms or feet cut off by the edges of the frame? Should they be? Is there too much head room,

Figure 1.11 An important part of balancing content within the frame is paying close attention to the background. Once recognized, background problems are as easy to avoid as moving the camera a little, this way or that. City and county firefighters of Roanoke, VA, battle a house fire at 7th Street and Dale Avenue in the adjacent town of Vinton, VA. (Photo by Josh Meltzer, *The Roanoke Times*)

making the picture awkwardly weighted and diminishing the subject? The frame of a camera offers only a small amount of space to work with. Don't misuse it, or let it go to waste. Seek the perfect balance between the content that can be captured, and the size and shape of the space available to capture it. As the saying goes, Content is king.

Control the Background

An important part of balancing content within the frame is paying close attention to the background. It is a natural tendency to zero in on a subject and disregard all else, but most background problems are merely distractions that take away from a photograph. Always be alert to what is behind the subject. A poster on the wall or a desk lamp might not be much of a distraction in the moving world of the present, but once an image is captured, every quirk and error of composition will be there to see. David Sutherland, who first formulated the *fill the frame, control the background, and wait for moments* mantra and has taught photojournalism at Syracuse University for more than thirty years, said of his beginning photography students, "Never as 'happy snappers' have they ever looked beyond their subjects to see what is behind."

Lights in the background should also be avoided. Fluorescent lights can look like bright, hovering spaceships in a picture. Unless the bright rectangles serve as graphic elements, they surely are not going to be content, and the

Figure 1.12 Terrence Palmer (left rear) and his groomsmen get dressed in the basement of Exousia International Church before his wedding ceremony in Roanoke, VA, in August of 2010. (Photo by Jared Soares)

camera should be moved to keep them out of the image. Lights move viewers' eyes away from the subject, which should be the center of attention.

Once recognized, background problems are as easy to avoid as moving the camera a little, this way or that.

"When I say, 'control the background,' sometimes you control it by eliminating everything you can, and other times you control it by putting all the details that you need in it, to help set the scene," Sutherland said. "I call it photographing the stage that our actors play on. Sometimes the stage is really important for the understanding of the audience."

Wait for Moments

Being a photographer requires some interpersonal skills, which develop over time. A photographer needs to build up good enough relationships with subjects to understand body movements, identify emotions, and anticipate reactions. Sometimes the better moments of a shooting session arise from the relationship that develops with your subjects. They understand you, and you them.

This working relationship is fertile ground for moments. Moments are fleeting, by definition, but they are the gold that the photographer is panning for. "A moment is when the action is at an emotional peak and we see humans at their highest and lowest, happiest and saddest," Sutherland said.

Figure 1.13 For this shot the photographer waited until the smiling boy could be placed in the exact center of the action of the other children playing. The boy's smile takes the photograph to the next level, focusing the fun and excitement of the overall image. (Photo by Sam Dean, *The Roanoke Times*)

It will not be possible to see a moment and then fiddle with technical things like exposure or focus. Those things need to be taken care of in advance. The photographer's mind needs to be calibrated to understand when a moment is coming, based on what his or her eyes are seeing, so that the signal to shoot can be relayed to the brain in time. Like shooting the ball through the hoop in a fast-moving basketball game, it is an intuitive process in which everything seems to come together out of focus and willpower. Great compositions include great moments. Great lighting in composition happens during great moments. The essence of being a photographer is to feel all of the elements come together, and to capture a great scene that goes to that next level, transforming a pretty picture into a storytelling picture.

Adopt the mantra, and think about how to take a picture in this order: Fill the frame. Control the background. Wait for moments. Arching over all three actions is the matter of content. Does the subject have substance? Does it have real value? Will this photograph be worth a viewer's time? Will it hold the viewer's attention? Will there be visual impact? Is the image artful? This is the content a photographer must seek out and deliver to the viewer.

The concept applies to video as well, if in a slightly different way. The videographer is also waiting for moments to occur, but will capture them as they take shape (before) and resolve (after). The videographer is able to capture the onset of the moment, the moment itself, and the moment's aftermath.

LEARN THE MANTRA

- **Fill the frame:** Put everything that you want the viewer to see in the frame. Make sure there is a reason for all that is included.
- **Control the background:** Are there elements in the background that are distracting, or that will detract from the viewer's experience looking at the image? Or does the background enhance the storytelling qualities of the image?
- **Wait for the moment:** Look for meaning as you follow the action in front of the lens. It is hard to define, but it is the engaging, telling, and emotional content that we relate to as human beings.

 ### Exercise: Photographic Composition

Your assignment is to "Shoot the Five Senses." Look for images that represent either one or all of the senses: touch, taste, smell, hearing, and sight. Shoot a lot of images, at least fifty.

Make sure to think about the mantra while shooting

- Fill the frame
- Look for moments
- Control the background

Look for vantage points above or below eye level to make these images

- Step out of your comfort zone; meet new people.
- Make a point of talking to the people you photograph. Prepare for this in advance if you need to.
- Use your legs to zoom. Do not use a digital zoom that does not zoom optically.

Evaluating Photographs

While photography for many people is about recording the world as they see it, there needs to be "some kind of methodology and rubric to value it at a higher level of execution," said the Poynter Institute's Kenny Irby:

> The documentary storytelling and reporting that I have participated in, and the legions of folks who have gone to school and studied and practiced at a level where it is about service . . . It is about sharing understanding for the world to make decisions, not just to experience in the moment . . . That's the challenge that we have: making sense of it, not only in media organizations but in the societies that we live in.

The photography department at the *Washington Post* had their own system of talking about photographs that were to be used in the newspaper, called "The Language of Photography in the Newsroom." Designed by former assistant managing editor for photography Joe Elbert, the system gave *Post* photographers four categories of images to keep in mind as they shot their assignments. Three-time Pulitzer Prize–winning photojournalist Michel du Cille, who was an editor at the paper when the system was being used, said, "As picture editor, I used it regularly as a system to teach our staff (including a top word editor) and others the language of photographs."

The Language of Photographs

A handout the picture editors distributed to the photography staff listed the four categories into which journalistic photographs can be divided:

Category 1: Informational

This is the lowest standard for photos. The photographer was there, pressed the button, and got an image. This type of photograph does not say much more than that the shooter arrived on time and that the event actually occurred. But it can also be a photo that identifies things in the most basic, factual way, such as a CEO standing in his office, the sign outside a corporate headquarters, a piece of real estate that is for sale. Sometimes scoffed at by photographers who want to do more to show their talents, the informational photo is nonetheless an inescapable element of photography.

Figure 1.14 An informational photograph presents things in the most basic, factual way. (Photo by Mitch A. Franz)

"The best way to describe [it] is fairly basic, not fancy, creative, or super-creative. But it is a basic, here-is-what-we-are-looking-at photo," said du Cille.

That being said, offering informational pictures only, or settling for them when better content is possible, will lower standards. "We will shoot informational pictures, but we know when they're needed and do not see them as standard," du Cille explained.

Category 2: Graphically Appealing

These photos usually occur when a photographer gets an informational assignment, and then tries to "jazz things up" through clever composition, angles, blurs, or other effects. "These images are intellectually appealing but don't have much emotional impact," du Cille said. In other words, they can make a viewer look and think twice, but don't leave much of an impression.

Category 3: Emotional

This kind of photograph shows the subject in an emotional light, or the mood and style of the shot elicits some kind of emotional reaction from the viewer.

Figure 1.15 Shapes and patterns within an image can make it more interesting. Nearly thirty of Andrew Gillespie's Roanoke Catholic School classmates shaved their heads to support him as he lost his hair during chemotherapy treatments for osteosarcoma, a type of bone cancer. (Photo by Josh Meltzer, *The Roanoke Times*)

Figure 1.16 The Olympic Games offer plenty of instances of winning and losing, and either one is an emotional event. Emotion intensifies a photograph and the story it is telling. (Photo © 2010 Andrew Burton)

It could be a child crying while getting a flu shot, or the reaction of a rabid football fan to a touchdown. Images like this take patience and intuition to capture, and they create real excitement, joy, sadness, or tension in the viewer. Human beings tend to be innately sensitive and fine-tuned to the emotions displayed by other humans, and photos like this play on that instinct for high impact and a lasting effect.

Category 4: Intimate

This is a scene that feels very personal and private, in which the viewer might feel almost voyeuristic. But since it is a photograph, the viewer is allowed this intimate, insider view. They may forget that they are looking at a photograph, so captivating is the subject and moment. Such images usually occur only after large amounts of time have been spent with a subject. The person being photographed has become comfortable with the photographer's presence and allowed them to capture a very unique moment. "You know it when you see it," du Cille said.

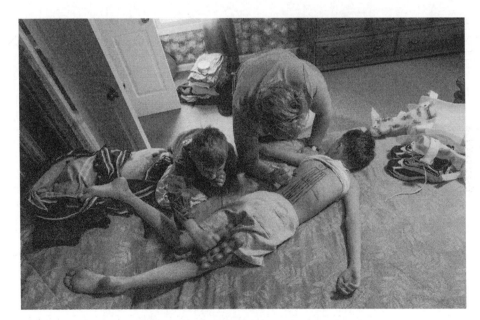

Figure 1.17 When subjects are so caught up in what they are doing that they forget the photographer is there, very intimate, up-close, and personal photographs are possible. Cooper Tyree runs a toy truck along his brother Jacob's legs as their mother refreshes the marker diagram for her son's radiation treatments for a tumor in his spinal cord. Jacob eventually lost the use of his legs, but he went on to become a nationally ranked wheelchair basketball player. (Photo by Seth Gitner, *The Roanoke Times*)

Exercise: Four Categories of Pictures

Take a minimum of fifty different images over the course of a week that are examples of the Four Categories of Pictures.

You'll definitely need to venture out of your comfort zone to get these images. They are not likely to be found in your everyday life. You may need to do some thinking and make prior arrangements to find topics that will yield images that qualify for the higher levels. Shoot indoors and outdoors, at night and during the day.

Make sure to shoot five separate situations that have the following traits: *Then, move into combining more than one of the traits in the same photograph.*

- Informational
- Graphically appealing
- Emotional
- Intimate
- Combination of one or more of the above*

* Extra credit

Chapter Summary

We're humans—we all think visually by default.

How much has photography changed in the past few decades? We used to have photo albums to preserve our "Kodak Moments." Pictures were regarded as a priceless commodity. Whenever there is a fire or flood, one thing that always seems to get mentioned is images that have been lost forever—print images that were never scanned and sent to the "cloud" of distributed digital storage.

These days, however, everything is photographed from every angle, by virtually everyone. Flickr is filled with images of people's new shoes, and the dishes they eat at every meal. Wearable cameras, perhaps improvements on the now-defunct Google Glass, will make everyone's daily life a photo album or even a broadcast show. When entire lives are being recorded, it makes for a lot of visual noise. To stand out from the masses and be a true visual storyteller requires a finely honed visual skill set that separates you from the pack. It's something that cannot be acquired purely via the latest technology.

It used to be that professional journalists were just about the only ones recording images of newsworthy events. This role is being increasingly taken up by "citizen journalists," people who are on the scene with a camera and a means to broadcast what they shoot—that great, "tweetable" picture.

Since today's photographic space is so enormous, photography is not purely about pretty pictures, the processes of people doing things, or stuff arranged on a table. It takes deeper digging to find emotional value and content that explores the more intimate and human moments of life. Learn to do this digging, and capture what gets dug up, and the scene in the viewfinder will become meaningful to the viewer. Go beyond button-pushing, and into the realm of the visual storyteller. It takes skill, practice, and understanding to get deeper and more meaningful images.

 ## Review Questions

1. What are some major forces currently shaping the way images are made and used?
2. How is a "moment" defined?
3. A pleasing kind of light is coming through a window. How can it be shot to take a viewer to the next level?
4. What does it mean to "fill the frame"?
5. What are some things that make an image graphically appealing?
6. Have you ever been in a situation that would generate an emotional image? What kind of situation was it?

 ## Key Terms

Camera phone – A digital camera built into a cellular phone. Camera phones have contributed to an explosion in digital photography.

Composition – The arrangement of subject(s), surroundings, and background in an image.

Color – An essential element of photography that results from the different powers and wavelengths of light across the spectrum. Color can have a large impact on the mood, feel, and even meaning of an image.

Distance – The space between the photographer and subject. Distance can have a large effect on the mood and meaning of an image.

Emotional image – A photograph that portrays vivid human emotion, and subsequently evokes it in the viewer.

Fill the frame – To strive for the perfect balance between meaningful content and the space available to capture it.

Graphically appealing image – An informational image in which an attempt is made to present the subject in a creative, interesting, attention-grabbing, or otherwise insightful way.

Informational image – A photograph that records a person, place, thing, or activity, nothing more.

Intimate image – A truly rare and powerful photograph conveying emotion and meaning that a viewer could not otherwise experience.

Light – Photography is the recording of light hitting our world and everything in it. It makes photographs possible. Knowing its qualities and behavior is essential to multimedia storytelling.

Moment – A time, sometimes very brief, when subject, activity, composition, and light all come together in harmony to capture the emotional essence of a scene.

Sources

Amaria, Kainaz. Conversation with author, April 9, 2014.

Cartier-Bresson, Henri. *The Mind's Eye: Writings on Photography and Photographers.* 1st ed. New York, NY: Aperture, 1999.

Colton, Jim. Conversation with author, December 3, 2013.

Danziger, James, and Barnaby Conrad. *Interviews with Master Photographers.* New York; London: Paddington Press, 1977.

Davie, Michael. Conversation with author, February 23, 2011.

Davis, Mike. Conversation with author, December 4, 2013.

du Cille, Michel. Conversation with author, December 3, 2013.

Farlow, Melissa. Conversation with author, December 6, 2013.

Franklin, Tom. Conversation with author, December 7, 2013.

Gruber, John. Twitter post. Accessed after September 10, 2013, 1:55 p.m. http://twitter.com/jgruber.

Hicks, Wilson. *Words and Pictures.* New York: Arno Press, 1973.

Irby, Kenny. Conversation with author, December 9, 2013.

Johnson, Brooks. *Photography Speaks: 150 Photographers on Their Art.* 1st ed. New York, NY: Aperture Foundation; [Norfolk, VA]: Chrysler Museum of Art, 2004.

Johnson, Lynn. Conversation with author, December 9, 2013.

Koci Hernandez, Richard. Conversation with author, December 18, 2013.

Lock, Jeremy. Conversation with author, December 16, 2013.

Lynn, Bob. Conversation with author, December 6, 2013.

Newhall, Beaumont. *The History of Photography: From 1839 to the Present.* Completely rev. and enl. ed. New York,. Boston: Museum of Modern Art; Distributed by New York Graphic Society Books, 1982.

Pool, Smiley. Conversation with author, December 5, 2013.

Snyder, William. Conversation with author, December 2, 2013.

Sutherland, David. Conversation with author, December 9, 2013.

Vucci, Evan. Conversation with author, December 9, 2013.

2 STORY STRUCTURE
How Do You Tell a Story to Be Made into a Film?

In this chapter you will learn

- What a story really is
- Types of stories
- The basic requirements of a story
- Parts of stories
- Mapping a story with an arc
- How to structure a story with a beginning, a middle, and an end
- Differences between a report and a story

Introduction

All stories have the same basic characteristics. They have a place and time, whether it is "once upon a time," "a long time ago, in a galaxy far, far away," or simply "last week at my house." They have characters that display basic human traits and foibles, whether they are rabbits, toys, reindeer, teapots and candlesticks—or just humans like us. Every story also has a plot, or a sequence of events involving the characters and tied together by order of occurrence, cause and effect, or just chance.

Stories have other vital characteristics, but first let's get even more basic. Stories are about change, going from one state to another. That's because life is about change, and growth. But life can also be a confusing, fly-by-the-seat-of-the-pants thing that doesn't allow time to learn from what is happening around us. Perhaps that is why people like stories so much. They are a way to look at and make sense of life from a safe distance, from a comfortable chair or theater seat. They are literally "slices of life" we can enjoy and learn from, and in which we can invest our emotions with no risk of personal harm or loss. The struggles of the characters become our own for a time, even producing laughter or tears, and we see the catalysts that change their lives and move the action along. But at the end (or in the middle, for that matter) it is always possible to get up and leave the theater, shut the book, or turn off the computer, tablet, or television. Stories are therefore a valuable and sought-after commodity. Pretty much everyone is up for a good story.

Stories can be categorized in a number of ways. One very important division is fiction versus nonfiction.

Fictional stories are based upon a scripted, designed reality, usually for the purpose of education or entertainment. They do not seriously claim to be real. In the visual realm, they are often a collaborative effort of many people, including writers, directors, actors, cinematographers, and film editors.

Nonfiction stories in the visual realm are things like documentaries and news reports. The events are historical and actual, the characters real. A rough, flexible "game plan" or story structure strategy is usually mapped out before shooting begins, for these stories must be captured in the moment, without staging or even much planning, as they happen. To stage anything in a news report is to veer into the world of fiction and betray your viewers' trust, and even violate the rules of ethics.

So while fiction storytelling is a challenge to the imagination, nonfiction storytelling can seem even more difficult, especially to the beginner. It is one thing to imagine a story and put it down on paper, but another to go out and trap a real one in the wild, so to speak. Yet, as a visual storyteller, this is exactly what you will need to do. It takes effort and practice. It also takes a special kind of understanding.

A great way to build this understanding is to start with the freer, less constricting world of fiction, and see what makes made-up stories work.

Narrative Storytelling in Fiction and Nonfiction

Any business report or research paper benefits from narrative storytelling. Good narrative storytelling sparks the curiosity of readers or viewers, touches their emotions, and subsequently engages them. No matter what type of story it is—a news report, a profile, or a feature—adding narrative will pull the audience in.

In his book *Writing for Story*, Jon Franklin says, "Remember that narrative tells your story and that your story, like the people and events upon which it is based, is a living thing—and life is a constant change" (136–137). Being a "living thing" means a story also needs to happen naturally, in a way that makes the audience feel they are discovering it for themselves and not being spoon-fed or lectured to. An important mantra of storytelling is, "Show, don't tell." To put an audience into a scene, care is required in deciding what they should be shown or allowed to find out, and when. In multimedia storytelling, this is in large part a matter of visuals. Viewers would rather take in visuals and form their own comprehension of what is unfolding than simply take someone's word for it. In nonfiction especially, therefore, you need to "be there." To allow a viewer to experience something, you will need to experience it too, and share it with them. In fact, there is a lot to be gained by a viewer not even really noticing you are there, telling the story.

How Fiction and Nonfiction Storytelling Overlap

A journalism or public relations student may have little or no desire to "waste time" learning about fictional stories. They need to look past that. They need to realize that fiction storytelling is simply storytelling with full control: The teller of a fictional story can truly make all of the elements of a great story come together. In nonfiction, it is much harder (if not impossible) to arrange the facts to make the story you want. So when starting out as a storyteller, it is a good strategy to first master the elements of fiction before moving into the more challenging realm of nonfiction. The realms do overlap in some very important ways, and clearly share some characteristics. These shared characteristics are covered in detail in the sections that follow.

Setting

Fictional and nonfictional stories both have a setting: a place and time for the action to take place. Setting needs to be established early on, so that the audience does not become lost or confused. People have an inherent need for this information before they can give themselves over to a story. The discussion of cinematic shot types found later in this book includes the all-important establishing shot, which begins nearly every film, fiction or nonfiction. Once viewers know where and when the action is taking place, their attention can then be directed more fully to the next vital element: the characters.

Characters

Characters are a component of every story. They have strengths and weaknesses, and traits that can range from divine to irritating. They are good guys, villains, sidekicks, tyrants, saviors, idiots, saints, party animals, victims, or stern judges, or any other kind of person imaginable. They are people we know or can imagine knowing. They are equipped by life and history (either real or imagined) with their own personalities and quirks. They have a hand of cards they have been dealt. This hand can be very interesting. It can also change.

A strong character can even drive an entire story. As a protagonist goes through various trials, tribulations, and transformations, the character-driven story (as opposed to the plot-driven story) follows and turns on his or her actions and reactions. The character can change the focus and direction of the story, and their decisions often determine which way the story will go. If a character has a choice whether to take a job or a cross-country trip, their choice will take the viewer on a journey either way. If a character is struggling emotionally with a massive problem, we ride along and find out whether the problem is overcome and how. If the character is heading for a major fall, we go along for the ride.

In the 2009 film *Slumdog Millionaire,* a street kid in India wins the jackpot on the Hindi version of the television game show *Who Wants to Be a Millionaire?*

After he wins he is accused of cheating. The entire movie follows the boy, Jamal Malik: his past in the slums of Mumbai, and the ways he learned the answers to the quiz show's questions. We see all the events in the film for how they affect or are affected by him.

Character-driven stories are very common in news video journalism. Often an issue is explored through a character affected by that issue.

Opposite the protagonist can be the antagonist—simply the character who presents an ongoing or eventual obstacle to the protagonist. This would be Gollum or Sauron to Frodo Baggins in the *Lord of the Rings*, Voldemort to Harry Potter, the Joker to Batman, or any number of less fantastic, more human enemies.

While it is tempting to say that nonfiction stories must always have human characters, while fictional ones can also star animals, machines, toys, or supernatural beings, it isn't that simple. Every nonhuman fictional character is really just a human in disguise. No actual rabbit can wisecrack like Bugs Bunny. No plastic toy has the inflated self-image of Buzz Lightyear. They are all people we have known, or can imagine knowing. Think of the Scarecrow, the Tin Man, and the Cowardly Lion in *The Wizard of Oz*. They are just caricatures of real men whom Dorothy knows from her real life in Kansas.

By the same token, it's not a given that every nonfiction story must have human characters. Imagine a documentary about an old, abandoned car that is rediscovered and made new again. We may find ourselves feeling sorry for that car. We might feel happy when it wins a contest. We might have warm feelings about its return to glory. Still, it is the viewer who is imposing these human emotions of sadness or joy on the car—an inanimate object. It is safe to say that characters represent humans, with human emotions and personalities.

The Lead Character

A strong and clearly drawn lead character is very important to a story. The storyteller must know this character inside and out—must know the cards the character has in his hand, even if the character himself doesn't know what they are. In nonfiction settings it is not realistically possible to know everything about the main figure, but the storyteller must know the traits that will affect the outcome of the story. This can take some delving into human nature.

Everyone knows the poorly developed, stock, or two-dimensional character, and it is even worse to do this to a nonfiction story subject than a fictional one. Invest thought, respect, and research into your characters, even if they are minor players, and especially when they are actual people who do not want to be stereotyped. Suppose you are doing a short film that involves some interaction with a "typical college jock." Go beyond making him coarse, dumb, or haughty. Give him an unlikely strength, like speaking French, or a weakness he is trying to hide, like extreme shyness. If you are doing a story that involves a janitor, there will probably be a bucket, a cart, and a mop. But as simple as it sounds, janitors can be fascinating people. Maybe the janitor's night job is cleaning rooms at a school, and during the day he is putting himself through school, or she is learning to be a tattoo artist. Possible plot points could include the janitor's difficult home life with several children, school, and the decision to be away from family in order to try to make a better life for them.

In short, if your lead character is fictional, take the time to give him or her some interesting or unexpected characteristics. If your project is nonfiction, seek out the deeper traits and personalities of the subjects with whom you are working.

Keys to Good Character Development

The following are traits of characters, looked at in both the fiction and nonfiction contexts:

1. **Backstory:** In fiction, it must be created. In nonfiction, learn about the subjects of the story to be told. How did they find their way into this story? What made them the people they are? What are the origins of the character traits that affect the course of the story being told?
2. **Strengths and weaknesses:** What are they best at, worst at, and why?
3. **Personality:** Personality comes straight from a person's way of looking at life. Try to sum up a character's outlook with a quotation or saying, which could be as simple as, "Always leave them guessing," "Rules are made to be broken," "Winners never quit and quitters never win," "Life's a bitch and then you die," or, in the case of Forrest Gump, "Life is like a box of chocolates." Let the statement shape your character's response to every situation. For real people, seek out this kind of statement, even asking them outright what life means to them, what they want out of it, what they are looking for.
4. **Supporting Characters:** These say a lot about main characters. With whom do they surround themselves? With whom do they get mixed up or fight? Whom do they admire, and who admires them?

Story

Story, as the title of this book suggests, is kind of a big deal. It is a topic requiring subtopics, which it will get. Fictional or nonfictional, stories are what it is all about.

It is tempting to think that simple processes can be stories by themselves. A woman wakes up in the morning, she goes to work, she has lunch, she goes home—and the process is repeated day in and day out. A doctor treats a cancer patient according to a set regimen. A man builds a bookcase. Life is full of chronological sequences like this, which can be recorded. But that does not make them stories.

So what differentiates a story from a process, or from a simple sequence of events?

The difference is this: Stories take the viewer to new places. They tug at the emotions; they engage and make the viewer feel for the characters involved—characters all trying to play with the cards they have been dealt. This engagement is created through story structure, the backbone of all great stories from fairy tales like *Little Red Riding Hood* to motion pictures like *Gladiator* or *The Dark Knight*. Story structure is the organization of selected, key events into a meaningful sequence called a plot.

Even writing a term paper (or a textbook) requires an organized plan; you must perform research, make an outline, impose order that a reader can easily follow. The outline does for the finished product—and, more importantly, for its audience—what story structure does for stories. Without structure, stories become simply profiles about people or processes. The inner feelings, desires, and hopes of characters go undeveloped and unexplored, because we do not relate to the characters, don't care about them, and don't see them reacting to the situations they encounter. It is the problems characters run into that really define them, and involve the viewer.

Look at yourself. What have you gone through to get to where you are now? Did you have to overcome anything? Did you have difficulty with tests, like the SAT? Were there financial obstacles, biases, rivalries, or character flaws to be overcome? What still needs to be conquered? The college experience is a transformation from high-school youthfulness to adulthood (ideally) and a successful career. College students take classes that help to transform them into work-ready people. A lot of things can stand in the way of that. Forces both external and internal challenge us every step of the way, as the people we are, holding the cards we do.

We encounter problems. We must react to them. It is problems that show what we are made of, and that transform us.

Another word for problem—and the essence of a problem—is something called *conflict*. Conflict is an essential part of what is called the *story arc*.

Story Arc

The best stories seem like spontaneous, magical things, catching us in their action and emotion and becoming our reality for a time. Still, they can always be mapped out or diagrammed. The visual representation of a story is called its *arc*. An arc breaks down a story into its individual parts, but also shows how each part contributes to the changes that occur over the course of the narrative, changes that can sometimes be extreme.

In James Cameron's 1997 film *Titanic*, some big changes occur. Some are physical and geographical. The magnificent ship leaves Liverpool and heads west across the Atlantic. Eventually it hits something, stops going west, and then goes downward. That progress can be shown as a map, or an arc. But meanwhile, other arcs are tracing paths through time. Romantic tension blooms between Jack and Rose over the course of several scenes, each with its own small, inciting conflict. Class tension flares up between Jack and Rose's

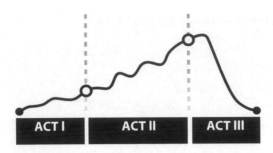

Figure 2.01 The visual representation of a story is called its *arc*. An arc breaks down a story into its individual parts, but also shows how each part contributes to the changes that occur over the course of the narrative. (Illustration by Chris OBrion)

mother, fed by the cultural and socioeconomic conflicts of 1912. A male-rival conflict arises between Jack and Rose's arrogant fiancé. This is a whole different map. It is the emotional map, and it springs from what makes each of these characters tick. It comes from what each of these characters wants most of all, colliding just like ships into icebergs.

So the story arc is a visual representation of something in the story. The tension level. The emotional level. The uncertainty level, caused by the clash of people against people or against other forces. It can take many and various shapes, but its basic form is a series of conflicts leading up to a supreme conflict that effects permanent change on a character or characters. In *Titanic*, with everything else that is going on, the character of Rose is being transformed from a timid, trapped little girl into a unique and independent—if permanently scarred—woman. The night of the ship's sinking marks the end of many people and ideas—a whole way of looking at life. For Rose, however, it is a transformational rebirth, a blooming. The name of her character was probably not chosen randomly.

Exercise: Story Arc Worksheet.

Choose a popular fairy tale, movie, or television show and map the key points of its story. Graph the amount of tension in the story with a line that rises and falls, creating a story arc.

What is the setting? _____
What are the names of the characters? _____
What is the beginning? _____
What is the middle? _____
What is the end? _____
Plot point 1: _____
Plot point 2: _____
Plot point 3: _____
What are the surprise(s) or turning point(s) of the story? _____

An Introduction to the Three-Act Structure

So we have seen that all stories have a beginning, middle, and end. This fact translates conveniently to a common model in fiction: the three-act structure. The number of acts can actually vary, but generally this structure provides a simple, straightforward framework that allows a story to be built in a dramatic way. Think of a story this way:

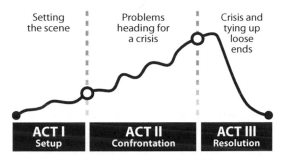

Figure 2.02 The visual representation of a story, called its *arc*, can be broken up into three separate acts. (Illustration by Chris OBrion)

Act I: Setup

- Physical and historical scene is set.
- Characters are introduced, with their situations and what "makes them tick."
- Situation (or problem, or conflict) is introduced.

Act II: Confrontation

- The characters begin to respond to the situation/problem/conflict, based on what makes them tick.
- The characters begin to strain, collide, and encounter challenges.
- Tension builds; problems snowball.

Act III: Resolution

- The characters come upon their final obstacle.
- The main character and that character's greatest enemy meet and clash.
- The story is resolved; the outcome of clash has its effects on the world and the characters, and the audience is satisfied.

Proven Structure

The three-act structure is a sturdy and proven strategy for engaging viewers. Act I and Act II naturally tend to move more slowly than Act III, when cause-and-effect tends to kick in, but this is a type of pacing that viewers expect and understand. It is not a rigid model. Climax can come at the end of Act II, or somewhere into Act III.

Within this basic structure, as the outline above indicates, are storytelling sub-elements that will be discussed later: vignettes, mini-conflicts, dialogue, flashbacks, montages, historical facts, minor characters, description. These all serve to add color, humor, and context, keeping viewers engaged and watching.

Example: Basic Three-Act Structure

To see the three-act structure in action, take a look at the children's story "The Three Little Pigs." There are four main characters: the eponymous pigs, and a villain, the wolf.

ACT 1

We meet the pig characters in their peaceful forest world and learn of their problem: having no shelter. We get to know each pig's personality/outlook on life through the way each intends to build his shelter. They are all distinctly different.

ACT 2

The pigs build their shelters according to their personalities, which range from hasty, thoughtless, and carefree to slow, deliberate, and cautious. The Wolf then enters the scene and puts each pig's shelter/outlook on life to the test. ("I'll huff and I'll puff, and I'll blow your house down!")

Figure 2.03 The children's story "The Three Little Pigs" is a good example of the three-act structure in action. (Illustration by Chris OBrion)

ACT 3

Only one pig's shelter/outlook survives the showdown. Luckily, it is strong enough to save the others and even defeat the Wolf, although in some versions of the story, the less forward-thinking pigs become dinner. The listener is left to ponder the message of the story.

Act I: The Setup

This is a good time for a closer look at each part of the three-act structure, beginning with Act I, also called the setup. It is here that the viewer finds out where and when the story is set and meets the characters. The more focused this setup is, the more quickly the viewer will enter the world of the film and become emotionally involved with the characters. Every spoken word and occurrence, everything the characters do and talk about at this stage, should be setting up what will come later. Give the viewer only enough information to start the story at a good pace. Resist the temptation to reveal information—say, huge experiences in a character's past that make them what they are—that could emerge later in a more natural way. Giving too much information at the outset can bog a story down and kill the tension and mystery that grab viewers. For the same reason, do not trouble viewers with irrelevant details, or characters and incidents that lead nowhere.

The setup should also kick-start a sequence of events that gets the story moving forward. Getting things moving quickly is especially important with web video, in which the final running time is likely to be only three to five minutes.

Don't forget that multimedia storytelling is a visual process, and to show rather than tell, even from the very beginning. You should not feel that you have to use voice-over or narration to explain things.

Examples of Setup

In director Alfonso Cuarón's 2013 film *Gravity*, the story opens with one suited astronaut working diligently on the Hubble Space Telescope while the other jets around making jokes and small talk. No one tells the audience anything, but both characters are perfectly introduced through visuals, actions, and the content of their brief conversation, perfectly believable for two trained people working in space. Then we hear mention of something that has gone slightly wrong elsewhere in orbit. The story is in motion. What happens after that will reveal much, much more about these two people.

Venturing farther out into space, look at the 1977 film *Star Wars*, in which several plot lines need to be set in motion. After the initial action sequence we meet the character Luke Skywalker, stranded in a boring, chore-filled, rural life in the middle of nowhere on the fictional planet Tatooine. He is restless and feels destined for bigger things. He is depressed about how this seems hopelessly out of reach. Through the routine chore of buying a couple of used robots, he is pulled into a galactic struggle in which we (and he) discover what he is made of. The robot-buying sequence helps set the scene while lighting the fuse on the plot at the same time.

For examples of a more formulaic approach, look at primetime television crime shows such as *Law and Order*, *CSI*, *Criminal Minds*, and others. Episodes tend to begin with unsuspecting people out for an evening stroll, usually in an urban environment, and if these characters do not fall into some kind of distress involving crime, then they meet someone who has. The criminal incident becomes the inciting incident. The rest of the show is about how that inciting incident is found to have occurred, and leads through smaller conflicts and setbacks (often new crimes that present new clues and puzzles) to an ultimate conflict with a perpetrator.

Exposition

Exposition is the addition of backstory to a script. It can be difficult to pull off without falling into telling instead of showing. There are different ways of going about it. In both fiction and nonfiction, for example, a narrator can take the viewer from scene to scene and help to connect the dots. Think of Burl Ives as Sam the Snowman in 1964's *Rudolph the Red-Nosed Reindeer*, talking right to the viewer and filling in the plot with comments and songs.

In story-driven, short-form documentaries with no narration, interviews with characters can serve this function. A lot of information can also be conveyed through natural sound, devices like the montage (to be covered later), and fly-on-the-wall, cinéma vérité–style footage which simply allows a viewer to soak up the atmosphere and scenery. Exposition can also be done through text on the screen, such as the rolling, here's-where-we-are-in-the-story text that opens *Star Wars*. Other methods include flashbacks, where the viewer is given glimpses of previous, explanatory events, or events in another time and place. A fairly recent development in television comedy is the fake documentary interview, as in *The Office* or *Modern Family*, in which a character voices his or her thoughts right to the camera during a sit-down in an out-of-the-way spot.

The Narrative Question

Every type of conflict involves a force that a character or characters must overcome. This force, and the way it is overcome, make up the *narrative question*, which builds tension within the story. It keeps the viewer engaged and determines how the characters will react to the various plot points they encounter. As tension is built through plot points, a story comes into being. The viewer's engagement builds every time a plot point occurs, raising the tension. The viewer begins to ask questions of the story itself, like, "Who done it?" "Are they going to win?" or "How will she ever get out of this?" Such questions heighten the drama and make it more and more difficult for the viewer to stop caring and disengage. Other narrative questions are more subtle and inwardly focused, such as, "Will [the main character] fall in love at the end, or will she be denied what she thought was the love of her life?" or "Will he find meaning in this suffering that has been forced on him?"

Strive to create narrative questions, and seek them out in nonfictional situations. They hook the viewer into needing to learn the rest of the story.

Conflict

All good stories, fiction or nonfiction, include a conflict in some way, shape, or form.

As human beings we experience conflict almost daily. Little children vie for toys or parental attention. We fight with our own consciences and fears when there are choices to be made. We battle for promotions, wealth, influence, lovers, glory, approval. It was mentioned earlier that all characters have things that make them tick—things that they want more than anything. These desires often clash. Is the character up against someone who is trying to achieve the same goal? In nonfiction it might be as simple as a sports trophy, although the best sports conflicts also contain elements of history, underdog status, socioeconomic challenges, physical challenges, or even racial conflict—there is something bigger at stake than just a win or a loss.

Who or what stands in a character's way? Sometimes it is the actual character. Sometimes it is society. Does someone else's goal stand in opposition? How confident is the character of victory? Is that confidence justified, or is this character in for a shock?

Stories are often made up of many small conflicts that build up to one main conflict. This isn't because someone made up this rule and it must be followed. It's because this is what *works*. It keeps viewers glued to the story, unable to disengage even if they want to. Smaller conflicts, occurring chapter by chapter or scene by scene, build the character's involvement with and connection to the story. They also enthrall the viewer, who must stay to find out who wins.

The following list gives some basic categories of conflict to watch out for.

Types of Conflict

1. HUMAN VS. SELF

This is internal conflict. The character is trying to get past something inside—a character trait, a phobia, a bias, a weakness—that is blocking the realization of a personal desire.

An example of this is the 2005 film *The 40-Year-Old Virgin*, in which the main character, Andy Stitzer, played by Steve Carell, has issues with insecurity when others in the movie find out that he is celibate, and not by choice. Andy's bout with his inner self is the internal conflict that drives the story. The supporting characters in the movie devise a plan to help Andy get past this obstacle in his life after he meets a woman named Trish. These supporting characters are essential to moving the story along, as the main character would not be moving in any direction at all without them. In his book *Supporting Character Secrets*, William C. Martell writes, "Supporting characters aren't just thrown on the page to give our protagonist someone to talk to in this scene, or someone to kiss in that big scene on page 73; they are part of the story itself" (131). *The 40-Year-Old Virgin* shows how they can be valuable allies as a character fights with something inside himself.

Another example is the film *1,000 Times Goodnight* (2013), which is about a woman named Rebecca, a conflict photojournalist who has a husband and two young daughters. She must leave behind her family every time she travels to a war zone. The story has her struggling with an internal conflict in which she must decide whether to go with her passion for telling stories that she feels need to be told through images, or to stay with the family she loves and does not want to lose.

Now picture a nonfiction piece about a heroin user or alcoholic who is dealing with addiction, a terrible struggle that often does not end well. On the surface this might seem like a case of human vs. drug. But a drug is not a character with a will of its own, or even a natural force. It would be a conflict of human vs. human appetites and inner pain—human vs. self.

Watch the trailer for *The 40-Year-Old Virgin*: http://bit.ly/40yearoldvirgin

Watch the trailer for *1,000 Times Goodnight*: http://bit.ly/one-thousand-times

2. HUMAN VS. HUMAN

Human-to-human competition is a big part of human existence, and it is one of the most common conflicts in both fiction and nonfiction. We are trained from childhood to compete against others in virtually all pursuits, to win and be the best. As our lives go on, our goals are bound to clash with the goals of others. Characters clash in the same way. Some could be seen as heroic and good, pitted against villainous and evil, but often things are not so black-and-white. Sometimes both characters have a dastardly goal. Sometimes both are striving for what they believe to be good. Sometimes the clash can even be a running joke, as in the television show *Seinfeld*, in which Jerry is locked in a long, mysterious feud with his mail-carrier neighbor Newman. No matter what the episode's plot or situation might be, Jerry always greets his rival with a venomous, "Hello, Newman," which is followed by his neighbor's mocking, scoffing, "Hello, Jerry!"

In the 1976 film *Rocky*, a hardworking, humble underdog's desire to be the best he can be collides with the desire of another fighter, Apollo Creed, to be famed and celebrated. While one could argue that Rocky is in conflict with many things, including himself, his battle with Creed has us cheering for him with the crowd at the end. The Bible is filled with vicious rivalries and conflicts, even between siblings like Cain and Abel, Jacob and Esau, and Joseph and his jealous brothers, as are the plays of Shakespeare and all of classic literature.

In the HBO series *Game of Thrones* (2014), Brienne of Tarth is a female knight who battles male opponents. Tarth proves herself worthy as a warrior by fighting in a tournament. She eventually becomes the bodyguard to Lady Catelyn Stark and becomes her "Sworn Sword," vowing to protect her.

Watch the trailer for *Rocky*: http://bit.ly/rockytrailer

Watch the trailer for *Game of Thrones*: http://bit.ly/gameofthronestrailer

3. HUMAN VS. SOCIETY

Sometimes society itself conflicts with a character's goals. Many nonfiction news stories are based on a "character" or subject who has come into conflict with societal norms—usually the law. Crime—in movies from *Bonnie and Clyde* to *Thelma and Louise*—is a huge source of fictional stories. Sometimes characters confront more negative social forces than the law, such as Abraham Lincoln battling the institution of slavery in Steven Spielberg's *Lincoln*. Sometimes it is a societal bias that creates the conflict. In the 1993 sports film *Rudy*, a small-in-stature football player earns a chance to play for the practice squad at his dream school, Notre Dame. Over and over again, Rudy is told that a person his size can't play football. He goes up against this societal norm, and ends up earning so much respect from his fellow players that they pressure their coach into letting him suit up for a game. In *The Hunger Games: Catching Fire* (2013), protagonist Katniss Everdeen is up against a violent society that treats its citizens cruelly. Katniss comes to symbolize freedom from a ruthless government system. It's her quest to be an agent of change that gets the people on her side.

Watch the trailer for *Lincoln*: http://bit.ly/lincolnmovietrailer

Watch the trailer for *Rudy*: http://bit.ly/rudytrailer

Watch the trailer for *The Hunger Games: Catching Fire*: http://bit.ly/hunger-games-catching-fire-trailer

4. HUMAN VS. NATURE

This conflict is present in every news story about storms, earthquakes, droughts, or people trying to save their homes from floodwaters. Human beings are in constant conflict with the natural world—with forces ranging from meteorites to microbes.

In the 2000 film *The Perfect Storm*, the crew of the Andrea Gail, a fishing boat, go up against an unusually violent storm that finally claims the vessel and all aboard. The movie puts the characters up against nature and its brutal force, unaware of the sheer magnitude of the storm that overwhelms them. The 2003 docudrama *Touching the Void* tells the harrowing story of two happy-go-lucky young British men who decided in 1985 to climb a mountain in the Peruvian Andes, got in way over their heads, and somehow managed to survive.

In the film *Gravity* (2013), lead character Dr. Ryan Stone is an astronaut faced with a seemingly impossible challenge: returning to earth from orbit after an orbital catastrophe kills everyone else on her mission. Alone in space, she must conquer her own fears along with nature at its coldest and least forgiving: the vacuum of space.

Watch the trailer for *The Perfect Storm*: http://bit.ly/perfectstormtrailer

Watch the trailer for *Gravity*: http://bit.ly/gravity-trailer

Act II: Inciting Incidents

Act II is often the longest of the three acts. The setup has been mostly accomplished, the characters have been established, and now it is time for some action to happen and for the narrative question to be intensified. It is a time of conflicts, twists, and building tension.

"Action" can be thought of as events, called *inciting incidents*, along a story arc. Another name for inciting incidents is *plot points*. These points keep the viewer engaged while raising the stakes for the characters. As the viewer gets more and more invested in the storyline, these incidents continue one after another in a distinct order, building engagement.

A storyteller needs to make the viewer empathetic to what characters are going through—to make the viewer care for the protagonist. Each inciting incident plays a specific role in pushing the story forward. The second inciting incident will push the story into the third inciting incident and so on, setting the stage for Act III. The character or characters are so enveloped in the story, with no hope in sight, that the viewer is now very connected and craving some kind of resolution.

In the previously mentioned crime show example, the next event to occur after the initial setup would be a set of detectives or forensic experts being assigned to the case. The experts follow the clues that they find, some arising from additional crimes. Each crime and clue becomes an inciting incident, as does each "break in the case." Each of these incidents becomes the substance of individual scenes. Inciting incidents do not have to have dialogue. They can be visuals that show action to move the story along.

In the 1999 movie *The Matrix*, Act II begins in a completely different reality from Act I: Neo has been sucked in, and his entire life proves to be something other than what the viewer—not to mention Neo himself—could ever have imagined. The inciting incidents keep coming, building up to the "reality" that not only has Neo been living in an evil and sinister reality that he never knew existed, but that he is the one and only man who can change this reality. The director keeps hinting at the future and the truth through characters like the Oracle, and pitting Neo against the forces of tyrannical control, personified by Agent Smith, through spectacular action sequences. The film is a tour de force in audience engagement.

 Watch the trailer for *The Matrix*: http://bit.ly/matrixmovietrailer

Examples of Inciting Incidents

Take a look at the plot points in Act II of Pixar's breakthrough 1995 animated film *Toy Story*, after the audience has been introduced to Woody the cowboy doll and the other toys, and we know that Andy, their owner, will be having a birthday party soon and then moving shortly thereafter.

- *Plot point:* The toys send the toy soldiers out on a scouting mission to find out about Andy's birthday presents.
- *Plot point:* One of them is a Buzz Lightyear action figure, which is so cool that it sets up an immediate, intense conflict with Woody about who will be the leader of the toys. Buzz is new and technological, in conflict with Woody's more traditional qualities.
- *Plot point:* Woody accidentally knocks Buzz out of the window, causing him to be falsely accused of murder by the other toys.
- *Plot point:* Buzz is able to confront Woody at a gas station on the way to Pizza Planet, and they fight and fall out of the car.
- *Plot point:* After Buzz crawls into a toy-lifting game at Pizza Planet, he is spotted and captured by Sid, Andy's sadistic, toy-mutilating neighbor.

And so on.

The inciting incidents arise from Woody's character, who thinks he must be the one and only love of Andy's life but sees that slipping away, and that of Buzz, who while heroic and flashy, lacks awareness of his own real abilities. He does not even know he is a toy. The tension between them grows and grows, until they are forced into a much larger conflict with Sid, where they must work together to survive dismemberment—or worse.

What makes the story so engaging and believable is the organic way the characters' weaknesses (Woody's lack of confidence, Buzz's lack of a clue that he is a toy) set up the inciting incidents, which all intensify the conflict between them, and drive them inevitably into the final conflict where both their existences are in question.

 Watch the trailer for *Toy Story*: http://bit.ly/toystorymovietrailer

Act III: Climax

After the story has built up tension through plot points there comes a point where the tension needs a release. This is the climax, and it usually occurs in Act III, with an ultimate struggle that resolves the conflict, for better or worse. The main character or characters come face-to-face with their ultimate opponent(s), and the outcome determines the new, changed shape of the world after the story has ended. It is where a character wins or loses, and where the story should reach an end that, even if it is not completely happy, is satisfying to the audience.

The Surprise or Turning Point

Before a climax comes a reversal, that redefines the story and makes things appear in a new light. Remember the fairy tale of "Goldilocks and the Three Bears." Goldilocks tries out the porridge, the chairs, and the beds in a mysteriously empty home. It's a cozy and pleasant place, seemingly put there to provide for all her needs, even offering a choice as to what she would like best. She is so content that she falls asleep. Then what happens? The bears come home, putting everything about the house and the story into a whole new light. This is something for the nonfiction filmmaker to seek out in true stories: *the fact that puts things in a new perspective.* In the modern-day story that frames the film *Titanic*, think of the moment when we learn that the elderly Rose still has the massive diamond in her possession, after all these decades. Her remembered story takes on a whole new reality. The film has an array of climaxes, but the moment with the elderly Rose and the diamond precedes her death, and her symbolic return to the sunken ship to be with Jack forever.

In *Toy Story*, the self-important Buzz Lightyear sees a commercial on television, while he and Woody are captive in Sid's house. The commercial is for a toy: himself. It is a devastating moment. Buzz sees that he is not what he thought himself to be, or how he portrayed himself as being to others. He is crushed and broken, a fact reinforced when he attempts once again to fly and snaps off his cheap, plastic arm. He is still the character of Buzz in the film, but his self-awareness changes the entire story. Woody becomes the force that must rebuild him. Buzz's realization of the truth—his tragic fall, to put it in literary terms—is the only thing that can make new growth and resolution possible.

Then comes a twist, one of many in the film: The hideous creatures that Sid has made out of mutilated toys . . . turn out to be friendly. They help to reattach Buzz's arm. They, too, are not what they seemed to be. And it is not a bad thing.

This turning point steers us inexorably to the climax, in which Buzz and Woody together confront a threat greater even than Sid: being left behind when their owner, Andy, moves away. They do confront it, together and in spectacular style, and the outcome is positive and satisfying.

Examples of Climaxes in Films

- *The Hangover*, when the guys make the trade in the desert but get the wrong Doug in return.
- *The Dark Knight*, when Batman saves the life of Commissioner Gordon's son by defeating Harvey Dent, but with a twist: He casts himself as a villain at the same time.
- In *The Shawshank Redemption*, Andy Dufresne breaks out of prison after years of suffering abuse, and we learn of his relentless, secretive years of planning and working toward his escape. The audience finds out something that utterly changes the entire story. They have been given just enough clues to form a subconscious suspicion, and the reveal makes everything fall into place.

These are the moments the visual storyteller values most highly of all.

 WATCH MOVIE TRAILERS ONLINE

To watch the trailer for *The Hangover*, go to: http://bit.ly/thehangover trailer

To watch the trailer for *The Dark Knight*, go to: http://bit.ly/thedark nighttrailer

To watch the trailer for *The Shawshank Redemption*, go to: http://bit.ly/ shawshanktrailer

Resolution

After the climax comes the resolution of the story; on the arc this is called the *falling action*. The main character has an opportunity to realize what has happened, to look and see what he or she went through to get to that point. All (or some of) the consequences of what has happened are revealed, for the story has given the world a new shape. A sense of equilibrium returns, but it is a new equilibrium. It shows that change does not end the world. Will the main character live happily ever after? Is there something new in life that everyone must grow accustomed to? A main character does not always need to win. Sometimes victory is not what anyone anticipated. Will he or she try again? Is this not over yet? Does anyone even know?

Nor are all endings happy. The important thing is not to drag the viewer on or leave them hanging or unsatisfied. *Romeo and Juliet* does not end simply with two dead teenagers, who were once madly in love and didn't have to die. It ends with an entire town having to ponder how they have acted, and who has suffered needlessly for it.

For a more modern example, look at the film *Inception*, in which the viewer is forced during the resolution to consider that maybe the entire story was nothing but a dream. In Jeff Jensen's article "Christopher Nolan on His 'Last' Batman Movie, an *'Inception'* Video game, and that Spinning Top," on the website EW.com, *Inception* director Christopher Nolan explains:

> It's not a mistake. I put that cut there at the end, imposing an ambiguity from outside the film. That always felt the right ending to me—it always felt like the appropriate 'kick' to me . . . The real point of the scene—and this is what I tell people—is that Cobb isn't looking at the top. He's looking at his kids. He's left it behind. That's the emotional significance of the thing.

Types of Stories

It has been said that there is nothing new under the sun, and this is true of stories. It might be one of the reasons human beings like stories so much: We like to see new characters dealing with the universal experiences of being human, all in their own unique—and maybe even new—ways. There is nothing wrong with basing a story on a time-tested model, much as its structure can be based on that of the three-act play. Audiences don't necessarily need something completely new, and that is fortunate. What they want is something to which they can relate, and in which they can invest emotion.

So there are many types of stories to choose from. Or perhaps you already have a story in mind, which fits into one of the following categories.

The Hero's Journey

This story structure, described by Joseph Campbell, an American writer, lecturer, and mythologist, is so common and widely used that it gets its own

Figure 2.04 The Hero's Journey is a story structure based on elements that are common to the various mythologies of human history. (Illustration by Chris OBrion)

section. Campbell's ideas are based on structures common to the various mythologies of human history. As the hero embarks on the journey, the choices that he or she makes, and the directions in which he or she leads, determine the character arc. It's important to note that although Campbell used "hero" and the male pronoun to describe the mythic journey, he believed that this universal story structure applied equally to men and women. Following his usage, I use "hero" here as a generic term for both male and female protagonists. Since the model is so common, its key steps are given here. These descriptions are borrowed from Stuart Voytilla's book *Myth and the Movies: Discovering the Mythic Structure of 50 Unforgettable Films.*

The Ordinary World

The viewer gets to meet the hero as an ordinary human being. He or she is not superhuman but normal. It's not until the next stage that this character becomes the lead. The world in which the hero lives is in stark contrast to the world that he or she is about to enter.

Call to Adventure

The initial inciting incident of the story arc. The hero gets some kind of information that calls for action.

Refusal of the Call

The hero thinks twice about what is involved and has doubts. He or she worries about what would be left behind.

Supernatural Aid

Some mysterious force makes itself known to the hero, adding such importance to the call that refusal is no longer an option.

Crossing of the First Threshold

The hero ventures into the new world of the unknown.

Tests

The hero learns the skills needed to move forward on the journey, and to be transformed. Failure is common.

The Ordeal

The hero might question him or herself or reflect upon what he or she is about to do. Maybe the hero will even think twice about the trip he or she has embarked upon, and is then rejuvenated into pressing forward.

The Reward

The hero obtains what he or she sought out to win, but nonetheless has to stay vigilant, since what has been won can be taken away.

The Road Back

The hero begins the re-entry into normal life.

The Resurrection

The hero completes his or her initial mission. What the hero set out to do at the start is resolved.

The Return

The hero returns to where he or she started the journey as a true hero, integrating what has been learned with everyday life.

Exercise: The Hero's Journey

Watch *Rudolph the Red-Nosed Reindeer* online or obtain a copy and watch it.
    Identify at least four elements of the Hero's Journey in this hour-long children's television classic.

Other Types of Stories

The following are basic plot patterns that are also commonly used in fiction stories.

Quest

The hero is in search of something, looking for something long-lost or something new. Elements of the Hero's Journey may be present, but this is a simpler form.

Nearly all of the action of Steven Spielberg's 1981 film *Raiders of the Lost Ark* revolves around Indiana Jones' quest for the ultimate archaeological treasure, the Ark of the Covenant, which came directly from God. He must deal with natural dangers, rivals, puzzles, snakes, and Nazis to complete the quest.

Love

Human romance and intimacy are the goal, with all of the rivalries, complications, biases, fears, and even illnesses that can stand in the way. Film examples of this form are countless.

In the 2008 movie *Twilight*, Bella Swan, a mortal, falls in love with a vampire, Edward Cullen. The fact that Bella is a mortal introduces a huge obstacle to their love. Disney is a great source of classical love stories, such as *Beauty and the Beast*, *Tangled*, or *The Little Mermaid*.

Revenge

The story is driven by a main character's need to avenge a wrong by seeking out the one who did it. Although Inigo Montoya is not the main character in 1987's *The Princess Bride*, he is defined by his quest to avenge his father's death and by his repeated pronouncement, "My name is Inigo Montoya. You killed my father. Prepare to die." In 2005's *V for Vendetta*, the title character spends the film getting large-scale revenge on the government that tried to make him into a super soldier. *Munich* (also 2005) follows a group of Israeli agents seeking revenge for terrorist acts at the 1972 Olympics.

Adventure

This is the traditional journey story, in which the lead character sets out to discover new lands. Quite often this can be the wanderer escaping from the past, or the graduating college senior looking to start a new life.

The 2009 Pixar film *Up* is a relationship story about a young man named Carl Fredericksen who meets a girl named Ellie. The two fall in love and dream of going to a waterfall in South America. Seventy years later Ellie has passed away, but Carl still wants to keep the promise he has made. When Carl is told he needs to go to a retirement home, he devises a plan to sail away to South America in his house, tied to a large number of balloons. That journey makes this movie a classic adventure story.

Although the characters in the *Lord of the Rings* trilogy are really on a quest to destroy a ring, the character of Bilbo in 2012's *The Hobbit*—the story that started it all—goes out strictly for the adventure of it.

Chase

An element in many stories, the chase portrays one force pursuing another, with lots of potential for twists, turns, and setbacks. The hero can be the pursued or the pursuer.

The Bourne Identity (2002) is the story of a man with an erased memory, found by a fisherman. The movie unfolds as the main character, Jason Bourne, tries to rebuild his memory based on clues that he finds along the way. His quest becomes a chase with the revelation that he is being hunted to be killed.

The year 2002 also saw *Catch Me If You Can*, in which an FBI agent chases a clever con man around the world, finally enlisting him to catch other check forgers.

Rivalry

This is the human-on-human conflict made into an entire, ongoing plot. It can be teams vying for a title, lovers vying for a lover, or robots like Optimus Prime and Megatron in *Transformers*, once friends but now enemies after Optimus stole the rank of "Prime" from Megatron.

Another example is 1995's *Toy Story*, already discussed in detail, in which Woody, the leader of Andy's toys, finds himself competing for that position with the newer and flashier Buzz Lightyear.

Power

This is where the hero may start as an ordinary person and turn into a hero that has gained supernatural powers, or someone who achieves powerful financial or social standing. Any number of comic book–based films follow this model, including *Captain America* and *Spider-Man*. In *Willy Wonka and the Chocolate Factory*, from 1971, and remade as *Charlie and the Chocolate Factory* in 2005, Charlie Bucket, a very ordinary boy, has a stroke of luck and gets to tour a magical candy factory. His integrity and character are put to multiple tests, and when he passes them all he becomes the heir to the magical factory.

Dodgeball: A True Underdog Story (2004) is about a different type of rise to power: the struggle against what seem like impossible odds. The story is about the owner of a fancy gym called Globo Gym name Bruce La Fleur, who tries to take over a smaller gym called Average Joe's. Winning a dodgeball competition is all that stands in the way of the Globo Gym takeover, and the little guys . . . well, that would be a spoiler.

Allegory

Allegory uses a fictional situation to symbolize a real one, such as *The Dark Knight*'s 2008 exploration of the moral problems and traps of the War on Terror.

Another example would be 2009's *District 9*, by South African director Neill Blomkamp, who explored his country's past system of apartheid with a tale of extraterrestrials who come to earth only to be marginalized and forced into poor living conditions. In a 2009 article in the *New York Times*, culture reporter Dave Itzkoff writes:

> The plight of the film's crustaceanlike extraterrestrials can be easily read as a metaphor for the persecution of South African blacks under apartheid. But, Mr. Blomkamp said he was also trying to comment on how the country's impoverished peoples oppress one another. While *District 9* was being filmed in the Chiawelo section of Soweto, Alexandra and other townships were ravaged by outbursts of xenophobic violence perpetrated by indigenous South Africans upon illegal immigrants from Zimbabwe, Malawi, and elsewhere.

Parallel Storytelling

According to James Scott Bell (180–193), parallel storytelling is when two or more story arcs are going on at once: for example, multiple characters are experiencing the same event, commonly a large disaster or cataclysm such as the alien invasion in *Independence Day* (1996). A different approach is that of Quentin Tarantino in 1994's *Pulp Fiction*, in which four different narratives unfold, each with their own heroes and villains. Parallel storytelling is very common, often leading up to a climax in which the story lines begin to collide and intersect with one another.

How Fiction and Nonfiction Differ

After surveying the major elements of fiction, which can be looked for and utilized when reporting nonfiction stories, it is time for a look at the attributes of nonfiction.

An upcoming "Meet the Pro" section later in this chapter looks at the reality television series *Intervention*, and includes a conversation with its creator. *Intervention* provides an important example of a fictional structure—in this case, a five-act model—being "populated" with nonfiction people and situations to create a compelling and entertaining television show. It is a model for what this whole chapter is about: understanding fiction stories as a way to produce better nonfiction stories. Later chapters will go into nonfiction storytelling in much more depth.

So let's take a closer look at nonfiction stories, those that feature real people living in real life. They can take the form of television news items, newspaper stories, or documentary films. Nonfiction is based on truth, and the fact-finding involved in finding that truth. It's a crucial way of reporting and analyzing real-life events, and it is all around. Often the ideas presented are direct, specific, and very relevant to a viewer's own life. The way in which a visual nonfiction piece is presented can even alter the attitudes of its viewers. But it does so in a very different way than fiction does.

Nonfiction visual stories like documentaries benefit from "in the moment" storytelling, in which the recording happens right as events occur. It's best to be there when things are happening instead of talking about them after the fact. This presents challenges. Also, nonfiction stories tend to have ups and downs that are difficult to control, much like human nature. Sometimes you may be groggy; other days you are full of energy. Nonfiction stories don't need to be brought to life. They are already living, breathing entities that need to be found, pursued, and approached closely enough for capture.

An understanding of fiction structures lets you, as the filmmaker, craft your piece in ways that keep viewers interested. In nonfiction the facts cannot be changed, but rearranging their order is a possibility. This is especially useful when telling stories that must compress time, as a great many films do.

Reports vs. Stories

It is interesting to note that both fiction authors and nonfiction authors (the latter are usually referred to in the news world as "reporters") both see themselves as writing "stories." This says a lot about storytelling. News items are also known as "reports," however, for their straightforward and factual content. Missing are the contrived story arc, the plot points, and usually the tension and emotional involvement of a fiction story. It is "just the facts" that viewers are expecting, and that is what they get.

News reporters usually don't write like scriptwriters. Instead they use a structure based on the "five Ws": who, what, where, when, and why. They strive to put this information in their first paragraph, called the *lead*. They want to deliver the most basic, most important parts of the article to the reader as quickly and effectively as possible. They want to start off with what makes the story news. This style of writing is called the *inverted pyramid*, which reflects the way information becomes less vital and important as one moves farther down into the story. After the lead comes the body of the article, containing interviews and an overview of the topic. The ending might contain information that is less important still, such as the history or origins of the story, which the reporter deems unessential but helpful to the reader for the background and explanation of the topic it provides.

In *Writing Tools: 50 Essential Strategies for Every Writer*, author Roy Peter Clark explains the differences between reports and stories: "Reports convey information. Stories create experience. Reports transfer knowledge. Stories transfer the reader, crossing boundaries of time, space, and imagination. The story puts us there" (124).

Clark reminds us that writing is broken down into the "famous" five Ws—who, what, where, when, and why—for the way these words help "convey information with the reader's interests in mind" (127). He also uses the five Ws to build an important bridge between reporting and storytelling—so important that it could be taped to the bathroom mirror of every visual storyteller:

Roy Peter Clark's Breakdown of the Five Ws

- "Who" becomes character.
- "What" becomes action (what happened).
- "Where" becomes setting.
- "When" becomes chronology.
- "Why" becomes cause or motive.

 Exercise: Report vs. Story

Pick up a newspaper and find an article about a current event. Go through it and identify one fact and one central character in the story.

1. Identify the basic five Ws (who, what, where, when, and why) as described in Clark's breakdown.
2. Could the report have been presented as a narrative? Could the narrative have been a report? Which would have worked better?
3. What would have to be done to the story to turn it from one into the other?

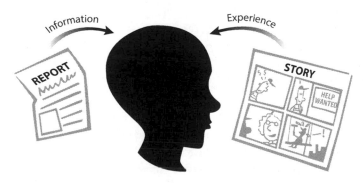

Figure 2.05 It is interesting to note that both fiction authors and nonfiction authors (the latter are often referred to in the news world as "reporters") both see themselves as writing "stories." (Illustration by Chris OBrion)

The Fusion of Fiction and Nonfiction

The fusing of nonfiction and fiction is a common thing—simply look at the film *Titanic* for a prime example. For the purposes of this book, however, this fusion means something different: It means using the elements of fiction to tell a nonfiction story—whether a news report or a more involved documentary— more effectively.

This means seeking out character, seeking out conflict, and seeking out story arcs in the real world. Visual news features and reality television do this, with varying levels of success, and that is why a video news producer and a reality TV show, *Intervention*, might be helpful in illustrating the process.

MEET THE PRO

Evelio Contreras, Video Producer, CNN Digital

Evelio Contreras is a New York City–based video producer for CNN Digital's Original Video team. Previously he worked as a videojournalist at the Washington Post, *the* Las Vegas Sun, *and* The Roanoke Times. *His work has been recognized by the National Press Photographers Association, the Society of News Design, and the*

Figure 2.06 Evelio Contreras is a New York City–based video producer for CNN Digital's Original Video team. (Photo by Deborah Brunswick)

Capital Emmys. He has coached students and taught multimedia workshops, including NPPA's Multimedia Immersion and News Video Television Workshop.

Contreras grew up in Eagle Pass, TX, a small town on the Mexican border. It was there, working at El Gram, a bilingual newspaper, that he developed an interest in telling stories about ordinary people doing extraordinary things. He enjoys meeting new people and finding new ways to tell their stories.

Evelio Contreras thinks about story structure every time he tackles a nonfiction assignment for CNN. "You should have 95 percent of the work done prior to shooting a story," he said. "You need to have identified themes, planned your shooting, and understood what is going to happen before it happens." Contreras believes that researching a story prior to shooting will

---

(Continued . . .)

(. . . continued)

help in the long run, allowing the reporter to "focus on what is happening in front of the camera."

"I don't want to leave much to chance, except for transformational moments, " he said, referring to a story's turning points. These are the moments when the character being followed does something unexpected, or runs into an unexpected situation, and their response transforms them and their story just as a turning point can transform a fictional story. It's usually possible to predict how things will affect people, either positively or negatively, but sometimes things happen that aren't expected. When a diehard fan is watching a football game, it is known that one team will win and one will lose. What is not known is how that specific fan will respond. The reaction could well be a transformational moment. If that fan is a main character, the visual storyteller needs to be ready.

Out in the field, the story is always in the back of the reporter's mind, the deadline is often looming, and the facts don't always fit into an exact, most desirable form of the story arc. For Contreras, it's not about making that exact, formulaic arc. He has his own system. "I think of five points in time for my story," he said. "I definitely think about the beginning and the end. I plan my shoots, but I always make a commitment about how I want my story to end. If not, I will shoot for eternity and never know when I am done."

Since he has planned his story ahead of time, Contreras knows he does not need to shoot everything he comes upon. "I just need to identify the struggles that my character is going through," he said. "As my character embarks on their journey, I need to identify the roadblocks and obstacles that are holding my character back."

"Think about the most common story out there, your life. Say you went by the story, 'I had a bad day.' If you go through your day and mark each thing you did as a struggle—you woke up, you put your clothes on—you will have multiple instances where things will be going wrong. For example, you can't find your keys or your lunch is taking too long, or you were late to work—all of these are conflicts throughout your day; these build to a punch line. That punch line is the climax."

Contreras wants his viewers to be enveloped in his films so that they watch the whole story. "You are trying to grab people to watch your work for five, ten, or fifteen minutes," he said. "You need to think about transformations, struggles, and responses. What you expect to happen does not always happen. You want a profile with a surprise, something to validate the human experience."

MEET THE PRO
Sam Mettler, Executive Producer, A&E's Intervention

Emmy-winning executive producer Sam Mettler is the creator of the gripping real-life series Intervention. *However, Mettler spent his early years on much lighter fare. He has been a comedic writer, actor, and occasional stand-up comedian, with guest-starring roles on* The Drew Carey Show, The Norm Show, *and multiple television commercials. He built on these experiences and an early 1990s stint as a morning radio host in Syracuse, NY, rising to the small screen with writing credits on* South Park, *MTV's* Head-Trip, *and Fox's* Misguided Angels.

Figure 2.07 Sam Mettler is the creator of the gripping real-life series *Intervention*. (Photo courtesy of Sam Mettler)

To watch clips from Intervention, *go to: http://bit.ly/interventionepisodes.*

Success in any aspect of Hollywood does not come easily. People working their way up in the screenwriting business may have to do whatever kind of work they can find to support themselves. Sam Mettler worked in IT, fixing fax machines or copiers, until he was able to produce his own show.

Mettler knew from an early age that he wanted to work in the television industry. "I spent a lot of time in front of the TV, watching comedies, immersing myself in them, and spending a lot of time trying to laugh instead of dealing with a tough home life," said Mettler, who tried his hardest right after college to put his scripts in front of whomever would read them. "Paramount had a lot of television on the lot. I tried to get anyone to read my stuff," said Mettler.

Many writers work their way in by becoming writer's assistants, typing up what other people come up with. "By being in the room and becoming part of that team, eventually they will get their stuff read," said Mettler. "Maybe add a joke here and there, and then, God willing, if they are decent they will get, like, one script. Maybe they will get another. And then maybe they will be hired on staff."

Mettler got his start working on a reality TV project at about the same time that *Survivor* was becoming a hit on television. It was then that Mettler came up with the idea for the show *Intervention*. "It started out as a joke; my father wears too much cologne: 'Old-fashioned spill and flap.' My wife and I were walking, pushing our stroller in Beverly Hills, and I smelled my hands, and it was my dad. My dad had pushed the stroller three weeks prior, and the cologne was still on the handlebars. I called my sister: 'We've gotta do an intervention with the cologne,' and the idea popped into my head."

Mettler put together a pitch for MTV right around Sept. 11, 2001. The terrorist attacks on the World Trade Center and Pentagon made it

(Continued . . .)

(... continued)

impossible to pitch his show, however. "New development was at a halt—no one wanted anything remotely sad on television. It sat on my desktop for two years," he said. Then Mettler got a call from a friend who told him to send his pitch.

"I made it deeply personal, for someone in my life where an intervention should have happened, but it didn't, and three weeks later I was producing the pilot," he said, adding that he was suddenly thrust into the position of producer, something he had never attempted before. "I took on every role: I cast it, found the interventionists—I developed the format for it, what the show would look like, what the hook would be, found our first subjects, our addicts. I directed it in the field," he said.

The show itself is no longer on the air, but it ran 14 seasons with 194 episodes on A&E and won the 2009 Emmy for Outstanding Reality Program after getting multiples of nominations. It was shot all in cinéma vérité style, very much the same as.shooting journalistically, with no setting up of events or added fictional elements. "In terms of vérité, it really needed to be, 'We're not choreographing a drug addict using drugs,'" Mettler said.

The idea of *Intervention* is really a hybrid of documentary and reality television. Everything leading up to the intervention is a documentary and is filmed in cinéma vérité style. The intervention is then added by the show, and the interventionists are real and doing what they know how to do. "That's where we are inserting ourselves," Mettler said, "and that's where it becomes . . . reality television." Mettler said that the interventions were really happening, and would have happened the very same way whether cameras were capturing the action or not. "We really don't interfere. We're there to follow an addict through their life, without constructing a story that isn't true," he said. "It's one of the reasons *Intervention* worked really well."

Mettler believes in storytelling. "All of my projects, while there is a larger vehicle—drug addiction and intervention, will-they-or-won't-they-go—within that there is a more specific story and conflict. Or, what is wrong with this person? What did they want? And how do they get what they want?" Mettler said he created a story map and template for each and every episode. "We don't have people read the lines. It is a script based upon hours and hours of interviews," he explained.

The interviews are very much the thread of the entire show. The subjects would tell the show producers what their lives were like every day, from the moment they got up to the moment they went to bed. They would also tell the backstory of all of the critical moments in their lives.

When interviewing the subjects, Mettler said, building trust was the most important thing, and simply being able to listen to the person talk. This was not done through a list of questions, he said, but by "being empathetic, by giving back. If someone is at an emotional point, being able to empathize with them so they feel like they are being heard and understood . . . they will give more."

(Continued . . .)

(...*continued*)

"The follow-up question is so important," he continues. "If someone gets to an emotional point in an interview, you [ask] every single emotional question you have, even if it is from a different point in their life. Don't lose that moment. Even if it's another part of the interview, move it up. It is extremely important when you have those fragile moments to hold on to them and to work with them, so that while they are in that 'mind space' you can really get all of the important emotional parts done," said Mettler, who explained that he always did a pre-interview over the phone prior to the on-camera one.

Since the subjects have already revealed their backstories over the phone, they have spoken of traumas that have already been processed. These backstories do not change. "Then you get them to repeat those quotes—to say it a different way. Those moments in the backstory will be particularly emotional, based on chronology or tone," said Mettler.

Broken down into acts, *Intervention* episodes had a five-act format that was very specific. The interviews were plugged into the template format, and worked to uphold the overall story arc. The show would begin with what Mettler terms the "cold open," or essentially a trailer montage of the entire show that provided a glimpse of what the viewer was about to watch.

The Five-Act Structure of A&E's *Intervention*

>   **Act I**—This is the introduction, the anatomy of an addict. This is the backstory from birth to the present, with the important moments where things went wrong. It leads up to the present, when things are at their worst.
>
>   **Act II**—This is a more free-flowing act; call it "a week in the life of the addict." There are documentary scenes of the family conflict, based on what was revealed over the backstory. This is the conflict and the trauma of the backstory playing out today, and what those scenes look like.
>
>   "We'll have a couple of scenes," Mettler said. "Mother and daughter, friends. You see how this trauma that hasn't been processed . . . It still lives in their daily life. We act out that traumatic conflict. 'How will things change? Can they change both the family and the addict? Are they stuck? Who will they get unstuck?'"
>
>   **Act III**—This is the spiral. It is the lowest point in the week of shooting. The drug addict does something very self-destructive. This is the time for the pre-intervention, the family training, where the family discusses the intervention and what the family must do to keep the intervention going.
>
>   **Act IV**—Now the intervention is coming, with a cliffhanger: Will they or won't they go into treatment?

(Continued . . .)

(...continued)

> **Act V**—This is the closure, the answer to that yes-or-no situation. Most of the time the answer to treatment is "yes." It is the first moment of the first day of the rest of their lives. Then there is a follow-up a month or so later, showing where they are now.
>
> Mettler knows that *Intervention* involved shooting illegal and unsafe situations. "Safety-wise, if something bad happened . . . these people are using drugs whether we are there or not. This is a problem they've had for years. They're pros. The likelihood of something happening is diminished. [But] we've had to call in for ambulances and such," he said.
>
> The show had no problem finding and enlisting subjects, he went on. At the end of each episode, a message would inform the audience that if they knew anyone who needed help, they could contact the producers. "At the end of an episode, we could have 500 submissions," Mettler said.
>
> Though the show was not considered fiction, it was still cast by the producers to cover people whose lives were dramatic. "A drug addict fits that bill perfectly," said Mettler. "Their lives are inherently dramatic, minute by minute. There are moments throughout their life—shame and guilt from the day before they are in withdrawal, they need to use, they are sick—another moment they need money. What are they going to do to get the money? It's literally a drug-addict life: moment to moment."
>
> Though *Intervention* won the Emmy for Best Reality Program, Mettler knows the difference between it and a show like *Survivor*. "It's a difference between reality and realness. Some are shot so beautifully that they lose their realness. They can be shot so beautifully that it looks overproduced," he said. "The difference between reality TV and true documentary is the insertion of a produced construct. Putting people on an island, when they wouldn't necessarily be on an island, is reality TV. Going to an island and shooting people who are already there is a documentary."

Chapter Summary

Stories are at the heart of good film production. All stories have a beginning, a middle, and an end. These stories can be plot-driven or character-driven, or they can be stories of rivalry, love, power, adventure, or pursuit, and very often they are combinations of many of these elements. The characters' reactions to events, within a setting, will create a story arc that keeps viewers engaged. The events, plot points, or inciting incidents—whatever you wish to call them—of a story are fueled by conflicts of various kinds, whether internal or external, and will drive the story forward. The audience can be kept engaged in the storyline through surprises, twists, turns, and carefully withheld revelations about character, setting, and backstory. Near the end of the story, the action will reach a climax and conflict will come into the open and be decided. The resolution that follows will leave your viewers feeling satisfied, and as if they have been through a change.

This chapter touched on the concept of using the elements of fiction stories to tell nonfiction stories, with a detailed example. The structuring of nonfiction stories will be covered in more depth later.

Review Questions

1. What is a story?
2. What plot elements make up the traditional story arc?
3. If you were about to start work on a fictional story, what three basic parts are you going to think about before you start?
4. Describe the differences between a report and a story.
5. What is a narrative question?
6. If you are making a video that is going to be only two to five minutes in length, what must you do to engage the viewer quickly?

Exercises

Fiction Exercise

From the list below, choose one set of three elements and combine them into a 250-word, written story. Draw an arc charting out the plot points, the beginning, middle, and end, and the climax. Use your imagination and try to avoid clichés.

- A tent, a campfire, eerie sounds
- A pair of shoes, a bed, and a note
- A dog, a neighbor, and a lawn
- A computer, a window, and a chair
- A telephone, a remote control, and the sound of raindrops
- A treasure chest, a hat, and keys
- An ex-boyfriend, a letter, and a photograph

Nonfiction Exercise

Choose one of the following questions and answer it as truthfully as you can in a 500-word essay. Think visually as you plan and write.

- Describe a sound from your childhood. What was it? When did you hear it? What does it bring to mind?
- Do you ever think about growing old?
- What did you accomplish last year?
- What relationships have had the greatest impact on your life?
- What would have happened if you had not left the house this morning?
- If you could follow someone around for one day, unseen, who would it be and why?

⚙ Key Terms

Action – Events that occur during the course of a story.

Backstory – Events or elements of a story that an audience must know about, but which do not happen during the story.

Character – The main, human element of a story (even when the character is not portrayed as a human).

Character-driven – When a particular character's goals and decisions steer the story.

Conflict – The problem that drives a story, when a character cannot get what he or she desires. Also, the second part of the three-act structure, in which the action of the story unfolds and builds.

Climax – When tension reaches its highest peak in a story.

Development – Changes that occur in characters and plots as stories are told.

Exposition – The practice of revealing backstory, by one of several methods.

Fiction – Events that are chronicled but that did not occur in real time, or to real people. Made-up reality.

Five Ws – Questions that should be addressed in a report: who, what, where, when, and why.

Inciting incident – An event or action that changes the course of a story. Also called a *plot point*.

Narrative – Elements related to an audience that tell a story.

Narrative question – The unresolved tension that keeps an audience attached to a story.

Nonfiction – Events that did occur, in reality, to real people.

Plot-driven – When events, or the actions of many different characters, steer the story.

Plot pattern – Established story models that are used again and again, such as revenge, chase, quest, or allegory.

Protagonist – The main character of a story, whose progress the audience follows.

Report – A chronicle or narration of nonfictional events.

Resolution – The third part of the three-act structure; also called *falling action*. The establishment of a new normal after the end of conflict.

Setting – The place and time in which a story takes place.

Setup – The first part of the three-act structure, in which setting, characters, and conflict are all introduced.

Show, don't tell – The practice of allowing an audience to witness action, rather than be told about it.

Story – A sequence of information relating what happens when characters come into conflict with what separates them from their desires.

Story arc – The rise and fall of emotional tension over the course of a story.

Three-act structure – A structure that provides a simple, straightforward framework to build a story in a dramatic way.

Sources

Bell, James Scott. *Plot and Structure: Techniques and Exercises for Crafting a Plot That Grips Readers from Start to Finish*. Write Great Fiction. Cincinnati, OH: Writer's Digest Books, 2004.

Clark, Roy Peter. *Writing Tools: 50 Essential Strategies for Every Writer*. New York: Little, Brown, 2006.

Contreras, Evelio. Conversation with author, July 2, 2013.

Jensen, Jeff. "Christopher Nolan on His 'Last' Batman Movie, an 'Inception' Videogame, and That Spinning Top." EW.com. Accessed July 10, 2013. http://insidemovies. ew.com/2010/11/30/christopher-nolan-batman-inception/.

Franklin, Jon. *Writing for Story: Craft Secrets of Dramatic Nonfiction by a Two-Time Pulitzer Prize Winner*. New York, NY: Plume, 1994.

Itzkoff, Dave. "A Young Director Brings a Spaceship and a Metaphor in for a Landing." *The New York Times*, August 6, 2009, sec. Movies. Accessed March 16, 2015. http://www.nytimes.com/2009/08/06/movies/06district.html.

Martell, William C. *Supporting Character Secrets*. Studio City, CA: First Strike Productions, 2012. Kindle ed., location 131.

Mettler, Sam. Conversation with author, July 26, 2013.

Voytilla, Stuart. *Myth and the Movies: Discovering the Mythic Structure of 50 Unforgettable Films*. Studio City, CA: Michael Wiese Productions, 1999. Kindle.

3 THE VISUAL STORYTELLER'S TOOL BOX

What Kinds of Equipment Are Needed for Gathering Multimedia Content?

In this chapter you will learn

- The types of video cameras available
- Differences between a video camera and an HDSLR
- How the camera works
- Basic use of a video camera
- Proper exposure with a video camera
- Types of video shooting accessories
- Types of audio gathering tools

Introduction

Technology is part of everything we do as multimedia storytellers. You can work with gear that costs thousands of dollars, or that costs only hundreds—and also serves as your phone. All this gear comprises the multimedia tool box, and just as hammers and screwdrivers come in different varieties and levels of quality, so does technology. Each tool does something specific, such as a framing hammer as compared with a roofer's hammer. Tools can also vary greatly in sophistication, such as a multispeed power screwdriver compared with a simple flathead.

This chapter will introduce both still and video camera systems, and how to use each to make visual stories. Do not worry about whether the technology currently at your disposal measures up to what is discussed here. The technology described in this chapter is only a sampling of what was available at the time the book was published. Technology changes rapidly, as do the prices of gear, so keep that in mind. We will try to concentrate on aspects of equipment and its use that do not depend on month-to-month or year-to-year technological advances.

If you are using this book in a college classroom for an introduction to multimedia storytelling, there is no reason why "prosumer" (suitable for either the professional or the consumer) gear would not be perfectly adequate. It is important to understand the differences, however, between this prosumer equipment and what is available in the professional realm.

We've made an effort to make the discussion here as easy to understand as possible, without getting overly technical. Quality multimedia storytelling depends not so much on knowing exactly how things work as it does on making them work for you.

The Multimedia Camera Kit

There are many different types of cameras from which you can choose to shoot a visual story—everything from traditional still cameras that also shoot video, to mobile phones that do the same, to small video cameras that also shoot photographs. Most modern brands of camera create high-quality images that are very suitable for both video and stills.

This book assumes you have a camera at the ready, be it a mobile phone, small digital camera, or high-definition single-lens reflex (HDSLR) model. Although smaller, non-HDSLR cameras tend not to allow much manual adjustment, it is important for you to know how to adjust your camera manually. Knowing the basics of camera function and operation will help you to be a better visual storyteller.

There are also some essentials that go with a camera; take a look at the following list, which includes items that will be discussed later.

Multimedia Camera Kit Checklist

A good basic camera kit for gathering multimedia content consists of the following:

1. HDSLR camera that shoots both still photographs and video
2. Small, on-camera microphone that fits on the camera's hot shoe
3. Tripod
4. Over-the-ear headphones (preferable to earbuds)
5. Memory card (Even if there is built-in memory, use a card. This will ensure that you have a backup of your footage and images.)
6. Charged battery

While there are many different camera brands, this book assumes you have a prosumer HDSLR, mini HDV, or mobile phone that shoots HD video and images.

The Camera

Your camera itself could be anything from a low-cost camera phone, like an iPhone or Android, to a high-end, high-priced 4K model, intended for cinematic use. The following sections give a basic overview of cameras currently in

Figure 3.01 A good basic camera kit for gathering multimedia content consists of head-phones, video camera, external light, and external microphone. (Photo by Seth Gitner)

PAL	Phase Alternating Line: format with a frame rate of 25 fps for broadcast television used in video cameras primarily purchased in Europe.
NTSC	National Television System Committee: format with a frame rate of 30 fps for broadcast television used in video cameras primarily purchased in the United States.
H264	A codec primarily used in mobile phones and tablets.
mov	Container format for holding audio, video, effects, or text, primarily used by Apple Quicktime.
m4v	Format used for video files in the iTunes store.
mp4	Container format that can be played on tablets and on the web; an international standard usable on a wide range of players.
mp3	Type of audio file used by portable audio players. The quality of the music file degrades as it is compressed to fit more music onto storage media.
HD	High definition: frame size equaling 1920 x 1080 pixels or 1280 x 720 pixels with frame rates ranging from 23.98 fps to 60 fps.
SD	Standard definition: in the United States the screen size is 720 x 486 pixels, which means a 4:3 aspect ratio with a frame rate of 29.97 fps. In Europe, the screen size is 720 x 576 pixels, which means a 16:9 aspect ratio with a frame rate of 25 fps.

Figure 3.02 Abbreviations of technical jargon used in this chapter.

use, from the one that is likely in your pocket all the way up to those used by professional news organizations. This book tends to concentrate on cameras in what is known as the "prosumer" realm—those that can serve either the professional or the casual consumer—and do so while staying within a budget of a few thousand dollars.

Prosumer HD Video Cameras

Several options exist in the prosumer category, which can be defined as units costing up to $1,500. What's the difference between a prosumer camera and a still camera or mobile phone that also shoots video?

For one thing, dedicated video cameras are different from their still camera counterparts in the way that the lens is constructed. Many HD video cameras, like the Panasonic HC Series or the Canon Vixia series prosumer models, have lenses that are built into the camera body, which allows quicker auto-focusing and greater ease of use. As one would expect, prosumer models offer much more image control and storage capacity than still cameras or phones. Their lenses zoom using built-in optics. They also have a digital zoom capability, although this tends to degrade image quality as it is applied. They may also have internal hard drives that can hold a lot of HD footage, built-in headphone jacks and microphone jacks, plus image stabilization and a tripod socket. Many of these cameras have touch screens that allow for rack focus (covered later) and many other options through use of software menus, as well as preset modes for a variety of effects and shooting conditions. Prosumer cameras also tend to be constructed of very durable materials, with bodies of magnesium alloy instead of plastic, and have better weather sealing. In other words, they can withstand a lot more use and abuse.

They are, in short, everything that a multimedia storyteller needs, at a reasonable price. For this reason many colleges teaching multimedia production opt for prosumer models; they offer features and capabilities found only in dedicated cameras. But that doesn't mean they aren't seeing some competition from the other options.

Figure 3.03 A prosumer camera has at least HD-quality video but does not have the ability to record two-channel audio with XLR inputs. (Photo by Seth Gitner)

Mobile Phone Camera

Mobile and smart phones are everywhere now, and offer an ever-increasing array of capabilities. While they are always near at hand and definitely economical, the cameras in these small units simply do not have the kinds of features offered by prosumer cameras. On most mobile phones the zoom is going to be entirely digital rather than optical, with the inevitable loss of image quality when it is used. To get different focal lengths requires add-on hardware, such as Premier Systems USA's Olloclip. Likewise, adding a microphone requires a device like IK Multimedia's iRig. For a tripod connector, the best bet might be to use an enclosure like the PhoGo by DiffCase. By the time the costs of all these add-on features are added up you might be approaching the cost territory of a prosumer camera, which would most likely take a lot more punishment than a mobile phone. It would also offer more built-in functionality, and the simple ability to make a phone call while recording.

Microphones are discussed later in this chapter, but for the time being it needs to be said that the microphones in mobile phones are better suited to telephone use than to the recording of high-quality audio for broadcast-level video. As Stan Alten and Doug Quin write, in their book *Audio in Media*:

> Built-in mics often have a limited frequency response, usually up to around 8 kHz; and while the range can adequately cover the human speaking voice, it is not optimal for other situations. Furthermore, the preamplifier circuit in the built-in mic input is not typically designed with high fidelity as a consideration and can generate an unacceptable level of self-noise.

While prosumer cameras are superior to mobile phones in most film-shooting situations, the portability and universality of camera phones gives them a definite role, as does their growing flexibility.

Professional Video Cameras

Most users of this book will not have ready access to cameras above the prosumer level, but it's useful to know the differences between prosumer cameras—which you are most likely using—and what the professionals use.

For the most part it is optics, handling, and stability. Some professional cameras used for electronic news gathering (ENG) work have a lens that costs several thousand dollars, attached to a camera that rests on the user's shoulder. A shoulder brace allows for better stability than is possible with a handheld camera.

Larger cameras also offer more possibilities with codecs (the types of files that are recorded), allowing higher quality footage to be obtained. Still,

Figure 3.04 The iPhone and other mobile phones are increasingly becoming tools to gather video content for use in journalistic news reporting. (Photo courtesy of Apple)

some broadcast outlets have actually forgone the use of shoulder-carried cameras for smaller, more prosumer-type cameras that are lighter, less costly, and more versatile.

One of the biggest considerations for these larger, higher-end pieces of ENG equipment is cost. With lenses and camera together, a rig for one camera operator, such as JVC's GY-HM790 or the AG-HPX600 P2 camcorder, could cost over $10,000. Both cameras shoot digitally and are shoulder-carried.

Another difference between professional and prosumer cameras is audio capability: professional models tend to have XLR inputs for microphones and better overall audio controls, which are advantageous in professional news situations. They can also offer neutral density (ND) filters, which help cut down the amount of light that enters the camera without affecting the color of the scene.

Figure 3.05 Higher-end, more professional video cameras have capabilities beyond those of prosumer models, such as the ability to record two channels of audio at the same time. (Photo by Seth Gitner)

HDSLR Cameras

HDSLR cameras offer power, exposure options, and superior image quality, making stories look nicer overall while keeping costs reasonable. They are also small and easily portable.

Even though the small footprint of HDLSRs is enticing, along with the high-quality video that they can produce, these cameras aren't so good for "run-and-gun" video journalism, much of which is better captured with a prosumer HD video camera or high-end ENG gear.

"Sports video with HDSLR can be [hard] to do," said James Gregg, a multimedia photojournalist at the *San Diego Union Tribune* who also says he has not shot much hard news with the HDSLR. "I shot NCAA for a season; it made me learn my gear."

One of the problems with using an HDSLR on a daily basis for news gathering is similar to that with mobile phones: A number of attachments are necessary to reach the functionality of a video-type camera. Just having the ability to shoot HD footage is not enough; there also needs to be the ability to capture broadcast-capable audio, something readily obtainable with a video camera that has a shoulder brace, audio meters, and XLR audio connectors built in.

HDSLR gear is more of a mix-and-match—whatever works for the shooter. Gregg said, "I use a JAG shoulder rig. I have a couple of ball heads and a fluid head with Gitzo tripods. I don't use a tripod as much as I should. I push myself to use one 50 percent of the time. I have this urge to move my feet. Often I use a Zacuto viewfinder, along with the fluid head arm in my armpit; that gives me three points of contact [with my body] to help with stability."

Gregg said his tried-and-true lens for everyday work is a Canon EF 24–105mm f/4 L IS USM. "It offers everything I need to get tight shots and to shoot tight with a perspective difference," he said, adding that he has never wished after shooting with the lens that he had less depth of field, usually achieved by using a lens with an aperture of 2.8 or smaller. "It allows me to work with one camera and one lens," he added. "Keeping the gear simple allows me to focus on my story and being thoughtful about how my images can communicate that."

Camera companies are responding to a need for a hybrid unit that offers both interchangeable lenses and built-in audio meters and connectors, and which does not require the purchase of additional hardware to give video-camera functionality. Canon has a series of cameras that have built-in XLR ports that use HDSLR lenses and genlock (technology that allows synchronization of several video devices being used in production), making them more plug-and-play and ready for a studio environment or a satellite truck. Known as the C Series, these cameras, like their close cousin the HDSLR, are not at their best in "run-and-gun" types of news situations.

There are tradeoffs to using a dedicated video camera with a built-in lens rather than HDSLR interchangeable lenses. HDSLR lenses provide the feel of still-photo framing and allow shallow depth of field, but the zoom is not as smooth as that of an ENG-style video camera.

The C-Series cameras come in three versions that range in cost from $5,500 to $15,000. "I like it because it gets me back to a video camera," said McKenna Ewen, a multimedia producer at the *Washington Post* newspaper in Minneapolis, MN. Ewen says he likes how all of the accessories that need to be added to an HDSLR are now built right into the camera, including ND filters. "I am not dealing with the 'Frankenrig,' or syncing audio in post, which when working on deadline can save me an hour or two," he says. Ewen says he feels like he "fundamentally" shoots better with it.

"When I shot with an HDSLR the audio storytelling suffered. I was too worried about the technical things . . . to make it work. It's better with a C100. It's like I can get back to the storytelling," he said.

As the industry and the technology evolve, new and better gear will result. The most important thing is to make sure to choose a camera that allows the story to be told to its greatest potential. Having high-quality gear is nice, but it doesn't necessarily make the crucial difference. Whether using an iPhone or an HDSLR, you're still shooting in high definition. It's just the capability and the amount of control with the camera that is different. The camera is only a tool, and, as always, that is secondary to having a good story to tell.

NIKON

The Nikon company has gone through the evolution of film-based cameras through digital and into digital with video capabilities. Their cameras are used by a wide range of professionals working for entities as varied as *Sports Illustrated* and NASA. This manufacturer offers a wide range of cameras capable of shooting video for multimedia.

As of the writing of this book, Nikon's top-range camera is called the Nikon D4, and it features Full HD 1080p video at various frame rates—suitable for use in broadcast—and a 16-megapixel full-frame sensor capable of shooting still images at a rate of 11 fps. The company has dubbed it their Multimedia HDSLR. It offers a small form factor, low-light ability, and NIKKOR lens versatility. Nikon has been making lenses for about seventy-five years, and has a range of lenses from 10mm to 800mm with a full range in between.

CANON

Offering a wide range of both still and video cameras, including those in the aforementioned C Series, Canon U.S.A. Inc. was the first company to offer HD video-gathering capability built into an HDSLR camera. Canon has been in the broadcast ENG business for a long while, so it was not a big stretch for them to add this capability to their cameras. The 5D Mark II was their first offering with video capability, and since its release the company has produced several other cameras that offer video capability, including their latest high-end model as of the publication of this book, the 5D Mark III. This model features a 22-megapixel full-frame CMOS sensor and 1080p30 video recording, and is capable of shooting still images at 6 frames per second.

Figure 3.06 The Nikon D4s system has interchangeable lenses and the ability to shoot both still photos and HD video. (Photo courtesy of Nikon)

Figure 3.07 The Canon 5D Mark III has interchangeable lenses and the ability to shoot both still photos and HD video. (Photo courtesy of Canon)

Full-Frame vs. Crop Sensor Camera

With 35mm-based film cameras the standard size of the image area is 24mm × 36mm. But now, with digital cameras, there is a variety of types of sensors. Some sensors—usually in more costly cameras—mimic what a full-size 35mm film camera "sees," while less expensive cameras have sensors that can only see a selected portion of the image projected off of the lens, giving the appearance of magnification and resulting in an apparent focal length increase or a narrower field of view. Canon has manufactured sensors of different dimension focal planes, including full-frame, 1.3, and 1.6. Nikon cameras have a crop size of 1.5, also called DX. There are different image sensor sizes to complement different lenses.

There are two different types of 35mm HDSLR camera available. There are full-frame cameras, which have sensors that are much larger, with a larger number of megapixels, which in turn allow a higher quality image. These tend to be more costly than smaller, APS-sized sensors (Advance Photo System), which are cheaper to manufacture and have fewer megapixels. Whether a camera is full-frame or APS-sized refers to the size of the sensor in the camera.

Understanding the frame size of your camera helps you to better understand the focal lengths of your lenses. For example, placing a 35mm lens on a full-frame camera would result in an effective focal length of 35mm, but on a DX camera you would multiply the 35mm by 1.5, creating an effective focal length of 52.5mm. When choosing a lens to use with HDSLR, it is important to understand these factors.

Full-Frame vs. Crop Sensor Cameras

Whether your camera has a large image sensor, enabling full-frame photos, or a smaller sensor that results in a cropped photo can have a big impact on composition.

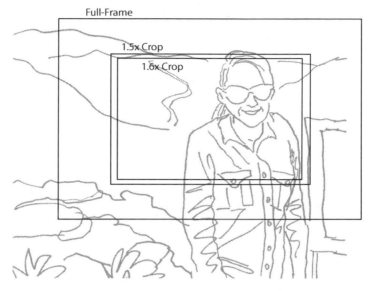

Figure 3.08 Some sensors—usually in more costly cameras—mimic what a full-size 35mm digital camera "sees," while less expensive cameras have sensors that can only see a selected portion of the image projected off of the lens, giving the appearance of magnification and resulting in an apparent focal length increase or a narrower field of view. (Illustration by Chris OBrion)

4K and the Future of Video Technology

Houston-based freelance videographer Jerry Hattan, who works with clients across the country on video projects, has used all different types of cameras and formats in his thirty years in the news business. He described the challenges of reconciling camera capabilities and cost with his clients' desires:

> They call asking, 'Do you have this camera?' That request might only be due to that particular camera manufacturer's marketing, or only because somebody told them that camera was the best to use . . . The life of a freelancer is changing all around me . . . every manufacturer is trying to beat the other guy.

Freelancers are at the beck and call—and sometimes the whim—of the client. Still, Hattan says,

> Part of my job is to educate people on what they may actually need for a shoot. It's hard to talk to them on the phone and explain why 4K is overkill, or why that 'cool camera look' may not be what they actually

want—especially if they don't have twenty-five terabytes of storage space for the footage.

When Hattan started freelancing in 1994, he used an Ikegami V55 Betacam SP Camcorder with a $58,000 price tag. This did not include lens, monitors, batteries, lighting, audio, or other accessories. The beta format lasted as "the format of choice for twenty years," he said. "It made a lot more sense to buy a camera then."

Hattan is trying to figure out how to keep up with the times and shoot in the formats clients are now asking for. He later purchased a Canon C300 digital broadcast camera that seems to fit his needs and budget at $16,000, a cost significantly below those of the Sony and the Panasonic full-size cameras he already owns:

> It's for making movies. It's not as fast as a broadcast-style camera, where you have a wide-ranging zoom. If you need to change focal lengths in the middle of a shoot you must stop, change lenses, and begin again, but the pictures are gorgeous.

Still cameras are capable of shooting larger still images than video equipment. Some HDSLR cameras can shoot still images of more than 20 megapixels while shooting video at only 1920 × 1080, the playback resolution of HD television. What if these huge images could also be brought to life in video? A recent trend in video camera formats is 4K, which is twice both the vertical and horizontal resolutions of HD. Shooting this size video has its benefits, especially with televisions that have 4K capability, but editing footage like this requires a huge amount of storage space.

Professional cameras for 4K, intended for cinematic applications, have costs ranging from $10,000 to $50,000. Most of these units are far beyond the reach of most educational programs, but one has to remember that there was a time when HD video was not possible on mobile phones. Who knows what the future might hold?

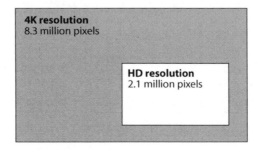

Figure 3.09 This illustration shows 4K video size compared with HD video size. (Illustration by Chris OBrion)

Lenses

Every lens has a specific focal length that is either fixed or zoomable. Lenses are the optical devices—mechanical "eyes," in fact—through which a camera "sees" the world it will record. A wide range of lenses is available for cameras. Usually lenses are tied to a brand—a Nikon lens will not fit on a Canon camera and vice versa. They also vary according to coatings and sharpness. Though every lens has its own ratings, usually the particular camera you are using determines the types of lenses to buy.

At the start of this chapter we explained the differences between DX, APS, and full-frame cameras. Understanding the type of camera you are using is very important when choosing a lens, since different focal length lenses will have different general uses, depending on which type of camera sensor is being used.

Prime lenses are considered higher-end and have a fixed focal length, meaning they are not zoomable. They are known for minimal depth of field and a good *bokeh*, the out-of-focus portion of an image that results when a lens is used at its lowest depth-of-field setting.

The term *depth of field* is often applied when using HDSLR cameras for video work, because before these cameras featured video capabilities, the capacity for varying levels of sharpness did not equal that of dedicated video cameras. In Leslie Stroebel's book *Photographic Materials and Processes*, depth of field is defined as "the range of object distances within which objects are imaged with acceptable sharpness" (160).

Most lenses purchased as part of a kit are low-cost items that make the kit affordable. Specialty lenses like fisheyes and macros usually have a higher price and tend to be used for specific applications. Most lenses also allow for filters to be attached. Some of these are used merely as lens protectors;

Figure 3.10 Professional photographers can often be found using long lenses at college and professional sporting events to shoot action sports at a distance. (Photo by Lawrence Mason, Jr.)

others, like a neutral density (ND) filter, used frequently in HDSLR videography, will reduce the amount of light allowed into the camera. Filters have a wide range of cost. It is worth considering that if a prime lens costs in excess of $1,000, putting a $25 filter in front of that lens might be like buying a $10 pair of sunglasses on the street. They do the job, but they are nowhere near as sharp as a $150 pair of Ray Bans.

Types of Lenses

NORMAL LENS

A normal lens for a 35mm full-frame camera is in the range of 40 to 60mm. This is a lens that has the same perspective as the unaided eye.

WIDE ANGLE LENS

Any lens below 40 mm, the extremes being as low as 8mm, which is considered a fisheye, is considered a wide-angle lens. Many journalists use a 16mm or 17mm lens in tight, cramped areas such as the front seat of a car while doing a ride-along with a police officer or a video story about a singing bus driver. These lenses can cause distortion in the corners of the frame. A wide angle zoom often covers a range of 17mm to 35mm.

PORTRAIT LENS

An 85mm or 135mm lens on a full-frame 35mm HDSLR camera is often used for portrait photography. The lens is perfect for this application because of its smaller size and the capacity for a faster f-stop speed. When shooting a portrait with this lens, the area behind the subject can easily be rendered out of focus by using a shallow depth of field.

Telephoto Lens

Any lens that is 200mm or greater is considered a telephoto and has specific uses. A 300mm lens, for example, is very good for sports photography. A telephoto lens with a "fast" aperture allows for the image background to be compressed and blurred out, making the subject stand out noticeably. In sports photography this is a great benefit: the action can be separated from a distracting background. These lenses tend to be very bulky, and often require either a tripod or monopod for support. Remember that when using a 300mm lens on a camera that is DX or APS, the lens focal length is more than the specified length of the lens due to the size of the sensor within the camera.

NOTE: As already mentioned, when putting lenses on cameras with APS-sized sensors there is a multiplication factor that needs to be associated with the focal lengths of the lenses.

Figure 3.11 A telephoto lens allows the photographer to shoot high-speed action sports. When being used to shoot these events a telephoto lens should have an aperture of f2.8 or f4, allowing for low-light photography and/or a compressed background. (Photo courtesy of Nikon)

Figure 3.12 Though large in size, a 300mm lens is a workhorse when it comes to shooting action photos, as of a fast-moving gymnast. (Photo © 2008 Andrew Burton)

Camera Memory

Before there were digital memory cards, there was film. Film would be exposed to light admitted through a lens, which would record an image. The film image was then "developed" with chemicals in a darkroom and made into prints. Technology has now shoved film to the wayside, and today's cameras capture images on an electronic sensor called a *charge-coupled device*

(CCD), allowing them to be recorded onto a memory card and subsequently uploaded to, manipulated on, and printed from a computer.

There are several different types of card, varying according to the type of camera you have. Secure Digital (SD) cards, Compact Flash (CF) cards, and Personal Computer (PC) cards are all used for professional applications. CF and SD cards are standard for HDSLR cameras.

Memory cards come in several different types, and it is important to obtain a card—either CF or SD—that is designed for what you are going to use it for. For example, video is very memory-intensive and requires a card that holds 16 GB or more. The card needs to have a high read/write speed, so as not to get bogged down. Remember that the camera is capturing video at 30 frames per second; the faster the card, the less work the camera has to do.

CF cards are very sturdy and can take a reasonable amount of abuse. They have no moving parts, the contacts are on the inside, and they can be written to and reformatted repeatedly. The speed of these cards ranges from 8× to 133×; the higher the number, the faster the read/write speed.

SD cards have contacts on the outside and are about the size of a postage stamp. Their speeds range from 2 MB/sec to 10 MB/sec.

The most important thing to think about when considering cards is their read/write speed. It's the manufacturer's choice whether a camera uses the CF or SD format, with professional cameras offering both options. It's important to understand that both types are very good options, and that this should not

Figure 3.13 A side-by-side comparison shows the difference in size of a CF (Compact Flash) card and an SD (Secure Digital) card. (Photo by Seth Gitner)

determine the type of camera you buy or use. You should just make sure that the card you have is fast enough, in the case of shooting video, to both capture and upload footage to a computer quickly.

Choosing a Digital Photo Editor

The world of photography has gone completely digital. The once-long process of getting the film developed and waiting for the prints—which might then prove to be junk that you didn't even want to keep—has become an essentially instantaneous process. Now photographs can be instantly taken and viewed, the bad ones erased, and the good ones copied an infinite number of times and instantly published to the world.

The same holds true for moving pictures, or video. What was once a slow and very laborious process, in which the user would edit tape-to-tape, is now a fast, flexible, and feature-rich environment where the possibilities are virtually unlimited, even for the beginner.

There are many different ways to work with digital still images, from software like Adobe Photoshop or Lightroom, or Apple's Photos. At one level, digital editing makes it quick and easy to fix—or at least greatly reduce—flaws in lighting or composition. Most images benefit from a little bit of color correction, especially when they are going to be printed. On another level, however, image-editing programs have a whole new power: Along with changing the colors or exposure of a digital image, it is also possible to digitally manipulate its content, combine images, remove whole people from the frame, add anything, and generally alter what was once the "reality" of a photograph.

Whatever piece of software is being used, however, the principles of storytelling remain the same.

Photo Editing Software Choices

Adobe Photoshop

Long known as the gold standard for working up photographic images, this software is also a powerful tool for designing websites and creating digital art. It is excellent for compositing—combining multiple images into collages or whole new images. It has advanced capabilities for lifting complex images out of their backgrounds, and for fixing cosmetic imperfections in advertising and commercial photography.

In photojournalism, Photoshop is used to adjust the tones of images for printing in a newspaper or magazine, or for publishing on the web. Its powers of image manipulation have also made news on more than one occasion, when images have been altered to change the news or tell a false story. For the purposes of journalism, this software should be used only to alter the colors, tone, and printability of images, and not their content.

Figure 3.14 Adobe Photoshop is a great tool both for compositing images and for toning images for print or online use. (Adobe product screenshot(s) reprinted with permission from Adobe Systems Incorporated)

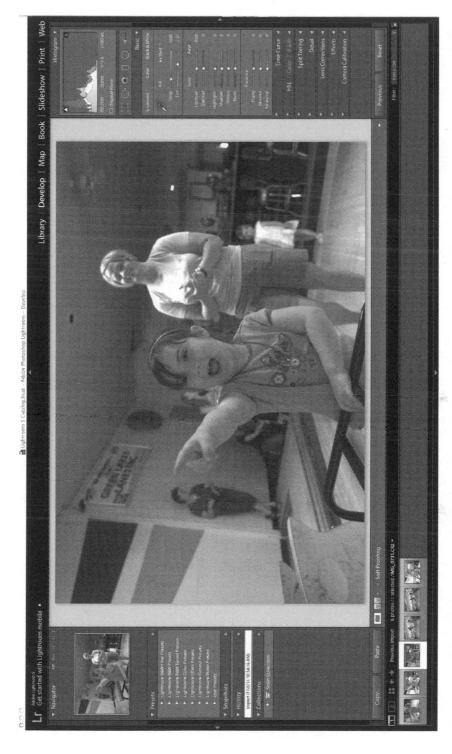

Figure 3.15 Adobe Lightroom can be used both for cataloging large volumes of images and for toning camera RAW images. (Adobe product screenshot(s) reprinted with permission from Adobe Systems Incorporated)

Adobe Lightroom

It is always best to shoot images at the highest quality setting possible. Lightroom is made specifically to work with "raw" image files—the unprocessed information that comes straight from a camera's CCD. These large files provide a great deal of latitude in exposure and other properties during the post-processing phase. Color balance can be changed along with tonal range, and the changes can be made instantaneously without losing information from the image file. Lightroom is a powerful piece of editing software that allows not only the precise editing of images, but also helps in the organization of large sets of images so that they can be meta-tagged and searched for later on.

Imaging Software for Mobile

Now that many images are being captured with mobile devices, software built into mobile applications is being used to make the adjustments once possible only on a desktop or laptop PC. The latter still offer much more screen space and image quality to the serious image editor, however.

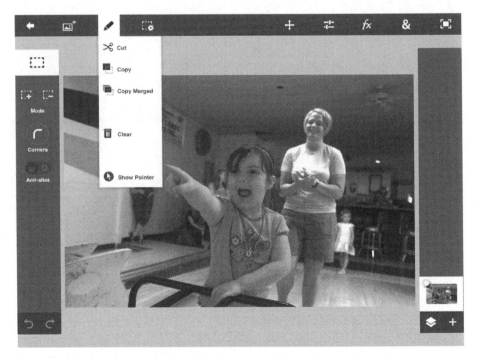

Figure 3.16 Since the invention of the iPad thousands of apps have been developed to do all kinds of things, including toning and retouching photographs. Software such as Adobe Photoshop Touch was developed to do the same things on mobile devices that its more powerful cousin does on laptops and desktops. (Adobe product screenshot(s) reprinted with permission from Adobe Systems Incorporated)

Using Your Camera

Battery Power

Surprisingly, this needs to be said: Charge your battery. It's a basic part of planning a shoot. Never be caught without power. Do not expect to keep a camera plugged in while shooting. You do not want to be attached to a wall. Also, do not depend on someone else to do the charging. If the battery is not charged prior to a shoot, you are dead in the water and will not be able to do much of anything.

Exposure

All cameras—even those in mobile phones—create images from light that reaches the sensor. All DSLR cameras use three settings to change the amount of light hitting the sensor, also called the *exposure*. These settings are shutter speed, aperture, and ISO/ASA. Exposure is a vital factor when shooting either video or photographs. Without properly exposed images and footage, you are not able to produce a high-quality final piece.

Current technology is very "smart," which means that setting a camera on automatic will usually result in acceptable image quality. Still, the camera's automatic settings can be fooled, and this can result in an undesirable or improper exposure. It's best to understand the basics before embarking on a story. Proper exposure depends on the shutter and the aperture working hand-in-hand. When using a mobile phone camera app—depending on the app being used—exposure can be changed. It is common for the focus area of the phone to act as an exposure meter as well, reading the amount of light falling on the area where it is placed. Some third-party apps offer separate focus and exposure areas.

Shutter Speed

The shutter is built into the camera, and controls the length of time that light hits the sensor. Shutter speed can range from one second or more to 1/4000 of a second and up. Most HDSLR cameras work in half-stop increments as a default, meaning that for each level of shutter speed the duration of light is cut in half, or doubled, exposing the sensor to more or less light.

Shutter speed controls the amount of motion blur within an image. To capture a long streak of car lights in a night shot, hold the shutter open for a long time—a low shutter speed. When photographing high-speed action in sports, on the other hand, a high shutter speed will capture a sharp image of a rapidly moving subject. A slow shutter speed will capture motion as blur. Common settings for shutter speeds include: 1/8, 1/15, 1/30, 1/60, 1/125, 1/500, 1/1000, 1/2000, and 1/4000.

Video: Shutter Speed

When shooting video, the denominator of the shutter speed—that is, the fraction of a second that the shutter is open—should be double the frame rate. For example, if the frame rate is 30 fps, the shutter speed should be 1/60 sec. If the frame rate is 60 fps, then the shutter speed should be 1/125 sec. Failure to follow this rule can result in a choppy-looking video. The faster the shutter speed, the sharper the image will be, but a skip will be visible during playback. Only in special circumstances should a slow shutter speed be used, to show things like the moving blades of a helicopter or the swing of a baseball player's bat.

Existing Light Exposure at ISO/ASA 400	*Shutter Speed*	*Aperture*
Bright or Hazy Sun or Light Sand or Snow	1/500	f/16
Basketball, Hockey, Bowling	1/125	f/2
Bright or Hazy Sun (Distinct Shadows)	1/125	f5.6
Cloudy with No Shadows	1/500	f5.6
Stage Shows	1/60	f2.8

Figure 3.17 This chart lists ASA/ISO ratings for common activities.

Figure 3.18 When you are shooting high-speed action, a slow shutter speed will help to show movement. (Photo © 2008 Andrew Burton)

FIGURE 3.19 When shooting high-speed action, a fast shutter speed can capture individual water droplets flying from the hair of a spinning diver. (Photo © 2008 Andrew Burton)

Exercise: Test Your Shutter Speed

This exercise is about changing shutter speed to make a correct exposure with an HDSLR camera. Find a friend to photograph, then line them up so that they are looking at the camera and have them jog in place. Use the camera's shutter priority setting and shoot a few images, varying the shutter speed for each exposure. Check the quality of the images on the back of the camera, or transfer them to your computer. Look at the images' meta information, which is embedded in the files, to determine which image was made at which shutter speed. It would be helpful to use software such as Adobe Bridge or Camera Bits' Photo Mechanic to perform this task.

Again using the camera's shutter priority mode, shoot some photographs of your friend jogging perpendicular to your camera position. Make sure they are running at the same pace each time you take a photograph. For each exposure, vary your shutter speed from slow to fast.

1. What are the results?
2. Which exposure is the sharpest?
3. Can you see how the change in shutter speed changes the range of motion that is captured?

Aperture

The aperture is in the lens, and along with the shutter controls the amount of light hitting the sensor, or CCD. In a traditional HDSLR camera, the aperture is a ring of thin blades forming an opening that controls the amount of light that reaches the sensor. It can be controlled through different f-stops, which range from f1.4 to f22. The smaller the number the wider the opening, resulting in more light hitting the sensor, and vice versa. It is preferable to have a lens that has a wide-open aperture of f2.8 or less.

Lenses with wide openings admit more light and are typically more expensive than zoom lenses, which have minimum wide-open apertures of f4 or f5.6 (lenses that tend to be sold in camera kits). These lenses double or triple their minimum apertures as the focal length is extended, thereby allowing less light into the camera. For example, a 35mm f1.4 lens will allow a higher shutter speed in low light without a flash, for available-light photography.

 Exercise: Test Your Aperture

This exercise is about changing aperture to make a correct exposure with an HDSLR camera. Find a friend to photograph, then line them up so that they are looking at the camera. Using the camera's aperture priority setting, shoot a few images and check their quality on the back of the camera, or transfer them to your computer. Look at the images' meta information, which is embedded in the files, to determine which image was made at which aperture. It would be helpful to use software such as Adobe Bridge or Camera Bits' Photo Mechanic to perform this task.

Again using aperture priority mode, shoot some photographs of your friend at the front of a classroom, about four to six feet from your camera position. For each exposure, change the aperture stop by stop, from f2.8 to f22.

1. What are the results?
2. Can you see a difference in the edge-to-edge sharpness of your image?
3. What happens to the background as you vary the aperture from wide open to smaller?

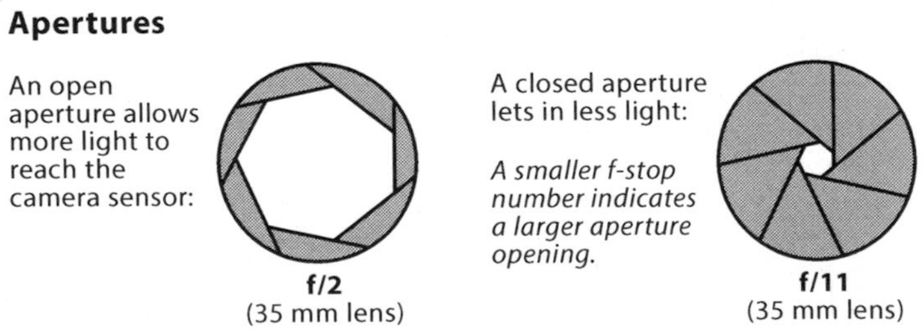

Apertures

An open aperture allows more light to reach the camera sensor:

f/2
(35 mm lens)

A closed aperture lets in less light:

A smaller f-stop number indicates a larger aperture opening.

f/11
(35 mm lens)

Figure 3.20 The difference between a large aperture (left) and a small aperture (right). (Illustration by Chris OBrion)

ASA/ISO

You also need to know how to control a digital camera's sensitivity to light. In the days of film, before cameras went digital, each roll of film had a specific American Standards Association (ASA) or International Standards Organization (ISO) setting. ASA/ISO was the speed at which the film was rated. A low ISO meant it was rated for brighter light (ISO 64 to ISO 200), while a higher ISO meant one could use the film in low light and get properly exposed images (ISO 400 to ISO 1600). With digital, the capabilities of the sensors have surpassed those of film—digital camera sensitivity ratings can go upwards of ISO 12,000 with good results. These higher ratings do have a downside, however: the higher the rating, the more expensive the camera.

On some cameras higher ratings result in more *pixelation*, or noise, in the resulting image. On film this was called *grain*. There is a certain amount of give-and-take to all photography, however; this is why it is good to understand as much as you can about your chosen tools. Mobile phones do not have the ability to have their ISO changed manually. Generally, the ISO is determined automatically, making low-light photography in available light without a flash difficult on these devices.

 Exercise: Using ISO

Set your camera on its Program setting and find a room with light entering through a window. Make sure there is a dramatic change in light level when you turn the room lights on or off. Using the ISO menu, shoot images at different ratings with the lights both on and off.

1. Do you notice a difference in the exposures that the camera can make?
2. Is there a difference in the quality of the exposures?
3. Do you see any graininess or pixelation in the images?
4. If so, at what ratings can you detect these imperfections?

ISO/ASA	
100	Bright, Sunny Days
200	Sunny days for common picture taking of friends and family
400	Sports Action in Sun where a higher shutter speed is needed
800	Ideal for existing light photography indoors
1600	Ideal for Sports action in existing light photography
3200	Best for shooting in dimly lit situations without flash

Figure 3.21 A list of common ISO/ASA settings that the camera needs to determine the amount of light sensitivity for the meter.

Review: Exposure

- Exposure is the amount of light that hits the sensor and makes a digital image. It is a combination of shutter speed, aperture, and ISO/ASA sensitivity.
- Slow shutter speeds allow more time for light to hit the sensor and generate an image, which is useful in low-light situations but doesn't capture motion well.
- Fast shutter speeds allow light to hit the sensor for a shorter interval, useful for capturing action in well-lit situations.
- Shutter speeds are usually in this range: 1/15, 1/30, 1/60, 1/125, 1/250, 1/500, 1/1000, and higher.
- Aperture is directly related to the amount of depth of field in an image.
- A smaller aperture (f2.8 or below) is a wider opening and will allow more light to hit the sensor, but it will also result in a shallower depth of field.
- An aperture of a higher number (f16 or higher) will allow in less light. It will be a smaller opening, but also sharper around the entire frame.
- Aperture has a lens-opening size range of f2.8 f4.0 f5.6, f8.0, f11, f16, f/22.

Color Balance

Did you know that the sky is not just "blue"? It can be cyan, or turquoise, or royal blue, or cerulean, or violet, or any number of other shades, depending on the time and conditions. The same goes for white, which is seldom pure, but rather can be cream, very light blue, gray, or even pink. The brain processes the signals from the eyes and decides to make this color the "white" for this situation.

A camera, even though it has an "auto" function for setting white balance, cannot really know what color is what. To avoid situations like those that occur when shooting under fluorescent lights—when footage may turn out to be a weird shade of green—it is important to know about white balance. While cameras have different ways of adjusting this, generally you can hold a piece of white paper in front of the lens (so that it is reflecting light from the primary light source), push the white-balance button, and set it for the lighting type of every shot you take. White balance applies to both video and stills. Digital cameras must have their white balance adjusted.

It is possible, of course, to adjust color balance through software in post-production, but doing so can add considerably to production time. The computer will have to be left to process all those changes. When on deadline in a news situation, it's always best to get the correct white balance at the outset.

Color is measured in degrees Kelvin. Here are some common lighting situations with their Kelvin measurements:

- Sunlight – 5500K
- Fluorescent – 4000K
- Tungsten bulbs – 3500K
- Candle – 2000K

Focus

All cameras have a focusing system of some kind. Focus is based on distance: If you photograph a subject that is three feet away, and set the focus on three feet, that subject would be in focus. The same holds true for ten feet. Farther out than that, the focus would be set to the infinity symbol; the lens then puts everything in focus.

All cameras made nowadays have autofocusing mechanisms that measure the distance from the camera to the subject, which provides enormous help in focusing. In low light the autofocus can be "fooled" and function poorly, however, and this is when it is important to understand how to focus manually. It is also important to use manual focus when shooting video interviews. On these occasions the subject is often off-center, and many auto focus systems read the center of the image. This will cause a camera to automatically focus on whatever is behind the subject, such as the wall. This is called *back focusing*, and is a common pitfall of autofocus use.

Figure 3.22 Focus is determined by distance. Every lens has a distance meter on it to help the photographer determine focus when it must be done manually. (Photo by Seth Gitner)

Even when not shooting video—say, when using an HDSLR to shoot still photos—built-in autofocus is useful. In these cameras, the technology has reached a point where autofocus works so quickly that there is no way—especially when shooting sports—that it can be improved upon manually.

Many HDSLRs disable autofocus when video is being shot, which can make things difficult. Smaller prosumer cameras generally have good autofocus, but depending on the camera, manual focusing may be a challenge. Some smaller cameras have touch screens that simplify focusing on different objects within a frame.

 ### Exercise: Focusing

This exercise is a about testing a camera's manual focusing mechanism. Secure the camera to a tripod.

Place a coffee mug on a table with a blank wall behind it. Using a tape measure for precision, and the manual focus controls on the camera, do the following:

1. Place the mug one foot from the camera lens, adjust focus accordingly, and take a photo. Review the photo on the LCD on the back of the camera.
2. Move the mug one foot farther away, take a photograph, and review the image. Do the same up to five feet, adjusting the focus each time you move the mug back. Notice how the image stays in focus. Now repeat the exercise, only this time without changing focus. What happens?
3. Now focus the camera on the wall behind the subject. What happens to the subject you were photographing? What does it look like?

Light Metering

All cameras have a built-in light meter that measures the light being reflected off the scene being photographed. Many newer cameras have special, multipoint metering systems to automatically measure this light. Many camera systems have meters that are center-weighted, meaning that they concentrate only on whatever is at the center of the viewfinder when measuring reflected light. Spot meters are even more precise, allowing the user to assess certain points in a scene and measure the light falling on particular areas. Average-weighted meters measure the light reflected off an entire scene, averaging the measurements to give an overall meter setting. The light meter will help in determining the right exposure for an image. Let too much light hit the sensor and the image can be overexposed. Not enough light results in underexposure. Small variations in exposure can make or break an image—video or still.

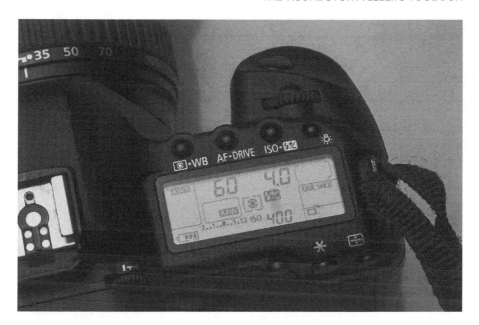

Figure 3.23 Most cameras have a digital readout on top to help the user understand whether an image will be under- or overexposed. (Photo by Seth Gitner)

Strobes

There is a common misconception that images taken indoors should always be taken with a flash. Professionals know that this is not the case. Most small cameras have a function that automatically pops up the flash when a sensor determines that more light is needed to get a properly exposed, in-focus image. The resulting image usually has a dark background and subjects that are washed out, often with the familiar phenomenon of "red eye." A better way to take a photograph is to turn the flash off and use existing light; the result will nearly always be more pleasing.

Some low-light situations do not allow this type of photography with a smaller, handheld camera. In a very dim room or outdoors at night, using a flash may be the only way to get the image recorded to the sensor.

Using a camera with manual exposure capability provides a lot more control. When you are outside at night and need to get a photograph without a flash, using available light only, use a wider aperture and a slower shutter speed to allow more light to hit the sensor, in addition to raising the ISO/ASA of the camera. If the situation allows it, use a tripod.

Depth of Field

Suppose you are on vacation, and you come to a place in mid-afternoon with a beautiful view. To take a photograph that would be sharper overall, it would be best to use an aperture of f5.6 to f8. Using an aperture of f16

Figure 3.24 The image on the right was made with a flash; that on the left was made without. Note that the flash image is sharper, but also note the shadows. It's commonly thought that taking better photos involves pointing a flash at a subject. It's actually better to take a photograph without a flash, using available light. A flash can overpower the exposure, resulting in a flat, blown-out look with a dark background. (Photo by Seth Gitner)

or f22 would allow more depth of field, but most lenses also lose critical sharpness at f16 and f22.

To get an image of someone in the foreground, with the background out of focus, use a lower aperture setting with a wider opening. An aperture of f2.8 or f4 would help to blur the background and put more emphasis on the subject.

If, for example, you want to photograph somebody with a blurred background, also known as *shallow depth of field*, set the aperture to a wider opening and a higher shutter speed. This would produce the desired blurring of the background. Sports photographers shooting still images prefer to use this shallow depth of field, as it helps to make whatever they are shooting stand out. Some photographers may also use a shallow depth of field to layer subjects within the frame, blurring the subject that is closest to the camera while keeping a point of focus on the rear subject. This is usually just a matter of preference when shooting an image.

Video: Depth of Field

Generally, the lenses used in small video cameras make it difficult to achieve a low depth of field. Unless you focus on a subject that is extremely close up or very far away, there are minimal options for producing a shallow depth of field, in which foreground objects are out of focus at the same time that background objects are in focus, or vice versa. These cameras tend to cost a lot less than cameras with interchangeable lenses, however, and are still very suitable for many video applications.

Professional-grade, ENG video cameras, with lenses that cost up to $15,000, have large apertures and a wide-ranging zoom. Many filmmakers are opting for HDSLR to shoot video, though, since costs can be lowered by using lenses originally intended for still photography.

"Don't get distracted by the shallow depth of field," said Rick Gershon, a freelance director of photography and cinematographer based in Brooklyn,

Figure 3.25 When shooting with a telephoto lens, an aperture such as f16 or f22 will result in a background that is in focus. (Photo by Seth Gitner)

Figure 3.26 When shooting with a telephoto lens, a wide-open aperture such as 2.8 or smaller will result in a photo with a background that is out of focus. (Photo by Seth Gitner)

NY. "It can easily become a gimmick. It is a great tool but needs to be done with purpose. Good storytelling and solid photography cannot be replaced by shallow depth of field."

Video: Frames per Second

On average in the United States, video cameras shoot anywhere from 24 fps to 60 fps, and different settings have different uses. A high frame rate (an HDSLR camera will usually allow 60 fps) is better for video that will be played back in slow motion, or when shooting something like a high-flying, fast-moving BMX bike acrobat or skateboarder.

Hollywood filmmakers generally shoot film at a rate of 24 fps. Images shot at this frame rate, when looked at individually, tend to appear blurry. When played in a theater at full speed, however, the result appears sharp. Many HDSLR cameras that shoot video can be set to shoot at a rate of 24 fps, making the video look "film-like," but it is recommended that first-time videographers shoot at 30 fps, since this is a sharper frame rate, allows more latitude during viewing on the web, and is easier to work on with a nonlinear editor (NLE). It's important to note that when editing video in the timeline of an NLE, all the video footage should have been shot at the same frame rate.

Camera Supports

Unless a shaky effect is desired in a video, it's best to keep the camera still and steady. With small cameras in particular, this can be difficult. There are a number of devices to help with this, notable among them being the Steadicam, a brand of a sophisticated device that isolates the movement of a camera from that of the operator carrying it, creating the illusion of a camera that is weightless and flying through the air.

Tripods

It is a good rule of thumb to always use a tripod. Shaky video is undesirable unless it is a vital part of the story being told. The viewer will notice it instantly, and it's also annoying to try to piece together an edit in post-production with video that is shaky and unsteady.

There are many options when it comes to purchasing tripods, from very cheap to very expensive. In the end, all you need is something that fits your budget, is easily portable, and can hold the camera steady for long periods of time.

The cheapest brands of tripod fulfill their simple task, but in general they will break down under constant wear and tear. It is therefore a good idea to once again look at the prosumer option—midrange models that can be used by professional and casual consumer alike.

Tripods have heads that allow the camera to be both panned from side to side and tilted up and down. In addition, they come with camera plates that attach to the underside of the camera. These plates make it easy to pop the camera off the tripod between scenes for handheld use.

Most tripods also have a built-in bubble level, making it simple to level the field of view and keep the scene from being tilted. This is, again, a great benefit in post-production. Additionally, some tripods have heads that are on a ball mount, allowing easy leveling of the tripod separate from the legs. Lacking a head like this, tripod legs need to be manipulated one at a time to get the bubble in the center of the level.

Also, be careful about where the tripod is set up. Look for level ground, out of the way of foot traffic and the possibility of being tripped over. Remember that there is going to be an expensive piece of equipment sitting on top.

When its legs are folded in tight, a tripod can also be used as a monopod (see the following section). In "pack" journalism, such as at a press conference in which journalists are following around a politician, a tripod can hold a camera up high for a shot from above.

Steadying Devices and Accessories

BEAN BAG

You can either build this yourself, filling it with sand or beans from the grocery store, use ankle weights, or purchase a bean bag with a carry strap. A bean bag can be placed on most any surface, such as a boulder, vehicle, or fire hydrant, providing instant stability for the camera.

MANFROTTO 585 MODOSTEADY 3-IN-1

This "three-in-one" product acts as a shoulder support, a camcorder counterbalancing stabilizer, and a table tripod.

TRIPOD BRACED AGAINST BODY

A lightweight tripod with its legs opened, but without full extension, can be braced against the body to make a kind of makeshift Steadicam.

SHOULDER RIG

There are all sorts of shoulder rigs; essentially, this is a device that steadies the camera so that you can look through the viewfinder while the camera is braced against the shoulder.

COWBOY STUDIO SHOULDER MOUNT SUPPORT PAD

Made of plastic, this inexpensive rig is very versatile and puts pressure on the user's shoulder to hold the camera steady.

Figure 3.27 Less-expensive tripods will usually do the job, but don't expect the quality of a more expensive model. (Photo by Seth Gitner)

Figure 3.28 A higher-end tripod for video will often have a fluid head that makes panning and tilting easier and smoother. (Photo by Seth Gitner)

Monopods

Another way to keep a camera steady is with a monopod, a single-legged mount or pole that rests on the floor. These can often be seen attached to the cameras of sports photographers on the sidelines, usually for the purpose of offsetting the weight of a very long telephoto lens. Monopods are also very useful with digital video cameras—especially small ones that lack a shoulder brace. These cameras, though small in size, can be tiring on the arms when held at a certain level for extended periods of time. A pan/tilt or ball head can be present on a monopod, and can help to make shooting more fluid.

Slider/Rails

The advent of HDSLRs in particular, which increased the ability to get high-quality video easily and affordably, has resulted in many new attachments that add movement to video.

One of these is rails or a slider, in which a camera is attached to a track, along which it moves smoothly. Rails are a great way to keep a shot moving, so that a scene is not at a standstill for a long period of time. This is useful

Figure 3.29 A monopod can be used when shooting HDSLR video to help steady a camera on the move. (Photo by Seth Gitner)

Figure 3.30 A slider is a tool that moves the camera along a path for a long tracking shot. (Photo by Ethan Backer)

for stories in which there is a lot of process to be shown—things that involve building or following some procedure. Smooth, subtle movement can help keep things from becoming monotonous and keep the viewer engaged.

Lighting

Have you ever gone outside on a fall day at sunset and seen light glowing on the homes in the neighborhood? The orange glow lights up everything it touches, producing a distinct mood. The visual storyteller needs to be sensitive to this, to natural light as it falls on a scene. Different kinds of light can be utilized to vastly improve photography and video. Everything from interviews to documentary visual storytelling is enhanced by attention to available light sources.

Not everyone has access to studio lighting kits and other ways to achieve fancy lighting effects. To make high-quality video without a painful hit to the wallet, shoot an interview with the subject close to a window, but without the window in the shot. A large, nearby window can be the perfect way to get side lighting that enhances a portrait or interview. To make the shot even better one could position a reflector, such as a light disk, but there are cheaper options. A piece of white poster board or foam core could do the job; position it so that it is on the other side of the subject from the window. The light reflected from the board will fill in the shadows of the subject's face.

Never discount daylight as an abundant, effective tool for making a portrait or an interview more interesting.

Figure 3.31 A light disc can be used to bounce light back onto a subject. (Photo by Mark Carlson)

If tungsten lamps are available, "bounce" these lights off a white board, wall, or ceiling. This will diffuse the light and make it more manageable. Pointing a bare-bulb desk lamp directly at a subject can result in light that is too harsh. If studio lighting is available, make sure to use the diffusers that might have come with the lighting kit, such as umbrellas or reflectors.

Microphones: The Basic Audio-Gathering Tool

Strong audio is essential to multimedia production. Audio is the backbone to video storytelling, and it is collected with microphones.

There are over 200 kinds of microphone available, but for our purposes we will center on four types with varying pickup patterns and uses. Think of microphones the way you think of lenses for a camera. Just as lenses of different focal lengths are used for different shots in photography, different types of microphones fit different recording situations. It is also important to understand the settings at which audio is being recorded—just plugging a microphone into the camera does not guarantee good audio.

Microphones capture both desirable and undesirable sound. Strive for the desirable. Undesirable sounds are things like cars whooshing by during an interview, air conditioners humming, refrigerators buzzing, RF noise that can make a wireless transmitter go awry—virtually any distracting noise that does not further the story. Desirable sounds are what the storyteller wants and needs to capture with a microphone: spoken words, sounds that enhance the story, and natural, ambient sounds that will help to put and keep viewers in the scene.

Omni-Directional Microphone

These microphones pick up a lot of sound, in a 360-degree pattern from all directions with the microphone at the center.

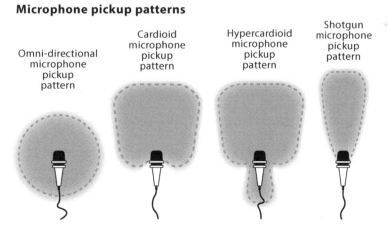

Figure 3.32 Different types of microphones have different pickup patterns. (Illustration by Chris OBrion)

Cardioid Microphone

Commonly used for vocals and speech, this microphone is unidirectional, or good at rejecting noise that comes from behind, such as sound that the camera operator may make.

Hypercardioid Microphone

This type of microphone has a large, frontal pickup pattern and a smaller pickup pattern behind, so that its entire pattern resembles a figure eight. Since it rejects sound from the side, this kind of microphone is ideal for voices on broadcast news reporting.

Shotgun Microphone

This type of microphone is standard for anyone shooting video, and especially news video, since it allows for sound to be gathered from a short distance. To return to the camera lens comparison, this mic is the telephoto lens in your audio tool box. It can be used to capture dialogue from a subject some distance away, and is directional—it can be pointed at a specific location. Like the cardioid, it picks up sound that is in front of it while rejecting sound at the sides. It also tends to pick up sounds to its rear, however, making it necessary for the camera operator to keep noise to a minimum. It needs to be understood, though, that while a telephoto lens brings objects closer within the frame, a shotgun microphone will not magnify a distant sound, but only make it more distinct.

Handheld Microphones

The preceding types of microphones can all be handheld, and they are generally built to withstand a lot of punishment since they are used in daily news-gathering.

If a shotgun microphone is being used for news gathering along with a handheld microphone or a lavalier microphone (see Figure 3.33), the shotgun with a wind screen is used on the left (A channel) and the lavalier or handheld would be on the right (B channel). In this type of situation the shotgun would be gathering ambient audio from the scene.

The handheld microphone can also be used off-camera, with a coiled cord attached. When acting in a one-man-band capacity, needing to interview people quickly but also obtain good audio, the operator can hold the camera in one hand and the microphone in the other.

Tips for Using Handheld Microphones

- For on-camera applications, it's best to hold this microphone at chest level, pointed toward the reporter's mouth.

- Use a wind screen, even if the microphone supposedly has one built in.
- Try to hold the microphone at its center, so that your hand is away from both the microphone element and the connector at the opposite end.
- Be careful not to rearrange your fingers while recording, as this can produce handling noise.

Figure 3.33 When reporting on camera, use a microphone pointed upwards toward the reporter's mouth. (Photo by Seth Gitner)

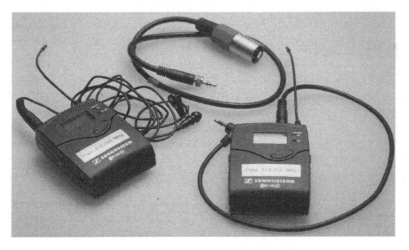

Figure 3.34 A wireless lavalier microphone set has both a transmitter and a receiver. It can transmit some distance. (Photo by Seth Gitner)

Wireless Microphone

A wireless microphone is connected to a transmitter that sends an audio signal through the air to a receiver, which is connected to the camera or a handheld audio recorder. The audio that is recorded tends to be more candid than audio captured with an ordinary shotgun or stick mic.

Lavalier Microphone

Also known as a *lav*, this microphone is designed to be worn on a subject's upper body. Also called a *lapel mic*, it tends to be discreet and inconspicuous to viewers. Lavalier microphones come in various pickup patterns and allow audio to be gathered "in the moment." They can also be wired or wireless. Wired lavalier microphones tend to be a lot more dependable; the wireless variety is subject to interference that can block or degrade the signal. For sit-down interviews, a wired model is definitely recommended. Make sure to place the wireless microphone six to eight inches below the subject's mouth, with the wire running up the person's shirt and out of view of the camera.

Tips for Using a Lavalier Microphone

- Position it fairly close to the subject's mouth.
- Be aware of a rubbing noise that can result if the microphone is up against a collar or shirt.
- Make sure the microphone is securely attached to the subject before recording.
- Attach the transmitter to the subject's waistband or have him or her put it in a pocket. Try to hide the cable that is connected to the wireless transmitter as much as possible by coiling it up and placing it in a pocket.
- Try to avoid bending the cable at the mini-plug connector; these tend to break under repeated stress.
- Check that the frequency on the transmitter matches the frequency on the receiver.
- With all cameras, it is important to test the quality of the audio going into the camera before starting a shoot.

HDSLR-Specific Microphones

There are microphones specifically built to be used with prosumer video cameras and HDSLR cameras. These units have built-in shock mounts, are battery-powered, and have shoe mounts that allow them to be attached directly to a camera. Though not as high in quality as broadcast ENG-style microphones, they do a fine job for what they are. They do tend to be very susceptible to mic handling noise, however, especially since they are attached to lightweight cameras.

Figure 3.35 The microphones built into both HDSLRs and video cameras tend not to pick up sound very well. It is recommended that an additional microphone be plugged into the camera to help pick up more desirable sounds and fewer extraneous ones. (Photo by Seth Gitner)

Microphone Accessories

A variety of microphone accessories are available to help in obtaining the best possible sound quality. Remember that bad sound is unusable sound, whether shooting for journalism or entertainment.

Shock Mount

Microphones "hear" movement that is within close proximity, and especially when something is touching the mic. To minimize this kind of noise, use a shock mount. These mounts hold the microphone suspended in midair with special rubber bands, dampening any vibration that could cause unwanted noise.

Pistol Mount

A pistol mount is ideal for handholding a microphone at times when you are not carrying a camera, for a radio piece, for example. Shaped like a handgun, the mount can be fitted with a shotgun microphone to obtain very focused sound. Some pistol grips allow the microphone to be put at the end

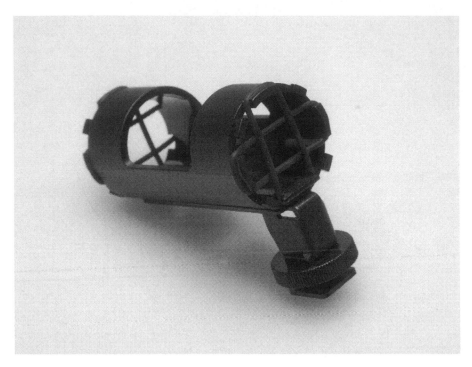

Figure 3.36 A shock mount holds a microphone suspended to cut down on handling noise. (Photo by Seth Gitner)

Figure 3.37 A pistol microphone mount can be held in the hand to record ambient sound within a scene. (Photo by Seth Gitner)

of a monopod or boom pole; that way a sound recordist can hold the boom above a subject for good audio.

Wind Screens

Wind is a microphone's worst enemy. Even the smallest breeze on a mic can sound like a hurricane on a bright and sunny day. To avoid this, use a wind screen, a foam tube that surrounds the microphone and prevents this extraneous noise. Many different types are available. In common use are the "dead cat" variety, shaggy, furry-looking socks of various sizes that fit over shotgun microphones, and "blimps" or "zeppelins," which are essentially large cages covered with sound-permeable material that ensure still air around the microphone.

XLR Connector

This three-pin connector is commonly found in professional video cameras and cabling, mixing boards, and amplifiers. Able to transmit both audio and low-voltage power, XLR cables are commonly found in news situations where a "mult box" is used, which allows multiple operators to record one source of sound, such as a microphone on a stage.

Broadcast news multimedia journalists often carry a six-foot XLR cable as a backup in case they have problems with batteries in a wireless microphone or problems with wireless frequency transmissions.

Figure 3.38 Wind screens on microphones keep out unwanted air-movement noise that can mess up a recording. (Photo by Seth Gitner)

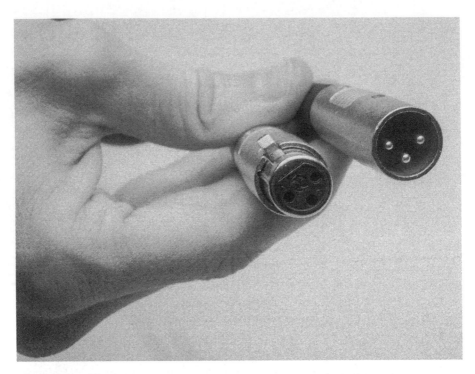

Figure 3.39 XLR plugs connect microphones to cameras. (Photo by Seth Gitner)

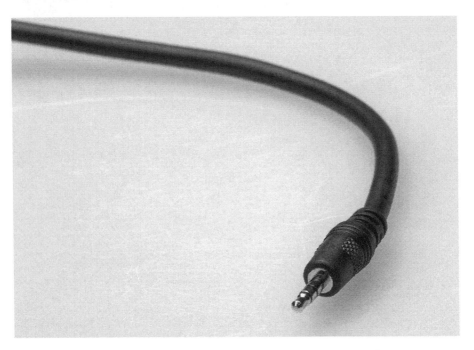

Figure 3.40 Mini plugs are very common in HDSLR and prosumer cameras, serving as both headphone and microphone jacks. They plug into the camera but are not as secure as the XLR or ¾-inch plugs preferred by professionals. (Photo by Seth Gitner)

Mini-Plug Cable/Jack

This is the same kind of jack found on a portable audio device or mobile phone. These connectors tend not to hold up very well, and can easily break if not handled with care. Many HDSLRs and prosumer cameras have this type of jack built in.

Batteries

Some microphones have built-in power. If these batteries are not maintained and replaced, the result is poor or weak sound. Check battery status before every shoot.

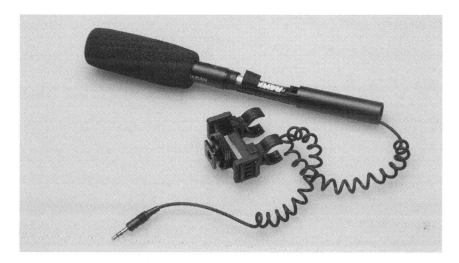

Figure 3.41 Microphones not powered by the camera need to be powered by an internal battery. (Photo by Seth Gitner)

Figure 3.42 Phantom power is the term for microphones being powered by the camera. (Photo by Seth Gitner)

Phantom Power

Some higher-end video cameras allow the camera to power the microphone, which is known as *phantom power*. This option is noted on the camera as "+48v."

Headphones

It's rare that a person would not have a pair of earbuds for listening to music; these ubiquitous "headphones" come bundled with portable audio players and mobile phones. While economical, they are not well suited to listening to audio while recording for a film. More suitable is a pair of headphones that covers the ears and blocks out any sound other than what is coming through the microphones. Some headphones cancel out extraneous noise—useful if you are flying on a puddle jumper and want to watch a movie, and can barely hear it through your headphones over the sound of the propellers. The problem with using noise-canceling headphones in recording is that while the headphones might cancel out the sound of an air conditioner for your own ears, the camera will still record it, and when you get back to edit the video you will have a problem.

Also, be careful with volume when using headphones, especially any that are placed inside the ear. As Stan Alten and Doug Quin write in their book *Audio in Media*:

> It has been found that listening to headphones at a loud level after only about an hour and a quarter can cause hearing loss. One recommendation

Figure 3.43 Over-the-ear headphones are preferable to earbuds. When recording video it is better to cover your ears to make sure that what you are getting on the recording is free of extraneous noise. (Photo by Seth Gitner)

is called the 60 percent/60-minute rule: Limit listening through headphones to no more than one hour per day at levels below 60 percent of maximum volume. You can increase daily listening time by turning down the level even further. (69)

Audio Recorders

Sometimes, especially when working with HDSLRs, audio might need to be recorded separately from the camera itself. These situations require a handheld audio recorder, much like radio reporters use. When using one of these devices, make sure to always record at the highest quality setting. For filmmaking, record at 48k. This ensures that if the audio is combined with audio from a video camera, the two types will match.

As with video cameras, never use the internal microphone of an audio-only recorder. Try to use a broadcast-grade microphone. This will ensure audio of the highest quality.

The memory cards used in cameras are also used in audio recorders. Since audio files are not as large as video files, it is not necessary to compress them in formats like mp3—save that format for songs on your audio player that you listen to while exercising. Compression on an audio recorder will only degrade the quality of the recording.

On a similar subject, there are two types of audio recording: lossy and lossless. *Lossy* refers to audio in which information has been thrown out to compress the data on a memory card. *Lossless* is the highest quality possible, and should be the goal when recording. The same terms and concept apply to photography, only the data are for images rather than audio.

Some Tips for Common Audio Level Settings

1. Do not let your audio peak, where the meter is driven to the maximum.
2. Keep dialogue and important sound at or near −6db.
3. Keep background at or near −18db.
4. Anything below −18db will not be delivered by many sound systems. Try to mix your sound so that it is at least loud enough to be heard on a laptop computer.

Audio for Video

Having good quality microphones for recording audio is essential to making a quality film. Make sure to use a camera that allows an additional microphone to be plugged in, and once again, never use the microphone that is built into the camera. These built-in units tend to record anything and everything, including the pressing of buttons on the camera.

Once a higher-grade microphone has been plugged into the camera, the levels will need to be set. Make sure that the camera has audio indicators that move as sound is picked up by the microphone. Every camera is different, but for the most part a mic level should be set within a range of –12 dB to –6 dB. This will allow enough room for a peak or two, if they should arise. Avoid over-modulated levels, which tend to be red in the camera's indicators. In post-production, the difference between good levels and over-modulated levels can be seen in the waveforms in the video editor.

It is important to note that there are different types of audio signals that can enter the camera, such as a mic level and a line level. *Mic level* is the lowest signal; this is the signal that is often boosted using Phantom power, to bring the signal up to a line level. *Line level* is the highest strength audio level; examples of this can be from typical home stereo components, such as DVD or CD players.

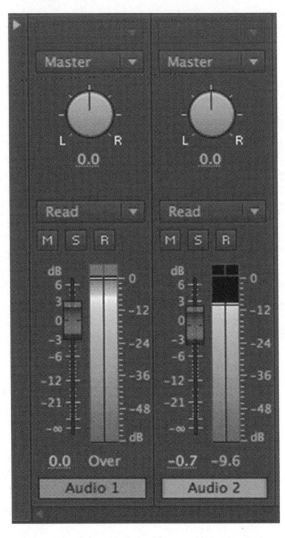

Figure 3.44 When playing audio in the video editor, check the levels to make sure that they are not peaking or are not over-modulated. (Adobe product screenshot(s) reprinted with permission from Adobe Systems Incorporated)

Chapter Summary

Students who study multimedia storytelling have more powerful, more affordable tools at their disposal than ever before. You can start with the smart phone that's very likely in your pocket, and move quickly to more powerful, more flexible prosumer cameras that might be available in a school program. Some students might even already have their own HDSLRs.

Knowing about all the current types of cameras, along with something about how they evolved, will allow you to put the technology into perspective as it continues to change rapidly.

You may be lucky enough to have access to the highest quality gear out there, or you may have access only to a mobile phone. You may come upon less than half of the items mentioned in this chapter during the course of your introduction to multimedia storytelling. Either way, it's important to know what the options are. The process of filming, for whatever genre it might be, is bound to introduce snags and challenges that can often be resolved with higher quality gear. As you gain expertise, you will want to enhance your work with the options that better gear provides. Imagine filming a hockey game with a standard camera with a built-in microphone. Now imagine filming the same game with a GoPro camera mounted on the referee, paired with a lavalier microphone. Your viewers would hear firsthand the scrape of skates on the ice, the sticks smacking the puck, the profanity flying faster than the punches being thrown. Knowing the tools available helps you to shoot the story that you want to shoot.

Still, remember: These items are just tools in the toolkit. The final product, the images shot and the story told, is what will affect the viewer. Anyone can use cool gadgets or shooting techniques. Making a story that resonates is the ultimate end.

 ## Review Questions

1. What is the difference between shutter speed and aperture?
2. What is the "temperature" of daylight in degrees Kelvin?
3. How far underneath a subject's chin should you attach a lavalier microphone?
4. What recording level should you aim for when using a microphone?
5. How do you cut down on the amount of wind hitting a microphone on a windy day?
6. Other than using a tripod, what is another way to support and steady a camera?
7. What rating (high or low) ISO/ASA would be best to shoot a photograph of someone indoors, in low light?
8. What are the two types of memory cards used in digital cameras?
9. What is the difference between a full-frame sensor and an APS-sized sensor?

 ## Exercise: Still Photo Exposures

It is important to know what exposure to use when shooting photographs. There is no wrong answer, as long as the photo is not over- or underexposed and you get the desired image.

A small aperture such as f16 will keep everything in focus in the frame from front to back. Shooting wide open, such as f2.8—a large aperture—allows manipulation of the depth of field within an image. Show movement by using a slow shutter speed, or freeze the action with a fast one. The desired end result should determine what the settings will be.

Make four images of the same scene, using the extreme settings of shutter and aperture given below. Make sure to adjust the ISO accordingly.

1. One image with a slow shutter speed, showing movement
2. One image with a fast shutter speed, showing captured action
3. One image showing a large depth of field
4. One image showing a minimal depth of field

Use human beings in your photographs; try to avoid inanimate objects. Feel free to "set up" your photos, as this exercise is primarily about learning to work with exposure.

Exercise: Visual Scavenger Hunt in Video

Using a DSLR's video function, shoot footage that expresses or captures at least three of the following words:

- Work
- Love
- Joy
- Water
- Cold
- Time
- Danger
- Hope
- Sensuality
- Dark

You do not need to put these video clips together in one timeline. Rather, make one 15- to 30-second video clip for each word.

- Be thinking of light, color, and composition while shooting the sequence.
- Use a tripod.

Key Terms

48 kHz – Standard audio sampling rate for audio in video applications.**

4K – Twice both the vertical and horizontal resolutions of HD.

Aperture – Aperture controls the amount of light hitting the sensor.

APS-sized sensor (Advanced Photo System) – A light-gathering sensor that is cheaper to manufacture, with fewer megapixels. Whether a camera is full-frame or APS-sized refers to the size of the sensor.

Bokeh – The out-of-focus portion of an image that results when a lens is used at its lowest depth of field setting.

Cardioid microphone – Commonly used for vocals and speech, this microphone is unidirectional, or good at rejecting noise that comes from behind, such as sounds from the camera operator.

Depth of field – The range of sharpness from foreground to background relative to the primary focus point.

ENG – Electronic News Gathering.

Full-frame sensor – Cameras that have sensors that are much larger, with a larger number of megapixels, allowing a higher quality image.

H264 – A codec primarily used in mobile phones and tablets

HD – High definition, screen size 1920 × 1080 pixels, the ratio of the screen being 16:9.

HDSLR – High-definition single-lens reflex.

Hypercardioid microphone – A microphone with a large, frontal pickup pattern and a smaller pickup pattern behind, so that its entire pattern resembles a figure eight.

Lens – The optical "eye" of the camera through which light passes to the sensor.

Line level – The normal level or strength of the audio signal output from most electronic devices.

m4v – Format used for video files in the iTunes store.

Mic level – Lower than line level, it needs to be amplified to achieve a higher output.

Mini plug cable jack – The same kind of jack found on a portable audio device or mobile phone.

Monaural (Mono) – One-channel audio (right or left).

mov – Container format for holding audio, video, effects, or text, primarily used by Apple Quicktime.

mp3 – Type of audio file used by portable audio players. The quality of the music file degrades as it is compressed to fit more music onto storage media.

mp4 – Container format that can be played on tablets and on the web; an international standard usable on a wide range of players.

NTSC – National Television System Committee: format with a frame rate of 30 fps for broadcast television used in video cameras primarily purchased in the United States.

Omni-directional microphone – These microphones pick up a lot of sound, in a 360-degree pattern from all directions with the microphone at the center.

PAL – Phase Alternating Line: format with a frame rate of 25 fps for broadcast television used in video cameras primarily purchased in Europe.

Phantom power – Some higher-end video cameras allow the camera to power the microphone, known as *phantom power*. This option is noted on the camera as "+48v."

Prosumer – Intended for either the professional or the casual consumer, within a budget of a couple thousand dollars. A video camera is considered prosumer grade if it has a lower quality lens or it has restricted audio capability. Professional cameras tend to be more durable, since they are used heavily and in harsh environments.

SD – Standard definition, screen size 720 × 480 pixels, the ratio of the screen being 4:3.

Shock mount – Holds a microphone suspended in midair with special rubber bands, dampening vibration that could cause unwanted noise.

Shotgun microphone – The standard type of microphone for anyone shooting video, and especially news video, since it allows sound to be gathered from a distance.

Shutter speed – The length of time that light hits the sensor.

Stereo – Two-channel audio (right and left).

Wind screen – A foam or fur tube that surrounds a microphone, blocking wind noise.

XLR connector – A three-pin connector commonly found in professional video cameras and cabling, mixing boards, and amplifiers.

** "A sampling frequency of 48 kHz means that samples are taken 48,000 times per second or each sample period is 1/48,000 second. Theoretically, the higher the sampling rate, the greater a system's frequency range" (Alten and Quin, 143).

Sources

Alten, Stanley R, and Douglas Quin. *Audio in Media.* Boston, MA: Wadsworth/ Cengage Learning, 2013.

Ewen, McKenna. Conversation with author, June 22, 2012.

Gershon, Rick. E-mail conversation with author, November 15, 2010.

Gregg, James. Conversation with author, March 27, 2013.

Hattan, Jerry. Conversation with author, June 2, 2013.

Stroebel, Leslie D., ed. *Photographic Materials and Processes.* Boston: Focal Press, 1986.

4 THE INTERNET AND SOCIAL MEDIA

How Are the Internet and Social Media Affecting Visual Storytelling?

In this chapter you will learn

- The basics of Twitter, Vine, Pinterest, and Instagram
- Digital content strategies for journalism
- The ideas behind information graphics
- Developing a digital content strategy
- The basics of website structure, architecture, and construction

---

Introduction

In the days of analog communication, when media consisted of the four separate platforms of print, television, film, and radio, content was being delivered just as it still is now. Fiction, nonfiction, comedies, dramas, sporting events, and journalism were all pushed out to audiences through these media, with things like advertising, public service announcements, and public relations tending to piggyback on the content that audiences were more willing and eager to consume.

Sometimes advertising was built into comedy and drama. It has long been a prominent part of sports. Advertisers even found ways to push their messages through cooperative journalists, and still do. In fact, the ultimate prize for a public relations professional is to get a news media beat reporter to cover a topic that a PR agency has been hired to push.

There are plenty of places to learn about the creation, development, and uses of the Internet; that is beyond the scope of this book. For our purposes, it is enough to say that today, with the Internet as part of the equation, anyone with a computer and some know-how can push their own content to an audience, whether it be entertainment, journalism, persuasive advocacy, or anything else that people will watch. The challenging part is assembling the audience—rounding up the watchers. This is where the explosive phenomenon of social media comes into its own.

Just as computer users can now be their own content publishers, they can now grow and use social networks to make their content known to an ever-widening audience. Likewise, traditional companies that once depended upon the advertising industry can now be their own media corporations. Along with advertising, they are able to push their brand's message through social media and other means of digital storytelling, the end result being many more eyes on their product or message. Now comes the real power of the Internet and social media. It is interactive. The audience can weigh in, and make a difference. If content is well done and appealing, it will be retweeted, shared, and reposted many times over. The shelf life of that content can become virtually endless—a big payoff for relatively little expense.

Consumers of traditional, legacy media are creatures of habit. The reader gets the newspaper in the morning, reads it, and then puts it in the recycling bin. Now, however, with the Internet, content no longer has to have such a short lifespan. Stories now have lives of their own. They also have their own distribution lines, and the supercharged word-of-mouth publicity machine of social media. Stories can be shared among friends and colleagues, saved, imitated, and re-shared months later in a face-to-face conversation. The life of a story can go on as long as that story remains relevant.

Social Media and Messaging

When ads are placed on newspaper pages, there is little doubt that they are ads. When an ad is pushed through Twitter, however, the message can be seen as news, PR, or an ad. "Twitter isn't paid for, but you can work with Facebook and put together a strategy to pay for it," says Tracy Rock, vice president and account director at the Publicis Kaplan Thaler advertising agency in New York City. "But the message itself is unpaid—Facebook and Twitter amplify and push out content."

Gaining influence in the social media space is more important than just adding followers to a Twitter account. Influencers have the ability to spread messages quickly and easily.

In today's social media world it is important to get one's message out to the top influencers in a particular area, such as someone with a large Twitter following that is interested in the topic at hand. Ideally, your content should be the first thing people think of when they are talking about a certain topic. William Ward, director of education strategy at Hootsuite Media, Inc., explained how different influence can be exerted on different platforms:

> Now there's a nontraditional media format with people who are influential in different spaces. People that were influential on one platform may not be influential on another. Somebody might be really influential on

Instagram . . . but then you go over to them on Twitter; they are not very influential. And then on Facebook . . . there might not be much going on.

Someone with something specific to say, based on a certain product category or industry, might need to identify with a specific social media platform. "Fashion is really popular on Tumblr and in Facebook, and electronics is more popular on Twitter," Ward explained.

Social media services enable companies to push their messages the way they want them to be heard, without the middleman of a newspaper or television station. Many times the audience does not know whether the content is being disseminated through a public relations or advertising campaign, or just spontaneously.

Social media are therefore becoming a very large component of promoting a brand or product, utilized by many companies and groups to build identity in the marketplace. The viral nature of social media also has a multiplying effect, giving anyone the capacity to get their name out to millions of people, not merely through text but through visuals as well. With Twitter owning the six-second-video app Vine, and Facebook owning the fifteen-second-video app Instagram, the ability to push video on social media is becoming mainstream.

Through online social photo sharing networks like Instagram, marketers have the potential ability to get their messages in front of new audiences that are based primarily online. Brands are now able to push their campaigns worldwide simply through visuals. Brands are becoming their own media companies, with no need for traditional media outlets to get the message out.

And, it is very easy. Instagram has a program that helps business users interact with their image-sharing network. The company publicizes ways for marketers to utilize a network through a page called "Examples of Brands on Instagram," providing examples of successful approaches to advertising and marketing.

Deploying the Story on the Social Network

Social networks are about connecting users. They function in a unique way, with users serving as both the consumers *and the producers* of content. This makes a social network into a kind of self-maintaining system with a life of its own—the creators need only to set it up, sit back, and let users and their interactions be the driving force. The more users who come, the more users will be attracted by the size and diversity of the growing user base. Lots of users means lots of potential for new or rekindled relationships, status, news, gossip, romance, business connections, jobs, influence, intrigue, family interaction, or anything else that humans seek from one another.

And, of course, stories. Lots of them.

A social network's biggest challenge, therefore, is providing a natural, intuitive environment inside which users feel comfortable to do their thing, and do it often.

They must readily be able to post their thoughts and their images, and/or comment on the thoughts and images of others. They must have the freedom to explore and be heard. The flow of information should be fast and free; content needs to move at a swift pace and change constantly. The environment must allow for a constant exchange of ideas in real time. Conversations must be allowed to develop. These conversations will be the lifeblood of a successful social network.

The first step, however—the most crucial conversation, so to speak—is the creation of buzz. The first, initiating conversation must be about the network itself. Something must make people want to dip a toe in the water, or just jump right in. Something must create the impression that *this is the place to be*. To put it another way, before it can get people talking about any and every subject under the sun, a social network must itself be a topic of conversation.

This is not a book about starting social networks, however; we're concerned with storytelling. Still, before moving on, let's take a look at the mother of all social networks.

Facebook and Social Networking

There isn't a lot to be said about Facebook that most users of this book do not already know.

For our purposes, it is enough to say that Facebook is currently the predominant social network worldwide. It has become a powerful company, always changing and evolving new ways to tie people together (and to advertisers), some more successful and popular than others.

Conceived originally as a way for college students to network, Facebook has grown into a truly vast array of mini-sites representing individuals, groups, causes, businesses, governments and government agencies, hobbies, politicians, media outlets, and even pets and zoo animals (presumably with some help from humans).

According to an article by Shea Bennet on the website Media Bistro, "Facebook remains the number one social marketing tool for brands, with 83 percent using that channel this year, and 88 percent targeted for 2014."

Every company that has a niche audience would be well-advised to harness Facebook and its avenue to millions of users. The capabilities that Facebook offers corporations through its API are virtually endless.

As social media and social networks evolve, their importance in daily life only increases. According to Facebook's company information website, they had 802 million daily active users on average in March 2014, with approximately 81.2 percent of daily active users outside the United States and Canada. Numbers like this make Facebook the undisputed king of social networks.

For the purposes of multimedia storytelling, Facebook allows the development of a steady group of "subscribers"—an audience—to which content can be pushed and from which "Likes" can be harvested. This wide-reaching, low-overhead, self-perpetuating audience can be a huge asset for journalists and brands alike.

One useful feature of Facebook for web developers is the Open Graph protocol, which utilizes the "Like" button. When a user clicks "Like," the data is passed to Facebook that this particular piece of content is considered good by a real, human user. Unlike search engines, which depend on algorithms, the "Like" button provides a different kind of assurance that content is worthy of reading or viewing. This ranking within Facebook therefore has a very real value.

This functionality can be accessed from outside the Facebook network, too: Journalism websites and other content publishers can place a "Like" button on their own sites, allowing users who are signed into Facebook while reading a particular story on a site to ascertain who of their friends has already viewed the article and "Liked" it.

Poynter.org's Jeff Sonderman explains: "What Facebook has done is change the definition of 'sharing.' It's the difference between telling a friend about something that happened to you today and opening your entire diary."

Much of what news organizations are doing is experimenting with ways of distributing their content to the masses. At one point, content was simply read in print—a "subscriber" who got the newspaper every day was simply a "reader." Now, with analytics, it is possible to know exactly what readers are reading and sharing, as well as who they are.

According to Facebook:

> At Facebook's core is the social graph: people and the connections they have to everything they care about. The Graph API presents a simple, consistent view of the Facebook social graph, uniformly representing objects in the graph (e.g., people, photos, events, and pages) and the connections between them (e.g., friend relationships, shared content, and photo tags).

This gives applications the capability to use Facebook as a form of distribution for their content.

The Open Graph has its own capabilities as information architecture. Any application that connects with Facebook through the Open Graph has the ability to draw specific profile content from users. For example, information about the author of this book can be found at: https://graph.facebook.com/sethgitner.

The Social Community

According to Frederic Stutzman of the University of North Carolina,

> Social network communities facilitate the sharing of identity information in a directed network. Compared with traditional methods for identity information disclosure, such as a campus directory, the social network community fosters a more subjective and holistic disclosure of identity information. (Abstract)

According to the 2012 Nielsen report "State of the Media," Americans spend 23 percent of their time online on social networks and blog sites. The data goes on to say that women are more likely to visit Facebook than men, and that the network LinkedIn is frequented more by males than by females. The report also says,

> Social networking is indeed a global phenomenon. In a look across a sample of ten global markets, social networks and blogs are the top online destination in each country, accounting for the majority of time spent online and reaching at least 60 percent of active Internet users.

This information suggests that social networking is more popular than ever and is a major driver of the Internet. Australia leads the way, averaging seven hours, seventeen minutes per person.

What Is Twitter?

Like Facebook, Twitter, a microblogging service that sends out "tweets" of 140 characters or less to users, has become a fixture of daily online life. The service can be used to promote videos, news, websites, and other content. Twitter provides a constant stream of textual information that lets users "subscribe" to the postings of other users and be subscribed to by them. Twitter uses hashtags (#—the pound sign on a numeric keyboard) to identify messages on a specific topic, and hashtags can be tracked. Brands often use them to identify specific campaigns and to check engagement for a particular topic. Because of its immediacy, simplicity, and wide reach, Twitter is a popular way for citizen journalists to post reports and photos of news events immediately after they happen, or even as they happen.

Twitter Basics to Gain Influence

- Make short statements that grab attention quickly. What would *you* want to read?

Figure 4.01 Twitter is a microblogging service that sends out "tweets" of 140 characters or less to users. (Twitter)

- Place links to infographics, videos, or sites to reference.
- Use hashtags (#) that are trending or relevant to the content.
- Be interesting enough to be retweeted; mentions in other tweets will attract more followers.

Exercise: Tracking Twitter

Choose one of the following five Twitter accounts:

1. The 1010 Project | Twitter: @the1010project | Website: the1010 project.org
2. Create The Good | Twitter: @createthegood | Website: aarp.org
3. American Cancer Society | Twitter: @AmericanCancer | Website: cancer. org
4. The Humane Society of the United States | Twitter: @humanesociety | Website: hsus.org
5. The Leukemia & Lymphoma Society | Twitter: @llsusa | Website: lls.org

Use one of the tools below to monitor the performance of the Twitter account you choose. Note your observations and thoughts about the trends that you see from the Twitter accounts.

- Tweetreach: http://www.tweetreach.com
- Twitalyzer: http://www.twitalyzer.com
- Tweetstats: http://www.tweetstats.com
- Twubs: http://twubs.com/
- Hashtracking: http://www.hashtracking.com
- Twitaholic: http://twitaholic.com/
- Twitter Counter: http://twittercounter.com/

Note the following about the Twitter accounts:

- Total followers?
- Followers from week to week?
- Tweets per day?
- Popular hashtag(s)?
- Do they host a tweet-chat?
- Give two examples of tweets sent out.

What Is Vine?

Vine is a very recent form of short-form visual storytelling. Owned by Twitter, it is a visual form of the same service, only limited to six seconds of visual activity.

Figure 4.02 Vine is a video form of Twitter, on which posts are limited to six seconds of visual activity. (Vine)

The service was first met with skepticism; people wondered who would bother to watch a six-second video. "Vines" have since become a very popular way of sending short video messages, however.

In the Vine app, a movie is taken only when a finger is pressed to the screen of the mobile device. You cannot shoot a vine with a camera that is not a mobile device.

Exercise: Vine

Find a partner, grab a piece of paper, and shoot a six-second video of the process of your partner folding a paper airplane. Make sure that the sequence has a definite beginning, middle, and end.

What Is Pinterest?

Social applications such as Pinterest have quickly taken hold as ways for public relations professionals to get their messages out to the masses visually. Pinterest is a scrapbook of sorts, that allows users to "pin" photographs and items from other sites onto virtual "pinboards" or collections, which can then be shared with like-minded people. These collections can serve as reminders related to weddings or other social events, cooking, crafting, home decor, or any other hobby or interest. When searching for items on the web that match your personal clothing style, for example, Pinterest offers an alternative to bookmarking. Rather than adding another bookmark, you can "pin" a specific image to a Pinterest board for later viewing. The images then can be saved to a "wall"— a wall possibly made up of items from brands from all over the Internet. Images posted to Pinterest are not uploaded to the service itself; they are linked from another site. This means that posting your own images to a Pinterest board requires uploading them to a blog or photo sharing website first.

Figure 4.03 Pinterest is a scrapbook of sorts that allows users to "pin" photographs and items from other sites onto virtual "pinboards" or collections. (Pinterest)

Exercise: Pinterest

Pinterest is a convenient way to catalog visuals you may want to use later. Think about what you might like to eat for your next meal. Create a Pinterest account, if you do not already have one, and then make a pinboard of items that would make a great meal. Make sure to grab items from all of the food groups to make it healthy and tasty.

What Is Instagram?

Instagram is an online photo sharing network for mobile devices that allows users to take photographs and then instantly upload them to the service. The application offers various filters for users to enhance their images. As in other kinds of social media, users have the ability to subscribe to or "follow" other users and "like" their images by clicking a heart-shaped icon.

Examples of Instagram in Strategic Communications

- Popular musician Jason Mraz held an Instagram photo contest to promote his single, "I Won't Give Up." Mraz picked twenty-five winners from thousands of entries, all of which needed to have the hashtag #iwontgiveup. The contest was won by a 19-year-old from Lynchburg, VA (Hernandez).
- The National Press Photographers Association used an Instagram photo contest to promote one of its conferences (http://contest.multimediaimmersion.com). The images were judged by respected picture editors and photographers, and the winners of the contest received prizes.
- When starting up an organization, you can always take photos of your officers the usual way, against a white wall. Or, you can shoot them on Instagram and post the images via social media for a livelier, more immediate effect that says something interesting about your organization.
- Planning an event or convention? Set up a game in which invitees post an image of some iconic place or thing from the place where they live, via Instagram, with a specified hashtag.

Social Media Content Strategies

"I think a great strategy for viral video is through analytics," said William Ward, the education strategy director at Hootsuite Media, Inc.:

> You can identify who the social influencers are. These are the people who have larger reaches or audiences and are actively engaged. . . . You can target those people, to get them to be more proactive and to share that

(specific) story. If you build a relationship with that person over time, and they know who you are as a brand or a person or a company, and they like your product, then you can connect with them.

It is important for strategic communications professionals to understand the basics of storytelling, but when working with those in the journalism world, building relationships with beat reporters and journalists is a very important capability as well.

As social media become a larger and more frequently used part of the strategic communications tool box, agencies are learning how to provide prepared tweets and headlines that can be easily shared, complete with bullet points that clearly explain the tweets themselves. Prior to this, agencies would fax press releases to newspapers that were, in fact, already-written stories. These pseudo-news stories would rarely be printed verbatim in the paper; normally they would be assigned as "story topics" by editors to reporters on specific beats, or possibly assembled in digests.

Imagery in Social Media

Something that has been known about print media for some time is that when a photo is paired with a newspaper or magazine story, there is a greater chance the story will be read. In newspaper journalism, daily editors' meetings are held to determine what the lead photo should be on a newspaper or website front. The lead image is a quick read for any publication, giving the reader an instant grasp of the big news of the day. Print newspaper editors are constantly thinking about what the "above the fold" image is going to be for tomorrow's paper, because that image is what a potential reader will see in the window of the newspaper box on the corner or at a convenience store. Single-copy sales like this help drive up daily readership.

Now, with Facebook for example, the same thought process holds true. A post with an image attached has more power to be seen. According to Socialbakers.com, a July 2013 report found that 93 percent of the most engaging posts on Facebook were photos.

The same thing is happening on Twitter: imagery is enabling more social media success. According to a 2014 report from simplymeasured.com, using photos in a tweet will increase user engagement: "Tweets that include photos and links receive 150 percent more engagement than brand averages. Visual content is effective on Twitter, driving more engagement on the content that brands post."

In April of 2014 Twitter redesigned their user profile pages, enabling inline images that were uploaded to pic.twitter.com to be seen without the user having to click a link. This makes Twitter a visual medium that now exceeds the limited power of 140-character posts, along with giving new meaning to the old adage, "a picture is worth a thousand words." According to Belle Beth Cooper at blog.bufferapp.com, the site performed its own test of 100 tweets (without any retweets) comparing the averages of tweets with and without images. The results: "Tweets with images received 18% more clicks than those without."

Social Media in Journalism

It is important to realize that journalism is not all long-form writing, being on camera, or even updating websites, and that there are other avenues through which to distribute news to an audience. Social media have given this fact a whole new meaning. Facebook and Twitter, for example, provide ways for journalism companies such as newspapers and television to reach a huge and important audience: one that is online but not necessarily reading print, watching television, or visiting their websites. Understanding just how to utilize social media to help report the news is not optional; it is a requirement. In journalism, "You need to learn how to craft the perfect headline . . . writing a tweet uses a lot of the same skills that writing a headline does, but there is nuance to it that takes an understanding of the platform," said Lauren Bertolini, a product manager at Gawker and the former social media manager there. Prior to Gawker, Bertolini was the senior social media editor for NBCUniversal. It's important for journalists to understand how to use tweets from other people in their own stories, and to provide attribution. Also, understanding what can and should be retweeted during a news story is a big part of using social media in journalism. "We are not going to retweet unsubstantiated tweets," Bertolini said.

It's also important to keep a Twitter feed fresh. "We're not going to . . . every two hours post the same link," Bertolini said. With an ongoing story, it is also best to keep the Twitter feed focused. Don't interrupt a Twitter feed about a breaking news event with tweets about other, run-of-the-mill new stories.

In spot news, often the best Twitter account to follow is that of the reporter on the scene where an event is occurring. What usually happens is that reporters will post content from their own Twitter accounts, and that content will be retweeted by the news organization, which probably has more followers. Of course, the reporter who is on the scene of a major event will have a good chance of picking up new followers and gaining an audience, too.

A journalism brand itself—the newspaper or TV station—may have a social media editor whose job is (among other things) to follow social media throughout a shift trolling for news and retweeting content from reporters in the field. The reporters in the field, in turn, should make it part of their job to follow on Twitter the agencies and prominent accounts of people they cover. A police reporter for a newspaper in New York City, for example, would stay tuned in to the New York City Police Department at @nypdnews. "Give people a sense that when news is breaking, they can follow you and they will get some insight into what is happening," said Bertolini. "If I know that you are the person who knows what is going on, you're the first person to go to when I want to read the story the next day." Twitter gives journalists a unique opportunity to establish that kind of reputation. The more breaking events you can be first with on Twitter, the more likely users are to see you as the go-to source of news.

Journalists also need to understand what a #hashtag is. Hashtags provide a way to find posts from different accounts that are talking about the same thing. When watching the World Cup on television, for example, and wanting to find out what's going on with the United States team, the right hashtag on Twitter will provide information right up to your exact moment. Someone will be tweeting it. If you are wondering why a certain star player is not in the game, rather than going to a search engine to find a news story that may or may not mention the reason, Twitter will likely have a conversation going on that might explain it. On a smaller scale, say you are unable to get to that high school football game on Friday night—the one that's not important enough for any larger news outlet to cover. Someone will be tweeting it, and you'll likely have the play-by-play. "Twitter is your news feed—true, on-the-pulse, raw feed—of updates," Bertolini said.

Nor will you be lacking for pictures. Twitter also has a way to receive images in their real-time stream of tweets, called twit-pic, on which you can also broadcast your own images via the network. The site displays each image in a feed on your Twitter page. These images make Twitter a quicker read and a more complete news experience.

As Bertolini said of her role in journalism at Gawker Media:

> I love the mission-driven focus—the idea that you have a readership that is coming to you with a specific need and purpose, and you're fulfilling that purpose for them, and you are answering questions they need answered and uncovering truths that need to be uncovered. That's a real valuable way to spend your life.

Other ways to use social media in journalism include using a platform such as Twitter to crowdsource story ideas, or to find people who might have something to do with a particular topic. When doing a story about the potential risks of tanning beds, it's possible to use a platform like Twitter to crowdsource someone who may have gotten skin cancer after too much tanning. It's a way to reach out to the community at large to find both subjects and sources. It could also work to build video stories, since it can be very hard to find that initial person who will allow you into his or her life with a camera.

Whether one is working for a large television network in New York City or a small newspaper in the Midwest, imagery on social media is increasingly important. At the *Macomb Daily* in suburban Detroit, MI, social engagement editor Mary MacLeod runs the newspaper's Facebook account. She said that since she took over the social media position, the number of "likes" for the page has increased fourfold, going from around 2000 "likes" to over 8000. The newspaper does not use the site to crowdsource stories, but more to promote stories already published on the newspaper's website. One photograph that she shared on Facebook has garnered over 16,000 shares: an archive image of a store called the Plum Pit. "We ended up doing a news story about the fact that it went viral," said MacLeod. "If I would have just had text and a generic photo with that I don't think it would have gone viral."

The *Macomb Daily* also has a Twitter account with over 16,000 followers, which MacLeod runs. "I use photos on Twitter and get better results there as well," she said. "It's interesting that at this juncture, where photos and visual journalism is so important, and it is what gets shares and the 'likes' and so forth, that photographers are being laid off. It's just kind of ironic."

MEET THE PRO

Matt Gelb, Philadelphia Phillies Reporter @magelb: *The Philadelphia Inquirer*, **Philadelphia, PA**

Matt Gelb is a staff writer at The Philadelphia Inquirer, *where he covers the Phillies and major league baseball. Born and raised in the Philadelphia suburbs, he attended Syracuse University and graduated with degrees in history and newspaper journalism. Gelb worked at the* Cape Cod Times *and* The Star-Ledger *prior to joining* The Inquirer *in August 2009.*

Figure 4.04 Matt Gelb is a reporter for *The Philadelphia Inquirer* who covers the Philadelphia Phillies. (Photo courtesy of Matt Gelb)

Covering a sports beat for a newspaper—better yet to be covering a major league baseball team— would be a dream job for many writers. Matt Gelb is the Philadelphia Phillies beat reporter for *The Philadelphia Inquirer.* Gelb covers both home and away games, and in the 2013 season he covered seventy-two of eighty-one away games. But despite the fact that he works for a newspaper, his job reporting involves a lot more than just writing. These days, a reporter needs to do more. He can be found shooting video, doing on-camera stand-ups, shooting photos/Instagrams, and keeping his 21,000-plus Twitter followers up to date with the latest information about Phillies baseball. "It's weird, because when I first broke in, the first paper I worked at when I was in high school was a small suburban paper. The circulation was no more than 12,000," Gelb said, comparing his present-day Twitter feed to the newspaper's number of subscribers.

Gelb's Twitter feed is not where he posts play-by-play game action from a Major League Baseball (MLB) game: "Play-by-play has its value at certain levels, like the high school level, where people don't have access to a TV or radio broadcast and really are relying on your account of what is going on." Gelb said he uses his feed differently, posting insider information about the Phillies and other items he finds out about the team as a beat reporter. Technology has automated play-by-play tweeting of America's favorite

(Continued . . .)

(...*continued*)

pastime and made it faster than any reporter or announcer; with mobile phones, die-hard fans can follow the game using the MLB app. "I think of myself as watching the game on the couch with a Phillies fan, and I am trying to give my insights as to what they are watching," Gelb said.

A look at Gelb's Twitter page reveals that he follows only 135 or so other Twitter users, but actually that's a little misleading. He uses Twitter lists to organize those whom he follows, combining major league beat reporters on one and minor league feeds on another. He says he also follows agents, scouts, and other members of the media, looking for news items and tidbits of information that could lead to possible stories. The Phillies organization itself uses Twitter to push its own messages to the news media. Gelb explained:

> The Phillies started a media-only account. They don't even send press releases out anymore... They tweet all their transactions; they tweet out the lineup every day. It's a protected account only for media members. No more email press releases, no more texts; they just do it on Twitter.

As for how much he tweets, "I like to try to limit myself to fifteen tweets, not including replies, a day," he said. "Don't waste words, or in this case don't waste people's attention. If you think it's worthy, go for it or be smart about it—if you think it is valuable and people will like it." Gelb sees Twitter as a way to interact with fans; he has even befriended a local Philadelphia police officer who follows his account. He also believes less is more:

> I think that the less you tweet the more meaningful they [tweets] become. I think the more you overwhelm someone, it turns people off. I try to maintain this happy medium where I am at the pulse of what is going on but I am not inundating people with minutia.

Gelb studied journalism in college and signed up for Twitter his senior year, at the suggestion of one of his professors. He never took a photo class, but he uses Instagram regularly in his reporting, taking pictures in and from the press box, pictures in the dugout, and other scenes he may find interesting. "My goal is to show people the behind-the-scenes, the everyday life of a baseball team," he said.

Social media has its place in journalism, but at the same time, people like Gelb are usually centered first and foremost on their roles as news reporters. "Social media is a big part of my job, but my writing and my reporting is still paramount to me," he said. "I do like taking photos and I do like tweeting—I like interacting with fans—but where I gain the most followers and most notoriety is when I do good reporting and good writing, no matter what the vehicle is or the medium to disseminate that."

Stories and the Viral Nature

"Storytelling is essential in doing social media effectively," says Anthony Rotolo, a social media consultant. "To feel involved and to feel heard, if you are continuously telling a story . . . at least in some way it feels real." Rotolo gives an assignment each semester in which students attempt to make a video that has the ability to "go viral," or spread spontaneously through social sharing on its own merits. As he explains,

> When I first started doing social media and working with companies, a lot of times you get asked, 'Can we make something go viral?' In the lesson, I say that question is inherently flawed. I try to teach that you really can't guarantee to make that happen.

Rotolo has had some success with at least two projects in which students have made videos that play to a particular niche audience—Syracuse University alumni and students. In one of Rotolo's classes, student Hailey Temple produced a Carly Rae Jepsen "Call Me Maybe" lip-dub video that attracted over 100,000 views on YouTube. Temple, a junior dual-majoring in public relations and information management at Syracuse, explained how she did it:

> A story captures those important moments that connect people together. I filmed my subjects with important Syracuse landmarks in the background: the Carrier Dome, the Quad, and Ernie Davis Hall. These scenes would help connect the alumni to the video. Uniting people together through these scenes and moments is what ultimately made this video effective.

Many in the strategic communications industry are hopeful that companies will recognize the power of social media and try to take advantage of what it has to offer, but some misconceptions can lie in the way. Many companies expect their social media efforts to instantly go viral, but that can be an elusive target to hit. "There is a way to increase your chances of making it viral, and that's the storytelling, which is 85 percent of it. The other 15 percent is knowing the market that you're putting your product in," said Todd LaBeau, vice president and director of digital marketing at Lindsay, Stone & Briggs, an integrated public relations and advertising agency in Madison, WI. "Brands that have more fans . . . have more reach and a higher potential of being viral because they are reaching more people, while at the same time they're also very smart in when and where they place that video," added LaBeau.

Figure 4.05 These photographs were taken and posted on Instagram by Richard Koci Hernandez. (Photo by Richard Koci Hernandez)

 Exercise: Instagram

Take and upload twenty-six *different* Instagram images over the course of a week that represent each letter of the alphabet—one photograph for each letter. Try to find real-world objects that resemble or at least suggest the actual shapes of the letters.

Make sure to take advantage of the software by adding and subtracting from the tonal quality of the images. You might be instructed to use a unique #hashtag such as #mmstoryatoz.

Infographics in Social Media

As the press release becomes outdated, new forms of distributing controlled messages, such as infographics, are taking hold. These forms of communication can convey more information than a photograph alone, adding visual detail to an otherwise flat topic or making comparisons through graphic highlighting of important pieces of information. Through shape, color, and design, information graphics make content more understandable and easier to grasp than it might be in a dense, long-winded, text-only press release. Infographics package content for quick and easy consumption.

Similarly, as our culture becomes more and more visual, long, text-only stories are becoming a thing of the past. Consumers seem to be opting for getting content quickly, but in fact turning data into information is nothing new. Many newspapers have in-house graphics departments that develop graphs, timelines, maps, and other diagrams both large and small that help reporters tell in-depth stories or explain complex topics.

"Infographics work in social media because they use visuals to tell the story, and visuals communicate more quickly with people," said William Ward, of Hootsuite. "They can read a 1,000-word blog post or a 100-word Facebook post or 140-character Twitter post, or they can look at the infographics. Visuals tell a story. It's a quicker way to get information, when done well."

The data-visualization, social media, and talent-sourcing website Visual.ly is a marketplace for visual content that is devoted to the sharing of infographics through social media. Users can copy embed codes, which are then easily entered into a content management system (CMS) or blog. The infographics on the site are diverse—everything from how to tie a bow tie to making place settings to a collection of all the sci-fi spaceships known to man. "The main ingredient that you need to get an infographic to go viral is luck," said Aleksandra Todorova, editorial director for Visual.ly. "You can create ten amazing infographics with great data and very good design, and they don't do much, but then the eleventh goes viral because a power Twitter account picked it up," she said. "Good design, good data, and good luck are a winning formula."

Infographics help PR professionals make data sets visually interesting. They assist in putting data comparison and research into easily digestible forms.

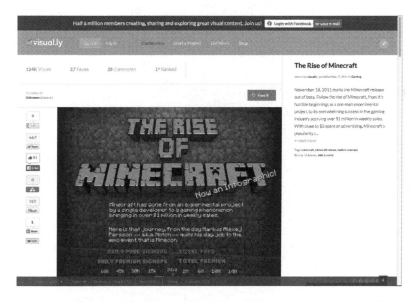

Figure 4.06a The data-visualization, social media, and talent-sourcing website Visual.ly is a marketplace for visual content that is devoted to the sharing of infographics through social media. (Infographic by Visual.ly)

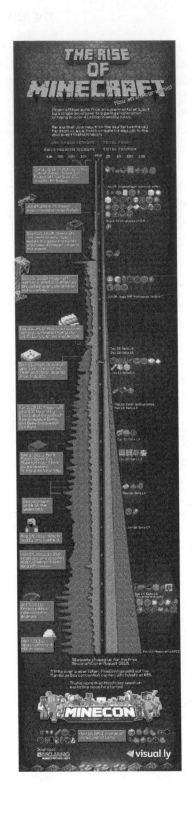

Figure 4.06b

They summarize statistics that could otherwise bore the audience, and even remove language barriers between the source and the viewer.

"From my perspective as the journalist behind the infographics, a good infographic is not just about design," said Todorova:

> You can have a very well-designed infographic with bad information—that's the worst of all, because people are like, 'this is so cool,' they start sharing it, and all of a sudden you have an infographic that looks great, and it has either wrong information or bad information . . . that is the most dangerous of all.

Infographics, Data, and Social Media

The quality of infographics in social media covers a wide range. "You need to go past the initial impact to show trends, patterns, or sales going up or down, and these are the reasons why," said Alberto Cairo, who teaches Information Graphics and Visualization at the School of Communication at the University of Miami. "Infographics should let me see a little bit deeper into the data. I will probably not like the graphic if it is just a bunch of numbers with a bunch of illustrations. That is not a good infographic," he explains:

> I have to say right away that many of the infographics that I see from PR and marketing agencies—90 percent of them don't look good. Many of them look great, but they betray the very word 'infographic.' They are just 'graphics' without the 'info' component. They don't provide insights into the data. They are just posters, or ads. Designing an infographic doesn't consist of just putting words, numbers, and visuals together. Infographics are about creating graphs, diagrams, maps, etc., that let readers explore the different dimensions of the story you're presenting.

Cairo said he believes a true infographic tracks trends and patterns of data, exploring the data and going deeper into it. It is not enough just to be fun or eye-catching, like many of the infographics shared on social media. "Infographics in social media today have an impact—many of them are beautiful, but they are shallow, trivial, and not insightful at all," he said. "As a consequence, they are completely useless. They get my attention for a second, and I move on."

ALBERTO CAIRO'S FOUR COMPONENTS OF A GOOD INFOGRAPHIC

Functionality – The graphic forms you choose to record your data should be adapted to the tasks that the graphic should facilitate. If you want to draw comparisons, use a bar graph; if you want to show changes across time, use a line graph; if you want to show geographic patterns in the data, use a map. Don't use a map to try to make comparisons. Maps are not suited for that. Think about what functions a graphic should have, and do so before you start.

Beauty – It's obvious a graphic needs to be aesthetically pleasing, and it can also be attention-getting and even fun. If it is merely functional, a graphic may not enjoy as much success. It could fail to attract initial attention and not get the chance to convey its information.

Insight – Many infographics these days are obvious and very trivial. They use a lot of space to tell us something we already know. A graphic should be insightful and offer a new view of things.

Ability to enlighten – You want to change your readers' thinking about important topics.

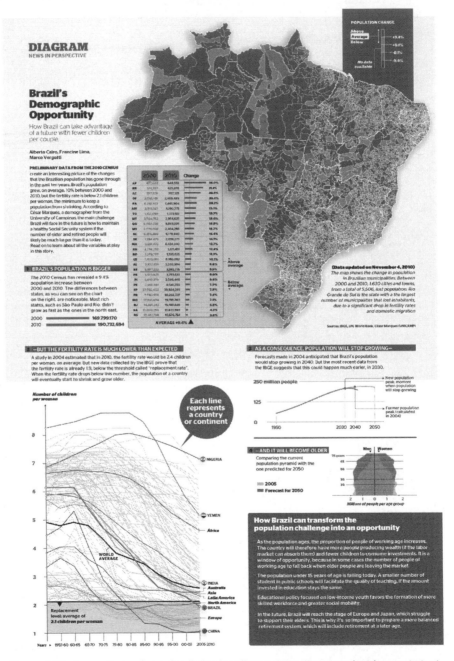

Figure 4.07 An example of an infographic by Alberto Cairo. (Reprinted with permission)

Exercise: Basic Infographic

Draw a picture of your day, starting with the time you wake up and ending with the time you go to bed. Use arrows to lead the viewer from one event to the next.

- Make sure to visualize as best you can all the processes involved.
- Think about your day along a story arc, but make sure to draw it out by hand.
- Don't worry if you don't turn out an artistic masterpiece.

Developing a Digital Content Strategy

A Digital Presence

A big component of strategic communications is distribution: Once multimedia content is produced and publicized, including through the powerful, relatively new channel of social media, how is that content best delivered to an audience? Whereas once the only channels for this kind of distribution were television and film, the dominant answer these days is the World Wide Web. The ways in which the web has completely altered publishing, public relations, information storage, entertainment, commerce, politics, and even national security constitute a vast subject that only grows larger by the month. For our purposes, at the moment, it's enough to say that you would be very hard-pressed to find a major brand or organization that does not have an established website. Twitter, Facebook, Pinterest, and other social media help to maintain one's presence on the web, especially in the case of individuals both well-known and not, but the most effective and readily available "home base" on the Internet for larger concerns is a dedicated site, or even sites.

Many websites, however, leave a lot to be desired as far as being able to deliver their content in a clean, intuitive, well-structured fashion. In strategic communications it is important that the audience not only be able to find content, but to readily grasp the mission of a website. For this reason all sites that represent a company or organization should have a mission statement that explains the reasons the organization exists. Everything the organization does revolves around this stated mission, as does everything undertaken by the multimedia storyteller working for that organization. Whether you are creating or redesigning a site, every page that you make, every photograph and video and piece of content you post, and each bit of text furthers the message of the mission statement.

Also, users have definite expectations about websites. According to Thad Allender, CEO and owner of GraphPaper Press, a WordPress theme design company in Brooklyn, NY:

> Everybody expects things to work. Really, when you're thinking about user experience, you want to make things as simple as possible. What does

the user expect? If you build something that the user does not expect to happen next, then you are going to have some friction. The user is going to be confused. Give the user what they expect. All of that is part of the process of thinking through the optimal user experience.

Tools to Make a Digital Product

There are all kinds of digital projects, from small to huge, from mere updates and expansions to large-scale redesigns and start-from-scratch launches. Some websites might just need an e-commerce solution added, or a redesign from an older, less-responsive version to one that is mobile-capable. Some websites might already have a WordPress blog as a backend, for example, or some other content management system, and they might not need much more than a redesign. But perhaps the client wants to start selling items, along with delivering already-established content. Many clients can make their own blog, but once a payment system and a database of products are needed, they may need help in figuring out a more sustainable solution.

As a digital storyteller, learning to code a website might not be an easy thing to undertake. It's possible to get in way over your head. "What's your level of commitment?" Allender asks:

> Are you interested in learning about how the web works, or are you just wanting to have a website? The easiest thing you can do is something like wordpress.com or wordpress.org, if you want to get your fingers dirty a little but don't need to know any code at all. There are other web tools that allow you to bypass code learning altogether and just get a website going.

And plenty of options are available. On the web it could be WordPress, Blogger, Drupal, or some other blogging system that makes it easy to present information in the digital space.

When it comes to mobile devices, however, it's a completely different ballgame. Either the system itself is designed with a responsive layout that automatically adjusts for the screen size of the user's device, or the content is native to the device itself. There are many different ways to go about delivering this type of content.

One option for making a mobile-specific app that has gained popularity in digital publishing is Adobe InDesign, which now enables the creation of stand-alone applications native to the devices they are on. Once only used for print publications, InDesign allows export through the Adobe Digital Publishing Suite (DPS), which can adapt digital products to mobile devices, including Apple's iPhones and iPad and Android-based devices.

At the *Arizona Republic* newspaper in Phoenix, AZ, a team of designers and editors produced an iPad-based publication using Adobe DPS. The tablet publication, called *AZ* and since discontinued, was the electronic resurrection of a former publication with the same name. *AZ* published twice a week, on

Monday and Thursday evenings. They also did several special editions, including one on spring baseball training with a unique cover story. A GoPro camera was mounted on a baseball catcher, and a sequence of a batter taking a swing at a ball was shot. "We then let the user move their finger and see the flight of the bat within DPS. It was so easy to do," said Dave Seibert, a photo editor for the *Republic*.

A tablet magazine screams out to be thought of differently from the way people think for print—even more so than a story for the web. The inclusion of interactive elements is much easier than on the web, where most sites are limited by a content management system that outputs stories automatically via an automated script. On the web, doing anything outside the ordinary usually requires a coder specially skilled in interactive features.

In DPS the options are all there within the system itself, with no hard-coding knowledge needed, only the visual assets to make the interactive elements work in the app. "The tools help you to be more creative; it is very flexible and fast. It is something that you can prototype with. In a matter of seconds you can put things together and pull it apart," said Seibert.

There are things to avoid, however. The DPS user should always be thinking about whether a clever interactive feature will push the story forward. Sometimes "cool" interactive elements will be only annoying bells and whistles that detract from or even derail a story. Chris Ballard, a former designer for the *Republic* who now works on the mobile design team at the *Washington Post*, asks himself:

> Is it intrusive rather than an inviting element? I look at those things and make sure the number one priority is story: Is this getting in the way as to how this person is telling the story, or is someone going to take in the story? Sometimes I scaled back on slide shows or a scrollable text frame or something where it really doesn't merit it.

DPS offers a quick way to pull together a lot of media elements, from slide shows to videos to graphics. It's an easy and quick way to take people where they might not otherwise go, or to show them something they haven't seen before. A presentation can have a panorama on one page, a slide show on another, and a little video piece on a third.

An interesting interactive that the *Arizona Republic* produced was a tall, scrollable page that allows the viewer to reveal the size of a basketball player as they scroll up in the application—something that would be impossible in print. Ballard explained the process:

> That was me sitting down with Dave and saying, 'What can we do that's a little bit different—something that is not 800 words—but what can we shoot and put together easily that would be a unique multimedia package?' [I thought] OK, well let's do a huge scroll frame and take advantage of the iPad comparing heights, and something that's a lot more fun.

"We call it a tablet magazine, not an app. An app is more technical," said Seibert.

There are growing pains involved with starting a new publication on tablet, as opposed to print. Print offers the chance for people to pick up a new magazine at the newsstand or doctor's office—not the case with a digital tablet publication. In an app store, a product is literally competing with every other digital app or publication out there. Would-be buyers have to search through literally thousands of available apps and publications. "People would pick up a newspaper at a grocery store just on a whim. You can't pick up a [digital magazine] app on a whim," said Ballard.

The Importance of Planning

Planning a website is as crucial and challenging a step in the process as actually building one. The more planning that goes into the site beforehand, the more energy can be devoted later to making a product that fulfills and even exceeds expectations.

Just as with writing a book, the best way to go about planning a website job is to create a detailed model or outline early on. When a good deal of time has been spent on thinking, categorizing, and organizing in advance, the actual execution of the project proceeds much more easily. Mistakes and missteps are much more easily corrected in the planning stage than when actually sticking things together, as is faulty or missing research, and a solid plan also frees up more time that can be devoted to making the best product possible.

Know Your Audience

When designing or redesigning a site, it is also vitally important to understand your audience. Whom are you targeting? In the case of organizational websites, one-size-fits-all is seldom practical or desirable. Organizations want to be unique, and they tend to be reaching out to specific people. Sites need to be designed for audiences of certain age ranges, with certain likes, dislikes, and cultural vocabularies, as well as specific levels of education and socioeconomic status. This may sound intimidating, but in fact this kind of information isn't something you need to go far to find. Most clients already have an idea of who buys their products, needs their services, or will want to support or be involved in their organizations.

Better Storytelling through User-Centered Design

At National Public Radio in Washington, D.C., what was once an over-the-airwaves-only media company has turned itself into a digital media company with a multiplatform strategy. The radio network has a dedicated team of visual storytellers that builds digital projects specific to the stories it works on.

The visuals team approaches projects with user-centered design as their central principle. As Brian Boyer, visuals editor for NPR, explained:

> We first ask ourselves . . . 'Who is our audience? Who are our users?' We ask ourselves . . . 'What are their needs? What are the questions they have?' Then we figure out what we are going to build. It's sort of a mind hack.

Boyer says he tries to avoid walking into projects just with cool ideas. User-centered design stops this sort of whiz-bang, bells-and-whistles approach from taking over projects from the start. "It's a check to stop people from building a shiny thing but build the thing that works for your audience," said Boyer, who added that this approach has helped projects not only from a "where the buttons go" perspective but from a content perspective as well.

Kainaz Amaria, the supervising producer for visuals at NPR, points out the usefulness of user-centered design for storytelling:

> This exercise is really helpful with big projects. You can have a ton of ideas, a ton of great ideas and a ton of bad ideas and nowhere to focus them. This exercise helps us to focus in on how to tell the story and what to focus on.

NPR's focus on user-centered design principles starts with the building of a prototype. "We try it out . . . on some people, we see if it works. If it doesn't work, we try it again, and that 'iterativeness' doesn't just apply to a single project," Boyer said. "I don't have a playbook for the team, except that I want to learn from what we did the last time and improve on it."

The multiplatform approach is built into everything NPR does: animated gifs, video, still photography, how the team builds out its projects. Boyer said he tries to avoid building templates for everything:

> That is a really great way to build something that won't work for you, based on the fallacy that you can predict the future, that you know what is going to work. Each project we build is bespoke, it is built to task, because every story is a little bit different.

One award-winning project that NPR worked on, which garnered them Documentary of the Year honors from Pictures of the Year International, is called "Planet Money Makes a T-Shirt." The team traveled to Colombia and Bangladesh tracing the journey of how a T-shirt is made, beginning with a cotton seed. The project, funded through Kickstarter, was very innovative in how it was presented. The user goes from chapter to chapter through various multimedia elements, but it can be viewed either in a sit-back-and-relax type of format or by clicking through the chapters. Amaria explained the storytelling design process:

> When we came back with all this stuff, we wanted to find the best assets we had. Video could not do it all; stills could not do it all; text could not

do it all. The way we structured it, the video is going to introduce different chapters in the process, to introduce the different people that came across the T-shirt, and then the drop-down is going to take you deeper into a scene or a topic . . . those are things that we do not want to get into in video but we thought were important to understand. . . .

The way I think of it is that we are all storytellers, and I'd rather our storytelling not be defined by a medium: pictures, video, charts, graphics. I'd rather we think about the story, think about the best way to tell the story, and so that is what NPR visuals does. . . . We collaborate with the newsroom. We see what stories are going on, what people are telling. Then we collaborate and figure out the best way to 'say' that story. Is it video? Is it photos? The combination? Is it thematic? Conceptual? Is it a linear narrative?

Behind all of this is the idea of innovating the user experience, making sure that what is built is what the audience will want and use to do what they need to do, whether it is buying airline tickets or a new jacket, or reading, listening to, or viewing a story. With that comes the ability to strive to do something different, but at the same time to make sure that the initial mission is always kept in mind. "The last thing that we want to put out is something boring. To me that is my enemy. We are always trying to challenge ourselves. I am not a purist about anything," Amaria said.

Logos and Design

Moving on to the visual aspects of website jobs, it's important on the web for clients to have a desirable, up-to-date design and logo. This can be a touchy subject, for logos and design are the public icons of an organization and changing them can be hazardous, or at least be perceived to be so. Artists will be involved, as will longstanding, time-tested designs and graphics that are intertwined with organizational identity. On the plus side, logos and design can be a fun and exciting part of the process.

David Miller is the senior graphic designer at the Adler Planetarium in Chicago. He uses mood boards—collages of images, text, colors, and even objects—to help get his creative juices flowing prior to working out a design. He wants his clients "to buy into where my head is at with a design" before he moves forward with the production:

A mood board can be broad or specific; it can inspire a look and feel—use color, shape, and texture and typography from around the web. I will often pull things from fashion websites or furniture design websites that I just think match the flavor I am trying to hit with the website . . . When you see a really cool modern chair design, maybe the curve of the back would look awesome in a project, or the seat pattern could inspire a project. You never know what might work.

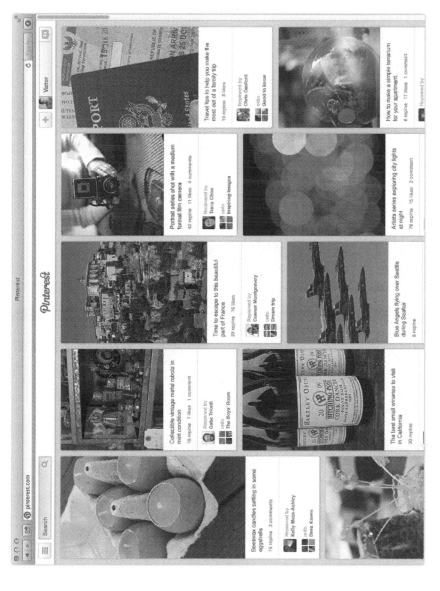

Figure 4.08 Pinterest is a handy place to save logos and other design assets to help inspire designers working on projects. (Pinterest)

Miller said he uses Pinterest as a digital mood board for his ideas. "It really boils down to line, color, and shape. Even typography is all about shape," he said.

Structuring a Website

Developing a Site Map

A map for a website looks like a company's organizational chart; it is where all the pages and sections are laid out and their relationships shown. Just as you would begin a story arc on a piece of paper, it is important to chart the site structure in a hierarchical form. It might even be best to start with an outline based on Roman numerals. This allows you to visualize what sections there are, how they can be arranged and subdivided, and other key information needed to make an engaging and easy-to-navigate website.

Site maps can be created on paper or a whiteboard, or with sticky notes on a wall, or cards on a table. They can also be created with a variety of software— any application that could be used to draw out an organizational chart can be used to draw a site map.

Exercise: Make a Site Map Diagram

Most websites consist of many, many pages, and the amount of content can be vast. It is very important to make a "map" of a site—whether a new site or one being redesigned—in the early stages of a project. At the very least, this greatly simplifies the process of creating navigational headings, labels, and other tools.

- Go to the website of your favorite grocery store.
- Draw an organizational chart of the main navigational elements and their subheadings.
- Make sure to start with the "Home" page at the top—or beginning—of your map.
- You only need to drill down three levels to complete this exercise.

The Importance of Grids

When you're not writing the code, making a website can actually be a relatively simple task. You pick a content management system, such as WordPress, download a theme, fill in some blanks, and go from there. When working for clients, however, things are usually not that simple. Not every company or organization can be served with an off-the-shelf design that can simply be downloaded and applied. Businesses in particular need sites that are unique and very distinguishable from those of competitors. Clients will usually want something that is custom-designed. So once a map has been made, it is time to move on to the next planning stage: setting a grid.

A *grid* sets the stage for the overall design template. It is nothing but a set of intersecting horizontal and vertical lines that form rows and columns, which

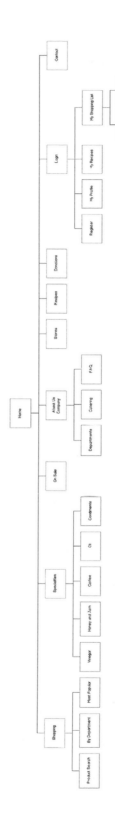

Figure 4.09 Site maps are a great way to illustrate the organization of a website or digital product.

help to keep the design orderly. Grids are usually based on a twelve- to sixteen-column format meant to provide a starting point for the design.

Many websites are built using templates and frameworks that have grids already built in, including Blueprint and Twitter Bootstrap, a responsive grid system that allows websites to be easily formatted for mobile devices. Grid frameworks allow designers to work more quickly and easily, since they include pre-made CSS styles that help to align objects on a page.

Before responsive web design became popular (using a web design that automatically reshapes a site to the size of the display device, be it a PC, tablet, or phone) web designers and developers would have to think about designing sites for multiple screen sizes.

"I would always say that it was more important to get the message right—to have a story for the end user—than it is to make your website look good at all display sizes," said Justin Winter, CEO of Winter Creative in Truckee, CA:

> Mobile is definitely a part of everything we do. Moving forward, people should use grids. The bottom line is that grid systems are a foundation of good design, things on web pages should line up, the display of all content across a site should be consistent. The alignment (of objects) on a website from a visual standpoint helps get the message across and to tell a story.

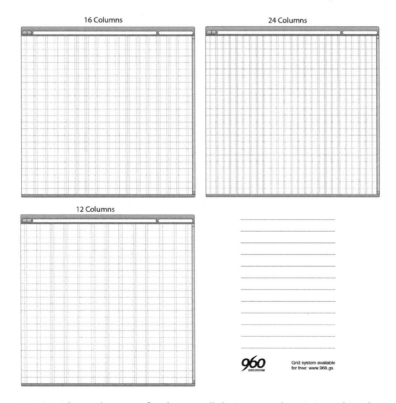

Figure 4.10 A grid sets the stage for the overall design template. It is nothing but a set of intersecting horizontal and vertical lines that form rows and columns, which help to keep the design orderly. (Courtesy of www.960.gs)

What Grids Do

In *Ordering Disorder, Grid Principles for Web Design,* author and former nytimes.com design director Khoi Vinh lists the benefits of using grids:

- Grids add order, continuity, and harmony to the presentation of information.
- Grids allow an audience to predict where to find information, which aids in the communication of that information.
- Grids make it easier to add new content in a manner consistent with the overall vision of the original presentation.
- Grids facilitate collaboration on the design of a single solution without compromising the overall vision of that solution.

The Wireframe

Once your client's old website—or plan for a new one—has been mapped out by an information architect and the grid has been set, the next stage is to create a wireframe. A *wireframe* is the blueprint from which the site will be built; it is the drawing plan, usually done by a designer collaborating with the information architect. A wireframe allows the client to "see" a site before it is built, functioning not unlike an architect's rendering, but it goes a step further in that it is also the diagram a web developer will follow, just as a building contractor follows an architect's blueprint. You are not yet building the website. You are getting the design down to a point at which it makes sense visually, functionally, and logically, so that in the next stage it can be coded and made to work according to the required specifications.

There are several options for building a wireframe. Starting with the simplest option, it can be done with merely a pencil and a piece of paper. Chances are, however, you will opt for (or switch to) a more powerful and professional tool. These include presentation software like Microsoft PowerPoint or Apple Keynote, or graphics and design packages such as Adobe Photoshop or InDesign. There is even cloud-based wireframing software available that provides more functionality specific to wireframes, such as individual widgets that represent common web elements, or notes that can be inserted to explain features and functionality. They might also offer importable custom icons and images to help give a wireframe its own identity.

Many of the cloud-based options are subscription-based and cost money, but the ease of use of tools—not to mention a more professional looking wireframe—can make or break the deliverable you are creating. It is all about generating a good-looking and functional plan that the client easily understands and that the web development and design teams can use to build out the site.

Things to consider when designing a wireframe include where logo(s) and navigational elements will be placed. What kinds of assets will be available to display the content? Will a rotating slide show lead the front page? Maybe specific products will need to be featured, and users can be directed to more information about them. A client may also want to add a footer, a customary location for copyright, site map, and contact information. As you draw out the wireframe, use either actual content or dummy content such as greeked text: the familiar *Lorem ipsum dolor sit amet . . .*

Use the grid to place various elements, including boxes and text. Just as newspapers and magazines have done for many decades, add dominant pieces of artwork—whether photographs or illustrations—to the page first. This tends to allow the remaining elements to fall into place in a natural manner.

Whether you use a pencil and paper or sophisticated software to make the wireframe, always remember that the purpose is to provide the designer and web developer with a basic scheme with which they can begin their work.

In *The Web Designer's Roadmap*, author Giovanni DiFeterici says that when drafting a wireframe, designers should ask themselves these four questions:

- What content needs to be on the page?
- How do the different pieces of content relate to one another?
- How might they possibly be arranged?
- How should the user interact with the content?

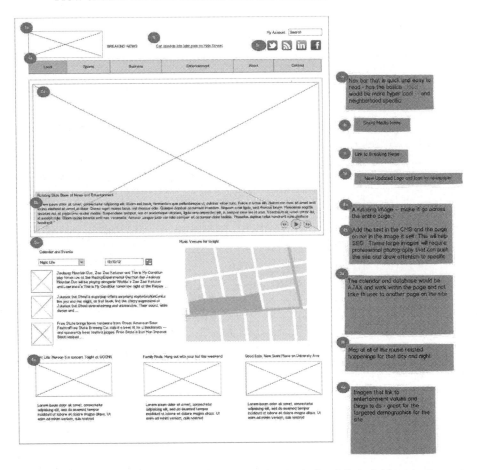

Figure 4.11 A wireframe allows the client to "see" a site before it is built, functioning not unlike an architect's rendering. It can also serve as the plan a web developer will follow.

When creating a wireframe, come up with multiple versions of how assets can be laid out on the page. Once again, it is easier to handle such things at this stage than later on, when content and appearance are being finalized. The more versions of the website you can represent in a wireframe, both for yourself and for the client, the better the site will be in the end.

Wireframes are an important tool when working with a stakeholder. They are the first step to helping a client understand what you have been up to, and where all the myriad parts fit into the overall architecture and strategy.

Exercise: Draw a Wireframe

Using a pen and paper, draw out a basic wireframe for the front page of a non-profit organization's website. The organization's mission is recycling plastic water bottles.

Be sure to include the following elements:

A. Logo
B. Navigation
C. Main photo
D. Body text
E. Footer

MEET THE PRO

Greg Hedges, Director of Strategy, Rain, New York, NY

Greg Hedges works as a strategist and producer at Rain, a digital agency. In that capacity, he works to cultivate creative strategies with an emphasis on user experience, design, and development. He has worked with clients including Walmart, PepsiCo, the National Retail Federation, Electus, Privacy-Guard, Plaza Construction, Consigliere, and Bosto-nia Group. Before joining Rain, Greg taught courses in graphic design as an assistant professor at the S.I. Newhouse School of Public Communications at Syracuse University. He is a graduate of the New-house School, with a B.S. in Graphic Design and an M.S. in New Media. He was also a partner at ThreeOneFive Design in Syracuse, NY. Earlier in his career Greg worked as a designer for Context Studio, as well as in-house for King Features, a division of the Hearst Corporation. Over the past thirteen years, Greg has built up extensive experience in various areas of development and design, including user experience, web design, identity, advertising, strategy, and typography.

Figure 4.12 Greg Hedges, director of strategy for Rain, New York, NY. (Courtesy of Greg Hedges)

Redesigning a large website can be a very large job, but it is work Greg Hedges enjoys. "I view the whole process as design—just different aspects

---

(Continued ...)

(... *continued*)

of design," he said, explaining that he has always liked both the information architecture aspect of web work as well as the design. "It satisfies both sides of my brain. I like to figure out ways to fix problems. Information architecture is fun—to work on the strategy overall."

Hedges was the point man on the team that redesigned the website of the S.I. Newhouse School of Public Communications at Syracuse University. He attended the school for both his undergraduate degree in graphic design and his master's degree in new media, and was also an assistant professor there. "For me it was a labor of love, something I know and care a lot about," said Hedges, who worked on the project with Newhouse communications director Wendy Loughlin. Loughlin was looking to build a website that had a content management system that allowed her and her staff to easily update content without having to go through a web developer. "The (former) website was not very good—it was not of the caliber we wanted it to be," she said. "We wanted something more sophisticated-looking and more elegant, that was easier to use."

The school had some requirements going into the redesign process. They wanted the ability to use a new content management system (CMS) that would be built in Drupal, an open-source framework for building complex websites. This required a complete redesign of the old site and the implementation of the new, Drupal-built CMS, which would be both easy to use and would allow the assignment of hierarchical roles for administrators, so that different people could have different levels of capability to update different parts of the site.

Hedges identified different stakeholders for the project, so that the initial conversation included prospective students, current students, faculty, staff, and alumni. As far as content was concerned, Loughlin herself was very interested in being able to post news, consisting of text and photos, to the site.

"Our main audience is prospective students. We've seen analytics that the most visited section other than the home page is the admissions section," she said. "We serve other audiences that include current students and alums."

A big part of the project was comparative analysis: Rain needed to compare the new site with the existing one. "The old site—it really wasn't targeted toward current students.... While you are a prospective student the goal of the site is to get you in the door. For the faculty, the site is a way to share research," Hedges said, or to provide contact information and generally facilitate connections with the media on areas of expertise. "For alumni, it is hoping to continue the relationship with the school, discuss renovations and updates, and make connections that could lead toward a donation or other form of involvement."

Hedges explained that students tended not to use the old site, so the new version was geared toward attracting students and giving them reasons to return and use it repeatedly. "If we made it useful for students during the time they are here, maybe they would come back to the site as alumni," he said.

(*Continued*...)

(... continued)

The project then rolled into the discovery phase, to figure out exactly what the client needed, Hedges said:

> It was a research and information-architecture phase, where we went in and had stakeholder conversations. We talked to fifteen or so faculty members [in a range of] roles, some adjuncts, the department chairs and deans, and we talked to current students.

They also set up focus groups that included prospective students and alumni, gauging what users might want in a school website. "We wanted to know what was falling short for them on their own website and what their dreams were for the new one," said Hedges.

There is an abundance of college sites on the web; the Internet is a major way to connect with alumni and prospective students. For the second group in particular, this means a lot of competition for eyes. The Newhouse School competes for students with schools like Medill, Columbia, and the University of Southern California. With so many major schools vying for the same prospective students, it was important for Rain to do another kind of comparative analysis, one that looked at other college websites, including both Newhouse's direct competitors and schools that simply had nicely designed websites. "We looked at it from a qualitative standpoint," he explained:

> We asked a lot of questions, about twenty to twenty-five questions with multiple parts. We looked at things like how well they use social media. Then we took an assessment of how recent some of the content seemed. We looked at how they engaged the users in different ways, from user-generated content to comments to forms to video players.

The overall idea of this process, Hedges said, was to understand what everyone else was doing and try to take the best parts, which were working elsewhere, and apply them to the new site. The Newhouse School wanted to "integrate a newsroom-based approach" he said, referring to how they wanted to disseminate information on the site.

The next part of the process was the site map, and a content audit in which Hedges' team went through the entire existing site. "We withdrew all the content [and] extracted a link, title, and associated metadata," said Hedges, who was looking at the commonalities among different types of content that already existed on the site.

"We created a section called My Newhouse—that's where current students can go to get information intended for them," said Hedges. He said that his team also came up with some major, new interactive capabilities, some of which were implemented, like faculty bios with connections to a professor's Twitter feeds. "Others were not implemented, or were targeted for later phases, such as videos of faculty members talking about their research areas, and interactive maps of the school," he added.

(Continued ...)

(...continued)

Before presenting the strategy report to the school, Hedges came up with a time line and a cost structure. Hedges said he generally does not introduce wireframes as part of this report, since he wants to hear from the client about the research before moving forward into the design phase. "I have pushed for wireframes to not be part of our discovery process," he said:

> The problem with doing wireframes in discovery is that you haven't really had a conversation with the client about what architecture you just put in front of them. You hope you've solved their problems, but you haven't really gotten anything back from them. To go into the work of the wireframes, for me, just doesn't make any sense at that point.

Hedges said there were some differing opinions from the stakeholders about labeling on the site. For example, he said, "There was a question: Was it 'The Career Development Center' or is it 'Career Development'? The center is a physical location in the school. We made decisions based on everything presented."

Other discussions included the grouping and labeling of departments, subject areas, and degrees offered. Conversations like these are essential to developing the information architecture of a website, he said:

> We find that when you're building sites you often end up doing it for a lot of the people within the building. You get influence from a lot of people you come in contact with. Sometimes they do not have the whole picture in mind with design.

Once the client had approved the strategy report, Rain was able to move forward with designing in Adobe Photoshop before building out the site. "We put up a client-review site so that we could walk through the design with the clients, asking for a few revisions," Hedges said. After the designs were made, they were passed on to the web development staff with detailed instructions on what needed to be built.

The project started in 2011, and the new site did not launch until 2013. For Loughlin, the overhaul has been a long time coming. She is looking to add more multimedia and pages with examples of student work. "It's a vast improvement . . . it's been good, and people are happy," she said.

"A lot had to be figured out," Hedges concluded. "Since it has launched we use it as an example of a project that has gone well, which balanced the needs of users versus the desires of the client."

At the end of the project, Loughlin looked forward to what she could do with a very capable and well-designed website. "I love the [print] magazine, because once it is printed and the boxes arrive I don't ever look at it because it's too late, and you are done. You don't ever have to revisit it; it's kind of nice," she explained. "The website is a blessing—and a curse—in that you can always improve it," Loughlin said, only half joking.

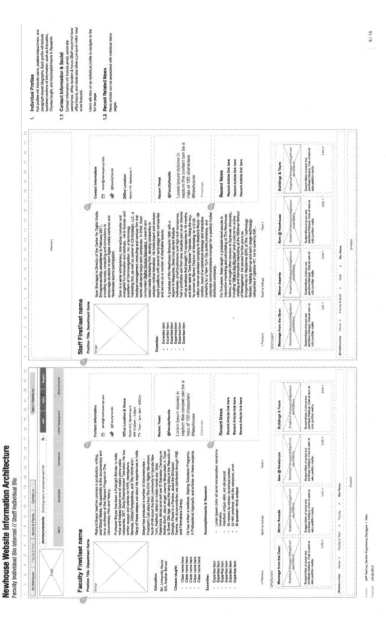

Figure 4.13 The wireframes for the redesign of the website of the S.I. Newhouse School of Public Communications at Syracuse University. (Courtesy of RAIN)

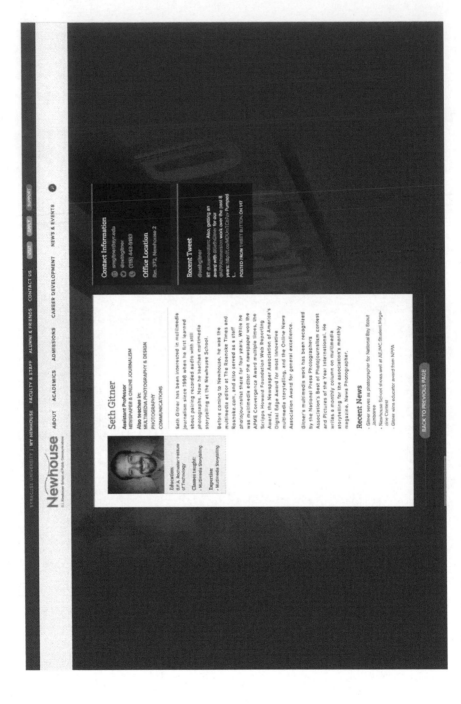

Figure 4.14 A Newhouse faculty page. (Courtesy of The Newhouse School at Syracuse University)

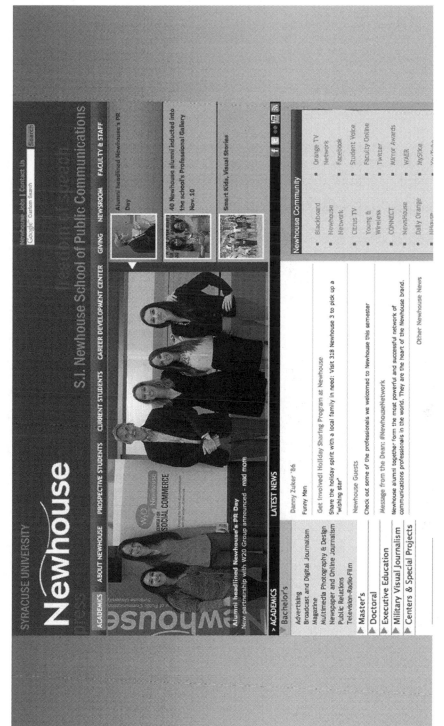

Figure 4.15 The "before" design for the website of the S.I. Newhouse School of Public Communications at Syracuse University. (Courtesy of The Newhouse School at Syracuse University)

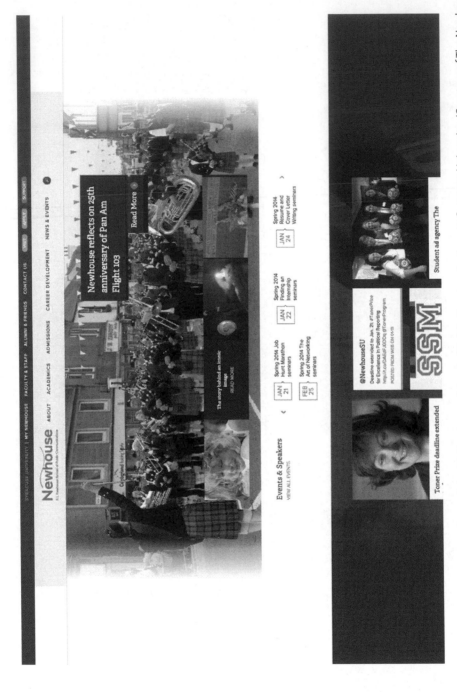

Figure 4.16 The "after" design for the website of the S.I. Newhouse School of Public Communications at Syracuse University. (Courtesy of The Newhouse School at Syracuse University)

Chapter Summary

The Internet has become part of everyday life. What we do, how we interact, who we share our photographs and video with, even what we say—has all become tied up with the social media that the Internet has made possible. It has become a part of who many of us are.

Also, the dissemination of information to the public is no longer solely the domain of legacy media such as print publications. These organizations have had to learn to harness and adapt to the ever-increasing reach and influence of social media, a task that has fallen to editors, sports reporters, local reporters, photographers, and other staffers. These individuals now have the ability to take their work global through the highly personal channels of social media.

Life and communication in the digital space are under constant redesign; the related media are constantly evolving as well. New technology is always being invented, resulting in new ways to disseminate and consume information. Just when all of the platforms possible seem to have been developed new ones pop up, such as wearable technology like eyeglass computers.

The digital communicator needs to stay abreast of these new developments, as well as master the existing ones, for social media are a powerful way of both telling and spreading the word about stories. No longer does a story need to be created and set out in hopes of attracting an audience. With enough knowledge and ingenuity, the audience can now be contacted directly and the story pushed right to where the storyteller wants it to go.

One mainstay of the Internet that seems destined for a long, useful life is the World Wide Web, and best practices exist for the planning, targeting, building, and maintaining of a digital presence on the web.

Review Questions

1. What are currently the most popular platforms to visually tell or push a story through social media?
2. What are two social media techniques that journalists might use to help tell a breaking news story on the web?
3. Explain the difference between a poster design and an infographic.
4. What is the significance of the Graph API?
5. What is the role of analytics in a social media strategy?
6. What are some important considerations when designing a website?
7. What is the difference between a web design and a wireframe?
8. What are some tools that are commonly used to build websites?

Exercises

1. Research a recent breaking news event and seek out hashtags that developed from the event. Study the tweets that come up and find those most relevant and informative about the event. Rank the tweets by their quality. Was the tweet related to a particular fact about the news event, or was it

only opinion? Was there a photograph attached to the tweet? Did the photograph have storytelling value? Is there a difference between the tweets from a recognized news source and those of a "citizen reporter"?

2. Go to a newspaper's Facebook page and analyze the photographs that have been posted there, paying attention to which images have the most "likes." What are the images of? Do the images presented have any news value? Use the criteria from Chapter 1: Were the images composed well? Would you consider the images to be "moments"? Are there posts without images that would be better with them? What kind of image would you have used on a particular post to help it garner more "likes" or shares?

 Key Terms

API – An application programming interface specifies how some software components should interact with each other. Specifically, this is how one website can connect data to another website.

Grid – A set of intersecting horizontal and vertical lines that anchor a web design.

Hashtag – A word that identifies a specific topic of conversation on a social network.

Infographic – An image, such as a chart or diagram, used to deliver information or data.

Instagram – An online photo sharing network for mobile devices that allows users to take photographs and then instantly upload them to the service. The application offers various filters for users to enhance their images.

Mood board – A collection of images and designs to help show stakeholders the design ideas and concepts of a website, so that a nondesigner can understand the thinking of the designer.

Open Graph – A protocol used to enable developers to read from and write data into Facebook from other websites, such as newspaper articles linking to Facebook.

Pinterest – A scrapbook of sorts that allows users to "pin" photographs and items from other sites onto virtual "pinboards" or collections, which can then be shared with people with similar interests.

Site map – A diagram of web pages that shows—and sets—the hierarchy of the website.

Social influencers – People who have gained enough followers and profile to drive awareness about topics with their social media posts.

Stakeholder – Someone, such as a client, who has a stake in the end result of what is being built or designed.

Strategy report – The final document that would be presented to stakeholders, containing the wireframes, site maps, design compositions, and anything else that pertains to a redesign or design of a website or digital application.

Twitter – This microblogging service that lets users send out "tweets" of 140 characters or less to other users has become a fixture of daily online life. The service can be used to promote videos, news, websites, and other content.

User-centered design – Design of a product where the needs of the user are the controlling principal, rather than style or "cool" features.

Vine – A very recent form of short-form visual storytelling. Owned by Twitter, it is a visual form of the same service, only limited to six seconds of visual activity.

Wireframe – The blueprint from which a website will be built.

Sources

Allender, Thad. Conversation with author, September 18, 2013.

Amaria, Kainaz. Conversation with author, April 9, 2014.

Ballard, Chris. Conversation with author, March 19, 2014.

Bennet, Shea. "93% of U.S. Corporates Will Use Facebook, Twitter, YouTube for Social Marketing by 2014 [STUDY] – AllTwitter." Media Bistro. Accessed October 29, 2012. http://www.mediabistro.com/alltwitter/social-saturation_b27169.

Bertolini, Lauren. Conversation with author, June 12, 2014.

Boyer, Brian. Conversation with author, April 16, 2014.

Brody, Roberta. "Credibility and Information Naiveté in Socially Networked Information." Paper presented at IEEE International Symposium on Technology and Society, 2008. 1–3. IEEE Xplore, 2008. doi:10.1109/ISTAS.2008.4559756.

Cairo, Alberto. Conversation with author, September 16, 2013.

Cooper, Belle Beth. "How Twitter's Expanded Images Increase Clicks, Retweets and Favorites [New Data]." *Buffer Blog*. Accessed June 25, 2014. http://blog.bufferapp.com/the-power-of-twitters-new-expanded-images-and-how-to-make-the-most-of-it.

DiFeterici, Giovanni. *The Web Designer's Roadmap: Your Creative Process for Web Design Success*. Collingwood, VIC, Australia: SitePoint Pty., 2012. Accessed March 16, 2015. http://www.books24x7.com/marc.asp?bookid=49342.

Facebook. "Company Info | Facebook Newsroom." Accessed June 28, 2014. http://newsroom.fb.com/company-info/.

Facebook. "Graph API." *Facebook Developers*. Accessed October 19, 2012. https://developers.facebook.com/docs/reference/api/.

Gelb, Matt. Conversation with author, June 13, 2014.

Hedges, Greg. Conversation with author, September 6, 2013.

Hernandez, Brian Anthony. "Jason Mraz Picks Instagram Contest's Best Snapshots [PICS]." Accessed March 12, 2012. http://mashable.com/2012/03/12/jason-mraz-instagram-winners/.

LaBeau, Todd. Conversation with author, September 6, 2013.

Loughlin, Wendy. Conversation with author, October 15, 2013.

MacLeod, Mary. Conversation with author, June 25, 2014.

Miller, David. Conversation with author, September 16, 2013.

Nielsen. "Nielsen: Social Media Report." Accessed December 4, 2012. http://blog. nielsen.com/nielsenwire/social/.

Rock, Tracy. Conversation with author, September 8, 2013.

Rotolo, Anthony. Conversation with author, August 29, 2013.

Seibert, Dave. Conversation with author, March 17, 2014.

Simplymeasured. "How Top Brand Marketers Use Twitter." A Simply Measured Twitter Study Q4 2014. Accessed January 21, 2014. http://go.simplymeasured.com/en0kJO03001XIn0a60GI20m.

Socialbakers. "Photos Make Up 93% of the Most Engaging Posts on Facebook!" *Socialbakers.com*. Accessed June 25, 2014. http://www.socialbakers.com/blog/1749-photos-make-up-93-of-the-most-engaging-posts-on-facebook.

Sonderman, Jeff. "With 'Frictionless Sharing,' Facebook and News Orgs Push Boundaries of Online Privacy." Poynter.org. Accessed September 29, 2011. http://www.poynter.org/latest-news/media-lab/social-media/147638/with-frictionless-sharing-facebook-and-news-orgs-push-boundaries-of-reader-privacy/.

Stutzman, Frederic. "An Evaluation of Identity-Sharing Behavior in Social Network Communities." Paper presented at CODE: Human Systems, Digital Bodies. April 6–8, 2006. Miami University, Oxford, OH. Accessed March 16, 2015. http://www.units.miamioh.edu/codeconference/papers/papers/stutzman_track5.pdf.

Temple, Hailey. E-mail conversation with author, August 29, 2013.

Todorova, Aleksandra. Conversation with author, September 16, 2013.

Vinh, Khoi. *Ordering Disorder: Grid Principles for Web Design*. Berkeley, CA: New Riders, 2011.

Ward, William. Conversation with author, August 28, 2013.

Winter, Justin. Conversation with author, October 7, 2013.

5 THE BUILDING BLOCKS OF VISUAL STORYTELLING

How Are Visual Images Created and Combined Logically to Tell a Coherent Story with a Beginning, Middle, and End?

In this chapter you will learn

- How to shoot sequences as the basic building blocks of a visual story
- "Shooting to edit"
- Some important principles of continuity, action, and composition
- Important things to avoid when gathering sequences and shots
- A variety of types of shots

Introduction

When writing a story you present thoughts selectively; you do not simply lay everything out or present the same thoughts over and over. You write meaningful sentences for each thought, then combine them with other sentences to create paragraphs that tell a story or make a point. The same applies to video storytelling. You need to shoot images that, when combined, tell a story that is both logical and organized.

Photographic images are captured in a fraction of a second by selectively aiming the camera at a subject. When you take video you are capturing many, many more images—30 frames per second, in most cases.

Ideally, when videographers shoot a sequence, they need to have planned out the shot in advance, either in their head or on paper, before touching the button. When shooting news in a nonfiction type of situation, of course, this kind of storyboarding cannot be done. The videographer cannot really plan out or "set up" a news shoot, but must shoot everything "in the moment" or "as is," which can make this kind of storytelling more challenging—or at least challenging in different ways—than what a fiction cinematographer or director does.

You might be tempted just to point the camera and go. This works with informal recording of friends and family, but telling a good visual story requires strategy in image-making. This applies to everything from choosing the right gear for the job to waiting for the ideal moment. Video storytelling is a means of communication that can influence opinions and change minds through stories that are engaging and informative, but it demands careful strategy and thought.

Shoot to Edit

Shooting to edit is a broad concept. It means that the storyteller or videographer must shoot all images and sequences with the editing and storytelling process firmly in mind. Good content cannot be gathered in a random, spur-of-the-moment way. You are going to need to edit what you collect, and use it to tell a story. Imagine shopping at the grocery store. You need to think about your breakfasts, lunches, and dinners for the next week, and not just randomly fill up your cart. Even if you don't know down to the last item what is needed, you have a pretty good idea, and can visit the right aisles with certain meals in mind.

Shooting to edit is the same kind of thing. Think about the final product while collecting the pieces. Visual storytelling is a process that requires a great deal of thinking in advance. Especially when shooting video, it is crucially important to have a grasp of the story being told before going out with camera in hand. The end goal is to make viewers feel comfortable and natural as they watch the final film. If a video is three minutes long and is being played on a website, the viewer should be left with the impression that it was only ten seconds long, or at least be too caught up in the content to be thinking about time. This can't be done with content that is collected randomly and somehow magically integrated at a later stage.

Just like you shop to cook, you must shoot to edit.

Starting the Shoot

Any creative activity needs a plan. In the realm of video storytelling and moviemaking, you can benefit greatly from all the years of experimentation that have already been performed by other people. Experimentation is always enticing, since plans can always be changed and rules broken, but the beginner's first task is to learn the rules and master them. There's plenty of time and opportunity to bend them later.

So, always be planning ahead. When beginning a shoot in the journalism and documentary world, you should be trying constantly to pin down the story at hand, what kinds of sound bites and images will contribute to telling it best, and what storytelling technique will accommodate them all. When planning out the shooting of a scene, especially as a beginner, it is important to shoot both A-roll and B-roll, shoot using the rule of thirds, pay attention to your axis of action, and shoot a variety of shots so that there is good continuity from sequence to sequence in post-production.

Now let's take a look at what all these terms mean.

A-Roll

A-roll is generally interview footage, both audio and video. It consists of sound bites and ambient audio gathered on scene.

B-Roll

B-roll is all the visuals that are shot, *excluding* interviews. This includes all the video, still images, and motion graphics that can help to tell the story visually. Despite its seemingly secondary status, it is best not to think of B-roll as less important than A-roll. The footage should be as high-quality as possible, with strong storytelling potential. Many first-time filmmakers think that B-roll is just visuals, but it's not. Remember that the microphone is recording audio as well, and that the ambient, natural sound being captured is as important as the visuals to the telling of the story.

Rule of Thirds

Just pointing a camera and pressing the button does not result in a nicely composed image. Whether the final image will have an aspect ratio of horizontal, vertical, or square, it is important to know where to place the subject within the frame for a pleasing final result. Most beginners' first instinct will be to place the subject at the center of the viewfinder, but a properly composed image should use the rule of thirds, a device that helps frame an image in a visually appealing way.

As a child, did you play Tic-tac-toe? Remember how the board was set up much like a number sign (#)? The intersecting vertical and horizontal lines that make up a Tic-tac-toe board can be used as a device to help compose an image. If that Tic-tac-toe board is superimposed on the camera's viewing area, subjects can easily be lined up along one of the axes. This technique results in better-composed images. The Tic-tac-toe grid divides the image into nine equal parts, but also breaks the image into thirds. Try not to put the subject in the center; the center tends to be the most unappealing part of the image area. Try instead to place the subject where the Tic-tac-toe lines intersect.

Many mobile phones have the rule of thirds actually built into their LCD screens. In electronic viewfinders such as those found in mobile phones, these guides can often be turned on and off.

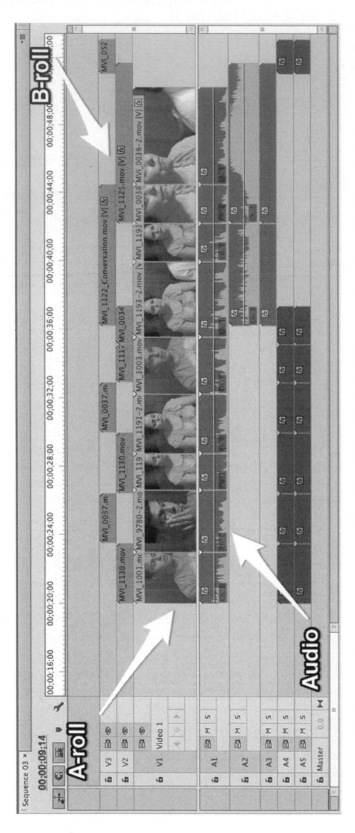

Figure 5.01 *B-roll* is all the visuals that are shot except interviews. This includes all the video, still images, and motion graphics that can help tell a story visually. *A-roll* is the footage from the interview. Despite the naming, B-roll is no less important than A-roll. Since we are telling visual stories, B-roll can sometimes be more important. (Adobe product screenshot(s) reprinted with permission from Adobe Systems Incorporated)

The Rule of Thirds

The Rule of thirds uses a Tic-tac-toe grid of nine rectangles to help you compose compelling photos. The grid, imagined or superimposed on your camera's viewing area, allows you to line up the elements of the photo to make them dynamic as well as balanced.

Figure 5.02 To produce better-composed images, a Tic-tac-toe-like grid is superimposed on the camera's viewing area. Subjects can easily be lined up along one of the axes. (Illustration by Chris OBrion)

 Exercise: Rule of Thirds

Using a mobile phone, shoot one photograph of each of the following scenarios. This exercise will assist you in understanding how to go about a shoot.

1. Shoot a photograph of one person standing in the center of the frame.
2. Shoot a photograph of a person standing on one of the lines in the rule of thirds. Most mobile phones have a function that allows you to overlay a grid that looks very much like the rule of thirds over your frame. Feel free to use this as a guide.
3. Evaluate the images. How do they look and "feel"? Do they have a different sense of balance?

180-Degree Rule

It is important while shooting to be attentive to where you are shooting from. The relationship between two subjects in a scene forms an "axis of action" from one subject to the other, and the camera should stay on one, consistent side of this axis. This is known as the *180-degree rule*. For example, when shooting two people eating dinner at a table, across from one another, the camera's various positions should all be on one side of that table. One of the diners should not be looking to the left of the screen in one shot, then looking to the right side in the next. "Crossing the line" or "jumping the axis" with the camera runs the risk of disorienting the viewer.

Sequencing

A series of planned shots serve as the building blocks for any visual narrative. A sequence consists of a variety of shots at varying focal lengths, such as tight,

The 180-degree rule

In this scene, the viewer feels like they are sitting in on a private conversation. As long as the camera stays on this side of the couple, the viewer understands that the man is "on their left" and the woman "on their right" ...

... but if the camera suddenly moves to the *other* side of the table (across the Line of Action), the viewer becomes disoriented. Now the woman is sitting on the viewer's *left*, and the man appears to be sitting on the *right*.

Line of Action

180 degrees

Figure 5.03 Known as the 180-degree rule, the relationship between two subjects in a scene forms an "axis of action" from one to the other, and the camera should stay on one, consistent side of this line. (Illustration by Chris OBrion)

medium, wide, and long. Think of shooting a sequence just like writing a story: It starts with "Once upon a time, in a faraway land," or "Last night, near the bus station on the south side of town."

While shooting video, be thinking constantly about this variety of shots. Visual variety is crucial when building a story. Starting with a wide shot allows a survey of the scene, after which other shots can be made within that scene. In the editing process the visual events are arranged into a combination—or sequence—of shots that tells the visual story. But the building-block shots must be obtained.

Think about this example: You are assigned to do a journalistic story about the retirement of a school principal who has worked at a school for thirty-five years. Do you start with the principal getting ready in the morning, as he has done for all of those years, or do you start with him driving into the parking lot for the last time? Will that shot be from the inside of his car, or outside? For the ending, will there be a shot of him driving home, or will it be an emotional goodbye to his teachers, or even a shot of the principal packing up his desk? When will close-ups be most effective? The possibilities are endless. And that's a good thing, as long as planning is involved. It will be your decision how to order the final piece, but it is vital to be thinking about this order, from a visual standpoint, long before the camera is even turned on.

We spoke earlier about the use of different lenses to frame up shots. Soon we will discuss the types of shots needed to put together both fiction and nonfiction stories.

Use a Tripod

In both fiction and nonfiction, it's important to lock the camera down to avoid shaky-camera syndrome. It might be quicker and more convenient to carry the camera around and get the needed shots "handheld," but trying to hold a camera weighing several pounds outstretched for a long time can be tiring. Today's smaller cameras and mobile phones can become awkward to hold steady for an extended period. Try doing leg lifts; it may look easy, but for anyone other than an exercise fiend, it becomes painful. Make tripod use a habit. It will prevent fatigue and yield better video.

Action/Reaction

All shots in a sequence are based upon an action and a reaction. Make sure to capture both.

> **What is the action? —> Something happens**
> **What is the reaction? —> How do people respond?**

When shooting a sporting event, the action could be someone scoring, or a great play, or a foul or bad call. The reaction would be fans or players cheering and celebrating, or booing accordingly. Sometimes the reaction shot is the one that says the most. For example, when a team wins a championship, the image that tells the story best might be a player reacting to the realization of what has just occurred.

Now let's look at some varieties of shots.

Figure 5.04 Action can be understood in sports photography as the photographer shooting a specific play during a game. Nebraska Cornhuskers guard Toney McCray (00) and Minnesota Golden Gophers guard Austin Hollins (20) and Ralph Sampson III (50) watch as a loose ball is picked up by a Minnesota player during the second half of a game that Minnesota later won. (Photo by Bruce Thorson)

Figure 5.05 Reaction in sports photography involves the photographer capturing an athlete's response to a win, loss, or other big moment. Nebraska Cornhuskers guard Brandon Richardson celebrates a victory over the Texas Longhorns. (Photo by Bruce Thorson)

POV Shot

The over-the-shoulder shot is important in character-driven stories, to show things from a character's point of view (POV). Using the example of a person in an office, working at a computer, you can position the camera behind the shoulder of the subject and point it at the computer screen to capture the subject's point of view.

This shot can be very interesting and fun. When shooting a sequence of someone making a peanut butter and jelly sandwich, for example, it might be fun to position the camera for a view of the sandwich coming together. Now imagine the other POV possibilities. Put the camera inside the refrigerator, very near the jelly, to capture their hand reaching for the jar. Hold the shot until the door closes, and you'll have a shot that ends neatly in the dark—from the refrigerator's point of view! If your subject throws a recyclable item in the trash instead of the recycling bin, position the camera inside the trash can and capture the item hitting the bottom. The POV shot can be a fun way to get alternative views of the same situation.

FICTION

POV shots can add a unique perspective to fiction and can increase tension and drama. The viewer is in the exact place of a character or an object, or even inside a refrigerator or a garbage can or a drawer. Plan ahead to add one interesting POV shot per scene to help break up the views.

Figure 5.06 Other types of POV shots include putting the camera where you know or think the subject might be going, such as in a refrigerator, and leaving it recording so that when the door opens the action is captured from a unique point of view. (Photo by Seth Gitner)

Figure 5.07 The over-the-shoulder shot is important in character-driven stories, to show things from a character's point of view (POV). (Photo by Seth Gitner)

NONFICTION

The same kinds of shots can be done, but it's trickier. You need to predict—sometimes down to the specific spot—when and where the action is going to happen. It's acceptable to ask people what they normally do, and then plan accordingly. That's different from setting up a shot outright. Remember that in nonfiction—and especially in journalism—it is very important to present *unstaged* reality.

THE RUGGED, WEARABLE MOUNTED CAMERA

One very interesting and relatively recent development in POV shooting involves the use of a small video camera contained in a waterproof housing. One such camera of this type is the GoPro, a palm-sized unit with a resolution of up to 4K. It has a very sturdy housing, plus a sensor that can shoot images of 5 megapixels or more. The batteries last up to two and a half hours, and a 32 GB SD card can be used. The camera has several different mounting options available, which allow for many different vantage points, and can take a ridiculous amount of abuse. It can be attached to a helmet or clothing, to a bicycle or surfboard, or even to a bird for a flight through the mountains. A GoPro has even been fastened to a hula hoop, for a previously impossible view of that activity.

Eric Seals is a staff photojournalist at the *Detroit Free Press* who often uses a GoPro in his video work. One of Seals' award-winning videos was shot on a radio-controlled car track: He simply mounted a unit on one of the cars and gave viewers the sensation of speeding around the track, hitting the jumps. He also mounted the unit on a pole and hung the pole out horizontally in the middle of the track so that the cars would drive directly into the shot.

Seals has even attached his GoPro to a balloon that ascended to the edge of space:

> Sometimes I watch TV and say, 'Wow, that was an interesting story.' For example there was a space balloon story on CNN where they launched a weather balloon into space with a camera attached. I wondered how I could localize that. I then Googled it and found some University of Michigan students who were doing an experiment much the same way. I then made calls, did a pre-interview with the professor and the students, then went out there and started shooting.

For the balloon story, Seals knew he needed a large enough memory card for a trip that was going to be over two hours long—a trip that would take the GoPro over 100,000 feet up in the sky. The camera returned to earth in one piece, with trip footage from beginning to end. "It's a workhorse camera," Seals said. "It's rugged and durable."

Still, Seals knows that the story is what matters, not the camera used to capture it.

"It's like candy," he said of using the GoPro. "You don't eat it all the time."

FIVE GOPRO TIPS FROM ERIC SEALS

1.   GoPro doesn't make your story better. It just adds a visual hook to your piece. It is the characters and your story focus that make the story.

Figure 5.08 Eric Seals is a staff photojournalist at the *Detroit Free Press*. (Photo courtesy of Eric Seals)

2. Think of using a GoPro like eating candy. It's sweet and gratifying, but too much is definitely not a good idea. Don't overfeed your viewers with it. Just tease them . . . give them just a little bit here and there, but only at the right places in your piece, for the right amount of time.

3. Out of the various GoPro versions, which has given me the most bang for the buck? The GoPro Hero 3 Black. It has a variety of resolutions, from 1080 to 4K for video or stills, better clarity in shooting in low light, and a number of mounts and many optional accessories.

4. If you're shooting video with the GoPro Hero 3 Black, a good setting is the 1080 at 30 fps. For stills, use the time-lapse mode. I do one frame every two seconds. Some people don't care for the fish-eye look that the GoPro can put out. This look can be fixed in two ways: (1) by changing the way the camera sees from "narrow" to "medium," or leaving it at "wide"; and (2) by using the free and downloadable GoPro Studio software, which has an option to remove the fish-eye look and straighten out the horizon.

5. Utilize the stills option of the GoPro. It can take 5-megabyte photos at rates from 1 to 30 frames per second, and it can fit into and go places you dare not put a more expensive camera.

 Watch the video of the remote-controlled cars: http://bit.ly/gopro-freep

Cutaway

Make sure to shoot *cutaways*, that is, other scenes within the overall scene that can be used to get from one shot to another during the edit. Shoot tight, medium, and wide shots of all cutaways, to ensure flexibility as you edit.

For example, if several people are outdoors playing basketball on a court, sequence the entire scene by getting shots of the hoop and the ball going through it; get shots of the faces of the players; get shots of their feet running up and down the court. A cutaway would be shots of the spectators, whether it is a child watching the game in awe or a mother proudly watching her son or daughter play. Shots that cut away momentarily from the main action help in the edit, for when two different scenes need to be combined for continuity.

Figure 5.09 The GoPro is a palm-sized unit with a resolution of up to 4K. It has a very sturdy housing, plus a sensor that can shoot images of 5 megapixels or more. (Photo by Eric Seals)

Interview Shot

In nonfiction storytelling, it is a necessity to shoot interviews. Most likely there will be only one camera to shoot with, so try to vary focal lengths. This makes interviews look better than they do with one, long shot at the same focal length. It's also important to give *lead room* in an interview, so that the subject is looking off to the side of the camera instead of straight into it.

What exactly is lead room? Whether shooting stills or video, use the rule of thirds as a guide. Positioning subjects off-center can grab viewers in new and exciting ways. For example, when shooting a portrait, place the subject to the right or left within the frame. The subject would be positive space within the frame, while the negative space would be the open area. Telling the subject to look into the negative area creates lead room within the image. Look for this practice in any video interview you see.

Tight Shot

It is important to get tight shots of a subject's face, ideally including both eyes and the mouth. It's a good idea to avoid shots of the eyes or mouth alone, although there are situations where this can be effective. For work such as this try using a longer lens, such as a 135mm or 200mm, which will make distant objects look nearer.

Super Tight

Super-tight shots are for showing details, and they also make good transitions to different sequences during editing. Good detail shots will help to maintain

Figure 5.10 When shooting an interview it is important to put the subject on either the left or right side of the frame and to have them looking and talking not at the camera, but out of the frame. (Photo by Seth Gitner)

Figure 5.11 You can never have too many tight shots. Tight shots are a great help in post-production, since they allow the editor to take the viewer anywhere. (Photo by Seth Gitner)

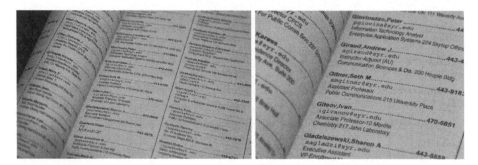

Figure 5.12 Shooting something as small as a name in a phone book with a tight shot is difficult. For very small subjects, shoot super tight. The viewer should be able to pick out one particular name, rather than seeing just a list of names. In this example, the left image shows what happens when the shot is not taken close enough. It is not easy to make out the name that is the subject of the photo. In the right image, the camera lens is zoomed in tight enough for a viewer to see that it's the name of the author of this book. (Photo by Seth Gitner)

continuity. Get as close as possible by using the macro function on the camera, usually marked with a flower icon. If the shot is of somebody tying up a sail-boat to a cleat, it is important to show just the hands, the rope, and the cleat. A tight shot can become a super-tight detail shot, such as a name in a phone book. Get in very, very close so that the viewer can distinguish one name from another. If someone is jotting a note down on a pad, get in close enough to capture what is being written.

Figure 5.13 It is important to get an assortment of shots at varied focal lengths, such as a medium shot in between a tight shot and a wide shot. A medium shot is often seen as a normal view. (Photo by Seth Gitner)

Tight shots also help to transition into and out of scenes. In post-production, a tight shot is often the best way to switch to a new setting.

Medium Shot

The medium shot is made with a lens of about 85mm. It is good for above-the-waist, head-and-shoulder shots, such as those that show a process or the performance of some activity, or someone talking on the phone while sitting at a desk in an office. It is a standard shot for showing people in conversation, and it also enables the characters' arms to be seen if they are gesturing.

Wide Shot

This broadly focused shot is very common in film and video. Usually captured with a wide angle lens, it shows the scene in its entirety while showing the activity of characters as well. In a scene with two characters in a dorm room, a wide shot could show the entire room, establishing place, with the characters present. It gives viewers a sense of where they are.

Try to capture a wide shot of the scene first off, so that you're sure to have it. If you are shooting video of someone sitting at their desk, it would be wise to shoot an overall extra-wide shot to give the viewer a feeling of where the story is taking place.

Figure 5.14 The wide shot is very common, but it should be used in conjunction with tight and medium shots in a sequence. (Photo by Seth Gitner)

 ## Exercise: Sequencing a Visual Story

When beginning a shoot it is important to think in sequences. What shots are needed to tell the story?

Using your camera kit and tripod, shoot a self-contained, active event of a friend sitting at a desktop computer or a laptop. Keep it simple, and make sure there is a beginning, middle, and end. When selecting a subject and character, keep in mind that you will edit this into a small story. You are thus shooting a complete piece, and despite the length, there should be a visual story. No soundtrack is needed for this exercise.

You will be creating a piece of fiction—a made-up story. It is more important to think visually than to try to shoot something happening in real life.

Take a variety of compositions for each step of the sequence: tight, super-tight, medium, and wide.

Not only do you want to assemble good sequences that contain a variety of shots, but the shots should tell the story: someone accidentally deleting a research paper, someone trying to prepare for a video job interview, someone trying to take an online test.

Procedure

1. Transfer the folder containing your shots from the camera to your hard drive.
2. Make sure the final edit has a beginning, a middle, and an end.
3. Export a sequence and review it.

4. Identify the beginning, middle, and end, and which shots form each part of the story arc.

Acronyms to Keep in Mind While Shooting

BOPSA – Bunch of People Standing Around

This happens when the action stops, and there is not much going on, and the videographer feels that he or she needs to be doing something to justify being there. So they shoot B-roll of people doing nothing. Try to avoid this temptation. If it must be done, perhaps for B-roll, try to shoot cutaways or detail shots that generate some visual storytelling value. This will pay off during the edit.

SLOBR – Serious Lack of B-Roll

On some shoots, there is just nothing going on. Or maybe you missed the action or event altogether, leaving only interview A-roll. This happens distressingly often, and in journalism it isn't permissible to recreate an event, or tell people what to do. This is a case where an ounce of prevention is equal to a pound of cure. The way to avoid it is to call a subject ahead of time, and strive to do things on the schedules of others rather than your own timetable. When the goal is to capture real moments, you need to be there when they happen.

AMD – Avoid Mindless Documentation

Shortly into some shoots, a videographer may feel as if he or she has shot it all and there is nothing new to capture. There is still a need to shoot, but it starts to turn into the same shots, over and over, and the documenting of pointless interactions. This can lead to a very frustrating edit, so avoid it.

Spray & Pray

This is shooting without any concern for what is being shot. The misconception is that with enough unplanned footage, something can be cobbled together in the editing process. This isn't the way it works. Not shooting planned, carefully considered sequences will leave you lost and empty-handed in the editing stage.

Camera Movement

When shooting video, always strive for movement within a frame. A viewer's eye is always tracking movement. Since subjects aren't always in motion, there are certain visual devices to avoid shots that are completely still.

The Rock Shot

A shot that is completely still is known as a *rock shot*; it's like shooting a rock. Nothing moves. Imagine a story about a lemonade stand, which might logically require a shot of a glass of lemonade. Just shooting the glass would be a rock shot. To avoid this, shoot a super-tight detail shot of a bead of condensation running down the side of the glass. This would get movement into the shot, with the added benefit of showing the coolness of the lemonade and the humidity of the day. When covering a breaking news story about a killing, there might be a police line that cannot be crossed, requiring other ways to shoot the scene of emergency vehicles and first responders. One way to introduce motion would be to shoot the yellow police tape moving in the breeze. Another would be to shoot revolving emergency lights, or to capture the accident scene reflected in the window of an emergency vehicle. In the latter example, it's not enough to just get the reflection. Wait until a police officer, paramedic, or vehicle moves through the scene. These bits of action will hold viewers' attention and propel them through the piece. Seek out motion.

The Tracking/Dolly Shot

Another way to keep the video moving is to use a dolly. Called a *tracking shot*, this is where the camera is physically moved along a set path. Film professionals usually use a wheeled cart that glides along a track. There are several inexpensive ways to get the same effect; one is to use a skateboard. Simply place the camera on the skateboard and gently move it across the floor. A smaller handheld video camera or HDSLR is perfect for this. The general idea is to show lateral movement; instead of having the subject move, the camera moves. A new, budget device that some web videographers are using is called a *rail*. It's a device consisting of a tripod socket mounted on a stand on a piece of metal track. The track can, in turn, be mounted to a tripod or set of tripods. This allows the camera to be raised or lowered and moved at whatever pace the photographer chooses. The viewer, of course, will not notice technology like this in use. They will be too involved in the story.

Static Shots

When shooting a video of a musical performance, it is important to get one shot of the entire piece from one vantage point. If two cameras are available, it is possible to get other views of the musicians playing—an assortment of tight, medium, and wide shots. This allows interesting views of musicians playing their instruments while maintaining the ability to cut back to a wide shot of the performance at any time. The same trick can be used for a press conference, shooting the entire event from a single location up until the question-and-answer session, and then getting tight, medium, and wide shots of the people behind the podium after that. This provides a selection of cutaways, making it easier to cut up the press conference and compress it to fit a newscast or online article.

Pan

Putting the camera on a tripod instantly creates options for making the shot more interesting. Depending on the quality and sophistication of the tripod, these options will vary. Most video tripods enable panning from side to side using an arm that extends from the tripod head itself. Panning shouldn't be done aimlessly; it should express something about the story. This is called a *motivated* pan, because there is a purpose in moving from one object to another in the shot. For example, when shooting a speaker at the front of a room, a pan from the front of the room to the back will convey the size of the audience. The same could apply to showing the size of a country estate, a factory floor, or a crowd at a sporting event. A motivated pan builds the narrative. A pan without motivation only shows focal points that have no aim or meaning.

Tilt Up and Down

A tripod can also be used to pan vertically; this is called *tilt*. This tilting action should also have a definite purpose. In an establishing shot of a building, for example, a tilt can emphasize the building's height or intimidating nature. Start low and work your way up. Again, make sure that all movements carry meaning and propel the story forward. Don't pan just for the sake of panning, or tilt just because the tripod allows it.

High and Above

Often there will be the opportunity to get high and above—to shoot from a second story window, a staircase, or some other perch. This point of view can add new meaning to a story. For example, to get a shot of a pastor preaching in a pulpit and also show the size of the congregation, a shot from a balcony could be the perfect solution. This can also be done using a *jib*, which is a crane with a counterweight on one end and a camera on the other. A jib allows a smooth transition from low to high vantage points and vice versa. With a jib attached to a tripod head, the camera can pan left to right as it ascends or descends, providing a shot with more movement.

Stephen McGee, an independent filmmaker based in Detroit, does a lot of film work in small teams or even by himself. McGee uses a crane on a lot of his shoots, and once he brought a crane along when shooting in Vietnam. To cut down on travel weight he left the counterweights at home and used locally available bags of rice instead. "Even the smallest movement is more beautiful than what you can do handheld," he pointed out.

Eye Level

It is important to vary the level of view. When shooting children or pets, for instance, shooting from eye level can give poor results. Imagine trying to get a shot of children painting in art class, only without taking up a position at their level. All of the shots would be of the tops of their heads.

Slow Motion

Occasionally during an edit it will be desirable to slow down or speed up a shot. Slow shutter speeds have nothing to do with slow motion in video. To get sharp slow motion in video, it's best to use a high-speed camera that shoots at a frame rate of 60 fps and higher. A high shutter speed is not nearly as important.

To show the form of an athlete in action, it is best to use a high-speed camera to get a sharp slow-motion image to begin with. Scenes may also be slowed down for storytelling reasons—think of the characters walking down an alley in the title sequence of the 1992 film *Reservoir Dogs*, and how the slowed-down motion makes it seem as if they are on a mission. This effect can be achieved in nonlinear editing software, but it's best to shoot it right the first time. It's unlikely that an entire movie would ever be done in slow motion, but that doesn't mean it can't be used creatively, to help tell a story.

Rack Focus

You have probably seen *rack focus* in action: it is when a subject in sharp focus in the foreground suddenly goes out of focus in favor of something else in the background, or vice versa. The idea is to draw viewers' attention to a different element of the same scene—to literally shift their focus elsewhere. This often can add drama to a scene, and a dramatic shift in perspective.

Exercise: Movement in Video

Using a DSLR's video function, create a "sense of place" sequence. Imagine you are creating the opening sequence of a video that will introduce incoming freshmen to your school's campus.

- Be aware of light, color, and composition as you shoot the sequence.
- Use a tripod—shaky cameras are not allowed except for a definite purpose.
- Shoot one sequence for each of the types of camera movements described above.
- Make sure to note what clips fall where in your visual story.

After you're done with your shoot, consider these questions:

1. Make sure that among all of your shots there is an identifiable beginning, middle, and end.
2. What were some problems you encountered?
3. What times of day did you shoot?
4. Do you feel as if you told a visual story that represents the campus and all it has to offer?

Editing a Sequence

Once all the needed shots have been gathered, they will need to be put together logically to tell a visual story. This is accomplished by working in a software application called a *nonlinear editor*.

Imagine a series of shots—tight, medium, wide, POV, and possibly an interview—that need to be made into a film. Try to think of the task as a puzzle with many pieces to assemble. The pieces start out in a bin, and must be taken from that bin and placed where they fit best in the puzzle.

Try not to overthink this process; edit the shots into something very clear and straightforward. If you're shooting a story about someone setting up a sailboat, the shots should include a wide shot of the boat club (the establishing shot), a second shot that takes the viewer out onto the dock, and a third that leads to the boat. The next shot could be a closeup of the subject untying the rope that secures the sail to the boom. This constitutes a visual story: a compilation of shots that shows a story or process unfolding. Recognize also that a process like this could take ten to fifteen minutes in real life. Since the video's total run time could likely be as short as two to three minutes, varying focal lengths will be needed among the shots to convey the passage of time. Each clip will need to be no longer than fifteen seconds or so.

As another example, picture a sequence about playing the basketball game Horse, an elimination game for two or more players trying to make baskets. Putting this together would require a series of shots of two people playing, along with at least one wide shot of the basketball court. Shot one would be a wide shot establishing the court as the place where the two players are—this is also called a *master shot*. The remaining shots will be within that same scene, but will be a variety of tights, mediums, and wides. Think about everything that makes up the game, from dribbling the ball to eyeing a shot, to reacting to a miss. All of these moments will help tell the story of the game.

The combination of all these shots is called a *sequence*. If you've played the game before, you know that it takes more than two minutes, so this sequence will need to compress time. Accomplish this by sprinkling the sequence with the "moments," discussed above. These moments will convey whether one person is winning over another, and the emotion evident in those moments will engage viewers. At the end of the game, the person who loses will hopefully exhibit the agony of defeat (or at least the mild disappointment of it), and the winner will look victorious.

Sequencing may be time-consuming, but it is not difficult, and thinking in sequences will help in the editing process later on. It will speed things up and help weed out the shots that don't work, so that what shines is the story.

Enter Frame/Exit Frame

During shooting there will be actions within the scene that need to be watched for, and that are vital to having a well-edited final product. Be attentive to characters; try to have them enter the frame and exit the frame at least once in a series of shots. This will allow easy cutting from one scene to another. Also, remaining with the basketball example, when the ball is shot at the basket and leaves the frame, a natural point is created at which to insert a shot of the ball going into (or missing) the basket. It's important to follow the action, and to anticipate what a viewer's eyes will follow in the scene.

When the subject enters the frame and walks away from the camera, this is a closing opportunity. If the subject walks toward the camera, this is another opportunity to transition to another scene. Always be alert as to how the viewer will be carried to the next scene; not paying attention to this could cost you important transitional shots. Always be looking for these moments, and be thinking about both the next shot and the final shot.

The more thinking that goes into shooting, the easier the edit will be in post-production. Once the project has reached the editing phase, it probably will not be possible to go back and shoot scenes again. It should be obvious, then, that getting sequences with an adequate variety of shots takes careful planning, and definitely makes better films.

Chapter Summary

This chapter covered the importance of variety in visual storytelling, some of its necessary components, and some things to avoid. As always, planning is key. Also important, however, is an alertness to what will be needed in the editing process to tell a complete and compelling visual story.

Many different kinds of shots and actions tell a story, and motion is a very important ingredient in storytelling. If a scene has no overt motion, there are clever ways to introduce it through camera movement, and equipment to help accomplish that movement.

Planning and putting a video together is different from building a still-image project, even if the same camera is being used for both. Time must often be compressed and events must make sense chronologically. It's also essential for the storyteller to gather all the kinds of shots needed to complete the "puzzle" of a visual story.

Looking at the big picture, shoot to build sequences. Think about what the beginning, middle, and end of a piece will actually look like. On a more micro level, use a tripod for consistent steadiness, pay attention to the axis of action, and always be on the lookout for transitional shots.

Review Questions

1. Explain the concept of "shoot to edit."
2. What is the difference between A-roll and B-roll?
3. Name three types of camera movement and describe them.
4. What two positions are involved in rack focus?
5. What kind of frame rate is best for capturing slow motion video?
6. What does POV stand for, and what can the concept be used for?
7. Draw a diagram of what "do not cross the line" means.

Exercises

1. Now that you have an understanding of the way a still camera works, it is important for you to practice using one every day. Document your day. Shoot photographs of what you do, your meals with friends, what you see on your way to class—anything and everything. Avoid posed, contrived shots. Document your life in the moment.

   • Download and review your images.
   • Break your edit down into a story with a beginning, middle, and end.

2. Identify a process that occurs somewhere in your daily life, and capture it using the concepts and techniques discussed in this chapter. It could be opening a store, cooking a meal, building/repairing something, cleaning/maintaining something, stocking shelves, exercising, etc.

   Think of this sequence as a how-to video for people who might have to perform the same process.

   Think of light, color, and composition as you shoot the sequence. Pre-visualizing and storyboarding your sequence prior to shooting is recommended. The video sequence must be between thirty and forty-five seconds long. The piece must have a soundtrack, whether natural, ambient sound, and/or royalty-free music.

   Use at least three different types of camera movements or techniques, such as:

   • Rack focus
   • Framing that includes tight, medium, and wide shots

- Motivated pan
- Tilt
- Varying depth of field
- Silhouette
- Slow-motion/speed-up/time-lapse

 ## Key Terms

180-degree rule – The relationship between two subjects in a scene forms an "axis of action" from one to the other, and the camera should stay on one, consistent side of this line.

Action – Whatever happens in front of the camera; whatever someone does that is the point of the shot.

AMD – Avoid Mindless Documentation: When you feel as if you've shot it all, and there is nothing new to shoot, don't be tempted to shoot whatever is there.

A-roll – Generally interview footage, both audio and video. It consists of sound bites and ambient audio gathered on scene.

BOPSA – Bunch of People Standing Around: B-roll of people doing nothing.

B-roll – All visuals that have been shot, excluding interviews. This includes all the video, still images, and motion graphics that can help to tell the story visually.

Clip – Once footage has been transferred to a computer, and in and out points have been established for each shot, the resulting files are called *clips*.

Cutaway – Make sure to shoot cutaways, that is, other, smaller scenes or details within the overall scene that can help you get from one shot to another during editing.

Enter frame – When a subject walks into a scene from outside of the frame.

Exit frame – When a subject exits a scene and is no longer in front of the camera or in the shot.

GoPro – A small camera with a 170-degree field of view that can withstand a beating and be submerged in water. Often used for POV shots, since it can be strapped to a person or attached to most anything.

High and above – A vantage point above a subject.

Medium shot – A shot with a field of view large enough to include everything above a person's waist.

Pan – Sweeping the field of view horizontally.

POV shot – The over-the-shoulder shot is important in character-driven stories, to show things from a character's point of view.

Rack focus – Changing focus from one subject to another, which is at a different distance.

Reaction – How people respond to whatever happens in front of the camera.

Rock shot – A shot where nothing moves within the frame.

Rule of thirds – Intersecting vertical and horizontal lines, like a Tic-tac-toe board, can be used as a device to help compose an image. Taking that Tic-tac-toe board and superimposing it on the camera's viewing area allows you to easily line up a subject or subjects along one axis. This technique results in better-composed images.

Sequence – A series of shots that serve as the building blocks for a visual narrative. A sequence consists of a variety of shots at varying focal lengths, such as tight, medium, wide, and long.

SLOBR – Serious Lack of B-Roll: This happens when you go out on a shoot and there is nothing going on, or you miss the action or event altogether. So all you have is interview A-roll.

Shot – Every time you focus a camera and frame up, and then record a tight, medium, or wide field of view, it is called a *shot*.

Silhouette – A silhouette is produced when a foreground subject is exposed against a brighter background, making the subject darker than the background.

Slow motion – A shot or a sequence of shots where action is slowed down, sometimes as a result of a higher frame rate.

Spray & pray – Shooting without thinking, and hoping it can all be worked out when you sit down to edit

Static shot – When shooting a video of a musical or other performance, it is important to get this shot of the entire piece from one vantage point, which can always be cut back to.

Tight shot – A shot that shows detail, helpful when there is a need to cut to different sequences during editing.

Tilt up and down – Panning vertically with a tripod, which can emphasize height.

Tracking/Dolly shot – Physically moving the camera along a set path. Film professionals usually use a wheeled cart that glides along a track.

Wide shot – Usually captured with a wide-angle lens, this shot establishes the overall setting.

Sources

McGee, Stephen. Conversation with author, October 7, 2013.
Seals, Eric. Conversation with author, September 6, 2011.

6 EDITING A VIDEO IN POST-PRODUCTION
Why Do Motion Pictures and News Video Utilize Specific Editing Techniques?

In this chapter you will learn

- Basic concepts and principles of editing
- Nonlinear video editing techniques to keep the viewer engaged
- The different types of cuts and transitions that are used to edit video
- Techniques to improve the audio in a final production
- Software options for producing video content

Introduction

It is helpful to think about video editing like building a jigsaw puzzle. There are many puzzle pieces (video clips), and they need to be assembled into a large image that tells a story. Unlike a jigsaw puzzle, there is more than one workable way to achieve positive results. Like a puzzle, however, there are ways that definitely don't work.

A lot is involved in putting together a sequence of images and scenes that works for the viewer. There is much more to it than placing a string of clips, one after another, in a line in a video editor. There are different types of cuts and different types of edits that will mean different things to the viewer. Using them correctly is a matter of logic, artistic sensibility, and following the conventions of visual storytelling (viewers have expectations, based on the visual content they have seen before). It might sound intimidating, but these intricacies are neither hard to understand nor hard to remember. Hands-on editing of content is the best kind of practice; that way you'll get the hang of it as you work and will soon be editing quickly and easily, without frustration.

One's first view of editing software can be one of those intimidating moments. What does all this stuff do? Go into it with an open mind and a solid understanding of the *why* of video editing, and in not much time you will be ordering, reshaping, and editing films, and in powerful ways that might not have seemed possible before.

The main foundation of video editing is essentially to put clips together into an order that makes sense logically. Once again, planning—the practice of sitting down and going through a process mentally to decide how things should turn out and what will be required to get to that point—is key.

Even with footage shot only fifteen minutes before it goes into the editor, for example at a news conference, there needs to be a plan for how the edit will tell a story. Editing provides virtually unlimited options, and starting to edit footage without a plan can easily lead into a never-ending spiral of trial and error. This is a common occurrence for the inexperienced. There isn't time for it.

So, where to start? Editing fiction begins with a shot list and a plan called a *storyboard*, which will be described in detail shortly. Also, in both nonfiction (journalism) and fiction, all footage should be logged, or categorized by type of shot, subject, people involved, time, location, and whatever other criteria help to keep things organized. Nowadays, this can all be done within the editing software itself. In fiction, the storyboard might already be done, and it can be a big help in making editing a smooth process with a definite plan. In news, provided that you were editing in your head ("shooting to edit") while gathering footage, there will also be a rough plan for the edited version.

Don't be too attached to footage. Remember that just because it was shot does not mean it has to be in the final film. If a scene simply does not work because of acting, direction, lack of action, lighting, or whatever, it can always be cut. One bad scene can bring down the overall quality of a film.

Essentially, editing is rearranging time. With a short film for a digital platform, what might be hours upon hours of footage needs to be compressed into an interval of maybe three to five minutes. It might seem impossible, but it is not. It is done all the time. Follow the shooting principles and recommendations in this book, and making a good film of this length, with a logical story that engages viewers, won't be that difficult.

Organizing the Edit

Organization is an early key to being a good video editor. In the editing context, being organized means meta-tagging and selecting keywords for your files prior to editing. The larger a project gets, the more video files and clips will be involved. Since editing is a process of putting together "puzzle pieces," a very, very large amount of time can be spent just looking for that one piece that fits perfectly and that you saw this morning, but have absolutely no idea how to retrieve now. And once it is found, what comes next? The time-consuming hunt for the next piece. If every forty-five–second piece requires a search through literally hours of footage, you'll quickly fall behind and not make deadline. So organizing footage ahead of time, while it takes significant work, ends up saving much more work in the long run.

Organizing should take place right after all of the video files have been shot and imported into the nonlinear video editor, a process also known as *ingesting*. Here are some best practices for organization:

Keyword your clips – It is possible to use many keywords for clips, but make sure always to notate—and *keyword*—the type of shot (tight, medium, wide, etc.)

Change clip thumbnails – The editing software will automatically choose a thumbnail, or small picture, for each clip. These can be changed to a visual that is easily recognizable.

Batch rename – Clips coming right out of a digital camera most likely will be named something like MVI_001.mov or DSC_001.mov, which makes them hard to recognize. Many software packages have a renaming function that allows these files to be renamed in bunches according to their content, like smithinterview_001 or treeplanting_001, or any other desired naming system.

Rate footage – While logging footage, do a quick, critical review of each clip. Maybe some scenes were shot from multiple angles, and one is better than the others. Think about rating footage on a scale of one to five, with five being the best. This provides an instant filter and reference system for the strongest material, without having to keep it all in mind. Some software will allow clips to be rejected or hidden from view. Maybe you accidentally shot one or two clips of the ground while you were walking. Rather than deleting these entirely, remove them from the bin so they do not get in the way during editing.

Add notes – While reviewing footage, there will be things that need to be noted or remembered that are specific to each individual clip. Each clip has a place within the editor for these kinds of notes, either to yourself or to whomever else will be working on the edit. Adding meta tag information to a clip is very important, such as label, nickname, and type, so that they will be easily searchable.

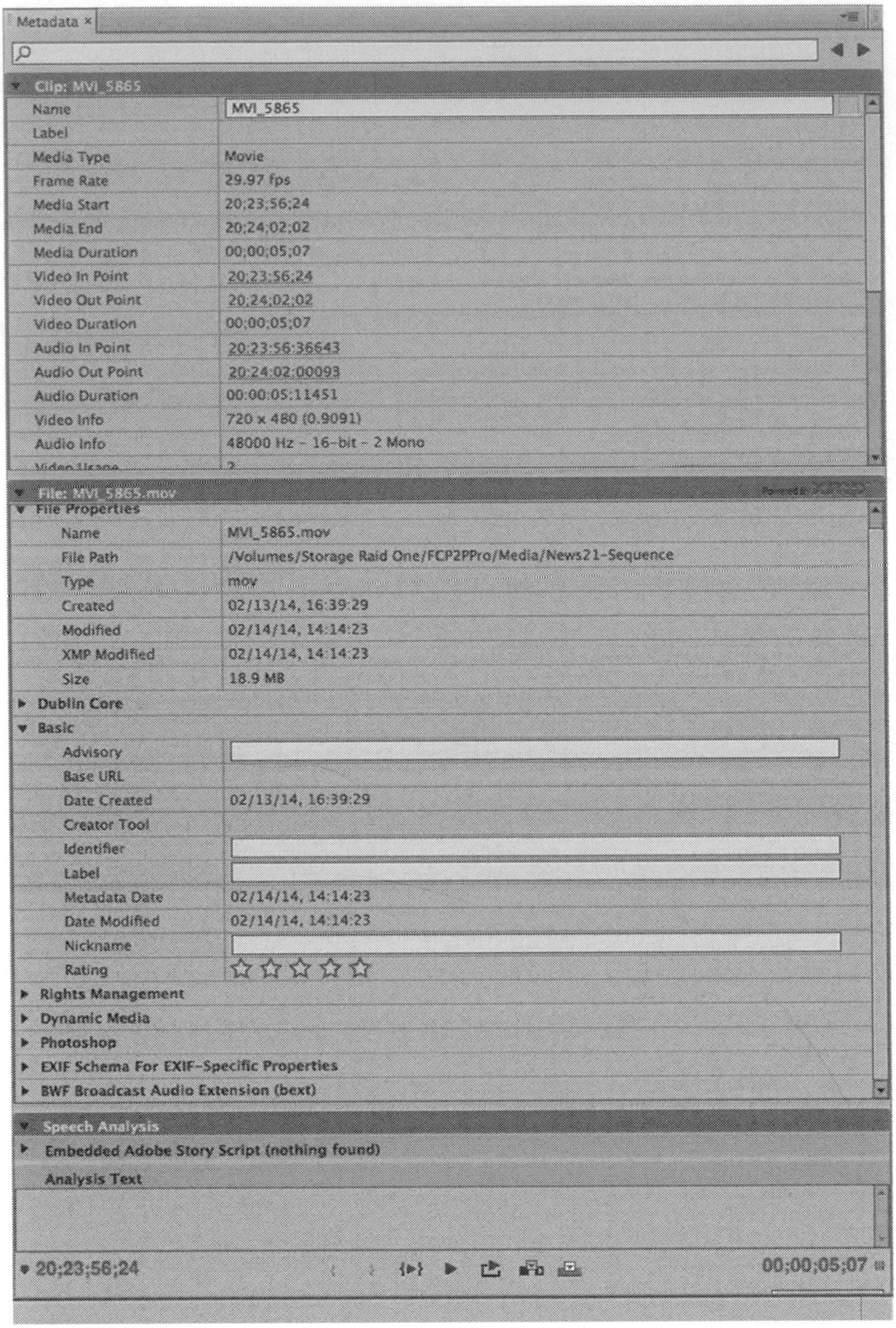

Figure 6.01 When beginning a video edit, being organized means meta-tagging and keyword-ing your files. Adding meta-tag information to a clip is very important; most NLEs allow the producer to add different types of information to clips, such as label, nickname, and type, so that they will be easily searchable. (Adobe product screenshot(s) reprinted with permission from Adobe Systems Incorporated)

MEET THE PRO
Debra Weinfeld, Editor, Los Angeles, CA

Debra Weinfeld works in Los Angeles as an editor on both television and film-based projects. She edited the movies Never Back Down *(2008) and* Never Back Down 2 *(2011). She has also edited television episodes of* Necessary Roughness *(seasons 1 through 3),* Covert Affairs *(season 4), and* Graceland *(season 1) for the USA Network. She is a member of Local 700 of the Motion Picture Editors Guild.*

Figure 6.02 Debra Weinfeld, film editor, Los Angeles, CA.

"On average I get between three and five hours of dailies a day—different cameras, multiple takes, all the footage they shot for that day," says film and television video editor Debra Weinfeld. Most television shows shoot an average of five to seven scenes a day, she said, which is about six to eight pages of script, although her workload is "sometimes only four pages if it's a big action scene, if it takes a lot of time to shoot." As she explained:

> In my experience so far, the more experienced the director is, if the scene doesn't call for it, they won't overshoot it. Mainly because they know what they want, and they know if they give too many options, their vision of the scene won't be in the final cut. They know exactly what they want, and what they want seen on TV in the end.

The footage comes to her already divided up into scenes, Weinfeld said. All she has to do is look at the script and put the scenes together according to it. As the crew is shooting the film, a continuity person writes down specific notes about each scene as it is shot. These notes are very important to the video editor as he or she puts the footage together. "They tell me what each setup was, how many takes were shot, sometimes preferences from the director—like, 'this is where I want to end,' or 'great ending,' or 'great reading of this moment,'" said Weinfeld.

She makes a point of not reading a script ahead of getting the footage, since scripts change and story lines are altered, with some scenes getting dropped. "I learned not to read ahead of time because I get disappointed when scripts change too much," said Weinfeld. "When the producers walk in and say, 'Oh, we dropped that story, now it doesn't make sense,' I can say I never knew that story existed, and it makes sense to me."

The process of making believable scenes in a fictional reality can be tough, especially when you may or may not have all of the footage you think you need. "I'll usually find my opening piece and then start looking at all the angles to see what would be the next piece," said Weinfeld, who

(Continued . . .)

(. . . *continued*)

lets some clips go longer than they should just so she can find the next angle to use in the edit. "Then I'll look to where I cut to another angle, cut to the other character, or pop in to get a little closer. Maybe I started wide, then I'll start looking for other shots," she said.

One cable television show Weinfeld worked on was USA Network's *Covert Affairs*—the episode is called "River Euphrates." The show is a spy drama about CIA officers who work missions around the world. In the episode Weinfeld edited, Annie, the lead character, comes out of hiding after seeing an ex-CIA agent get killed at a bus station. Annie's former boss, named Joan, who thinks Annie is dead, chases down a lead about some diamonds at a shop in Brooklyn, NY. Out of the blue, Joan bumps into Annie outside the diamond store. Weinfeld talked about how she edited the scene to make it work better:

> In that scene with Annie and Joan, I had to make it more of a "moment" because it went by really fast. So I added extra beats in, and I added the line of Joan saying, "You're alive," because it didn't *land*. It was way too quick the way it was shot.

As the editor, she has to think about where specific plot points fall within a scene to make sure that the viewer understands exactly what is going on—that the moment "lands." "It's a huge moment. Joan thinks Annie is dead, right up until this moment," she explained.

A big part of editing television shows is giving viewers a reason to stick with the show through a commercial break with a "cliffhanger" or a moment of emotional, which is called an *act out*:

> When we come back from the break they are back to business, instead of, 'My God, you are alive! Where have you been?' None of that happened. It wasn't scripted. It wasn't on the director. But there needed to be more of a beat. So I created beats on both sides, to milk that for a little more emotion.

Weinfeld said that creating those beats required adding extra shots, extending them, and taking the line of Joan saying *You're alive* from another shot. Weinfeld said she received a note from the network telling her about the situation, and that as the editor it was, "My job to just go in and figure it out," she recalled.

A lot of what she does depends on the director with whom she is working. The director, in turn, relies a lot on the skills and experience of the actors. "If it's bad, it's bad," said Weinfeld about acting:

> It affects everything. If the acting is bad the director struggles. The cinematographer can actually struggle . . . The first thing that makes

(Continued . . .)

(*. . . continued*)

> everybody's job easier is when the writing is good; the second thing is when the actors are good. Then the directors can do what they need to do to make the show work, and shoot what they need to shoot instead of trying to shoot around things that don't quite work.
>
> No matter who the actors and directors are, Weinfeld loves to edit: "Whether TV or film—I don't care. If I kept working in TV and never stopped that'd be fine. I just love cutting," she said.

Film Editing Techniques

During video editing, clips must be put together in a way that makes sense. A fiction piece might have scenes shot in multiple ways, many times, to acquire as many different angles as possible. There are certain editing techniques that film and video editors use to make a film look as smooth, fluid, and seamless as possible.

Each of these rules or techniques is a tried-and-true method. It is the case that rules are meant to be broken, but the prerequisite for that is knowing each rule well enough to break it, and to do so only sparingly. Use the following techniques and concepts to help tell the story.

Continuity

When editing a film, many different kinds of cuts and transitions will take the viewer from clip to clip, scene to scene. The challenge is doing this smoothly, without making the viewer feel jarred in any way. Ideally the viewer will not see clips and scenes, or any edits, and instead will remain caught up in the story. This is called *continuity editing*, and it comprises several techniques to keep viewers on the rails and riding along with the action.

Matched Action

Matched action is a good way to connect shots together in a way that makes the transition smooth or even engaging. For example, if a character exits one scene, try to have her enter the frame of the next scene moving in the same direction. Another example of a matched action sequence is a man sitting at a computer. A wide shot would show him typing at the computer; the next shot would show his fingers on the keyboard. The next would show what is being typed on the screen, followed perhaps by a shot of his face, wearing a bewildered look at what he just typed. Alternatively, a wide shot of a woman on the phone could be followed by a close-up of her face reacting to the conversation. Matched action provides a graphic line of continuity between shots, linking them together as if they were always meant to be.

Figure 6.03 Matched action is a good way to connect shots together in a way that makes the transition smooth or even engaging. (Adobe product screenshot(s) reprinted with permission from Adobe Systems Incorporated)

Figure 6.04 A natural way to transition to something interesting or important in the story is to follow a character's eyeline, to whatever the character is looking at. (Adobe product screenshot(s) reprinted with permission from Adobe Systems Incorporated)

Eyeline Match

In Chapter 5, which discusses shooting techniques, we stressed that every action has a reaction. When putting together a video, make sure that every time a character looks at something specific, whether an object, unfolding action, or just another character, the viewer doesn't have to wait long to see what the character is seeing. The *eyeline* of one character's action should lead to the other character's reaction. This way the viewer's curiosity about what is being seen is satisfied, and the movie director has a chance to show the audience something important. The point of view (POV) shot is a natural way to follow a character's eyeline to something interesting or important to the story.

Parallel Editing/Cross-Cutting

Often used in chase scenes or other tense situations, *parallel editing* or *cross-cutting* is where the editor cuts between characters in different places going through the same or a related experience. For example, if one car were chasing another, we might see the front seat of one car and then be taken instantly to the front seat of the other, and so on, back and forth. This cutting between actors in a situation helps build tension between two subjects while at the same time connecting them visually. The viewer knows that the scenes are connected because they are in order and usually short. Both scenes are part of the same, big, unfolding event.

Axis of Action

Editors need to obey the previously mentioned 180-degree rule, just as directors and cinematographers do while they are shooting. All of the action needs to stay on one side of an imaginary line perpendicular to the camera's line of sight, keeping the positions of the characters relatively the same. "Crossing the line" means running the risk of confusing or jarring viewers about who is where. Even though you may have footage shot from a different side or angle, as the editor you need to make sure that it is added into the film in the correct place, so as to not disorient the viewer. For example, think about watching a televised football game. The camera angle is always the same to the viewer, with each team facing a consistent direction during a given quarter. If the camera were to suddenly switch to the opposite side of the field, viewers would get disoriented and not know which end zone belonged to whom. If a camera angle does change, to show replay action of a disputed play, for example, broadcasters will often note to the viewer that the angle has been changed for that purpose.

Slow Motion

Slow motion is an interesting effect that can slow down athletes to show the workings of their muscles, show water droplets splashing in a kind of suspended reality, or show a character doing something difficult or momentous, when every second is full of significance. While extending a sequence, this technique can also degrade the quality of the footage, since the editor is literally "making a little go a long way." An editor can do this, for instance, by changing the speed of a shot from 100 percent to 75 percent. Slow motion footage is best captured using a high-speed camera, with the best results being achieved when the frame rate is at least 60 fps. This way the images are recorded at a faster frame rate than the rate they are played back in the final movie. That's a capability that tends to be limited to a select few cameras. Think about the example of a "moment" from Chapter 1—of a boxer landing a left hook that

Figure 6.05 Most NLEs have an option that allows the user to input a percentage to either speed up or slow down a clip. (Adobe product screenshot(s) reprinted with permission from Adobe Systems Incorporated)

knocks his opponent out. Imagine the moment when the boxing glove hits the jaw of the opponent, playing in slow motion. Sweat flies; flesh ripples. Slow motion in a movie can give a feeling of great power when done correctly.

Color Correction

First, it should be noted that the white balance inside the camera should be set for the current lighting situation whenever possible, by shooting a white piece of paper rather than using the actual lighting setting in the camera. This will make post-production editing simpler and quicker overall.

Sometimes color-correcting an edit cannot be avoided. It can consist of bringing down highlights, opening up shadows, or adjusting mid-tones to make the image exactly right for the viewer. Even with up-to-date hardware that allows very fast processing, adjustments like these work a computer hard and will likely extend a project's export time.

Color theory can be a complex topic, but the basics involve the following diagram. Essentially, if an image is too green, the fix is to add magenta. If the image is too blue, add yellow. If it is too red, the solution is to add cyan. As shown in the diagram, dragging the mouse from one end to the other will remove the color cast from a video. Some newer software programs analyze the color within a particular clip, then automatically remove the associated color cast. The problem with this kind of automation is that sometimes the algorithms that work the "magic" can be fooled, and they do the job wrong. Understanding the basics of color theory will help you do a better job color correcting your video.

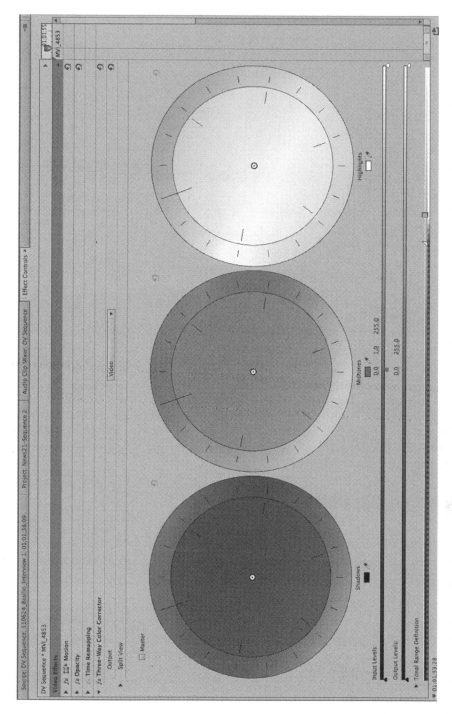

Figure 6.06 It is best to shoot video right the first time, using the correct white balance, but if you don't, nonlinear video editors offer color correcting options. (Adobe product screenshot(s) reprinted with permission from Adobe Systems Incorporated)

Stabilization

It is possible to remove shakiness from footage in post-production, but in no way is this a substitute for using a tripod in the first place. That being said, shaky video sometimes cannot be avoided, and it can be handy to have software that can deal with it. It can even make the difference between unusable and usable footage. The processing required to do this, however, will eat up a lot of computer time. Depending on the amount of footage that needs fixing, it might even be an overnight process.

Effects

Computer software allows for a huge range of "looks" and effects for video footage that would be very difficult or impossible to achieve through lighting and shooting alone. Apply these video filters carefully, though, so they do not upstage or distract from the story. Effects are usually as easy as dragging and dropping the desired filter onto a clip, although processing time can vary depending on the effect. Filters can add "flicker" for an aged appearance,

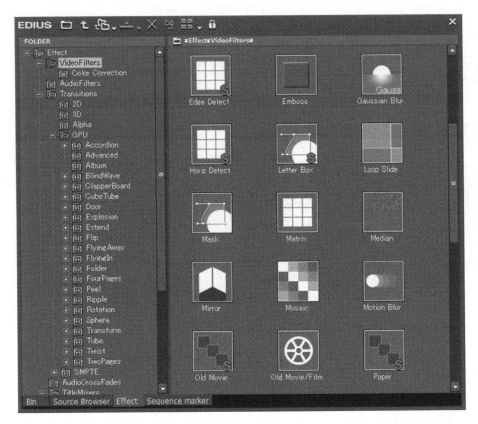

Figure 6.07 Video filters, also known as *effects*, can be as easy to apply as dragging and dropping the desired filter onto a clip. Filters can change the appearance of a clip, adding a vignette feel or changing the point of focus. (Screenshot courtesy of Grass Valley)

along with graininess and sepia tones, or they can add noise, lens flare, flashes, static, and a whole spectrum of other styles and effects.

Remember, however, that just because you have access to effects doesn't mean you need to use them. Approach them very cautiously. Use them only if they actually move the story forward, and be aware that they can actually be enough of a distraction to stop a story in its tracks. In other words, don't try to substitute the "coolness" of effects for solid content. See the next section for a rare example of when effects can be very helpful.

Flashback

Everyone knows the *flashback*—a sequence in a film when the viewer is swept back to some previous point in a character's life. We see some significant moment or achievement, or some incident that played a part in getting the character to where he or she is now. Flashbacks have elements of history and memory, like snapshots in an album that trigger foggy memories. In a story about a retiring principal, we might see a still image of the same character on her first day of teaching, or some other early point in her career. In a story about a police officer who has been working the same beat for a number of years, we might see that officer on the street as a rookie, or at a time when the neighborhood was a much better—or worse—place. It is an easy and time-tested technique to engage viewers and make them understand and care more about a character.

Flashbacks actually call for a change in visual style, and this is where effects (applied sparingly) can be key. Filters can be applied to evoke the passage of time through casts of color, murkiness, or even greater clarity. Still images can also be used, employing the *pan and scan* technique—also called the *Ken Burns Effect*, after Burns' well-known documentaries on war and sports—in which images slowly move within the frame as if one's eyes are drifting over them in a photo album or laid out on a table. This effect is done best when the image moves to a point within the frame where the viewer's eye falls naturally on its most significant content.

Montage

A *montage* is a technique in editing that conveys the passage of time with a lot of shots. It can also be used to connect random images and concepts in a linear fashion. Maybe there are several different shots that help tell part of a story, but there is no real, set order for the sequences to flow. A montage with cross-dissolves between the shots might be a good solution.

Famous montages include the detention scene in *The Breakfast Club*, in which the students are dancing in the library to "We are Not Alone" by Karla DeVito, passing the time during detention. Another is the scene in *Rocky* when Sylvester Stallone as the title character is training to box, running through the streets of Philadelphia and up the steps of the city's art museum. Rather than show day-in-and-day-out footage of a long process or undertaking, montages capture the prevailing mood of a long stretch of time when something is being endured, achieved, coming into being (like a romance), or falling apart. Doing this in conventional scenes could add an unmanageable amount of time to the film, so the director, with the help of the editor, provides the viewer with the quick, condensed version.

Another well-done montage to look at is the beginning of the animated Pixar film *Up*, in which the viewer is shown the married life of Carl and his wife, Ellie. It is a very effective and sad montage that ends with the wife's passing away. Once the montage is over, the viewer is able to understand Carl's frame of mind and accept his actions throughout the remainder of the movie.

Pacing

Pacing refers to the speed of the action in a movie—how many events and how much dialogue are packed into each scene, or into the total running time. Do a lot of things happen? Is the dialogue rapid-fire, racing from one situation to the next? Action movies and comedies tend to have faster pacing than, say, love stories, in which significant moments are more drawn-out and closely examined.

Pacing is another aspect of a film to keep in mind from shooting through editing. Try not to hang on to a shot too long. Directors will sometimes let a film slow down for more tender, emotional scenes, or pick up the pace for an action sequence. Pacing is a big factor in whether viewers become engaged in a movie or not. As you edit you need to feel these situations out and vary the pace accordingly. Few videos stay on the same pace for their entire length. Let the content dictate the pacing.

MEET THE PRO

Shawn Montano, Video Editor and Program Coordinator, Emily Griffith Technical College, Denver, CO

Shawn Montano has won five Regional Emmys, three Colorado Broadcasters Association awards, and an Edward R. Murrow award. He is the only person ever to win the title of Video Editor of the Year from the National Press Photographers Association four times. Montano also maintains The Edit Foundry, *an educational blog with an emphasis on video editing. In 2010,* The Edit Foundry *was named one of the 50 Best Blogs for Moviemakers by* MovieMaker Magazine.

Figure 6.08 Shawn Montano, video editor and program coordinator, Emily Griffith Technical College. (Photo courtesy of Shawn Montano)

"I love to make what somebody else shot better than what they envisioned or thought—I think I can make it better than originally planned," says Shawn

(Continued . . .)

(. . . continued)

Montano. "A photographer must constantly be thinking in sequences, thinking about the next shot and the last shot and thinking, 'How can I tell a mini-story with three shots?'" Montano explains sequencing like this:

> When you walk into a room, the first thing your eye does is take in the room, much like a wide shot would convey. Then your eye moves to a medium shot of, say, something like a person's face. Then it moves to focus on an item, maybe a pencil. That would be a tight shot. Your mind naturally builds sequences all the time.

Montano knows that when a photographer goes to shoot a news event, whether it's a public protest, a prisoner transfer, or a drag race, that the photographer must come back with enough usable images or sequences to tell that story visually.

Montano has some definite rules of editing:

Preserve Emotion – Never cut away from emotion. If you have a scene where your subject is getting emotional, do not cut away; stay on it for as long as possible. "Humans connect with emotion," Montano says. "You always leave emotion on the screen. Even if it is bad or shaky, emotion should override everything when you edit."

Seek Movement – "I am a huge fan of movement in every single shot," says Montano. "We are in a visual medium. Shoot movement in as many shots as you can. It enhances the presentation." For example, if you are going to shoot a sequence of a house, wait for someone to walk in front of the house. Wait for the action.

Predict Eye Movement – "Make your edit where the subject was last," Montano explains. "Place your viewer's eye in the frame where you want the viewer to be looking. Whatever is in motion on the screen, try to move the viewer's eye across the screen." Eye movement, in a nutshell, is the process of using whatever is in motion on screen to move the viewer's eye across the screen. Make your cut at a point where what is in motion moves your viewer's eye. As Montano says, make the viewer see what you want the viewer to see:

> If your subject walks from screen left to screen right and stops, find a shot for the next cut where the subject starts from the same place in the frame. Then, the eye is already looking where you want them to look.

Establish Rhythm – All video needs rhythm or pace; it keeps the viewer interested. "Turn the sound down, then, with a pencil, every time you make an edit, tap the pencil as if the pencil was a drumstick," recommends Montano. "With a good rhythm, the tapped beats between will be the same. If you feel a beat that is somewhat consistent, then you are hitting on a rhythm."

(Continued . . .)

(. . . *continued*)

> **Maintain Screen Direction** – Whenever you are shooting a scene you need to maintain all of your action on one side of the subject. If you are shooting two people at a table looking at each other, you want to keep each person's nose always pointing in the same direction. If you change that view, you could make it look like the two people are on the same side of the table. "You want a car's front end and back end to always be driving in the same direction; anything that is jarring is displeasing to the viewer," says Montano.
>
> **Enter Frame/Exit Frame** – "It's not what is at the beginning, it's what is at the end of the shot that's often more important," Montano emphasizes. "You don't need your subject to enter the frame and then exit the frame in the same shot. You can have them enter the frame in the first shot, then have them go a third of the way across the screen and then make your cut." In a first-time editor's video, the subject often enters and exits constantly. But, Montano says, "in that next frame, they can already be in the frame."

The Different Types of Cuts

Cuts

In news videography, cuts are key. They are the basic building blocks of sequencing. In video editing software, cuts are made with a tool called the *razor blade*. The cut is often compared to the natural human thought process. As one saying goes, "We think in cuts; we dream in dissolves."

For example, say you walk into an office and immediately look at a teacher, who is sitting at a desk and grading papers. Then you turn your head to the left to look at the window. Then your attention goes to a car outside, coming up the driveway. You keep cutting to the next shot, and so on. There is not a fluid panning and zooming over the scene. You take in one "shot" and then move quickly to another. There is no lengthy transition. Your eyes take in one set of information, and then the next, and your mind makes the connection between the shots.

Jump Cuts

Jump cuts can be described as jarring places where two shots that obviously do not go together very well—shots that have no continuity—have been spliced together. The mismatch can create an actual jump within the frame—it could be an interview in which the subject's head is in a different place than in the previous shot. In situations like this, it important to have enough B-roll or other shots that you can place in between the similar frames to avoid the jarring shot.

In broadcast journalism, jump cuts should be avoided most of the time, as they call attention to the fact that the viewer is seeing something that has

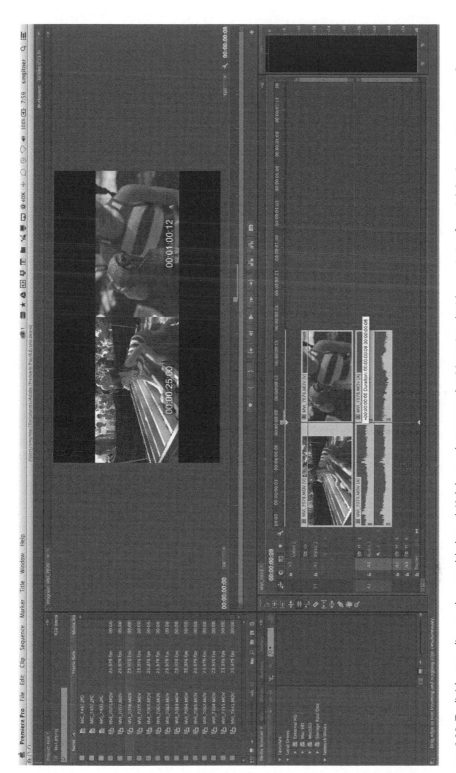

Figure 6.09 To divide up a clip, use the razor blade tool. (Adobe product screenshot(s) reprinted with permission from Adobe Systems Incorporated)

Figure 6.10 A *jump cut* is a mismatch between two frames within a sequence, which when played looks like an actual jump between frames. Note: When two clips are misaligned to make them look like one the image, the superimposed image in print is used to show this misalignment. (Adobe product screenshot(s) reprinted with permission from Adobe Systems Incorporated)

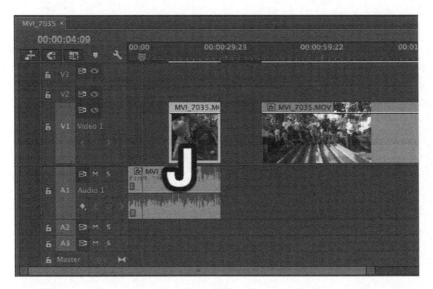

Figure 6.11 In a *J cut*, the audio of the next clip begins before the video of the first has ended. (Adobe product screenshot(s) reprinted with permission from Adobe Systems Incorporated)

been edited and pieced together. In some situations, they can be used creatively to "fast forward," or speed up the apparent passage of time.

J Cut

Normally, when video clips are placed back-to-back, the video and the audio cut at the same time, making the clips distinct and separate. A *J cut*'s name comes from the fact that it looks like the letter *J* in an editor's timeline. The audio of the next clip begins before the video of the first has ended. As viewers are still seeing the last image, they hear the audio of the next, which sparks their curiosity about what is coming up. It is a clever device to help viewers make the leap from one scene to the next without losing their attention.

L Cut

The *L cut* is another departure from putting video clips back-to-back and cutting both video and audio at the same time, only it is the opposite principle from a J cut. An L cut resembles an L in the timeline. It is when the editor lets the audio of a shot play a little bit beyond where the video cuts, so that the audio of the preceding clip plays underneath the next clip's picture. It is a device that helps make edits less visible, especially in conversations between or among characters. It can be used in a situation where a character is talking, to cut to the reaction of someone listening as the speech continues.

Say, for example, you are standing between two people talking, and every time a person speaks you turn your head to look at that person. This would feel very awkward and might even give you a sore neck eventually. If you held off moving your head back and forth, however, maybe anticipating a response from the listener while the first speaker is still going on, you would experience the virtues of the L cut. Viewers can put two and two together and still have an image in their head as to what the person looks like who

Figure 6.12 In an *L cut,* the editor lets the audio of a shot play a little beyond where the video cuts, so that the audio of the preceding clip plays underneath the next clip's picture. (Adobe product screenshot(s) reprinted with permission from Adobe Systems Incorporated)

Figure 6.13 Placing two different scenes in the same video frame can be an interesting way to show two stories going on at the same time, or the same story from very different points of view. (Adobe product screenshot(s) reprinted with permission from Adobe Systems Incorporated)

is asking the question. They can do this while they watch the other person's reaction.

This overlapping of dialogue is a great technique to use when actions and reactions really matter. Seeing someone react to what someone else says adds an element of emotional depth and interest to a scene, and the resulting filmed sequence will feel more like a genuine conversation.

Split Screen

Split screen is an editing device that is exactly what it sounds like. The viewer sees both parties in a telephone conversation, for example, on the screen at the same time. There is an added sense of drama and insight that comes from seeing the expressions and surroundings of two people who cannot see each other.

Transitions

When moving from one clip to the next, there are several editing options for bringing the viewer along. In video-editor speak, these are called *transitions*. There are almost too many to choose from, and like effects they should be used in moderation and only to advance the story. Using a clock-like wipe or a book-page flip might look "cool" in the editor, but there's a good chance this kind of transition will distract viewers and hinder a project.

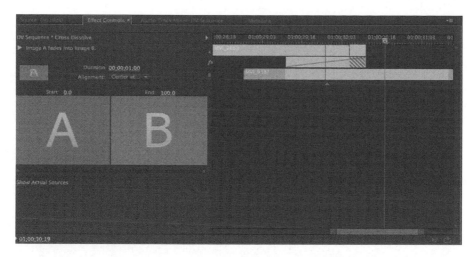

Figure 6.14 Transitioning between clips can be as easy as dragging and dropping a pre-made transition. A cross dissolve is when two clips are purposely superimposed and the opacity of the video image is changed to allow one clip to bleed through the overlaid clip. (Adobe product screenshot(s) reprinted with permission from Adobe Systems Incorporated)

Dissolve

Dissolves are always about change. The viewer is forced to think about what is coming next. Will it be a change from one scene to the next, or are we going to jump back in time or to another place? Remember also that video is part audio—visual dissolves can be paired with audio dissolves, which fade smoothly from one audio track to another.

Usually the two shots involved in a dissolve are related in some way. The dissolve is often used for a dream or to quickly show the passage of time.

Techniques and Ideas to Record Sound Effects

A fiction film is a designed reality. What happens on set can be changed at a later time, without the ethical restrictions of nonfiction. Particularly with audio, there is the opportunity for many do-overs. It's a little like playing a video game, where if things are not going well the player can always respawn and start the level over. Just because the sound for a scene was captured on location does not mean it has to be used. And sound should always be of the best quality possible.

"Production audio is always good as a scratch track. If you can nail it in production that's great, but usually the premium in production is making sure you get the dialogue," said Doug Quin, an associate professor of television, radio, and film at the S.I. Newhouse School of Public Communications. Quin worked as a sound designer for the 2001 movie *Jurassic Park III*.

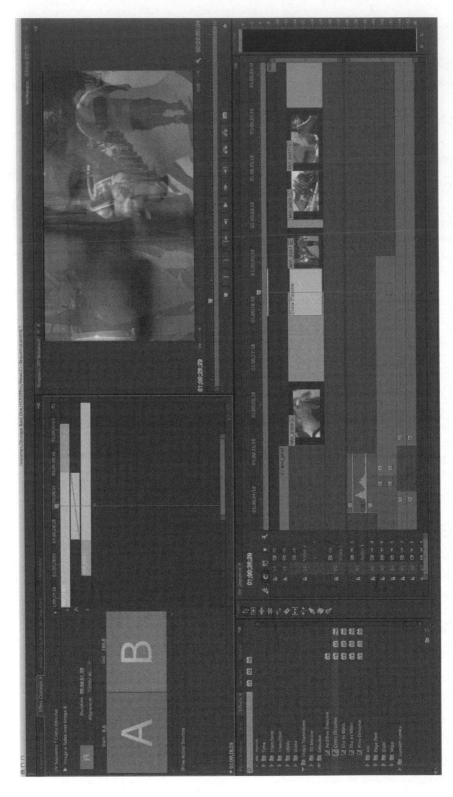

Figure 6.15 A cross-fade allows a smooth transition from one clip or track to another. (Adobe product screenshot(s) reprinted with permission from Adobe Systems Incorporated)

For example, if a scene involves an actor taking a sip of tea from a teacup, it might be important to capture the sound of the cup hitting the saucer—the very crisp and clear *clink* that would add something to a tense or awkward moment in the story. The best way to achieve that would be in post-production, by putting the microphone very close to a teacup and repeating the action of taking that sip until the recorded sound is just right. This is called recording a sound in *Foley*, after Jack Foley, who pioneered the technique at Universal Studios in the early twentieth century. These are sounds that were not made by what the viewer is seeing. The filmmaker, to provide the illusion of being right there in the picture, arranged for certain, distinctive sounds to be added later, synced to what is on the screen.

As another example, imagine a shooting situation that requires the sound of a waterfall. If a microphone were held up to the waterfall, the result would most likely be a recording of white noise. This is where a sound mix will come into play. It is possible to record multiple parts of one sound from different perspectives, and then mix them together in post-production to create a more layered, realistic waterfall sound. Maybe, for instance, you could take the sound of individual trickles of water, blend them together, then mix that with the sound of water flowing over rocks in a stream. Adding these different "voices" of dynamic water together can create a better approximation of reality, and provide a more realistic experience for the viewer. When recording fire, it might work best to start with a small fire, with its distinct crackling, and then build into a larger, roaring one. When recording wind, try capturing sound on a windy day inside a car with the window cracked just slightly. That way you can get a whistling or howling through the opening. Simply holding a microphone up in a strong breeze will yield nothing but the muddy distortion of wind hitting the microphone.

Today's technology offers a whole array of audio "sweetening" filters built into software, but just as with visuals, that is not an excuse to skimp on capturing it correctly in the first place. Just as you might turn up the ASA/ISO on a video camera to get more light into a video, but increase exposure and result in an undesirable grainy look, the same can occur with audio. The sensitivity of a microphone can be increased to pick up more sound, but doing so will add a distorted sound quality to the recording. Do not think that you can remove this undesirable sound in post-production. Record it right the first time.

"Do some location scouting with your ear to figure out the best place to record someone," Quin advised. "What is the best perspective, where you can reduce the amount of wind and ambient noise that bleeds into your recording?"

Sound Design

Fifty percent of a film is visual content, the rest is audio content. For the audio, pay attention to everything from dialogue to natural sounds.

Fiction offers a lot more latitude than journalistic situations, where everything needs to be gathered on scene. If you are covering a house fire for a television station, you need to record the sound of the actual fire from the scene. You can't recreate it later on a Foley stage, like you can for a fiction film. The consequences of recreating both sound and/or visuals in journalism can be the loss of your job.

Earprint Productions in San Francisco, CA, is a husband-and-wife team, consisting of Jason Reinier and Catherine Girardeau, that produces audio documentaries, podcasts, video, and sound design for interactive museum exhibitions. Their studio has worked on many different types of projects, from films to recorded museum tours. One piece they produced was for the SFO Louis A. Turpen Aviation Museum at the San Francisco International Airport; it was for an exhibit on the China Clipper, the first passenger flight in a fixed-wing aircraft across any ocean in scheduled service. The audio file accompanied photographs in a slide show. Girardeau and Reinier had to design a story based on oral histories about the China Clipper's flight, and in doing so they had to recreate what it might have sounded like onboard the plane, including the noises of final approach and landing. "They go into their dive," explained Reinier, "where engine sound takes over everything, shaking while landing—you have to imagine that space. You don't have a recording of that. You have to imagine the clinking of glassware and seats—that kind of clunking around." Each of these elements became a separate layer of the sound mix.

It should be noted once again that any type of recreation of sound, even though it may work wonderfully in the entertainment movie-making business, is not acceptable in journalism.

"The story is driven in this kind of 'verite' style, if you think of film," said Girardeau, "so it's not like we are just recreating it out of our heads. We're following a story and bringing a story to life in sound."

Post-Production Sound Sweetening Tips

When following these tips, always remember that you do not want to alter the sound of a file but merely improve its quality.

> **Ten-band equalizer** – This processor allows an editor to focus on specific qualities of a particular voice and enhance its quality.
> **Pop filter** – Sometimes a speaker on a track will "pop" their *P*s—this is called a *plosive*. There are not too many ways of removing this in post-production beyond recording it right the first time, by using a pop filter over the microphone.
> **Limiter** – A limiter increases the overall loudness of a voice. Use a limiter in post-production only, at the end of the "effect chain." This piece of equipment allows the level of a reference point to be raised, balancing out all the different levels of a voice and thus avoiding peaking.

Peaking is when sound is overmodulated. This happens when sound is not monitored by the user during recording. Once the sound is overmodulated it cannot be "fixed" back to the way it should have been when it was being recorded.

The Musical Soundtrack

Choosing a piece of music to go with a video can be interesting, but it can also be a mind-numbing experience. There you are, in front of the computer, scouring royalty-free music websites, looking for a piece of music that fits perfectly with the message of a film, and while there is always something that nearly does the job, it never seems to be just right. It can be a frustrating chore.

A lot of people don't think of music as an accompaniment but rather as something to be actively listened to. Choosing music for a film requires going beyond this, and being attuned to the kinds of music that work best in the background. To work with a video story, the track might need a certain rhythm, melodiousness, or to provide the right kind of ambiance. Each piece of music should be chosen specifically for the video it accompanies.

John Melillo is a New York music producer and supervisor whose job it is to find or make music for video productions. "It could be a storyboard, or something so simple as a tagline," he said of finding the piece that fits best. "It could be a series of still photographs that evoke something. We need to figure out musically what is going to enhance the story around this series of photographs." Melillo said he then searches out music that complements the emotions, pace, and rhythm of the story. "The tools and the essence of what you do really don't change, whether you are creating a web film or a sixty-second advertisement or a four-and-half-minute piece that explores a particular topic," he said.

Designing a soundtrack with music has its own peculiarities. "Laying a piece of music against film and making it mean something are two very different things," said Melillo:

> One might think that a fight scene is filled with drums and choirs. But if you just had a solo cello, interestingly enough, it creates a very different emotional quotient. Where the drums and the horns may have the valor and aggression of battle built into it, the solo cello all of a sudden humanizes that struggle, and perhaps, all of a sudden, you are noticing the expressions on the faces of the soldiers in a different way. Perhaps now you have decided you have the ability to explore what this perspective means from the context of a single soldier.

Not only is it important to find a piece of music that fits the visuals being shot, but you must be mindful of whether or not you have the rights even to use the music in the first place: "Even a TV station license agreement would be negotiated for what that license would be for, and it would strictly be broadcast on TV," explained Roy Gutterman, a communications law professor at the S.I. Newhouse School of Public Communications at Syracuse University. "I would presume that most of those licensing agreements now include online posting, and if they don't, then you probably see TV stations posting stories without musical accompaniment online," he added.

"We do the best job we can on the broadcast side, then we go back ahead of time and strip everything out and build it just for the web," said Bob Dotson, veteran reporter for the *Today Show*. On the television side of things the rights have already been figured out, but the web side is a different matter. This requires Dotson to find different music for the web version that may or may not be right for the piece. "It is like listening to your favorite song, and then going and hearing it being played by a Ramada Inn cover band out by the interstate," Dotson said:

> But we have to do it. That's fine by me. But if we can, [we] find something that matches the intensity and feeling of the original piece of music. If it were up to me, I would not use music much at all—I prefer to let stories work with natural sound. If you are really diligent at recording natural sound, you can immerse the audience in an experience that way.

ON MUSIC USE

During the National Press Photographers Association's Multimedia Immersion Workshop in 2014, past-president Alicia Calzada, a lawyer with Haynes and Boone LLP of San Antonio, TX, made the following points about the use of music in a multimedia piece:

1. There are at least three different potential copyright owners with music—the owner of the copyright to the lyrics, the owner of the composition copyright, and the owner of the sound recording copyright. Sometimes all three are the same copyright owners, but sometimes there is a different owner for each. In general, the same rules that apply to independent filmmakers apply to people who produce multimedia. To use music in a film, all rights holders to the music must agree to license the song. If any of the rights holders refuse, or even decline to negotiate, the music may not be used. Even if a piece of music is in the public domain, the performance of the music may be copyrighted, especially if it is a recently recorded performance.
2. Using music as background in an audiovisual piece requires something called a *synchronization* license. The sync license authorizes use of a copyrighted music piece in synchronization with an audiovisual work.

(Continued . . .)

(. . . continued)

> The license must be obtained from the owners of the sound recording as well as those of the composition and lyrics.
>
> 3. Many multimedia producers erroneously believe in a mythical "30-Second Rule" that allows them to include any song in an audio slideshow or video as long as no more than 30 seconds of the song are used. This false "rule" is a distortion of the legal concept of "fair use," which allows limited use of a song for purposes like commentary and education. Fair use is limited to the amount of a song it takes to illustrate a point. In a typical pop song, a musical phrase that's about 30 seconds long is enough to give a listener a sense of what the song is about. A classical piece may require a minute of music to get the same information across. Using more of a song than necessary to make a reviewer or educator's point goes beyond fair use. There is no clear line between just enough and too much, but using a song as a soundtrack is across that line and goes beyond fair use.
>
> 4. It is possible to license popular music from ASCAP for use on a website, but this license does not apply to music used in an audio slideshow or video. (See discussion of the "synchronization license" above.) Further, a license for using music in a television broadcast might not include the right to use the same music online, and vice versa.
>
> *Used with permission from Alicia Calzada and the NPPA Multimedia Immersion Workshop.*

Royalty-Free Music and Sound Effects

Royalty-free doesn't necessarily mean monetarily free. It may mean that you pay up front in lieu of paying a royalty each time the video is played. Also, music that is free when you're a student may not be free once you graduate. Likewise, music that can be used during a student-produced news broadcast may not be permissible in a free-standing video.

Freesound

Freesound is a collaborative database of Creative Commons licensed sounds. Users can browse, download, and share sounds that have been uploaded by users. Be forewarned: The site asks its users not to upload any copyrighted material. **http://www.freesound.org**

The Free Music Archive

The Free Music Archive provides free, high-quality music in a wide range of genres. The content on Free Music Archive is used under various Creative

Commons licenses. Anyone can download music from FMA for use in podcasts, videos, and other digital presentation formats. The music collections can be searched by genre or by curator. **http://freemusicarchive.org/**

Sound Bible

Sound Bible is a resource for finding and downloading free sound clips, sound effects, and sound bites. All of the sounds on Sound Bible are either public domain or labeled with a Creative Commons license. You can find sounds for use in podcasts, videos, slide shows, or other multimedia projects **http://soundbible.com**

Royalty Free Music

Royalty Free Music hosts music tracks that can be reused in numerous ways. The site charges the general public for downloads, but students and teachers can download quite a bit of the music for free. To access the free music tracks, visit the education page on Royalty Free Music. **http://www. royaltyfreemusic.com**

Jamendo

Jamendo is a source of free and legal music downloads. The music on Jamendo comes from artists who upload it themselves. While not all of the music is licensed for re-use, there is a substantial collection of tracks labeled with a Creative Commons license. As always, before re-using any of the music you download, make sure it is labeled for re-use. **http://www.jamendo. com/**

Incompetech

Incompetech is royalty-free music produced by Kevin Macleod. All you need to do is give him credit, and you can use his music for any noncommercial purpose. You can search for music by genre, "feel," or keyword. **http:// incompetech.com/m/c/royalty-free/**

Vimeo Music Store

This site basically sources music from the above-mentioned FMA, as well as Audiosocket, that can be purchased or downloaded for free. But it's all royalty-free. **http://vimeo.com/musicstore**

Youtube Audio Library

Download background music for your videos for free from YouTube for any creative project. **http://www.youtube.com/audiolibrary/music**

MEET THE PRO
Jon Menell, Video Editor, Los Angeles, CA

Emmy Award winner Jon Menell is a former television news editor who twice won the National Press Photographers Association Video Editor of the Year award. He left the news business in 2003 and now edits television shows, with credits including The Biggest Loser *(season 5),* Behind The Music: Guns N' Roses, The X-Factor, *and* America's Got Talent, *among others.*

Figure 6.16 Jon Menell is a video editor based in Los Angeles, CA.

"To me that is one of my most helpful guides: my feelings. That's the hardest part of the job," said Los Angeles-based video editor Jon Menell. "You have to stay a viewer while you're working. You have to keep your eyes fresh."

When editing pieces for *The X Factor* or *America's Got Talent,* Menell is doing it all—designing the story arc and many times taking one to five hours of footage, sometimes including an hour and a half of interviews, and editing it down into a one-minute and thirty-second profile with B-roll. Menell edits both the tryout shows and the participant backstories. He said he usually gets one day to go through all of the footage for each individual participant.

As the video editor, Menell is responsible for making all of his own selections regarding story pace, tone, dialogue, images, effects, and music. There's no one there telling him how to tell the story; that's his responsibility as the editor. Since he is editing shots of regular people and not professional actors or speakers, he often sees footage in which participants are nervous in front of the camera. Menell then relies a lot on the producer who is doing the interview with the participant, hoping they can get the subject to settle down and connect emotionally with the camera. "It's like a fishing trip," he said. "They just come back with a collection of what they said. My job as the editor is to listen through it, to pick out those gems."

Menell has also edited fiction-based content. As an assistant editor on the third season of *Rescue Me,* he edited in a junior capacity. "It . . . was written and planned and storyboarded and rehearsed and acted and directed and done—it's different than going into reality with much more of a documentary approach, where you are discovering what is really there," he said.

For live shows, "you're always still doing very basic character storytelling, which is revealing them to the audience in a compelling, sometimes surprising or funny or moving way," Menell said:

> I think generally the aim is to be as true to the person you are portraying as possible, but also to present [them] in a manner that

(Continued . . .)

(. . . *continued*)

> captures the audience's attention. . . . If it took them an hour to explain themselves to the camera, and you take that and accomplish that for them in less than a minute, or a little more than a minute, naturally things are going to get compressed quite a bit.
>
> Menell explained that when he creates stories for the live shows it's even harder, because he has to pack all of the information into a minute and five seconds. "It's always crazy to get everything to fit into that, with the twists and turns that they need fulfilled," he said.
>
> A good video edit will enable the audience to empathize with the characters, to connect with them, and to root for them, especially since the audience is spending a lot of time with them—even if it is in video form.
>
> Menell once edited a piece about a participant in *America's Got Talent*, Branden James, who is gay and whose parents had problems with that. James was in his thirties, but for the ten years preceding the show his mother had not been in his life. "His mom, who was the antagonist in a way, had come to support him in his career, but could not deal with his lifestyle choice . . . can't understand why he is gay," said Menell. As the editor of the piece, Menell worked through the footage to find "unexpected developments," he said, "shaping it tightly enough that it didn't just tell Branden's story; it also revealed something surprising about their relationship."
>
> Even with his years of experience, Menell said he finds it difficult to "find the language to convey [a story] in a way that doesn't turn it into a complete stereotype or shorthand cliché." He said his job is to delve into people's lives and find what makes their personality unique, and will make the viewer care about them. "Having it feel like a naturally breathing, evolving story, that's a big part of the job," he said. (2013)
>
> **Watch the video of Branden James:** http://bit.ly/brandenjames.

Video Editing Software Choices

There are many choices for editing in the video medium. We assume that you will be editing digitally, using a computer. Whether you are on the Apple Macintosh or PC platform, and whether you are using Adobe Premiere, Apple Final Cut X, Avid, or Grass Valley EDIUS, the techniques of editing video remain the same. No editor is simply better than another. They all have their strengths and quirks, and they all require a thick manual to really be understood backwards and forwards.

While each piece of software is different, they all have things in common. They all work in a nonlinear fashion, meaning that clips can be laid out any which way the editor pleases. Before nonlinear editing there was tape-to-tape editing, in which footage was laid down sequentially from start to finish. To go back and fix something at the beginning, you were stuck with having to go back and re-edit all the footage you had laid down since. It was possible to drop in a clip here or there, and make some changes to sound, but nothing like what a computer nonlinear editor can do.

For broadcast video editors editing tape-to-tape on a tight deadline, it was essential to know what the ending shot was going to be at the start of the editing process, and to keep it in mind throughout. "You had to start thinking ahead throughout the whole project," said Matt Rafferty of WJW-TV in Cleveland, OH, a two-time NPPA Cutting Edge Editor of the Year and winner of an Alfred I. duPont award for his editing skills:

> It really made you think as you were doing each edit. Is this really how I want the outcome to be? I would go back and I would watch it and see how it was going. . . . What am I going to use for my last shot? Because the last shot has to be something good.

Final Cut Pro and Final Cut X

Apple's Final Cut Pro was once very popular, and many editors used it to edit their films. When Apple decided that they needed to change the way people use their software, they redesigned the user interface into something that many users were not ready for. Previously, with the old Final Cut Pro 7, along with most other nonlinear video editing software packages, video clips and audio files were put into specific tracks to produce a video. In the new Final Cut X, Apple decided that it would do away with tracks and use *storylines*, a different way of organizing media within a timeline. Files can be placed anywhere in the storyline, and these storylines are sequences of clips that are then layered on top of and below a main, primary storyline that makes a video from beginning to end. This new system was a big change from what users had always known. Many editors looked elsewhere for their video-editing software needs.

Many longtime video editors found the switchover to X mind-numbing. However, if you have never edited before—and that is the audience this book is intended for—you can probably pick up the software much more easily. It has an easy-to-use database built in that enables users to easily and quickly find the clips they are looking for. The software also is great to use with HDSLR footage, in that it does not require users to transcode, or change the footage to a usable format, prior to editing. In addition, X allows real-time *scrubbing* (playback or review) of clips to help the user find in and out points. So while X may not shine with hardened pros, it can be very suitable in academic settings where students have no prior experience with the techniques of editing. If a pro says not to use it, take that with a grain of salt. It is a powerful editor that can do wonders, even in the hands of a novice.

Figure 6.17 Apple's Final Cut X is a nonlinear video editor that can be installed and used only on Apple computers.

Adobe Premiere

With Adobe's Creative Cloud feature, one monthly fee covers most of the company's software, including titles many students use such as Photoshop and InDesign. At student pricing levels, purchasing it is a no-brainer. While the user interface has not changed as Final Cut X has, Adobe has upped its game by adding many of the same features that X has, and more. It still has a semi-familiar timeline interface, however, that many editors recognize and prefer to stick with. One benefit to using Adobe Premiere is that it is cross-platform—it can be used on both PCs and Macs. Final Cut X is made for Apple only and forces users to buy Apple hardware.

Another benefit of Adobe Premiere is its ability to very easily integrate with other Adobe Suite products like After Effects, Photoshop, and Audition.

Avid

Avid is a nonlinear editing system that has been in the film and broadcast industry since 1987. The software uses hardware acceleration such as the Nitris DX/DNxHD (special computer chips that free up a system's processing and graphics hardware for other tasks, including playback and effects rendering) to quickly encode footage in real time for broadcast situations. In addition, Avid systems tend to be "turnkey" solutions, in which the high-powered computer hardware's specific function is to edit video—not surf the web or

Figure 6.18 Adobe Premiere is a nonlinear video editor. It is part of the Adobe Creative Cloud and can be used on both Apple computers and PCs. (Adobe product screenshot(s) reprinted with permission from Adobe Systems Incorporated)

Figure 6.19 Avid is a nonlinear video editor often used in the television broadcast news and film industries. (Photo courtesy of Avid)

do accounting or word processing. Avid Media Composer can also work on both the Macintosh and PC computing platforms.

Avid software can be found in many professional film production houses and broadcast editing facilities. The company has systems that allow footage to be housed on a server at a central location and be used by several video editors at once, which makes it a great solution for television stations where multiple people might be trying to edit a single piece of footage for different newscasts. For those whose hope and desire is to go into the film or broadcast industry, learning Avid could be time well spent.

EDIUS

EDIUS, made by Grass Valley, is a versatile software package for PCs. The company has been known to make software for broadcast production. People going into television news may use this software to put packages together. The package is compatible with broadcast server systems that allow video to be viewed and edited by several people simultaneously in a newsroom. The software's interface uses timelines, which will be familiar to those who have used Final Cut Studio. EDIUS also offers multi-format editing, which means working on video files from multiple types of cameras, all in the same timeline.

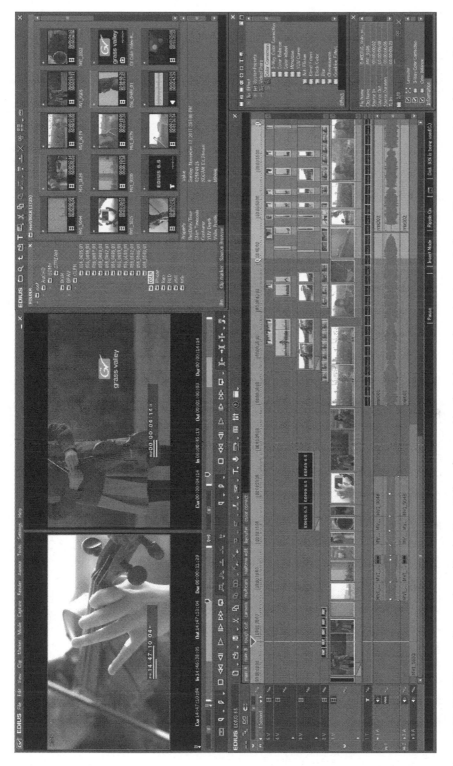

Figure 6.20 EDIUS is a nonlinear video editor by Grass Valley often used by the television broadcast news industry. (Screenshot courtesy of Grass Valley)

DOES THE STORY THAT I WANT TO TELL HAVE ALL THE ELEMENTS I NEED?

With the understanding that video editing is a process, and that there are reasons to use certain transitions in certain ways and that there is a certain thought process that needs to take place while editing, you can move forward with planning a video. Prior to sitting down to edit, think about the pre-production checklist below. Then, after producing your video, go back through it making sure that the post-production list has been achieved as well.

Checklist for Pre-Production

- One main character?
- A conflict or complication?
- A surprise or change?
- A resolution to the conflict?
- A "commitment" on the part of the storyteller? If so, what is it?

Checklist for Post-Production

- Has all of the footage been downloaded to a drive for safekeeping?
- Has all of the footage been logged with keywords and metadata?
- Have the music and/or sound effects been thought out?
- Is there a deadline? What is it?
- Has enough rendering time been factored in for your export?

Chapter Summary

Sitting down to edit a film, whether it is fiction, nonfiction, or something in the realm of strategic communications, requires thinking first and foremost about the story that needs to be told. Everything done with a video should have an element of storytelling. The techniques used to put a video together will contain certain visual cues that will help make that video become a story.

Effects, transitions, and the various bells and whistles of video editors are secondary. Don't do things in a video editor just because you can. Remember that everyone else has access to all these features as well. What they do not have access to is *your* story, your feel for that story, and your skills in telling it. These are the most important things you bring to any editing session. There should be a reason for each cut made and each shot included in the timeline. Software features are not a substitute for this.

Most of all, think about your viewers. Think about making them connect emotionally with your video. If the project is for the web, it might be better to consider how to get them to stick around longer than ten seconds, since there are so many other sites and videos competing for their attention.

Your storytelling matters, and it is editing that will give it impact, immediacy, and the ability to grab and hold an audience.

 ## Review Questions

1. What is meant by continuity in editing?
2. What is the type of editing in which audio of the next scene can be heard before the video is presented?
3. To run quickly and visually through the life of a character, what type of editing would you use?
4. Would it be better to use a tripod or to use image stabilization in post-production? Why?
5. In broadcast news, what type of editing is used more: jump cuts or match cuts? Why?
6. Which transition would you use to go from one time and place to another?
7. What are some differences between the ways sound can be used in fiction storytelling and in journalism?

 ## Exercises

1. Re-edit a Commercial
Find a car commercial made for television on YouTube or another video sharing website and download it to your computer. Import it into a video editing program. Rearrange the video in the editor using at least two of the editing techniques in this chapter. Change the visuals to say the same thing as the original, but not in the same order. Compare and contrast the videos.

2. Create Your Own Sound Effects
Sometimes using canned, already-made sound effects just won't work for a film. They don't sound like the noise that you will actually need.

Imagine a scene where the lead character gets in a car and drives away. Recreate the following sounds that the viewer would hear. Record each sound individually, and present each one as an audio file.

- Key unlocking door
- Door slamming
- Seat belt being put on
- Key activating ignition
- Car driving away

 ## Key Terms

Axis of action – An imaginary line perpendicular to the camera's line of sight, on which the characters' positions should remain consistent.

Color correction – Fixing improper color casts within editing software.

Continuity – Logical progression of shots in a sequence.

Cut – The building block of all sequencing. A quick change from one sequence to another.

Creative Commons – A specific type of license, including some limitations, for a piece of content that can be found on the web for general use.

Dailies – Specific video from a day's worth of shooting.

Dissolve – A gradual transition that moves the viewer to a different time or place.

Effects – Specific filters added to a video to alter or enhance its appearance.

Enter frame / exit frame – The points at which a subject enters and leaves the frame.

Eyeline match – Making sure that every time a character looks at something specific, the viewer doesn't have to wait long to see what the character is seeing.

Eye movement – The process of using whatever is in motion on screen to move the viewer's eye. Make cuts at points when motion stops.

Flashback – An editing technique in which the viewer is taken back in time.

Foley – Sound created and enhanced in a studio to replace sounds that occur in a story.

J cut – The audio of the next clip begins before the video of the first has ended.

Jump cut – A quick cut that has the feeling of discontinuity.

Ken Burns Effect – A technique that involves panning and scanning over still images. Rather than staying in one place on an image, the camera scans and zooms in on one area of importance.

Keyword – A specific naming mechanism that can help an editor find footage.

L cut – The audio of a shot plays beyond where the video cuts, underneath the next clip's picture.

Logging – The process of sifting through footage prior to editing to catalog content and make sure that all needed material is present.

Matched action – A way to link two separate shots visually in a sequence.

Meta-tagging – The tagging of each clip according to certain descriptive terms, to help in locating footage when it is needed.

Montage – An editing technique of assembled shots that can cover a large amount of time in a very short period within a film.

Musical soundtrack – Any music that goes along with a video. Often a soundtrack can help to set rhythm or pace.

Nonlinear video editing – The process by which video is laid down in a timeline or storyline and then moved around within editing software. Former methods of editing did not allow changes at the start of a video without rearranging the video as a whole.

Pacing – How fast a video or scene feels to a viewer. Directors adjust it to increase tension, or to allow breathing room.

Parallel editing/cross-cutting – Cutting between characters in different places going through the same or a related experience.

Rhythm – How a video keeps a beat within itself. A fast rhythm might be better for an action movie.

Royalty-free music – Soundtrack music for which there is no need to pay a royalty each time the video is played.

Screen direction – The principle of maintaining all action on one side of the subject.

Shot list – A record of all of the shots made during the filming of a video.

Sound design – The process by which sounds are developed and designed to enhance the viewing experience.

Sound sweetening – Changing sound to improve its quality.

Split screen transitions – An editing technique that splits the screen in half, enabling the viewer to see multiple characters or stories at once.

Stabilization – A software process that removes the shake from footage but is often time- and processor-intensive.

Sources

Calzada, Alicia. Conversation with author, February 4, 2014.

Calzada, Alicia. "Ten Takeaways on Multimedia." Presentation at the National Press Photographers Association Multimedia Immersion Workshop, May 13–17, 2014, Syracuse, NY.

Dotson, Bob. Conversation with author, November 1, 2013.

Gutterman, Roy. Conversation with author, June 23, 2014.

Melillo, John. Conversation with author, September 13, 2013.

Menell, Jon. Conversation with author, November 1, 2013.

Montano, Shawn. Conversation with author, July 26, 2013.

Quin, Doug. Conversation with author, November 1, 2013.

Rafferty, Matt. Conversation with author, October 31, 2013.

Reinier, Jason, and Catherine Girardeau. Conversation with author, October 28, 2013.

Storm, Brian. "Gathering Audio: Tips and Tricks from the MediaStorm Workflow." White Paper. MediaStorm, March 2005. Accessed May 28, 2009. http://mediastorm.com/sites/default/files/pdf/MediaStorm_Gathering_Audio.pdf.

Weinfeld, Debra. Conversation with author, November 22, 2013.

7 MULTIMEDIA STORYTELLING IN ENTERTAINMENT

How Do You Write a Script and Tell a Story Visually Within a Designed Reality?

In this chapter you will learn

- Ways to generate fiction story ideas
- How to organize and pitch your idea
- How to create writer's and director's treatments
- Story basics for short films
- Tips on how to develop characters
- The roles in a filmmaking crew
- Script formatting guidelines
- How to block and shoot a scene
- How to create the look, feel, and setting for a story script

Introduction

Whether producing a fiction film or a public service announcement, there's one reality that there is just no way around: There must be an idea, a script, and a plan. The idea needs to be worth all the time that is going to be spent on it, which is a lot. Without a good idea there is no story, which makes it difficult to create any kind of script.

Producing a short film is not an easy task, and it's not a task that should be undertaken alone. It is tough to approach fiction filmmaking as the proverbial one-man band. Fiction filmmaking is a process that takes several people contributing their energy and talents in a variety of roles. Producing a film therefore requires collaboration—the ability to work and get along as a team with one end goal: telling a visual story.

Whether the goal is a two-minute short film or a feature-length picture of an hour and a half, there needs to be a script from which to work. This is the time to think about what has been discussed previously about story structure, and where to apply it.

Starting requires an idea, and don't worry if you can't immediately come up with something excitingly original. There is very little that is new under the sun, and even clichéd premises and formulas can be built into new and entertaining films. Think about boy-meets-girl, underdog sports stories, runaway children, cases of mistaken identity, coming-of-age school stories, buddy cop stories, scary movies. They can seem clichéd, but most everyone knows a well-executed, memorable movie based on each of those models.

So don't be discouraged if your story falls into one of these categories. You're just starting out, and fiction filmmaking might not even be the final direction in which you're heading. The goal with this chapter is simply to provide storytelling tools that, if you were to study film or be assigned to make a short fiction film for the web, would be useful.

Story Basics for Short Films

This book is not really aimed at those who will be making feature-length films. It is directed instead at those who will be making short films, which are defined by the Academy of Motion Picture Arts and Sciences as having "a running time of forty minutes or less, including all credits." For the purposes of this book, we are talking about short films that are from three to ten minutes long, made by those who will be presenting these films primarily on the web and mobile platforms.

For a short film, it can be very helpful to break a film up into five "beats," a term for the points in a story when something specific occurs that transforms—or changes the direction of—that story.

1. Establish the lead character in the world; set the scene for the character. The character must be someone with whom the audience can empathize, such as the little blond-haired girl of "Goldilocks and the Three Bears," lost in the woods.
2. Give the story a hook, something that will get the viewer engaged quickly. This inciting incident is the "something happens" moment. The little girl discovers a mysterious but pleasant-looking cottage in the trees.
3. Now, start introducing problems that take the character in new directions. The little girl enters the cottage and discovers food, chairs, and beds. These are mini-conflict scenes in which she must decide between her own desires and more sensible action—scenes that keep the viewer connected to her character as she gets in deeper and deeper. The porridge is too cold, the bed is too hard.
4. The climax is when tensions reach a breaking point. The little girl has thrown away caution and fallen asleep, having found things that don't belong to her to be perfect for her taste. The bears come home.
5. The resolution of the story is Goldilocks fleeing in terror, but escaping with her life.

"In short films you have a resolution, and then you have a twist at the end, because all short films have some kind of twist," explained Juliet Giglio, assistant professor of screenwriting at State University of New York at Oswego, whose produced screenwriting credits include *Tarzan* (Disney animated feature), *Noah* (ABC television), *Halloweentown* (Disney Channel), and *Pizza My Heart,* an original teleplay for ABC Family. "I think it's standard for a short film to have a twist for a variety of reasons," added Giglio. "It makes the short memorable; it gets the audience talking after the film; it leaves the audience questioning what they just saw; it's thought-provoking; it sometimes has shock value."

In "Goldilocks and the Three Bears" there is definitely a twist: The pleasant little cottage with its "just-right" features actually belongs to frightening, dangerous creatures. The title is kind of a spoiler, true, but remember that this is a story aimed at young children.

Example: *The Black Hole*

This two-minute short fiction film, which has a single character, high entertainment value, and a very simple story structure, was directed by Phil Sansom and Olly Williams, also known as the Diamond Dogs. In the film, a sleep-deprived office worker discovers a mysterious hole and gets a little too greedy.

The opening shot puts the audience in the ordinary world of an office, deserted except for the main character, a young man working a photocopier. He inadvertently prints a black circle on a piece of paper, and when he puts his drinking cup on the circle it vanishes, leading him to realize that this is some kind of portal. He then goes through some mental gymnastics trying to figure out what is happening. He tests the hole in several ways, realizing that he can reach through it into seemingly any kind of object.

The next inciting incident is the man putting his printed circle up against a candy machine and reaching inside it to steal a candy bar. This reveals something about his character. A shot of his face conveys that he is starting to think about what else can he use this "black hole" for. He spots a locked door, places the paper with its black hole on it, and lets himself in by reaching through to the inner door handle.

The audience is then presented with a shot of a massive safe. The man tapes his black hole to the safe door and proceeds to reach through, removing bundles of cash. His plundering gets greedier and more and more enthusiastic, until he is reaching deep into the safe to get every last bundle. Eventually he crawls completely through the hole and inside the safe. But at this moment the tape holding the paper to the safe door gives way, having lost its stickiness. The paper falls to the floor. The audience realizes that the man has trapped himself inside the safe with no hope of escape.

The Black Hole shows that the shortest, simplest films have story structure. Each inciting incident in the film follows the last, with the stakes and the significance growing in magnitude. The first incident is a minor discovery, but the character's actions create the sensation of a snowball rolling downhill—things just keep getting bigger and bigger, and, like Goldilocks, he just keeps getting in deeper and deeper. The character's first and last impulse is to exploit his discovery for personal gain, and because his greed completely outweighs any thought of caution, morality, or what could go wrong, he ends up trapped and helpless . . . and maybe worse. In two minutes, the theme—and dangers—of human greed are illustrated and commented upon with the clarity of a modern fairy tale: If you get too greedy, you risk losing it all.

The Black Hole, directed by Diamond Dogs (Phil Sansom and Olly Williams)

To watch the movie: http://bit.ly/theblackholemovie

Where to Find Fiction-Based Story Ideas

Even though it can be fun, prospecting for ideas on which to base a screenplay can be difficult, to put it mildly. Many movies are based on writers' personal experiences, or something that they have researched extensively, and let's face it—not all of us have hilariously entertaining lives or know that much about sixteenth-century Scotland, or the Civil War, or whatever.

Still, with a little guidance, it isn't necessarily a long journey to find a story that can be written on paper. "For my own original material, it's people and situations in life that I find really interesting," said Erik Bork, a screenwriter based in Los Angeles who served as a producer for HBO's *Band of Brothers.* "If you want to learn about something, teach it or write about it—or so I've been told," he added.

Scriptwriting can often begin with focused thinking about life-changing events. Seek out significant events in your past life or those of people you know. Maybe someone is struggling to make ends meet by working two jobs. What kinds of challenges does this person face? It could be the basis for a script. A lead character's struggle to change, succeed, or simply get by introduces the vital element of conflict, which is what a story needs to work. Dig into your own childhood. Many stories can be found in childhood experience. Stories rife with struggle include:

- Experiences with death, whether of family members or simply of pets
- First encounters with violence or injustice
- Moments of extreme fear or embarrassment
- First encounters with sacrifice or love

Don't be afraid to borrow and tell other people's stories as well, such as those of relatives. Stories that are told around the table at Thanksgiving—sometimes repeatedly, from year to year—are told and retold for a reason. They have significance. Seek out that significance and use it.

Did you go through a relationship that had many ups and downs, which could be assembled into an interesting or revealing story arc? It doesn't need to have been a good one. Bad relationships often make great stories.

Also, read the news. News stories nearly always revolve around conflict and struggle, and they are interesting almost by definition. Otherwise no reporter or news editor would have jumped on them. They make excellent beginning points for a script.

Are there any stories that you like to tell to good friends? Do you have a story that could be told sitting around a campfire with them, and all would laugh at the outcome? What about jokes? Every joke is a story, with characters, conflict, and a surprise ending. Think about the challenges in your life. Are there any times when you went beyond your known limits and achieved or obtained something that seemed impossible?

Think about these questions in creating a treatment or synopsis, and keep them in the front of your mind as you work. Whatever story you decide upon, viewers will have to stay connected and engaged with it throughout the length of the film, whether five minutes or ninety.

Screenwriter John August's credits include the 2000 film *Charlie's Angels* and 2003's *Charlie's Angels: Full Throttle*. In a 2003 entry on his blog, johnaugust.com, he writes, "For all the talk of high-concept comedies or big-idea action tentpole movies, a screenwriter's daily life is almost entirely about coming up with the 'little' ideas that help get the story told."

John August's Techniques for Generating Story Ideas

- Figure out what the outcome needs to be, then work backwards.
- Decide what caused the problem in the first place, and whether it can be changed or cut.
- Look at the moment from another character's perspective.
- Quickly write several different solutions, then judge whether one or a combination of several best address the problem.

 ONLINE RESOURCES FOR GENERATING STORY IDEAS
Story Idea Generator: http://bit.ly/storygenerator
Science Fiction Story Ideas: http://www.writepop.com/category/1001-story-ideas

Scripting Characters

It is standard practice to have one main protagonist in a short film. The format does not allow a lot of time for character development, so try to avoid having more than one fully developed role. Even if the story is about a group of people, be they friends, co-workers, or just random people thrown together by events, there needs to be one person who is the recognizable focus or "leader," someone with whom the audience will empathize. When working with more than one character, aim for strong, contrasting personalities that are, as Juliet Giglio explained,

> opposite from each other. You don't want them all to be the same person . . . I call it the unity of opposites. For example, if you have two characters, and one is an introvert and one is an extrovert, they are very different from each other. This automatically makes the scene more interesting.

Think about the hit television show *The Big Bang Theory*. Both Sheldon and Leonard are both very knowledgeable about science, but they have completely different personalities. Sheldon is introverted to the point of obsession, thinking only of himself, while Leonard is a warmer, more empathetic character, to the point of being somewhat of a doormat. Yet they deal with each other as roommates and as friends, creating a modern-day "odd couple."

Character Description Sheet

Something that can help keep things organized when creating a short film is to write out character description forms or sheets. These are essentially brief bios of each character in the film. All characters should also have names. Even if they have only one line, they should have a name and an identity, just as everyone you see walking down the street in the real world has a name, a history, and an attitude about life. Try to avoid using the generic "customer in store" or "waitress in truck stop," which can lead to stereotypical cardboard cut-outs and clichés. Make the most insignificant-seeming character real, with an age and an occupation. To the audience, these small touches point to a larger reality in the story, making it more genuine and engaging. Make the generic "woman at the counter" into a 22-year-old music major at a nearby university who secretly wants more than anything to outdo her twin sister. She will come to life.

Example: Character Description Sheet

Type of Character: (Hero? Supporting character?)
Character name:
Age:
Place of birth:
Height:
Weight:

Hair Color:
General Appearance:
Key Friends:
Key Enemies:
Skills:

Setting and Location

Setting and location are two different things. Setting is where the story takes place, and it should be somewhere that fits the story. Sometimes it's important to know the specific location, such Miami Beach in the 1950s or Mars in 2245. For other stories it can be more vague, like Andy's suburban home in *Toy Story*, a modern office filled with cubicles, or the ambiguous town of Springfield in *The Simpsons*.

Location is where you will film the story. It is important to make this place your own, and not to let too much of its real identity leak in. Don't pick a place just because it's convenient. Think about the story and pick a place that will help to tell it convincingly. Once a location has been identified, modify it as much as possible to create a new reality. If it is a dorm room, try to remove anything that relates to the real person who lives there. This is a designed reality. Stick to that mission.

Sometimes a story will depend on historical facts to be accurate in setting; that is, it won't come purely from your imagination. This might require some research.

Also, when shooting a fictional story, it is unlikely that scenes will be shot in the order that they will appear in the finished product. Sometimes access to certain locations will be limited, such as outside of normal business hours. It is therefore very important for all of the actors to understand the script and play their parts accordingly. "You could be directing scene eighty-seven on day one, and the actors need to be where they need to be emotionally for scene eighty-seven," said Richard Friedman, a Los Angeles–based feature film director with twenty-five years of experience whose credits include *5th and Alameda* (2011) and *Halfway to Hell* (2013).

The same thing applies spatially. Just because the entryway to the campus library leads into the library doesn't mean it must do so in the film. In the film, someone can be shown going through these doors and, in the next shot, coming into an office, museum, or government agency. Similarly, a monument or playground tower shot from below, against empty sky, could pass for the spire of a 500-foot tall building.

Organizing and Pitching an Idea

So you have come up with a good idea for a film. Prior to writing a script, finding actors, and actually going out to shoot it, there is more planning and organization to be done. The importance of planning cannot be overstated.

Much time, money, and effort—not to mention patience and goodwill—can be squandered as a result of inadequate planning. You don't want to get into the laborious details of shooting without a firm, step-by-step plan that, while always remaining flexible, will act as a road map to the completion of the project.

There's something else at work as well. Storytelling doesn't happen in a vacuum, whether it is for a class or for a real-world client, and others are going to have to buy into and understand your story. Along with planning, this can take some ingenuity and salesmanship. It also involves some industry-standard tools.

Developing a Logline

For any story, whether fiction or nonfiction, it is important to develop a logline. Sometimes a story can be based on a theme, such as coming of age, fear, forgiveness, betrayal, or sacrifice. Capture this theme in a sentence, and you will probably have a good understanding of the story. In filmmaking this brief statement is called a *logline*. It might help to think about how to fit the story into a tweet on Twitter—140 characters to get in, get the idea across, and get out.

In the screenwriting world, the logline instantly communicates to others what a story is about. "Everybody is looking for that next great movie idea," screenwriter Erik Bork said:

> You need to distill it into a few words that make people get it, and get them to think, "Oh, that sounds like a movie. I am intrigued. I would want to see it. It sounds entertaining. Wow, I can imagine it already! I can imagine the poster and the trailer." It's got an obvious hook.

As Bork explained, a logline should quickly tell the reader who the main character is and what problem the whole movie will essentially solve, but not necessarily how that will happen. Remember, a story has an arc, and along that arc are plot points—significant events within the story that move it forward. Those won't fit in a logline. All that can be done in this small space is define the problem or challenge or goal—all elements of the conflict, as we discussed in Chapter 2—and get the reader interested in and relating to that challenge on an immediate, gut level.

A logline is essential to getting a screenplay sold, so it should "feel like it suggests a movie that could move and impact a huge audience," according to Bork. "That is the hard part. A logline is just the expression or description of that hard work that you've already done. The logline is that kernel of an idea underpinning what you hope will be a successful screenplay."

> ## WRITING A LOGLINE
>
> *The website scriptologist.com lists three factors to keep in mind when writing a logline, including words that are both active and descriptive:*
>
> 1. Who is the main character and what does he or she want?
> 2. Who (villain) or what is standing in the way of the main character?
> 3. What makes this story unique?

Examples of Loglines

Taken from the Logline Library on thescriptlab.com, these were written by the screenwriters. They are not necessarily the movie that was produced.

ARGO

A CIA specialist concocts a covert operation to produce a fake Hollywood movie to rescue six American diplomats during the 1979 Iranian hostage crisis.

BABY MAMA

A single businesswoman uses a surrogate to have a baby, but her plans go awry when the mother tries to con her.

BLACK HAWK DOWN

The U.S. military attempts a vicious strike against a Somali warlord with disastrous results.

BLOOD DIAMOND

In the midst of civil war and a dangerous diamond cartel, a diamond smuggler sets out with an African native to find a precious gem buried in the jungle.

THE BOURNE IDENTITY

A man with amnesia discovers he is a government assassin who has been targeted for death by the organization that employs him.

MEMENTO

An insurance investigator, suffering from a disorder that erases all short-term memory, struggles to find his wife's killer.

MEMOIRS OF A GEISHA

The daughter of a fisherman struggles to become a geisha in twentieth-century Japan with the hope of winning the heart of a man she loves.

THE PATRIOT

A former soldier—who has put his dark, bloody past behind him—joins the American Revolution when his son is brutally murdered by a British officer.

ROCKY

A washed-up boxer gets a chance to fight the world champ, but with the help of his lover, must learn to believe in himself before stepping into the ring.

XXX: STATE OF THE UNION

After being sprung from jail, an ex-Navy SEAL and street thug sets out to bring down a high-ranking general intent on taking over the country.

Story Bible

When writing a fiction narrative, whether it is a short story, a novel, or a scripted film, organization is vital. Drawing the story arc as a diagram is one way to make sure that all the necessary parts are there, but organization goes beyond that. Some writers make what it is called a *story bible*, in which all the information about a story is set out and categorized. This type of organization helps writers keep all the basics straight—elements that might otherwise be scattered throughout an entire script and hard to remember and keep consistent.

Story bibles include section headings such as:

- Logline
- Synopsis
- Characters
- Wardrobe
- Locations
- Progress
- Research

Writer's Treatment

Much more involved and detailed than the logline is the *writer's treatment*, a sales tool for a screenplay that introduces characters, summarizes the plot, and generally pitches the story. For a feature-length film this treatment could be several pages; for a television series it would describe both the pilot and future episodes. "I actually have my students summarize the whole story, almost like they are writing a short story—that's what the movie is going to look like minus flowery language," said Juliet Giglio.

When writing a treatment as one page or less, write it as a synopsis. As Sandy Eiges writes in her digital book *Hollywood Scriptwriting: How to Birth Your Idea into a Bankable Screenplay*:

> A working synopsis should be preliminary, including only the bare bones of your story, including the beginning, the middle and the end. This will function as a tent pole, to help you start putting together the major elements of character and plot. This synopsis may look very different by the time you finish the script, at which point you should revise it to reflect the completed screenplay. That would be your selling synopsis, which you will need in case a producer requests the synopsis before committing to read an entire script. Many do. (13–17)

Exercise: Writer's Synopsis

One way to come up with fiction story ideas is to use an app for the iPhone called Story Cubes. The app features digital "cubes" that behave like dice. On each side of each cube are pictures depicting different items, such as a plane, a castle, or a clock. When the phone is shaken the dice are "rolled," and the pictures that come up can be the starting points for a script or story. There is also a board game version of this application.

Using Story Cubes, shake up the dice and create a narrative based on the icons that come up. Write a 250-word writer's synopsis that summarizes the story into a readable piece of fiction—one that would give a producer a good idea what the story is about. Also write a logline for your treatment. There's no right or wrong here, just inspiration about how to come up with an idea.

Make sure to include the "five Ws"—who, what, why, when, and where—and define the audience for the story. The people to whom you are marketing a script need to know whom the project is aimed toward—who will ultimately be buying tickets.

- Who is your audience?
- What is the story about?
- Why will people want to see it?
- When does the story take place?
- Where does the action take place?

Scriptwriting

Now it is time to think about writing a script. This is what will translate the story to the world of film. You have reached into your own past and present, and possibly those of family and friends, and found a story that resonates. It's something that is brief and easy to understand, and does not require a ton of dialogue to get its point across, but it definitely has some truth or emotion to convey to the viewer. Now, get to writing.

Remember what filmmaking is: It is visual storytelling. Every scene and most pieces of dialogue will be captured visually by the camera. This is important to think about. In high school English class, when writing about personal experiences, you never needed to find people to act out the story. Now it is required. Their words will need to be convincing, realistic, and consistent with their characters. The pacing will need to be consistent with what people are used to in filmed entertainment, and the story will need to have continuity and logical cause-and-effect.

There are other aspects to consider. For a science fiction film, will it be possible to show a spaceship flying through space without it looking cheesy? Is there a location for filming that could pass for another planet? These are the things that the first-time screenwriter should be thinking about. For these kinds of reasons, basing a script on something in your own life might be more practical.

Also, be wary of the dull, obvious, and clichéd. Juliet Giglio said that surprise is the spice of life, or at least of scripts:

> Predictable? Here's the way to get around that: Always make sure that every scene has conflict—with twists and turns. You have to be surprised constantly. With clichés you are not going to be surprised. Some stories inherently have a predictable nature to them—that's OK. The challenge is to have interesting and surprising moments.

Scriptwriting involves a lot of minutiae about formats, styles, and conventions. A great way to avoid all the complexity of properly formatting a script is to use a software product. This will save a lot of time and be well worth the effort, because a script is definitely not the place to be looking unprofessional. "It's important to have a short script properly formatted," confirmed Giglio. "It has to be in the right format [or] it looks like amateur hour."

Never write camera directions into a script. Save that for the film's director to come up with. That will be part of the shot list and storyboard, to be discussed later in this chapter.

The script for *Pizza My Heart* was written by both Juliet and Keith Giglio. The movie, which aired on ABC Family and streams on Netflix, is about two families, the Prestolanis and the Montebellos, that run competing pizza shops in Verona, New Jersey. In keeping with the film's parallels to *Romeo and Juliet*, the families are archenemies.

When Gina Prestolani and Joe Montebello fall in love, they have to sneak around. A key scene in the film portrays both sets of parents finding out that their son and daughter are sneaking around and dating each other.

Giglio said that, like most scripts, the pages of *Pizza My Heart* were colored when it was in the production-draft stage. Once a script goes into production

Figure 7.01 Juliet Giglio, assistant professor of screenwriting at State University of New York at Oswego. (Courtesy of Juliet Giglio)

it is "locked," but changes can still be made after that. Each time there's a rewrite, it's printed on a different color of paper.

Here is the basic logline for the script, as provided by Giglio: "In the vein of Romeo and Juliet, PIZZA MY HEART is a comedy about two rival pizzeria families in modern day Verona, New Jersey."

Step Outline

One way to begin the challenging process of writing a script is to make a *step outline*. Once you have a writer's treatment, go back through it and describe all of the different things that happen to the main character(s). Each of these sentences becomes a step in an outline. It's an easy way to start figuring out if a story is working on a structural level. "It's a road map for a script and you know what works," said Giglio. "You don't go off course. It's like swimming in a lap pool."

Such an outline also helps to time a movie. When writing a script for a short film, remember that each page in the script generally equals about one minute of shooting time. If the goal is a six-minute movie, shoot for a six-page script.

Scriptwriting Software

It takes many hours to write a screenplay, even for a short film. It's an imposing creative task, and you want as few distractions as possible as you strive to make your characters and their stories come to life. Don't use a plain old word processor and proceed to get bogged down in the details of formatting and proper indentation. The screenwriting industry uses two main pieces of software, Celtx and Final Draft, although other applications are available, such as Adobe Story. The greater the functionality, generally, the higher the cost. Note also, however, that there is a free and limited version of each of these pieces of software.

Celtx

This is not just scriptwriting software. Celtx also helps manage the production process from scriptwriting through storyboarding to blocking and shot lists, all with only one software package to learn. The scripting capabilities make it very easy for the first-time user to write a properly formatted screenplay. The software is also free for both Macintosh and PC.

One benefit of using Celtx is that it supports team-based screenwriting, allowing several people to work on the same document at once. There are also mobile apps that sync with whatever is being worked on at home, so that if you come up with ideas on the go you can capture them and have them at your fingertips when you sit down to work again.

Figure 7.02 Celtx is screenwriting software that is both application- and Cloud-subscription–based. (Courtesy of Celtx)

Final Draft

This software, available for both Macintosh and PC, automatically formats a script to industry standards while the user types. The software also assists with tabbing and adds page breaks with "continued" and "more" as needed. Built-in functions allow for brainstorming, outlining, and structuring.

Figure 7.03 Final Draft is a software product that helps with scriptwriting. (Courtesy of Final Draft)

The software can also help to break down a script, with options for making character arcs along with note taking, revisions, and outlining with virtual index cards.

Formatting a Script

Fonts

- Use standard fonts such as Courier or Times New Roman, 12-point. Other fonts can make a script difficult to read, and it should look as professional as possible.

Page Numbers

- Every page gets a number followed by a period, in the top right corner.

Scene Headings

- Use ALL CAPS when writing out SCENE HEADINGS.
- Is the scene going to be an interior (INT) or exterior (EXT) shot?
- What is the location going to be? "ALEC'S HOUSE" or "THE CABIN"
- Is the scene going to portray DAY or NIGHT?

Scene Descriptions

- Write scene descriptions in the present tense, below the scene heading.
- Describe the location, characters, and action in a scene.
- Put words in the scene description in ALL CAPS for emphasis.

Dialogue Blocks

- Write the CHARACTER'S NAME before each line in all caps.
- Below the name write any dialogue cues, in lowercase in parentheses.
- Write how the dialogue should be delivered, for example, "(whispers)."
- Below that, write the actual dialogue that needs to be read by the actor.
- Sometimes dialogue can be broken by a scene description. Type the name again and then write "(cont'd)."

Transition Cues

- Transition cues describe the progress from one scene to the next. (ALL CAPS)
- Transition cues include: FADE IN, CUT TO, DISSOLVE TO, FADE OUT, CUT TO BLACK, FREEZE FRAME, etc.
- All cues are flush right, except for FADE IN, which is flush left.
- It is customary for writers to place a transition cue at the end of every scene.

Exercise: Scriptwriting

1. Write a script of the story for the synopsis that you wrote for the last exercise using the Story Cubes application. Use a software package such as Celtx, Final Draft, or Adobe Story to make sure the formatting is industry-standard.
2. Make a character profile for each character in the script, and make sure to give each character a name.

Things to think about while writing:

- Does the story have a clear beginning, middle, and end?
- Is there a clearly articulated character and story arc?
- Is the finished product of high enough quality to entertain an audience?

EXAMPLES OF PROFESSIONAL SCRIPTS

To download a professional script and see what it looks like:

The Internet Movie Script Database: http://www.imsdb.com

JoBlo's Movie Scripts: http://www.joblo.com/moviescripts.php

Table Reads

When a script is complete, it needs to be put through its paces. A good way to do this is to perform a *table read*. This is much like reading a play in high school. The parts do not need to be acted out, only divvied up among a group of friends or fellow students in an informal setting. Then, get ready to learn a lot about your script.

During the writing process, everything from the dialogue to the voices and mannerisms of the characters was inside your own head. Hearing it read aloud will provide a much better understanding of what has been accomplished, what might need to change, and whether the script works as a story. A character might sound much different "live" than when you were writing (Lawrence, "What Is a 'Table Read'?"). Each character should have a unique personality that comes through in every line. Returning to *The Big Bang Theory*, imagine if the lines of Sheldon and Leonard were swapped. It wouldn't take long to notice that something was wrong. Their personalities come through strongly in their every statement.

This is a moment of truth, when you might realize that not everything done in the drafting phase is masterpiece-quality. More feedback will come from those reading the individual parts, probably including numerous ideas about pacing, emotion, language, and character. This can require a thick skin, but it is also where great progress and breakthroughs are made. Ask the players about their parts—were they believable and easy to bring to life? Were there any situations or lines that jarred them or need to be removed altogether? Were the plot points identifiable, and in the right places?

Doing a table read is vital to the storyteller, because it's the first time that a work comes to life in the real world, outside one's own mind.

Storyboarding

Storyboarding is turning a finished script into a visual plan. Each planned shot should be drawn out as closely as possible to how it should appear on the screen. The result will appear something like a comic book illustrating key actions and moments. There is always room for change, but getting a designed reality into images on paper is a vital part of preparing to shoot.

Don't worry about artistic value. Use stick figures, if necessary. What's important is that the final video is being designed in its entirety, every shot being pre-visualized, all the thinking and strategizing being done now so that the technicalities of shooting can be focused on later. Also, while drawing a storyboard, label each shot by type: long, medium, close-up, etc. Use abbreviations for this, as suggested in the following section. The end result should be that anyone viewing the storyboard, and reading the script, should be able to visualize the action of the movie.

Extreme Long Shot (ELS)

The *extreme long shot* is often an establishing shot, where the setting can be seen in its entirety or nearly so. Think of the opening shot of a music concert. The viewer sees the venue in its entirety, along with the audience, and there might even be an exterior or aerial shot, as in the broadcast of a football game.

Figure 7.04 Extreme Long Shot (ELS). (Illustration by Paolo Libunao)

In a movie this could be a long pan across the main character's home territory or neighborhood. Think of a long, peaceful shot of the Shire in the *Lord of the Rings* trilogy, or a gray, sprawling city for a detective or superhero story.

Long Shot (LS)

Often done with a telephoto lens, a *long shot* compresses the scene into one focal plane and can show a character from head to toe while also showing that character's immediate surroundings.

Figure 7.05 Long Shot (LS) (Illustration by Paolo Libunao)

Medium Shot (MS)

The *medium shot* generally shows a character from the waist up. It is a standard shot for showing people in conversation, and it also enables the characters' arms to be seen if they are gesturing.

Figure 7.06 Medium Shot (MS) (Illustration by Paolo Libunao)

Close-Up (CU)

The *close-up* usually emphasizes a single subject or specific thing. Shooting lots of close-ups will help in the edit, for they allow viewers to be easily transitioned to a new scene.

Figure 7.07 Close-Up (CU) (Illustration by Paolo Libunao)

Wide Shot (WS)

The broadly focused *wide shot* is very common in film and video. It shows the scene in its entirety while revealing the activity of characters as well. In a scene with two characters in a dorm room, a wide shot could show the entire room, establishing place, with the characters present.

Figure 7.08 Wide Shot (W) (Illustration by Paolo Libunao)

Point of View Shot (POV)

The *point of view shot* is often made over the shoulder of a character, to give the viewer a sense of looking through that character's eyes, and seeing what he or she sees. It is a useful shot for generating empathy for a character, or in building suspense, among other things.

Figure 7.09 Point of View (POV) Shot (Illustration by Paolo Libunao)

Shot Angles and Movement

While drawing a storyboard, it is important to note the angles at which the camera will be situated for each shot. Will the shot be looking down on the characters? Looking up at them? At eye level? A bird's-eye view? Through a

Scene #	Shot #	Shot Angle	Location	Description

Figure 7.10 To stay organized and make editing easier, the production team should keep track of all shots taken, as they are taken

library bookshelf? Each angle has its own unique effect on the mood and progression of the story. All this should be noted on the storyboard.

The storyboard should also include notes about camera movements. Is the dolly moving in or out of the scene? Panning slowly across a landscape? Are you "tracking" the shot? Is there an upward or downward tilt? Is it a handheld shot, which can give the viewer a feeling of uneasiness, tension, or even chaos?

During shooting, a member of the team should be making what is called a *shot list*—a description of the location and other details of every shot made, including the abbreviation for what type of shot it is. This will help keep things organized through both the filming and editing phases of production.

Exercise: Draw a Storyboard for a Simple Fairy Tale

Draw a storyboard for the fairy tale "Snow White," making sure to include individual shots that cover the following story beats:

1. Introduce Snow White as a happy-go-lucky, beautiful girl.
2. The evil queen is jealous of Snow White's beauty.
3. Snow White heads out on a trek to collect flowers.
4. The evil queen has one of her huntsmen try to kill Snow White, but he fails.
4. Snow White runs off into the woods and finds the home of the seven dwarves.
5. Snow White settles down to live in the woods with the dwarves.
6. Snow White is tricked into taking a bite of a poisoned apple.
7. Snow White dies as a result of biting the poisoned apple.
8. A handsome prince kisses Snow White and brings her back to life.

Collaborating to Shoot a Scene

On the set of a film everyone needs to collaborate, so that all the jobs that need to get done are done. Communication is vital. Everyone on the set needs to know what is planned, so that each team member has an understanding of what needs to be done to make a scene work. Mike Mickens, a California-based cinematographer who shoots feature films and television shows, and whose credits as a cinematographer include *The New Normal* (2013), *Fred: The Show* (2012), and *Supah Ninjas* (2012) among others, explained the process:

> The process of making moving pictures is very collaborative, in which everyone is trying to put their best work up on the screen, from the production designer [to the] set dresser, property master, etc. It is a collaboration of very skilled craft persons.

In the real world, time is money. If you spend too much time trying to decide on the best placement for the camera during the actual shoot, you might be looking at a very expensive day, with people standing around waiting to be told what to do. Even in a student film, participants will not want to stand and wait, feeling as if their valuable time is being wasted. Detailed planning—doing the whole shot first in your mind and on paper—allows the crew to transition smoothly and efficiently from shot to shot without indecision.

Blocking

The director needs to plan on paper what the camera placement will be to cover the specific action that happens in front of the lens; these preparations will determine actual movement in the scene when it is shot (FilmSkills). According to Peter D. Marshall, as quoted on Frank Pasquine's blog for the New York Film Academy website, "Blocking a scene is simply 'working out the details of an actor's moves in relation to the camera.'"

Marshall's Five Important Blocking Tips

1. Having a shot list will help you during the blocking process. The shot list is like a map: It gives you a path to your destination but you don't always have to follow it.
2. Let the actors show you what they want to do first, then, when you make a suggestion, it is based on something you have already seen.
3. Where the camera is placed is determined primarily by what is important in the scene.
4. Blocking is like a puzzle: Directors need to keep working at it until the whole scene works.
5. In television and low-budget films, speed is essential. Block some scenes so that the action takes place in one direction (to avoid turning the camera around for reverses).

Lighting

What is the lighting going to be? Is there sufficient light on the set? Are you going to shoot with available light and outdoors, or indoors? Is the light from above, or behind, or from one side?

Direction

Before a scene is shot, the actors will need some direction as to what to do. Should they be walking toward the camera? Walking away? Standing in a certain spot? The possible movements are limitless, and the actors will probably have their own ideas, so it is best to spell it all out before starting the shoot.

Rehearsal

Rehearse the scene with the actors, especially if they are not professionals. Even when shooting digital, don't waste disk space and time (including editing time) on poorly acted scenes. Have the camera in place for at least some rehearsal time, to rehearse its movement as well and so that actors get used to its presence. The editing room is not the place to be repairing mistakes that could have been avoided in the shooting phase.

Shooting

Once things have been perfected through rehearsals, start shooting. Try shooting from a few different angles. This will provide some choice of alternate footage in post-production. If after shooting a scene you think something might have been amiss, make the needed adjustments and shoot again.

Creating the Look, Feel, and Setting for a Scripted Movie

Design

Be consistent with the look and feel of a production across the board. If you skimp on lighting in one scene, or if the rest of a film's production value is high while there is one obviously subpar scene in lighting, sound, or camera work, the audience will notice.

Be consistent also with the design of everything from the titles in the opening sequences to the credits at the end of the film. Many video editing software programs have default fonts that can be dropped into the edit; whichever ones you decide to use, be consistent. This will help make the finished film look as professional as possible.

Wardrobe

When recruiting actors for a short film, most likely you are going to be rounding up friends and fellow students. Make sure they wear clothing that fits their characters' attitudes, socioeconomic status, self-image, and degree of concern for appearance. Should their clothes be hyper-stylish? Frumpy or out-of-date? Expensive or cheap? Flashy or subdued? Sexy or modest?

People's clothing says a lot about their personalities, their jobs, and their outlook on life. If uniforms are needed, strive to make them look authentic, and not like badly-fitting Halloween costumes. Be careful also about clothing with logos or lettering, which could be a distraction if the college name, fraternity letters, or message don't fit the storyline.

Set Design

A short film might not require the building of much scenery, but remember that house and dorm-room decorations, like clothing, say a lot about characters. When using a ready-made location, check to make sure all the decor—along with the levels of neatness, clutter, cleanliness, and light—is consistent with the story. The characters are the decorators and caretakers of the places where they supposedly live.

Pay attention also to what sounds are present on the set, including such things as air conditioners, knocking pipes, birds chirping in the eaves, traffic outside, or the low hum of a light ballast. In college dorm situations in particular, sudden and unexpected noises from the elevator next door can ruin a shot. The more control you have over the noise level on the set, the better off you'll be. If you can't have that control, you can at least be ready and try to work around any problems.

Props

Look for real-world items to use in a film, unless of course the story dictates otherwise. People in 1969 were not using mobile phones—is it possible to find a dial model? Do some digging in secondhand or discount stores to locate believable, low-cost props that can be used or modified for use in your film, or find a place where more unusual or valuable items can be borrowed or rented.

Lighting

When shooting a low-budget short film, lighting can pose challenges. If the set is an office, the overhead lights may be fluorescent, shining down on the actors and producing deep shadows in the eye sockets that may or may not suit the story and mood. Find a way to shoot near windows with natural light or in a different room altogether that can be rearranged as an office. Make sure not to put a subject in front of a window, otherwise the camera may get fooled by the exposure and produce a silhouette. On the other hand, this could be a desirable effect for a scene.

Mixing common light sources can also create difficulties. Even if white balance is set indoors, a combination of halogen desk lamps, incandescent bulbs, and overhead fluorescents could prove to be a poor light mixture, making the final color in the film a bit "off." Try to choose one type of lighting, whether it is fluorescent, incandescent, or something else, and color correction in postproduction will be a lot easier.

Working as a Team on a Student Film Project

The real world after college (not that shown on the MTV program) is about collaboration and teamwork. There's not a job out there that doesn't require working with others and collaborating at least some of the time, if not all the time. Filmmaking is no different. Working in a setting like Hollywood requires working in collaboration with many, many people, but for the purposes of this book we will assume that you're on a team of two to five people, all collaborating on the goal of making a three- to five-minute film of sufficient quality to publish on the Internet.

Working in small teams usually means that team members need to play more than just one role. You may need to be the director as well as the lead or assistant screenwriter. You might have to act in one scene, and run the camera in the next. You might be in charge of both costumes and casting actors. Make sure to list in the credits everyone who has been involved in the film. This might be many more people than those first envisioned for the filmmaking team.

Student filmmaking might force you into roles at which you are no expert, but it's important to give it your best shot. A script will have to be written, but don't underestimate the power of others to provide help. You do not have all the ideas, or all the answers. Some people (whom we all know) may think that because an idea was theirs it is the best, and their minds cannot be changed. "That is the biggest lesson you can take away: how to work with difficult people without becoming difficult yourself," said Sullivan Fitzgerald, a graduate of the S.I. Newhouse School of Public Communications who was part of a team that won a Collegiate Emmy for an episodic web series called *The Complex*. Fitzgerald now works as a production assistant for the television show *Criminal Minds*. "You need to put your ego aside so that you can actually make something," said Fitzgerald, who wrote Episode 3 of *The Complex*, acted in the film, and helped build the sets.

Just as in the professional world, being a student filmmaker demands resourcefulness and compromise. When an actor is needed, sometimes it might be best just to use someone in your class rather than looking far and wide for a great master—whose schedule might not match your own. Also, it's important for a film set to look believable. Instead of trying to turn a dorm room or dorm common area into a coffee shop, it might be easier just to find an actual coffee shop and obtain permission to shoot there.

In *The Complex*, Fitzgerald and his classmates built a room to represent a superintendent's office, keeping it the same from week to week during filming rather than having to tear down and rebuild over and over. "You have to make it work; it's just one of the most frustrating things," he said. For one scene in Episode 5 the students built a Steadicam-like device that held a camera out in front of an actor, to capture his face in an up-close and personal style. "It was great. It worked fantastically. It was a style choice that we wanted to make and it paid off," said Fitzgerald, who agrees that collaboration is the key to success when making a fiction film. "The best lessons you can learn are how to work with other people. It's an art form. Emotional people get attached to things, and they may not want to let it go," he said.

 Watch *The Complex* on Youtube: http://bit.ly/thecomplexepisode5

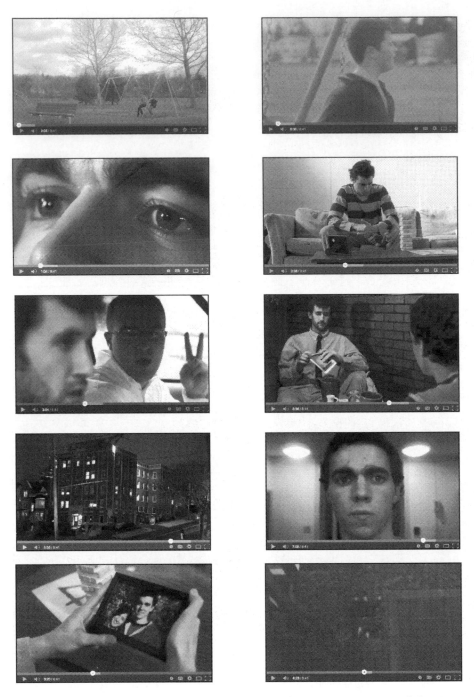

Figure 7.11 A storyboard of video poster images for *The Complex*. (Courtesy of The New-house School at Syracuse University)

Figure 7.12 A storyboard for *The Complex*. (Illustrations by Paolo Libunao)

Producer

Short, student films don't tend to have producers—or at least it's a role that gets mixed in with scriptwriting, camera work, or any other task your team needs to tackle. Producers do exist in the real world, however.

There is a difference between being an executive producer for a film and being the producer of a television show. For films, the *executive producer* is usually bankrolling the movie and handling the budget. In television, the *producer* is the point person who arranges the show from start to finish and hires the talent, makes decisions on the set and manages the day-to-day work. Producers can be thought of as the general managers or CEOs of the show, as they create the vision and hire the people to execute it.

Producers, whether of sitcoms or of reality shows, need to be aware of some basic show elements. "I think that with any genre television show—fiction or reality, it's no matter—any and every story you tell must have three rudimentary elements: beginning, middle, and end," said Brian Gadinsky, CEO of the G Group, which produces reality television. Gadinsky is credited as "creator" and "executive consultant" for *Sunday Best* on Black Entertainment Television. Gadinsky also produced the first season of *American Idol*, when Kelly Clarkson was the winner.

"I don't care if it's a game show or football game, basic storytelling is assured if you can follow these three rules," Gadinsky said. "One: Tell 'em what you're going to tell 'em. Two: Tell 'em. Three: Tell 'em what you told 'em." He went on to describe the unpredictability of the reality television genre:

> Being that it is unpredictable, because it is live, you work in what you think is going to happen, and then you have some contingencies if that doesn't happen, which is what I liked about it. You really don't know in a live contest . . . you don't know who is going to win the ball game. You don't know what is going to happen in *American Idol*. You have to be ready.

Gadinsky said that a turning point in his career was learning something from Mark Burnett, the executive producer of *Survivor*, while in Australia:

> One of the things I learned from him in terms of storytelling . . . He was filming the second *Survivor*. I went with him to the set, and as soon as one of the challenges ended he said to the cameraman to go over to the losers. He looked at me, and he said the loser story is so much more important than the winner. That's where the relatability is. That was a lesson I learned about storytelling in reality TV, and I carry that through: to really look for the heart and story, not just the "what happened."

Screenwriter

The *screenwriter* is the original person (or team of people) that comes up with the idea for the story and puts it down on paper. Screenwriters begin with a concept and shape it into something that could become a film. They must understand that what they create will need to be interpreted by numerous collaborators, who will transform what they have written into a motion picture, while simultaneously keeping the original idea, vision, and thought process intact.

As David Howard and Edward Mabley write in their book *The Tools of Screenwriting: A Writer's Guide to the Craft and Elements of a Screenplay*, "This vision is contained in the screenplay, a sort of blueprint for an extremely complex art form, an art form recorded in two dimensions that depicts three dimensions, an art form that has the additional dimension of time" (5).

Director

The *director* makes sure the actors do what is asked of them—the person in this role calls the shots, literally and figuratively. Collaboration can only go so far. Decisions must be made, and all teams need a leader. At the same time, both in amateur settings and professionally, collaboration remains key. It is important for directors to listen to their team members and to value everyone's opinion. You never know when one idea might spark an even better one, which can make a movie better. This thought process holds true in the real world too, at a place like Pixar. In the *Harvard Business Review*, Ed Catmull, president of Walt Disney Animation Studios and Pixar Animation Studios, writes, "Our philosophy is: You get great creative people, you bet big on them, you give them enormous leeway and support, and you provide them with an environment in which they can get honest feedback from everyone."

The director also works with the director of photography to help design the visual aspects of the film, considering suggestions and going with what works best. This is the director's role with everything creative about the film: listening to all of the specialists working on the project. At least in the professional setting, the wardrobe people got the job because they are very good at what they do—the same goes for makeup, cinematography, and so on. An important part of being the director is simply being able to listen, but while others are free to provide ideas and input, the director's vision for the film is the guiding force, and the director has the final say.

In addition, directors work with actors to get them to perform at the top of their game. "It's all gotta be good—you can't have a bad actor," said Richard Friedman, the Los Angeles director:

> Because if you have . . . ten great performances in your movie, and they're all fabulous, and you have one lousy performance, what does the audience talk about when they walk out of the theater? A lousy performance! Ultimately it is the director's responsibility to make sure that it all works, because who do they turn to at the end when they say that actor was terrible?

Cinematographer

In the motion picture world, the person who runs the camera is called the *camera operator*, which is pretty self-explanatory. The person who manages the picture quality, however, along with the lighting and scene design, is the *director of photography* (DP) or *cinematographer*. The cinematographer coordinates the crew working on the set in accordance with the director's vision for the film, and makes sure that everyone is in agreement as to what the film will look like. "I look into the director's brain and translate that into motion pictures," said Mike Mickens, the California-based cinematographer.

As Paul Wheeler writes in his book *Practical Cinematography*, "The prime job of the DP is to create the visual mood of the film, and this is primarily achieved by the use and control of light" (3). The cinematographer's judgments, Wheeler goes on to say, can directly and strongly affect a film's impact on the audience.

Audio Recordist

Most cameras have the ability to record audio with an onboard microphone, but as we discussed while covering audio in Chapter 3, this does not always give the best results. Most built-in microphones do not do a very good job.

Professional production crews are well-equipped with audio personnel, but think about filling that role in a short-film production as well. If the gear and the extra hands are available, an *audio recordist* can be designated to hold a microphone on a monopod or boom pole above the action, just out of the camera frame. The audio cable can either go right back into the camera, so that sound synced with images is recorded through the boom mic, or the audio can be recorded separately with a handheld recording device and paired up with the images later on, in post-production, with much better sound quality.

Audio is a major element of film, and it goes hand-in-hand with the visual content. Jeff Bradbury, an assistant professor specializing in audio for multimedia and film production at the State University of New York at Oswego, said this on the subject:

> I hate to say audio is more important than imagery, but how many people tend to watch movies and actually look away and still follow it? Because the audio is giving you clues as to what is going on when you don't even have to see it.

Gaffer

When making a film you are probably going to be shooting different scenes in different places, and each setting will probably have a different type of lighting. Not all of it will be good or even adequate. It's the role of the *gaffer* to hold reflectors or set up lights to make sure that the lighting in the scene meets the director's needs. On the professional level, the gaffer also understands how to lay cables and power cords and knows where to place lights and reflectors to achieve optimum lighting in a scene.

Like an audio recordist, a gaffer is a great role to have present on the set of a short film. Even without advanced training, the gaffer can hold a light stand so that it does not topple over in the wind, or hold a disc reflector to bounce light and make sure that shadows are filled in.

Casting Director

Finding people to act in a film might be the hardest thing you will undertake. Friends aren't always actors, nor actors friends. Still, competent acting is definitely a skill that increases production value, or harms things badly when it is missing.

Casting directors find the acting talent, and they match actors to the roles present in the story. Don't enlist just anybody to play a part in a film—obviously someone's age, gender, and often physical appearance will need to match the requirements of the role. On top of that, an actor needs to have some acting skills. It's a tricky job.

"Film casting directors look for actors with that certain quality . . . they demand the audience's attention," said Brette Goldstein, a New York City–based casting director who cast the independent films *El Camino* (2008) and *Hello Lonesome* (2010). "With film, especially a drama, an actor has to be compelling on a visceral level," she explained. "Unlike theater, where everything is so physical and vocal . . . with film it's often really visual; you watch someone not speak . . . just listen . . . just be," she added. "That takes on a whole different life. The camera doesn't lie. So much of casting is about the actors' presence and energy."

Video Editor

The *video editor* works on all of the footage in post-production. This person is very familiar with the script and the shooting, and in how to tell stories using visuals. Like the rest of the team, video editors use their own skills and talents to help realize the vision of the director.

The first edited version of a film is called the *video editor's cut*: The editor goes through all the footage and assembles the film according to how he or she sees it. Then comes the *director's cut*, in which the director can either start from scratch or, more often, modify the video editor's cut of the movie. The finished product is then shown to the producer and any other stakeholders in the film for their commentary.

"When I got into this business, if you made a movie you were special," said director Richard Friedman, of the difference that good editing needs to make:

> Just the fact that you made a movie. Not many people went out and shot one. Now everybody and their brother can make a movie, and put out a

movie. You can literally shoot a movie on your iPhone, and cut it, and put it out for the world to see. Which is a great thing. I think it is fantastic that you can make movies so quickly and so inexpensively. The problem is that everybody can do it. People need to be better than they have ever been, because there is a lot of competition.

Filming a Fictional Story

Filming a fiction piece takes hard and focused work, but the task is simplified when the acknowledged goal is a real story with a beginning, a middle, and an end. Journalists can benefit a lot from making fiction pieces. It helps them to become better visual storytellers. Building sequences based on made-up stories, and getting familiar with the elements of stories by putting them together yourself, can help you recognize real sequences in the field, in nonfiction settings.

Filming fiction involves many, many choices and decisions, and decisions eat up time. Plan thoroughly and meticulously, with decisions made in advance, so that you can concentrate on capturing the action when the camera is rolling.

Breaking Down the Shots: *Date Night* at the Metro Grill

Darren Durlach and David Larsen are a pair of former news photographers who now do corporate video storytelling. Building sequences and telling stories pretty much comes naturally for them. Harnessing the skills they learned shooting daily news, they now own a Baltimore-based company called Early Light Media that does advertising and marketing video.

"If you are shot-planning a commercial, [you] need to go in with a plan. Make sure that when you leave . . . you have all the shots to make the story," said Durlach, who has worked for both print media and television and is a three-time recipient of the National Press Photographers Association's Ernie Crisp TV Photographer of the Year Award. He has also earned more than twenty-five Washington, D.C., and New England Emmy Awards for his videography. "What is important to remember is that a lot of our news instincts come into play, and we get shots as we see them. Then the plan can change at any time as we think of something better," he said.

Durlach and Larsen filmed an advertisement for the Metro Grill restaurant in Richmond, VA, in 2013. The piece was for the restaurant's website and was called *Date Night*—each Tuesday the restaurant has a special for couples on dates. The videographers had originally planned to do a series of videos that were more like "how to's," filming bartenders making signature drinks and the like. Instead they centered on a video with a real visual story, in which a man and woman are going on a date and are going to meet at the restaurant. "I did a storyboard with stick figures and a reference sheet to make sure that we stayed on track," said Durlach. Since the restaurant was open for business during the shoot, the team tried to get releases from as many diners as possible

Figure 7.13 Darren Durlach, video storyteller, Early Light Media. (Courtesy of Darren Durlach)

who were already "on the set" but not officially part of the film. The duo said they mixed their news mentality with the idea of shooting a fictional film. When it was time for the couple to eat dinner the filmmakers told them to be natural and not to pay any attention to the cameras. "This is where I went into news photographer mode—not giving direction, just hanging out," said Durlach. The final piece turned out to be more of a silent film, in which the visuals told the story with the assistance of a soundtrack. There was minimal dialogue; the story was told through actions and the series of shots included in the final edit.

Now let's take a close look at what makes up *Date Night*, with some commentary from Darren Durlach.

Section 1: Anxious Beginning

The first series of shots portrays the man as nervous about calling the woman, and is in black and white. The viewer sees the man pacing in his apartment, fidgeting with his mobile phone, and finally summoning up the courage to make a call. The woman is also shown in this section, waiting for a call, then receiving it and saying yes. "I really wanted to display a . . . sense of feeling anxious about something," said Durlach. Deliberate jump cuts show "a disconnect that you feel when something is uncomfortable," he said. *Note: Jump cuts are generally not something that should be done in news photography, but like anything else in editing, they can be used as a tool to help your visual storytelling.*

Figure 7.14 *Date Night*: Medium Shot of the man, nervous about making the call. (Courtesy of Early Light Media)

Section 2: "Rule of Waldo" Montage

This black and white montage, split down the middle with the man on one side and the woman on the other, is a series of tight shots of feet, shower heads, shaving, hair being blow-dried, clothes on a bed, and shoes walking on pavement. The montage compresses time and quickly takes the viewer from the telephone call all the way to the restaurant. Durlach said he used an editing rule called the *Rule of Waldo*. "If you've ever read a Waldo book, you do not turn the page until you've seen Waldo. In order to see Waldo faster, you need to zoom in on him." Durlach said he learned the rule from John Hyjek, an NBC News video editor and three-time winner of NPPA's Editor of the Year award. Speaking to Regina McCombs for an article on Poynter.org, Hyjek explained the rule this way:

> What happens when you find Waldo? You turn the page, of course. You move on to the next illustration. In the same vein, in video editing, the moment you glean the important information, it's time to move on to the next shot.

The tighter the shots, the faster clips can be cut. "The wider the shot, the longer it takes the viewer to absorb the shot, because they need to sit on it a

Figure 7.15 *Date Night*: Split Screen of the man shaving and the woman doing her hair. (Courtesy of Early Light Media)

little longer," Durlach explained. "Six wide shots in a row would be a blob of nothing nobody would understand."

Section 3: A Wizard of Oz Moment

At this point in *Date Night,* the footage turns from black and white into color. "We wanted a *Wizard of Oz* moment [watch the 1939 movie to see this device in action] at the restaurant that highlights the restaurant, which is the purpose of the ad. We want to make you feel like you are at an exciting, wonderful, colorful place," Durlach said. The walking feet fade into color and there is a shot of the man and woman meeting in front of the restaurant with a hug, and the restaurant logo being revealed in the background. The shot has minimal depth of field, with the actors out of focus in the foreground.

Figure 7.16 *Date Night*: Split Screen of the man and woman walking to their date. (Courtesy of Early Light Media)

Section 4: "Have a Seat"

This takes the couple into the restaurant, where a hostess greets them in a POV shot from the couple's perspective. It then cuts to the opening of a bottle of wine.

Figure 7.17 *Date Night*: Medium POV shot of the hostess at the restaurant. (Courtesy of Early Light Media)

"She is the actual hostess at the restaurant. We shot it three different ways so that we have options in the edit bay," said Durlach, referring to the post-production process.

Section 5: "Let's Eat"

A shot of food cooking in the kitchen is paired with a dessert, and the satisfied look of the woman enjoying the dessert. When planning a film, don't forget to think about the wardrobe for the actors. "Basically the girl had a few different outfits. There was one that was racier and one more casual," said Durlach. "It's a bar and grill, not a highfalutin' restaurant."

Figure 7.18 *Date Night*: Tight Shot of dessert on the table. (Courtesy of Early Light Media)

Section 6: Awkward Ending

This sequence shows the end of the date, with a very awkward hug, and the man looking dejected. "The whole point is to be as awkward as possible," said Durlach. But the twist is coming up.

Figure 7.19 *Date Night*: Medium Shot from behind the man as he hugs his date awkwardly. (Courtesy of Early Light Media)

Section 7: The Twist

The woman surprises the viewer by walking back to the man and giving him a not-insignificant kiss, for a nice meal out. Or perhaps the Metro Grill has made the difference.

So as to not lose light during the shoot, the producers shot both the beginning and end together. "We did not shoot in order. We shot them going into the restaurant, then immediately turned around and shot the ending, then we shot the dinner. We shot the hug, like, four different times. One over his shoulder, one over her shoulder," Durlach said.

Figure 7.20 *Date Night*: Circular Transition of the man and woman in an embrace while kissing. (Courtesy of Early Light Media)

Chapter Summary

Producing a multimedia story for entertainment purposes is all about working together as a team—it is about collaboration. You cannot make anything more than the simplest movie by yourself. There are many roles involved in the process. In fiction, at the very least you need actors and the ability to talk and work with them, and you need people who will look after the myriad requirements of creating and capturing a story on film: leadership, acting, picking the wardrobe, deciding on lens focal length and lighting.

Planning is a necessity. You can't just start filming without having thought in detail about what you are going to do, in terms of either production or story. In the real world everyone gets paid, and you can't afford to have workers standing around while you think.

At the same time, think visually. Everything discussed in this book builds up to the filming of a movie. All of that must be brought to bear as a story is created and each scene is crafted to be just right.

If there is one paramount idea in visual storytelling, it is that detailed planning will put a story on the path to success.

REVIEW QUESTIONS

1. What is the difference between writing a treatment and writing a synopsis?
2. How are character description sheets and a story bible important to a screenwriter?
3. What is the function of a logline?
4. What are a few specific rules of formatting that make a script look and feel more professional?
5. Name three different types of shots that would appear in a storyboard and what they can do for a story.
6. Why are wardrobe and set design so important to the development of characters?

 Chapter Exercise

1. Write a three- to five-page script for a three- to five-minute short fiction film that will entertain an audience. This project will involve writing documents such as a synopsis, a script, a storyboard, and a shot list.
2. Write a synopsis of the story that covers the five Ws (who, what, where, when, why). Make it a page long, at most, and formulate a logline.
3. Draw up a step outline and map out your story as it would be told on screen.
4. In addition to the synopsis, write a three- to five-page script that is executable by a small team.

This project must be produced with the assumption that it will be shown as an after-school special on network television, meaning that it is G-rated. The final production cannot include nudity, profanity, or anything not suitable for young children. The soundtrack must include only royalty-free music and/or sound effects.

 Key Terms

Audio recordist – In charge of audio on the set. In fiction films, audio is recorded both on the set and off. Sound effects can be recorded and added later to make sure that their quality is of high production value.

Blocking – A plan on paper for what the camera placement will be to cover specific action that happens in front of the lens.

Casting director – Finds and evaluates actors to play the various parts in a film.

Character description sheet – A breakdown of the specific traits of a film character. At the very least, all characters should have a name, age, and gender. This makes them more real than the generic "boy" or "girl" in a script.

Cinematographer – Responsible for anything that goes through the lens of the camera. Works hand-in-hand with the director of the film.

Close-up – Used to emphasize a single subject or specific thing. Shooting lots of close-ups will help in the edit, providing transitions to take the viewer to new scenes.

Director – Runs what happens on the set with the actors. This is the person who visualizes the script and tells everyone else what to do, making his or her vision into a filmed reality.

Extreme long shot – An establishing shot, in which the setting can be seen in its entirety or nearly so.

Gaffer – Sets up the lighting and electrical rigging of the set.

Location – Where you will film your story. Just because it is a dorm room in real life does not mean that it has to be a dorm room in your movie.

Logline – A logline describes in very few words who the main character is and what problem the whole movie will essentially solve, but not necessarily how that will happen.

Long shot – Often done with a telephoto lens, a long shot compresses the scene into one focal plane.

Medium shot – The medium shot generally shows a character from the waist up.

Point of view shot – Often made over the shoulder of a character, to give the viewer a sense of looking through that character's eyes.

Producer – For films, the executive producer is usually bankrolling the movie and handling the budget. In television, the producer is the point person who arranges the show from start to finish and hires the talent, makes decisions on the set and manages the day-to-day work.

Screenwriter – The person or team of people who comes up with the original idea for a story and puts it down on paper.

Setting – Where the story takes place.

Short film – An original motion picture that has a running time of forty minutes or less, including all credits.

Shot angles – On a storyboard, this is the notation of the angles at which the camera will be situated for each shot.

Shot list – A list noting the location and other details of every shot. It also includes the abbreviation for the type of shot it is.

Step outline – A description of all the different things that happen to a character in a story, presented in outline format.

Story bible – A binder containing all the information about a story, categorized.

Storyboard – The finished script as a visual plan, with each shot drawn out as closely as possible to how it will appear on the screen.

Synopsis – A preliminary, bare-bones statement of the concept of a story, including the beginning, the middle, and the end. It is a starting point for putting together the major elements of character and plot.

Table read – The reading aloud of a script by several people. It is a great way to get feedback from those reading the individual parts, with ideas about pacing, emotion, language, and character.

Video editor – Responsible for putting the various takes of the shoot together after shooting has begun. The video editor will get dailies back from each day's shoot. The editor will then put scenes together in the order dictated by the script.

Wide shot – Shows the scene in its entirety, while showing the activity of characters as well.

Writer's treatment – A sales tool for a screenplay that introduces characters, summarizes plot, and generally pitches a story.

Sources

Academy of Motion Picture Arts and Sciences. "85th Academy Awards." Oscars.org. Accessed December 1, 2013. http://www.oscars.org/awards/academyawards/rules/rule19.html.

August, John. "Generating Ideas: A Ton of Useful Information about Screenwriting from Screenwriter John August." Accessed October 2, 2013. http://johnaugust.com/2003/generating-ideas-2.

Bork, Erik. Conversation with author, October 4, 2013.

Bork, Erik. "Loglines Don't Tease." Flying Wrestler. Accessed October 2, 2013. http://www.flyingwrestler.com/2013./02/loglines-dont-tease/

Bradbury, Jeff. Conversation with author, October 21, 2013.

Catmull, Ed. "How Pixar Fosters Collective Creativity." (Cover Story) *Harvard Business Review* 86, no. 9 (September 2008): 64–72.

Durlach, Darren. Conversation with author, October 11, 2013.

Eiges, Sandy. *Hollywood Scriptwriting: How to Birth Your Idea into a Bankable Screenplay*. Amazon Digital Services, 2010.

FilmSkills. "FilmSkills: How to Shoot a Scene Part I: Blocking." Published February 10, 2013. Accessed March 10, 2015. http://www.youtube.com/watch?v=y9_LW5H2EC4&feature=youtube_gdata_player.

Fitzgerald, Sullivan. Conversation with author, December 15, 2013.

Friedman, Richard. Conversation with author, November 12, 2013.

Gadinsky, Brian. Conversation with author, October 3, 2013.

Giglio, Juliet. Conversation with author, October 31, 2013.

Goldstein, Brette. Conversation with author, November 12, 2013.

Howard, David, and Edward Mabley. *The Tools of Screenwriting: A Writer's Guide to the Craft and Elements of a Screenplay*. New York: St. Martin's Griffin, 1995.

Lawrence, David H., XVII. "What Is a 'Table Read'?" Acting Answers. Accessed July 7, 2013. http://www.actinganswers.com/what-is-a-table-read/.

McCombs, Regina. "Blurring Boundaries: What Print Journalists Can Learn from Video Editors." Poynter.org. Accessed October 27, 2013. http://www.poynter.org/latest-news/top-stories/83168/blurring-boundaries-what-print-journalists-can-learn-from-video-editors/.

Mickens, Michael. Conversation with author, November 11, 2013.

Pasquine, Frank. "The 5 Stages of Blocking a Scene." By Peter D. Marshall. New York Film Academy Blog, June 18, 2009. Accessed March 10, 2015. http://www.nyfa.edu/film-school-blog/the-5-stages-of-blocking-a-scene/.

The Script Lab. "Logline Library." Accessed November 4, 2013. http://thescriptlab.com/logline-library

Scriptologist. "The Logline: What It Is, Why You Need It, How to Write It." Accessed July 7, 2013. http://www.scriptologist.com/Magazine/Tips/Logline/logline.html.

Wheeler, Paul. *Practical Cinematography*. 2nd ed. Oxford; Boston: Elsevier/Focal Press, 2005.

8   MULTIMEDIA STORYTELLING IN JOURNALISM

How Can Multimedia Storytelling Be Used to Tell True-Life Stories?

In this chapter you will learn

- Types of nonfiction stories
- Ways to research story ideas
- How to prepare for a video interview
- Audio storytelling in journalism
- Ideas for finding "characters" in journalism
- How to determine story structure in a nonfiction video story
- An introduction to telling stories for broadcast journalism
- Ethical considerations for journalism

Introduction

There will always be heroes. In sports there will always be someone who makes the game-winning play, and in life there are all manner of triumphs and episodes of heroism. There will always be winners and losers. The winners will often have great stories to tell, but often the losers do as well. The world of people is full of stories that no one invented—they actually happened.

Nowadays the platforms and technology to tell these stories are changing at a rapid pace. In journalism, the Internet has been a huge, new platform of choice for some time now, but mobile is increasingly prevalent, and the number of ways to distribute content is growing. Not too long ago the buzz-word was *multimedia*. Now the word to think about is *digital*, which includes everything untraditional, from broadcast to mobile to web. Digital teams now program apps for everything from mobile phones and tablets to set-top boxes like Roku and gaming systems like the Xbox. These e-platform relationships are making the delivery of news faster than ever before through social media and digital platforms.

The one thing never to lose sight of, however, is that multimedia content is storytelling. As the technology to produce content gets better and easier to use, it is still crucial to know how to generate stories that people will watch, and find characters to whom they will gravitate and relate.

Nonfiction Story Types

News-Driven Multimedia Reporting and Storytelling

Video storytelling is no longer the exclusive realm of the high-end broadcast camera operator who carries a $20,000 camera on his or her shoulder. The nationally distributed USA TODAY newspaper, based in McLean, VA, takes a "digital first" approach to everything they cover. "Our print reporters and digital reporters are the same reporters, so the person that I am teaching to do video is the person that is writing the cover story for the newspaper tomorrow," said Steve Elfers, managing editor for multimedia at the company. "There is no line between teams. We have a digital-first mentality here, and then the paper draws what they need of the next day's edition . . . Obviously we've never successfully played a video in the newspaper."

Now that all journalists can carry a mobile phone to shoot and report a story, and have the added ability to edit their footage on that same device in the field, journalism is changing. Traditionally, broadcast news reporters have needed to report both features and hard news, and to do both with ease. Now, people who go into journalism need to be capable in all things multimedia— whether they are working at a newspaper, television station, or digital-only media outlet. "You should know how to shoot, how to edit, how to effectively use social media, how to be able to tell stories, how to be able to write," said C. J. Hoyt, news director for WTOL11 in Toledo, Ohio.

In journalism, video has been adopted by all media outlets and is no longer limited to just broadcast television. Newspapers are making video a part of what they do every day, now that the web has made broadcasting so accessible and relatively easy. Much early newspaper video did not include a reporter track, but as newspaper video evolved, reporters and photographers realized that they needed to insert their voices to help tie pieces together. This became especially important in a deadline-oriented environment that was changing from putting out news the next morning, to putting it out right now.

At many newspapers video is not just for photographers but for reporters too. Nor is a lack of gear any longer an obstacle to video storytelling. Everyone in a newsroom can now take photographs and shoot video with their mobile phones—and in HD quality.

"If you are on the scene of something, you shoot a little bit of video and get it back immediately," said Danese Kenon, the assistant managing editor for visuals at the Pittsburgh Post-Gazette. "Everyone has this tool. Everyone can now visually report the news."

Timeliness is a major concern for websites and digital content providers in regard to breaking news. Journalists can now upload a photograph or video clip much faster than ever before. A journalist can shoot a video on a mobile device, edit it on an iPad or an iPhone, and post it to a website literally within minutes. A raw video clip doesn't have the quality of a well-polished, edited video, which might have involved hours at an editing station, but it can be available to viewers much, much more quickly.

Kenon is involved in the *Star*'s video training program, which teaches everyone at the newspaper how to report with video. "You can stay on the street and keep reporting the news . . . You get the information out there quick, tell what you know so far," she said.

Technology is also giving rise to new capabilities for live broadcasting. Both television and newspaper reporters can now go live using portable uplink kits, backpacks that contain multiple cellular phones that transmit a high-quality video signal back to a TV station or newspaper website. All that is needed is a reporter willing and able to report live. "It enables us to get a live shot faster and from more locations than we can do with a traditional live truck, particularly in breaking news situations or in situations where we need to be able to get to a particular location where a truck can't drive," said WTOL's Hoyt.

"It has given us a lot more opportunity to do things that we have not been able to do before," said Bob Redell, morning show reporter for KNTV in San Jose, CA, who has used a backpack uplink kit from the top of one of the arches of the Golden Gate Bridge:

> To push a button and be live 700 feet above the water, with the foghorn blasting, the mist of the bay coming in . . . it was amazing for us, it was just monumental, it made for good TV . . . To be looking down and seeing the suspension cables disappear into the fog, it was just one of the shots you don't get.

Figure 8.01 Bob Redell (foreground) transmits a live shot from the top of the Golden Gate Bridge. (Courtesy of Bob Redell)

VIDEO AT NEWSPAPERS

At newspapers across the country owned by Gannett, a program called "TurboVideo" was set up to train reporters and photographers on how to shoot video for news storytelling. Nancy Andrews, managing editor for digital media at the *Detroit Free Press*, explained how that effort went:

> The team came up with specific paradigms for shooting video, which include instances where a journalist would shoot raw video only. Another paradigm was the "look-live feature," which is a narrated cut piece. For example, if there was a fire last night, the journalist needs to add information that tells what is going on and give the viewer something they do not see or hear from the video itself.
>
> We trained over 1,500 journalists in the first three months of 2013. It was one of the funnest, most rewarding things I have ever done.

Andrews realized that the videos that the *Free Press* had been doing, many without a narrated track, sometimes needed more information added to them. "Not all videos that people watch on the web will have the added benefit of being seen with an associated text or graphic," she said. At times, especially in news-driven situations, it is difficult to get all the information from a subject that is needed to inform the viewer about the story. The reporter needs to gather information at a press conference, from a source, or even from a press release, write that information into a script, and track it over the images that tell the story.

"I think when you are reporting you should be able to tell great stories. It doesn't matter what the topic is; you've got to be able to tell a great story," said Hoyt. "I don't want people to get the idea that a story is only a story if it includes narrative, or characters, or things like that. Great storytelling is about effectively delivering content to the viewers so that they are engaged."

Many times reporters are just delivering the facts from the scene of a story as they find them out. This content can be delivered in multiple ways, from social media to video. "A lot of the time, those facts alone are very compelling. When you are telling someone what happened, you are telling them the story of that breaking news," Hoyt said.

Profile-Driven Storytelling

Profiles have long been a staple of newspaper journalism. They are great ways to introduce an audience to an interesting or influential person, and they are an important kind of story. Profiles can be of individuals or leaders of communities, but they can also be stories about places or businesses, or question-and-answer reports that give insight into specific topics. Profiles are also a great way for beginning storytellers to practice the craft and get a feel for multimedia storytelling.

A very common type of profile looks at somebody who does a specific job. Starting out is simple: Animals will always attract an audience, so search on the web for, say, "dog sitter." Armed with a list of dog sitters in the area, start calling them up and asking to do a story on them. It is not a story yet, per se—it's really only a profile. It does not become a story until more information about the dog sitter comes out—the route they followed to dog sitting, how they go about the job, how they find clients. Learning more about them will make it possible to build a story arc with plot points, reveals, and surprise, all of which help to tell an actual story. If the person being profiled truly has no interesting story—and this might merely be a sign of not having looked hard enough or having asked the right questions—you can still create a solid profile. But it is surprising how often intriguing backgrounds turn up.

"When making the choice to tell a story, it serves you and the story to find out what is life-and-death in it," said Stephanie Hubbard, a documentary filmmaker and teacher based in Los Angeles who is also a story consultant and story coach:

> So a student might state, "I am going to do a profile of a taco truck," and I'll ask them, "What is life-and-death about a taco truck?" I really encourage them to think about what life-and-death questions are contained in their story. It can be an emotional thing. What are the real kinds of deep, emotional issues that we can find in our world?

"What really makes a good story is a transformation," Hubbard went on:

> In order to have a transformation, your hero must lose everything and then realize that they can keep going. . . . A good place to start is to ask, "What does the hero want?" Ideally for your story, what the hero wants needs to be impossible to achieve. When they can't get what they want, they need to transform. Otherwise it's just a taco truck, and it's a guy talking about how he started this taco truck in 1983. Which is okay, but before you settle for no transformation, take the time to find it.

Character-Driven Dramatic Storytelling

Sometimes a profile is all that you will have time to do. Deadlines come quickly in the news business, and even when there seems to be all the time in the world, a deadline can be moved up or a new assignment can pop up when you least expect it. Producing a profile piece is not a bad or lesser thing. They happen a lot, especially in nonfiction news work.

When you start to embark on a profile of a person, however, always be thinking about going deeper. Look beyond the person as he or she tells you about doing this and that, and so on. Seek out and take that next step in your interview. "Learn to ask the why behind the why," said Bruce Strong, associate professor of multimedia photography and design at the S.I. Newhouse School of Public Communications at Syracuse University. "We are good at asking the first why—the surface-level why—but when you ask the second why, 'Why do you do that,' it becomes much more difficult." Strong said he defines story as "the tale of someone who wants something and who overcomes—or is overcoming—conflict to get it." In other words, there is a protagonist who has ambition, and who is willing to go through a transformation in order to achieve that ambition.

In character-driven dramatic storytelling, the person you are interviewing will most likely be the person that the story will be about. The person and his or her interactions with others will drive the storyline. To revisit the example of the dog sitter, what may have started out as a profile can easily morph into a dramatic story if, after you've learned about what your character does, you figure out the *why* of it, and then tell that story. For example, say the dog sitter's prior job was being an accountant, sitting in a silent, stuffy office all day. Then he was diagnosed with an ailment, which forced him to reassess life and realize that being an accountant was not his life's dream; he desired to work with animals instead. This is where a profile can turn into a character-driven story that has elements of transformation and drama. Eric Maierson, a producer at MediaStorm, a multimedia production company based in Brooklyn, NY, defined that last term this way: "Drama is a tension between what someone wants and what someone doesn't get."

Go beyond the standard "five Ws" (who, what, where, when, why). Make the reporting of these facts into the unveiling of reveals, each uncovering a little more about the character. Drama comes from conflict. A profile, while it tells a lot about a person, is most likely void of conflict. Once conflict arises, a real story starts to happen. In the book *Writing Dramatic Nonfiction*, William Noble writes:

> If conflict is necessary for fiction to work, why shouldn't the same be true with nonfiction? Conflict is a device for developing drama, and all writers—fiction writers as well as nonfiction writers—understand that drama and dramatic impact touch and hold readers. (26)

When looking for a character, don't settle for someone who just has a good story to tell. Find a character who would make a good story to *show*. It is the visual journalist's job to show a person's life through images, so try not to base an entire story solely on interviews about past events that you do not have any visuals to show. Interviews are important, but a character's visual moments and interactions—many of which can be nonverbal—will be just as important, and sometimes more so.

When writing a text-only narrative, talking about the past is much easier than it is for a visual storyteller, who must communicate with images. "Show me, don't tell me," says Strong. "Talk to that person and figure out something else that is happening in their life now, and how those things from his past play a role, but look for active things."

Maierson explained the importance of seeing dramatic interactions firsthand:

> Drama is the conflict that occurs when a person can't obtain what he or she wants, so this lack of resolution propels the character to try again, with ever-increasing stakes. You don't get what you want, so you try another method of trying to achieve that. It's that interaction between objective and denial-of-objective that creates the tension that makes us try to figure out what is going to happen next. [That] is always going to be more dramatic if we see that interaction happening firsthand.

To explain it a different way, it is one thing to have someone talk about a story that happened to them, like a police officer talking about chasing down and catching a thief on the street, and quite another to let a viewer actually be there, feeling the motion, hearing the police officer's running footfalls and breathless shouts. This in-the-moment experience is the drama that captivates viewers. Many times in character-driven nonfiction storytelling, the interview can act as the spine of the story, providing a framework for dramatic moments. Rachel Ballon, in her book *Blueprint for Screenwriting: A Complete Writer's Guide to Story Structure and Character Development*, defines the concept of a story's spine: "This is the skeleton that holds your entire foundation together . . . Without the spine or structure, you have no story, just unconnected scenes which become episodic" (35). Interviews are at their best, therefore, when they are providing context for vivid moments.

So, to take a story to the next level, think about going beyond just an interview. Visuals of a person going about his or her daily life will bring the spoken story elements together. Situations that the character experiences can build up drama in the story itself. While capturing your character's life as it happens, be a "fly on the wall" in the truest sense, in which the character ceases to be aware of the storyteller and goes about life as normal. In film this is called *cinéma vérité*. In their book *Audio in Media*, Stanley Alten and Doug Quin define the term: It means to "record life without imposing on it; production values do not motivate or influence the content. Whatever is recorded has to speak for itself" (317).

Look for situations that capture both audio and visual moments of characters revealing who they really are. Usually this means spending a lot of time with a subject. A fifteen-minute interview paired with some visuals won't suffice. There needs to be enough time for the storyteller and subject to get to know each other on a more human level, and "parachuting" into someone's life for a few hours usually won't accomplish this.

Character-driven dramatic stories can be quick-hit pieces that can be told in a day's shooting, as those often seen on the daily news, or they can be extended stories that take effort, patience, understanding, and, unavoidably, time.

Go beyond the initial, shallow formalities, such as "My name is John Doe and I do this for a living; it is a fun way to live your life," etc. If you can get people to open up, most likely they will respond to your interest in them and reveal still more about their own lives. "Look for the emotional elements, as few words as possible. First love, or the pain of leaving, or finding joy, something . . . that we can all relate to . . . Find the emotional core of the story," said Strong.

Once the subject has begun to open up, start to think about how that person has transformed or changed over time, moved from one state to another, or overcome conflict or adversity to become something different. "Understand not just what they do, but how they changed," Strong said. There are all sorts of directions to explore for the next part of your story, all kinds of questions to ask. Ask about the victories, defeats, and challenges they've experienced. Ask them where they think they might be now in life.

It is important when doing nonfiction stories to constantly think not just about the interview, but about the visuals themselves and how the interview will tie into them. Your ultimate goal is to show your viewers the subject's life, and to emotionally connect the viewer to the point that they are actively engaged and feeling for the character through the film. "Be willing to stand in the darkness and also celebrate victory with your subjects, the people in front of you. Look for present-tense stories; learn to find that emotional core that really ties all of your stories together," said Strong.

Finding Story Ideas

People whose everyday lives are spent sitting at home and surfing the web, or watching television day in and day out, never realize the sheer volume of stories that exist out in the real world. On the other hand, people who get out of their comfort zones and explore the world, and the people in it, find new ideas everywhere they go. It is difficult to teach the details of this—becoming a seeker of stories can require a big shift in thinking and temperament. It's an aspect of journalism that goes well outside the scope of this book. For now, here are some basic ways to start releasing your inner storyteller:

1. **Be curious.**
   You must see every day as a new day, all the time. Observe and think critically about everything you encounter.
2. **Check your surroundings.**
   Wherever you go, be aware of your surroundings. Does something stand out? Is anything new and different?
3. **Check local bulletin boards.**
   At local grocery or hardware stores, look at the bulletin boards in the vestibules. All sorts of possible story ideas can be found there, everything from someone looking to start a new business to someone looking for a lost dog or cat.

4. **Read the local newspaper and other periodicals, and watch the broadcast outlets.**

   Quite often, a one-off daily story would make a better in-depth story. Many times one news outlet won't be willing or able to follow through and make a story more in-depth. This is an opportunity to make contact and delve deeper.

5. **Localize a national story.**

   National news items often have a local angle, especially political stories that put people on opposing sides. Find the people who represent the different sides of an issue and tell their stories.

6. **Use Google and other search engines.**

   Do a search on an interesting topic. As mentioned above, a search for pet sitters will almost certainly yield local results, which can be followed up on.

7. **Ask people questions.**

   Journalists meet all sorts of people every day. When meeting new individuals, set out to learn as many things about them as possible. Ask them who is the most interesting person they know or knew. More than likely they will tell a story about someone, perhaps down the street, who could become the focus of a great, character-driven story.

8. **Listen to anyone and everything.**

   Be outgoing. Go to the coffee shop in the morning, ask to sit with the regulars, ask them about their problems and struggles. Find a fast-food restaurant where locals hang out. Just listening to people's views can lead to stories.

9. **Collect story ideas over time and write them down in a journal.**

   Always be collecting ideas, and then brainstorm with them. Look for common themes or connections that could contribute to a narrative. Often ideas will play off one another.

Covering Story Ideas

"The view from the editor's desk can be very different than the view from the field," said Jonathan Miller, executive director of the independent, nonprofit journalism cooperative Homelands Productions (homelands.org). Homelands gets grants from foundations to produce features and documentaries for public radio shows and the web. "Editors will often say, 'I like this story, I like the drama. Let's go with this guy as the main character. I like how he's fighting these people here. And let's go with this other guy for the opposite side,'" Miller said. "Then you go out as a reporter to do that story, and you find out that it's not quite so simple."

Sometimes an editor's or boss's idea for the direction of a story might not exactly match what is actually happening on scene. This is normal, but always make sure to relay the situation back so that your supervisors are not left expecting something they will never see.

Sometimes the person on whom a story will be based is not in any way what the editor had imagined. A decision might need to be made about whether to continue with the story, to attack it in a different way so it engages an audience, or simply to move on.

Story idea generation happens the same way for news media across all platforms, for all media. Editors or producers try to determine just what will be the news of the day, and when spot news is not breaking they still need content to fill their pages, paper or virtual, or their airtime. As Greg Bledsoe, a multimedia journalist who both shoots and reports his own stories for NBC 7 in San Diego, explained:

> Producers in the meeting—they always have something in their minds as to what they want. They wouldn't send you out on assignment if they didn't have an idea as to what the story is and how it fits into the newscast.

In broadcast journalism, a news producer plays the general role of an assigning editor at a newspaper. Producers are a big part of the decision-making process. Robin Clutters plays this role at Channel 4, KCNC-TV, in Denver, CO: "It starts out with our morning meeting. Together, collectively, we assign what everyone is going to do. After that I will go back to my desk and start selecting the rest of the stories to fill the newscast." As a producer, Clutters gathers story content from wire services, press releases, and news tips sent to the station, then sends reporters and photographers into the field to try to generate packages that can be aired for that evening's broadcast. "The pressure generally falls on the producer when the stories fall through," Clutters said. "If a reporter doesn't have something by one o'clock, then we will move on to plan B." Bledsoe also weighed in on the ever-changing nature of stories:

> The reality is that when we get out there and meet people and talk to people or find that nobody will talk to us, things change. The challenge as a reporter is to not let those preconceived notions interfere with what you go and try and do.

It is important to stay on the path and dig for a story. Get prepared with the necessary information, and know whom to talk to. Keep an open mind, and let a story unfold the way it really is. If the story ends up being something different from what was envisioned in the morning meeting, that's fine. Approach every story with an attitude of heading out into the unknown, to uncover what is really there, and be truthful about the events being covered. In addition, keep in mind that not every story will generate award-winning visuals. Sometimes it is a struggle to figure out what the visuals for a story should actually be, and you may need to resort to graphics. "I try to use graphics in an interesting way—I am not just throwing numbers up on the screen," said Bledsoe.

"Nine out of ten things we do in this life is just general news. Make something out of whatever you've fallen into. That is where the craft comes in," said

Bob Dotson, a veteran reporter for the *Today Show* on NBC. "If you become aware of the building blocks of your craft, then you can take what seems to be just an ordinary experience and really create an experience that people will remember."

Covering a Beat

Newspaper reporters often cover beats, or specific areas in which they have some history, expertise, and the all-important contact list. Stories on a given topic automatically fall to them. Sometimes beat reporting can include something as simple as covering the local board of supervisors, or regional tourism. Beat reporters tend to be aware of what will be discussed at the meetings they cover, and they have done their homework so that nothing takes them by surprise.

"I feel like I am really doing my job when I am tuned into things down on the ground," said Matt Chittum, who covers city government for *The Roanoke Times* in Roanoke, VA. Chittum said he wants to stay ahead of the process:

> When I hear about things from the residents and I take it to city hall and ask, "What about this?" instead of the other way around, where city hall takes some action and I go back into the neighborhood and ask, "What do you think?" . . . If I am writing about something that has already happened, and then I am going to ask people what they think of it when it is too late for them to effect any change, then I really have not done my job the best way that I could do it.

Chittum also tries to shape his stories outside the usual journalistic formula:

> The inverted pyramid is based on a total lack of faith—that the reader is not going to read to the end. I never bought into that . . . any time I get the opportunity to maneuver the information in a story into a position where I can tell it beginning, middle, and end, that is what I do.

Chittum explained that he often sees his stories in a cinematic way:

> There is drama and story in all kinds of things in a board of supervisors meeting . . . Write in a more visual way, so that you bring a reader into a story the same way the opening shot in a film does . . . You describe a wide shot and then you tighten until you get the focus of your story. It really is just bringing other artistic storytelling mediums and applying them to what we do.

Information/Data-Driven Stories

Data-driven storytelling does not have to be all charts, bar graphs, and databases. A story can start with data and then move in whatever direction the data leads. Part of thinking about data storytelling is figuring out how to categorize the data itself, so that it can be easily understood.

Think about how the data will need to be presented. Will it be observed data, collected in a qualitative way, such as the appearance, quality, and state of repair of houses in a certain neighborhood? *Qualitative data* involves description and categorization. Or will it be *quantitative data*—the assessed values, square footage, age, or likelihood of bank ownership of those houses? Quantitative data are hard numbers gathered from a source or from research.

Databases are great places to find stories, since compared and assessed data can say a lot about a community, organization, population, or trend. Once harvested from the data, conclusions can then be presented in a narrative form.

Data journalism also is about filtering complex information for specific data that can then be visualized in an information graphic. For the purposes of this book, data-driven journalism is regarded as a rich source of stories. We are not going to cover how to make data-driven web applications or how to make a data visualization; it is more important to think about how data fits in with the concept of story. Alison Young, an investigative reporter for *USA TODAY* in Arlington, VA, put it this way:

> I think if you look at the story in a holistic sense, the data is not the story, the data is a tool that helps you figure out the story. The data for me is a tool in the same way that interviewing someone is a tool, in the same way that going and looking at court records is a tool.

All of those things are the building blocks that ultimately result in the story, whether the story is told using text or video, or maybe even a photo gallery or an interactive presentation.

"My story ideas tend to come from reading the news, reading the reports, talking to experts, seeing trends, and then having those things raise questions," Young said. One project Young worked on for *USA TODAY*, called "Ghost Factories," arose from an article she found in a scientific journal. The story spoke of 430 factory sites throughout the country that time had forgotten. Young did not have a database from which to pull the data, so she created her own by going to some of the sites and collecting soil samples. "We were able to say pretty instantly how much lead was in the soil," said Young, who worked with a newsroom-wide team to present the data points on *USA TODAY*'s website, in interactive form. She was also able to get lead blood-test data from certain state health departments, and cull the results of children who were tested. "The story wasn't the data, but the data was sought out [as part of the reporting] to answer the question: Are there more children that are lead poisoned in the area around [a] lead smelter?" explained Young. "In that particular case the data wasn't good enough to help us answer that question. It is asking the question, 'Is there data that we can find that might help answer something?'"

Researching Stories with Data

Curiosity can take a story idea only so far. Even though video is a visual medium, and the goal is usually great characters whose stories can be told that way, a story might need to start with cold, hard data that points in the needed direction. Getting that data might require breaking out of that friendly, familiar comfort zone to do some reporting. From stories with a national scope to those with a more local focus, data sets can help focus a reporter's efforts and uncover real sources to interview.

"Data is a source, just like anyone else," said Matt Waite, a professor of practice at the College of Journalism and Mass Communications at the University of Nebraska. "It has flaws, it has a point of view, it has a reason to exist, and all of those things may not be what you exactly want them to be, but that is true about people as well."

Waite teaches reporting and digital product development. He was the principal developer of the Pulitzer Prize-winning PolitiFact.com, an independent fact-checking journalism website. He gave these tips on mining data for stories:

> So the way to find out stories in data, is to think of data as a source, and the searching, the queries, and the analysis you are doing is really just asking a question. It is just like interviewing a person. The questions need to be carefully worded so that you get a proper answer.

Waite said that when comparing data sets to reveal something like a decline in population from one year to another, it is important to avoid vague or

Figure 8.02 Matt Waite, a professor of practice at the College of Journalism and Mass Communications at the University of Nebraska. (Courtesy of Matt Waite)

ambiguous queries: "Data is not so helpful and not so intuitive, so if you ask it a dumb question, and you do so in-artfully, it will give you a dumb answer."

For example, a video story about the decline of a particular town could begin with a trip to a local restaurant, to seek out characters who can talk about the town's former days. It would also be possible, however, to dig deeper by searching accessible data. The key question would be, "What data would answer this question, and how can I chart this decline?" Begin by thinking about transactional data that may be available, such as sales tax receipts. With a data set from state or local officials, it would be possible to break down the sales tax revenue. To determine if a significant number of people are emigrating from the community and moving elsewhere, look at real estate data and check to see how long it takes for vacant properties to be filled, if they are filled at all. Check to see if the amount of rental housing is on the rise. Much of this information can be gathered from the census bureau. The day-to-day functions of government are tracked and recorded, and much of this information is available to the public.

As a visual journalist, look also for vocal characters at town supervisory and board meetings, who could provide good sound bites and have plenty to say on camera. But remember Waite's cautionary note:

> It is easy to go to the town council meeting and look for the loud one. It is much harder to find the data that presents what is going on, and then use that data to narrow in on somebody who might be able to talk about being in that situation.

Data isn't just a source of information for graphics, which help viewers digest complicated information. Data can actually kick-start storytelling. "The data will often produce the person in your lead anecdote. You can find the person that exemplifies the trend that you have found in the data. That data can guide you to that person," said Waite.

Wireframing a Story

Whether putting together a fiction or nonfiction story, there is a handy method to keep ideas in order that also provides a foolproof way to write a script or develop a storyline for a film. It isn't a detailed structure like a story arc; it's more of a sketch or "wireframe" that indicates where a story can and should go. (See "The Wireframe" section in Chapter 4 for more information on this concept.) Anne Lamott, in her book *Bird by Bird: Some Instructions on Writing and Life*, refers to a practice called the ABDCE formula (not quite the order of letters you're used to) for writing a short story, attributing it to a lecture by nationally acclaimed novelist Alice Adams (62). The following sections suggest ways to apply the elements of the ABDCE formula to visual storytelling.

A Is for Action

Start a story with some type of active moment. Find a way, through dialogue, sound, or visuals, to engage the audience to the point where they forget what they are doing and become fully involved in the story. Viewers should feel like they are there, experiencing just what you did while shooting the story. Seek out creative ways to draw the viewer in. If the story is about baseball, start out with the crack of a bat, spectators cheering, the sprinting, thudding, and panting of a runner rounding third. Put viewers in the scene. Engage them, so that it seems there is no better way to spend their time than by watching your film.

B Is for Background

This is where to introduce the main character, or hero. It's a perfect opportunity for viewers to learn about how the main character came to be who he or she is. It is also a good place to hint to the viewer about what the future might hold, or the people the lead character might come upon later. A good visual device for this is the flashback, in which the viewer is taken back in time. These are often transitioned to by using dissolves, a technique covered in Chapter 6.

D Is for Development

This is where conflict is introduced. The character starts to experience—or is shown to be dealing with—conflict that develops the story and further engages viewers. What is the protagonist up against? As the antagonist attempts to hold the protagonist back, the protagonist does whatever he or she can to keep forging ahead, further developing the story.

C Is for Climax

This is what the story has been building toward—a conflict of larger proportions. This can be the final opportunity for the main character to try to succeed in overcoming the antagonist, be it another person or a force. This is where the antagonist and protagonist will have their final battle—a sporting competition, trial, interview, or whatever—or where the two lovers finally meet. It's when the bulldozers arrive at the home someone has been trying to protect, when a key surgery or medical test is performed, when a young actor goes out onto the stage.

E Is for Ending

This is where the story is resolved, and the viewer is satisfied that the story has ended. This is called the *falling action*—the moment after the climax when things wind down. Neighbors cheer (or grumble about) the preservation of the house; the medical test results are dealt with; the actor receives congratulations for a great performance. Viewers get a satisfying view of the new world created by the story, but it doesn't mean they can't be left wanting more.

Audio Storytelling

"It really stands out when you use sound in a creative way," said Sam Eaton, a freelance multiplatform journalist who does work for Public Radio International (PRI) and National Public Radio (NPR):

> I always go into a story saying, "This is the way I want to structure it." I have the story in my head but it is constantly shifting. I look for detail popping up; maybe how I thought it is going isn't [working]. I try and see how I can redirect the story.

Eaton got his start doing radio, but he has transformed himself into a multiplatform, multimedia journalist in the truest sense. He can produce a written piece, a radio piece, and a video piece for multiple platforms, all from one story, and get them into national publications on television and the web. "The sum is greater than the parts. If I can tell the story in different ways and through different media, that is just more ways that I can tell the story," he said.

Planning out a story is just as important in audio as it is in a visual medium. "Early on, I learned the power of the outline," said Jonathan Miller of Homelands Productions:

> Even if it's just a list of scenes in what seems like a logical order. I've found it to be extraordinarily helpful, both before I start reporting and after I get back with my material. Of course the second outline often looks nothing like the first one.

Planning helps at both the story level and the scene level, explained Miller:

> In every scene you're trying to paint a picture. It's not that different from working with images—you need close-ups and medium shots and long shots. In some ways it's like a construction project, gathering individual sounds so you can combine them and layer them so they seem three-dimensional. But it can be pretty creative. When you go out with your microphone you're like a butterfly collector with a net. You have a pretty good idea of what you're looking for, but you keep your ears open for surprises.

So just as in video, audio requires meticulous care to put the listener into the place being portrayed. For an eight-minute audio piece, two to three minutes of ambient audio will be needed to keep the viewer mentally in that place.

"I love radio and find it to be really powerful," Miller said:

> Maybe it's just my social group, but constantly I am hearing, "Did you hear on NPR this morning that story about whatever?" I think people are really

touched by radio. We are wired to hear stories through the human voice. Also, when we consume radio we are almost always doing something else. So it insinuates itself into your life the way other media don't. If you're cutting carrots or washing dishes, the story seems to find its way into your brain more readily.

Adding Audio as Texture

Several times we have mentioned the importance of listening to the sounds around you, and constantly seeking appropriate natural sounds to go with images. This requires "seeing with your ears." The parts of a soundtrack that give a project real color, that put the listener "there" in the audio scene, are all the small, otherwise unnoticed sounds. In radio storytelling these sounds are called *actualities*, or "*nat*" sound, or *ambient* sound, and they lend authenticity and immediate reality to the story. For a story about a farm, for example, just imagine all the sounds that can be collected and used, large and small. There are tractors, the mooing of cattle, the rhythmic clicking of irrigation, gravel crunching under a truck's wheels.

In a document Stephen Hooker hands out for his talk at the Annual NPPA News Video Workshop in Norman, OK, the television photojournalist writes:

> Just as one looks for the shots that could be the opening or closing of the story, listen for the unique sounds that may trump a visual as the better choice for these key parts of the storytelling process. Edit sound like pictures: wide, medium, and tight. A distinctive sound will always make a distracted viewer look up and watch your pictures.

The wireless lavalier microphone is a clever tool for gathering these sounds, and can be used in innovative and unusual ways. Who said it needs to be clipped to a person? Place it near sounds and have it transmit them back to the camera. If a subject is working at a construction site, attach the microphone to the shovel to capture the harsh scrape of metal on dirt.

Editing an Interview Track

When doing a profile piece with a long interview, it will be mandatory to go through that interview to find the juiciest nuggets of information that help to tell that person's story. It's much like writing a profile piece for a newspaper: You are writing about a particular person and have amassed a lot of information about that individual, and you can't use it all. You need to go through your notes to find the best quotes to tell the story. This narrative audio track, your "A-roll," is also called the *spine* of the piece. "Audio provides the all-important narrative spine necessary for linear media productions," states a document produced by MediaStorm and called "Gathering Audio, Tips and Tricks from the MediaStorm Workflow."

In nonfiction work editing the audio first is often called a *radio edit*, in which the audio serves as the driving force behind the visuals. "I think it's important to start with a radio cut to get an idea of how the story makes sense and go from there," said Evelio Contreras, a video producer for CNN.

Relying on interview audio as the primary asset in storytelling has its drawbacks. If the final piece is simply an interview that drones on and on for two or more minutes, there's a real risk of boring the audience. Try to weave the interview into and around ambient sounds that will engage viewers and bring them into the story. "You should treat non-interview footage like a radio cut as well, to get everything down on paper and see it before you start laying it out," Contreras said.

It is also important to be precise with questions and in editing a piece together. Narrative-driven video is very popular among newspaper videojournalists. Essentially, it is video done entirely with natural sound paired with interview audio, and it contains no voice-over or narration. It often relies on the subject to tell the story, essentially giving the subject a voice. Since the interview is so key to the narrative-driven piece, it's important to do it right from the outset. According to MediaStorm's "Gathering Audio" document:

> Audio can help communicate information that may not be communicated as well via images or text. For example, emotion or humor that is heard in a person's voice through word choice, pauses or breaks in their voice, or music to create a mood, or ambient sound that transports you to a location.

Narrative-driven stories can have an authentic, documentary, "in the moment" feel, if done right. "The problem with natural-sound stories, in my personal experience, is that they are just not usually clear," said Scott Jensen, chief photographer at KING5 in Seattle and twice named as the Ernie Crisp Television News Photographer of the Year, the highest honor in the country given to a working television photojournalist by the National Press Photographers Association:

> You have a much better chance of creating a memorable story when you structure a story with objective writing, rather than trying to smash all of these pieces of sound together when you have no control over what the person is saying.

In television, speed is the number one priority. A package needs to be shot, tracked, and ready to be aired within hours or sometimes even minutes. As Jensen noted, "There are some fantastically produced nat sound stories online on Vimeo and newspaper websites, but my suspicion is that they are not putting these things together in five hours. I could be wrong."

Merely creating a story with just the audio, then laying in the visuals, is not necessarily the way to go about telling a true-to-form documentary video. Do not be fooled into thinking that just laying an interview over random video of a person doing things (B-roll) is as good as interweaving visuals with matched, ambient sounds. B-roll has its place in many videos, but there is an important difference between laying audio on top of visuals and shooting *cinéma vérité* footage with real moments. This real, in-the-moment content has a purer feeling, which serves to engage viewers and put them in a place that enriches their experience. Remember that the story needs to be pushed forward, with a story arc and plot points guiding the way.

ROB ROSENTHAL'S TIPS FOR RECORDING GOOD AUDIO

Rob Rosenthal is an independent producer and a teacher. He's the host for How Sound, the PRX (Public Radio Exchange) podcast on radio storytelling. He ran the Salt Institute for Documentary Studies' radio track for eleven years, and he is now the lead teacher for the Transom Story Workshop, which launched in the fall of 2011. This is a story he wrote for Transom.org, a website about radio storytelling (used with permission from Transom.org: http://transom.org/?p=27411).

Figure 8.03 Rob Rosenthal is an independent radio producer and teacher. (Photo by Ed Kashi)

Before the First Question

You have a story. Check.

You have characters. Check.

You have a sense of what you want to record for ambient sound and active tape (the close-up sound of people doing things). Check.

You've researched the topic and the people in the story. And, you've got a rough outline of how you think the story might be told.

Check. Check.

Now it's time to head out and start interviewing. What needs to happen before you ask the first question? Here's my preparation checklist, the tasks I tackle before I start interviewing. Follow this list and, while I can't guarantee a stellar interview or a perfect story, I do think it will increase your likelihood for success.

1. **Type out your questions.** I print them and bring them with me to the interview. More on that in a moment.
2. **Check your gear bag.** Got everything? Recorder. Mic. Extra batteries (that you've tested). Mic cable (ideally more than one since they're "the weakest link"). Headphones. A fully charged cell phone. Notebook and pens.
3. **Clothes.** Yeah. I know. I sound like your mother. But, do you have the right clothes on? A colleague recently told me they wore sneakers to a hog farm—oops! Also, I never wear sunglasses during an outside interview because I want to make eye contact. So, I always bring a baseball cap to shade my eyes.

(Continued . . .)

(*. . . continued*)

4. **Double check the directions and leave early.** Let's just say I hate being late. It's rude.

5. **Re-read your questions.** I almost never place my typed questions in front of me during an interview. I want my interviews to feel like a conversation. Having questions sitting in front of me is a distraction, a barrier to dialogue. So, instead, I'll re-read my questions just before I go in to do an interview. That way, they're fresh in my mind. I might read them in the driveway or sometimes I'll check them over a short distance from my destination so I don't look peculiar sitting in the driveway for a long time. When I'm done, I'll fold the questions up and put them in my shirt pocket. (At some point in my interview, usually when I've run out of questions, I'll pull the list out and make sure I haven't missed anything.)

6. **"Pull a Radiolab."** It seems like the folks at Radiolab start recording on their way to the interview—walking up to the door, saying hello, etc. If you do that, just be sure to tell your interviewee in advance that you'll be showing up with your gear on and recording.

7. **Politely take control.** Once you're in and you've said hello, it's important to ask for what you want—the best recording situation. You'll need to tell people what will work for you.

   a. **Avoid kitchens.** Refrigerators are bad news—too noisy. And, kitchens tend to be "echo-y." Usually the family room is best for a recording. Carpeting, cushy furniture, and curtains help absorb sound.

   b. **Become annoying, politely.** Ask to turn off televisions, radios, and cell phones. Keep an ear out for noisy computers. And, in some cases, you'll need to ask to close windows or turn off air conditioning.

   c. **Rearrange furniture.** If turning everything off didn't get you kicked out, now redecorate. It's important to sit close to your interviewee, usually directly across or catty-corner. I want to be so close to someone I can rest my elbow on my knee or the arm of a chair and still have the mic close enough for an intimate recording. Often this requires moving furniture. I can't tell you how many coffee tables and chairs I've moved. And, if I'm in an office, I nearly always ask people to get out from behind their desk. (By the way, I try to never interview someone on a couch. I find it uncomfortable because of the odd angle you have to sit at to be close and able to look them in the eye.)

      This all seems like a lot to ask a stranger. It feels like an imposition—an invasion, even. But, I always couch my requests this way. "I want to make sure you sound good. Can we . . . " As soon as you say, "I want you to sound good" people will accommodate your requests because they want to sound good, too. And, I say "we" because I think of my interviewee as a collaborator in creating the best possible conditions for recording.

      Of course, there's no such thing as a perfect recording situation in the field. If there's a noise you can't control, sit so your mic is facing away from the sound.

      Is it time to ask the first question yet? Nope.

(*Continued . . .*)

(...*continued*)

8. **Make idle chitchat.** Assemble your gear and talk about the weather, the dog, whatever. Don't ask questions related to your story yet. I've noticed photographers ask about photos placed around the house before they start shooting. It's a good idea. It gets people talking about personal subjects but doesn't seem invasive.

9. **Wear headphones.** It's the law. With your mic and recorder all set to go, put your damn headphones on and start recording. In addition to state and federal requirements regarding headphones, you need to assure a good recording. The only way to do that is to wear headphones.

10. **Slate the tape.** Right at the start, record the following: the date, the location, the name of the person you're interviewing, the subject matter. "Slating the tape" helps you quickly figure out what's on the file later.

11. **What's this all about?** There's a good chance your interviewee may not recall exactly what the interview is about or how it's going to be used. While the tape is rolling, tell them what you probably told them on the phone when you set up the interview, something like "Well, as you might remember, I'm producing a radio story for WXXX. It's about the decline in eel populations. Since you are a longtime eel fisherman, I want to talk with you about the fishery and the changes you've seen." They'll probably say, "Okay, sounds good," or something.

    Saying this on tape accomplishes a few things. First, it orients the interviewee. Second, it "activates" the part of their brain that stores info on the subject you're talking about. And, third, it's a recording of their permission. Of course, the fact that they're talking to you with a mic in their face suggests they are giving permission. But, since I don't use release forms (and most radio reporters don't), I feel like this is a good thing to record. To be honest, I usually don't get that on tape. That conversation tends to happen as I'm setting up my gear. But, I try to wait until the tape is rolling.

12. **What did you have for breakfast?** Set the recording levels with a throwaway question. "What did you have for breakfast?" is an old-school radio trick for getting someone to talk in a conversational voice. Adjust your recording levels as they talk. I never ask someone to count to ten or recite the alphabet to set the levels. That's not normal conversation.

13. **Who even are you?** This is the last step. Ask your interviewee to introduce himself or herself. "Could you introduce yourself? Tell me who you are, where you live, how old you are, what you do." That's another way to slate the tape. But, more importantly, you might be able to use their introduction in your story. And, sometimes, they'll reveal something about themselves you never considered.

Okay, are you ready? After all that, you should be! Go ahead. Ask your first question. Make it a good one.

Exercise: Ambient and Natural Sounds

Pick a room in your house, apartment, or dorm. Choose a place where you can control the overall sound. Once you've chosen a room, record thirty different sounds from that room that give a clear sense of what the room is like. Do not narrate during the taping. Listen for audible clues as to what the room is used for, what is in it, even its size. If a television or stereo is on, turn it off. Recording this sound for one take is fine, but don't have it as a constant background noise. You want to isolate each sound as much as possible.

1. On your video camera or mobile phone record thirty sounds that can be found in one room.
2. For each sound, record for ten seconds.
3. Do *not* announce at the start of the recording what room you are in. It's a game.
4. Make the people listening guess where they are and what the sounds are.

The Audio Slide Show

We started this book by explaining that the backbone to great videography is understanding how to see and frame up a scene. We showed that shooting video is not a very hard thing to do. But for many photographers who have been in the business of taking still images, and whose experience and expertise all lie in that area, there is an element of resistance. Shooting video was never part of the deal.

Keith McManus, a freelance documentary filmmaker and adjunct professor of photojournalism at Rochester Institute of Technology, has been shooting stills since 1965 and video since 1988. He talked about the differences between still photography and filmmaking:

> Photography is a single-dimension activity. Filmmaking has a more complex juxtaposing that doesn't exist in still photography. . . . Of course, still images can be taken out of the realm of the printed page and used in multimedia. In that case, the inherent quality of the still photograph's power to arrest time can be used to greater advantage with other forms of information. . . . By juxtaposing images, the order . . . you choose can create a description of an idea, a concept, an emotion, etc. . . . In filmmaking, it would be the layering that is possible of different sounds and pictures—a montage.

The advent of the audio slide show provided an introduction for still photographers to the world of film and video. After the invention of the HDSLR (an SLR camera that can shoot video in addition to stills), it was much each easier for still photographers to use the same gear they already had in their hands to take still photos and to pair these images with an audio track. It also needs to be noted that in the late 1990s, the decision to offer audio slide shows instead of video was more of a matter of available bandwidth than anything else. Pairing stills with an audio track took a lot less bandwidth than serving slow-loading video, which subjected users to a frustrating wait while the browser on their computer loaded the content.

In 2005, a photographer named Joe Weiss invented the software Soundslides, which enabled photographers to pair their photographs with an audio track in a cinematic way without knowing Adobe Flash or even anything about programming. With Soundslides, still photographers were suddenly able to go beyond the three-picture packages they were used to doing for stories in newspapers or magazines. They were no longer simply the photographer who shot the pictures while the reporter wrote the story. They could now tell a story that could stand on its own. With the introduction of an imported audio file came the dimension of time, which made it necessary to learn about things like the sequencing and pacing of images. Weiss' invention fast-tracked many photographers into becoming multimedia storytellers rather than just still photographers, along with adding new vocabulary to the medium itself. "I call them audio slide shows, not soundslides—I always have. It surprises me to hear them called soundslides," said Weiss.

The sound file is assembled using a multitrack audio editor such as Hindenburg, Protools, or Adobe Audition, which turns the process into a simple, intuitive matter of dragging and dropping audio clips into different parts of a timeline. If Soundslides is not being used, it is possible to use an NLE (nonlinear editor) video program to edit the sound, especially if the plan is to use the NLE for the final production.

Figure 8.04 Soundslides is software that enables the easy pairing of still photographs with an audio track. (Courtesy of Soundslides)

Will Yurman, a senior lecturer of journalism at Penn State University, produced a document for his classes called "Introduction to Audio for Photographers." In it Yurman writes:

> A well-edited audio track with strong images—video or stills—is a compelling way to tell stories. And gathering sound while photographing makes us better journalists by forcing us to spend more time and thought on a story. . . . Audio will almost always drive the story. Imagine watching your local news tonight. Would you rather turn off the picture and listen, or try to figure out what is going on by looking at the video without sound? . . . Sound has become a crucial part of storytelling on the web. Adding a soundtrack to your images gives depth to your storytelling. Good sound can make a story.

Just as photographers layer moments within an image to tell a multidimensional visual story, radio producers perform the same process with sounds. It is important for soundtracks in audio slide shows to be built so that the audio drives the story forward, pushing the viewer from one still image to the next, since there is no full-motion video to keep things moving forward. With no real movement to keep viewers' eyes moving from scene to scene—no enter frame and exit frame to serve as a guide—images have to work together with sound to keep viewers' interest. The audio is a much more important part of the slide show format than many people think when they first start to use it.

The audio slide show is a great way to introduce a budding multimedia storyteller to the importance of quality sound. The process of gathering audio in the field is harder than shooting video, because the still photographer must remain constantly aware of what is happening in the moment and what sounds will best complement the images being captured. The need for sound can be a significant distraction from taking good photographs, requiring an extra level of awareness on the part of the photographer that he or she has never had to deal with before. In addition, the photographer has to also become an interviewer while staying alert for ambient sounds and key visual moments. A good way to get around not having pertinent audio is to make sure to record audio for every scene that is shot. Imagine, for example, shooting images of a family preparing to sit down to eat dinner together, but the daughter is being impatient, so the mother steps in to tell the daughter to stop whining about being hungry. It'll be important to have audio from that situation to convey the audible conflict, but at the same time you will need images of the parents cooking or setting the table to pair up with the audio. Essentially, it's a good routine to get audio from every scene that you shoot.

The ultimate goal with audio slide shows is to have ambient sound mixed with interviews to carry things forward. You want to aim for *audio moments* that can carry complicated, layered images, paired with layered sound to give depth to the images. "An audio moment is something that is more than the moment; it explains and answers something larger," said Josh Meltzer, photojournalist-in-residence at Western Kentucky University:

> When someone is telling somebody something in an emphatic or emotional way, and that moment is more than a minute, it is saying something larger about the story. It is like when you look at a still image—it [a moment] allows you to look around the image, it allows you to feel the power of that specific millisecond. I think the audible moment is similar. It is a very important piece of the story that is very telling.

Imagine recording a story about a person who sings in a bar. You'll need to record just the ambient sounds of the bar for a few minutes, then use that sound to enhance the storytelling. Then you'd want to record the interview separately, in a quieter location than the bar itself. Then you will need to layer the interview with the bar sounds inside the multitrack editor.

Once the audio track is built, still images are laid in and paired with sound that corresponds to the situations in which the images were taken. It is important to think about creating audio slide shows in just the same way you produce strong video: by shooting sequences with tight, medium, and wide shots. It is very hard to make a high-quality slide show without considering—while in the process of shooting—what key, logical images will be necessary to push the story forward. The concept of "shoot to edit" is just as important here as it is when shooting video.

An important difference between video and audio slide shows is that the audio slide show is *asynchronous*, meaning that the audio is often not recorded at the same time the images are taken. This is usually because the person who shot the images also had to record the audio, and it is difficult to function as an audio recordist and a photographer at the same time. In addition, it isn't often desirable for the sound of a camera shutter to be audible in a recording.

When recording an interview it is acceptable to get a subject to say his or her name, but there is no reason to use "My name is" in every audio slide show. Omitting this will improve the pacing of a piece and prevent slide shows from appearing as if they all follow a cookie-cutter audio format. Feel free to use titling tools, such as *lower thirds*, or titles placed in the lower third of the player's frame. Templates for this are built into most NLE editors and Soundslides. If there is a need to clarify exactly who is talking in an audio track, it is common practice to label a slide in a slide show with something like "Voice of John Doe."

When producing an audio slide show, think about the images that will be used. The first images in the show should essentially set the stage, conveying things like subject, time, and location. We are still telling stories, even though it is still images rather than full motion video, and it will be necessary to think about crafting a story arc. Make sure to pre-edit images before bringing them into the editor. There are going to be times when "moment-less" images—more informational than anything else—will be needed to serve as transitions from one scene to the next. Images like this can be compared to B-roll in video. Avoid using images with poor composition just to fill out the sound. Just as in video, it's very important that the images chosen match the audio as closely as possible. A subject shouldn't be talking about what it's like to be on top of a mountain after a long hike while the screen shows an image of the hiker at home in his living room. Despite the asynchronous way in which the media were gathered, the image and the sound must still match.

It is common to mix still photography with video. Most often the interview (A-roll) is done in video while the still photography acts as the B-roll. "When you see the A-roll you can see the emotion, the inflection: you can pick and choose the best moments when they laugh, cry, pause, or they think about something," said Meltzer. He added that when using stills, the images have to be excellent to come off well in video:

> If you are using a still image, it has to be really, really good. You are asking the audience to look at something for three or five or eight seconds. It has to be really good. . . . The audience just doesn't have the patience to look at bad pictures.

Imagine a slide show about a woodworker. If there is audio of a saw cutting, show images of the woodworker performing this activity. The images can match without needing to be from the exact time the audio was recorded. Now imagine that the woodworker is making a toy boat, and it is time for the boat to be tested on the water. A good image to use would be a close-up of the boat finished in the shop. From this image, a transition such as a cross-fade could take the boat—and the viewer—from the wood shop to the pond, a transition of time and place. You will be surprised when making an audio slide show at how many cinematic constructs, usually associated with video, can be applied. The thought process is the same, only rather than motion video, the medium is still images. Avoid wild uses of transitions, cross-fades, cuts, and jump cuts. All of these storytelling devices have to be used properly, and only when appropriate. In addition, while adding a rock ballad to a high-energy video may pick up the pace a bit, it won't necessarily push the story along. Whenever possible, capture ambient audio on scene and use that to tell the story.

Meltzer also emphasized what can kill a story:

> The death of any story is boredom—becoming bored with it. Either I am looking at the same picture over and over again, or I am looking at the same picture too long, saying the same thing, not being surprised—all of those things are instant death for a story.

Interviews

Simply sitting down to talk with someone, and recording it at the same time, doesn't seem like a very difficult prospect, but it certainly can be. Print reporters have the luxury of being able to interview people without the distraction and intimidation of a video camera pointed at the subject.

When recording an interview on video, there is a lot more to think about than just the interview itself. The technology of both audio and video is probably the biggest hurdle—make sure that your gear is recording at the highest quality possible, that everything is set right, and that you've actually pressed the record button to start! Though all this may seem obvious, it's not. Cameras don't use the same system as traffic lights, where red means *stop* and green stands for *go*. It's the opposite: Red means you are recording; green means you are paused. So keep your wits together and concentrate. As challenging as an interview is, it's even more challenging to try to do it twice.

Camera Setup and Lighting for Interviews

When interviewing a subject on video, it is important to figure out a suitable and workable location, or how best to deal with the one at hand. You might be forced to shoot an interview in a poorly lit, windowless room. This can be fine if professional lights are available, but if they aren't, and the only camera available is a mobile phone with less exposure latitude than a prosumer camera, obviously things are going to be difficult.

"I've been in offices where a public relations person will suggest a room, and I will be, like, 'No,'" said Andrew Maclean, a freelance video producer based in New York City: "You'll hear the air conditioner or street sounds, especially here in New York City. I have asked people to change conference rooms, even if they are having a meeting in there. It works out, usually."

Maclean stressed that good lighting and sound are necessary for a good video interview. "These people are taking time out of their schedule for me, and I should do a good job for them," he said:

> We often don't know what we are going into. We have to think on our feet how to shoot it, how to light it, how to set it up. Every time I go into someone else's office, I am looking for window light, the best and the brightest. So if there is a good window light that is in or near a room that is quiet, convenient, and comfortable for everyone, that is the best option we can ask for.

If it's possible to place a light to the side of the subject, it will add texture to the subject. When using professional lighting, make sure to turn off any room lights before turning the lamps on. This will enable the lights to be positioned individually on the subject, so that the resulting image is exactly what is needed. Use the LCD screen on your camera to assist in this process.

If no other lighting is on hand, put the subject near a window that can act as a light source. Do not, however, put the window in the shot. The goal is only to add light to one side of the subject's face.

Suppose there is some alternate lighting available in the room, such as a desk lamp. Once the subject has been adequately lighted from the side, use a source like this to provide a little back light for the interview. When aimed at the back of the subject's head from behind, a light like this will separate them from the background and add depth to the image.

If the subject will be facing the opposite direction—providing it's possible with the existing light source—just make sure that the reporter is always in the center, between the light source and the camera.

This tried-and-true way of lighting an interview, in which the main light is placed on one side of the reporter and the camera is placed on the other, is known as a *reporter sandwich*. In addition to providing good lighting, this setup has the subject looking off to the side of the frame and not directly into the camera. The area that the subject is looking into is called the *lead room*.

Try not to put a subject up against a blank wall; this will make the image flat, when the goal is to add depth. Also try to avoid doing interviews in places where a lot is going on the background, such as people moving back and forth. This will be distracting to viewers.

As for the camera itself, use a tripod, at eye level with the subject. Do not try to hand-hold a camera for an entire interview. The camera needs to be "locked down" and as still as possible. In a one-man-band type of situation this is a real benefit—it will be possible to shoot while maintaining the ability to interact with the subject and monitor the camera's LCD screen at the same time. Interviews require a tripod.

The "Reporter Sandwich"

One way to get good lighting and an effective camera angle is to orient an interview in a "reporter sandwich" formation. The light and camera are on either side of the reporter, and directed at the interview subject.

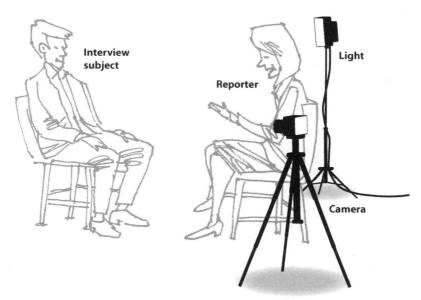

Figure 8.05 Good lighting is the key to making a good interview better. (Illustration by Chris OBrion)

Make sure the subject is sitting in a chair that does not have wheels and does not swivel. People tend to fidget when they are conversing or being questioned, and a movable chair will only magnify this. You want the subject to sit facing the interviewer, who is situated to the side of the camera.

Interview Framing

When doing an interview it is important to frame the subject nicely in the viewfinder. In an HD 16:9 frame, position the subject in the left or right side of the horizontal frame. Think about the rule of thirds, discussed in Chapter 5, and try to frame the subject so his or her eyes fall along the upper line. Be careful not to cut off the top of the subject's head; there should be space between the subject's head and the edge of the frame. Strive to keep a standard amount of space between top of head and frame for all interviews. This will keep the video consistent.

Also, while having a unique visual style is a good thing, for interviews it is best to avoid contrived looks that could detract or distract from what the subject is saying. Shooting an interview from a low angle, for example, won't necessarily create a very flattering look, especially if the subject is on camera for any length of time. The viewer will be peering up the subject's nostrils.

The "reporter sandwich" provides a dependable standard, in that the subject will be looking off to the side. Think about where the subject's nose is pointing. The reporter should be opposite the subject's nose.

Figure 8.06 Position the subject in the left or right side of the horizontal frame. Think about the rule of thirds. (Photo by Seth Gitner)

While interviewing the subject, be listening to the audio and at the same time looking into the LCD to make sure everything is in order. Don't be afraid to take a break from the interview to change focal lengths, which will add variety to the edit. Remember that as you interview you are building a relationship with your subjects. It is OK to ask them to sit up, fix their collars, or hold on for a couple of minutes while you make adjustments to the camera or audio levels. They are captive and in a situation run by you, but if you act like a professional they will usually treat you as one.

Interview Audio

Do not forget to make sure that the audio is working, and wear over-the-ear headphones. When getting started, ask the subject to state his or her name and occupation while audio is being recorded—this will show the audio levels. If your audio display has colors, aim for levels that are just above the green and into yellow—but not red, as that means your audio is *peaking* and will be distorted and unusable. The optimum settings for a good audio recording are in a range between –12 dB and –6 dB. This will allow enough room for a peak or two.

Depending on the gear available, recording audio in an interview situation can go a variety of ways. If you have access to gear that allows two tracks recording at once, put the lavalier mic on one track and an on-camera shotgun mic on the other. This provides redundancy; in case one mic fails you have the recording on the other track. The lavalier mic will be more natural-sounding, while the shotgun mic may pick up more of the ambient sounds of the room. Smaller prosumer cameras do not allow this, and only have one mic input: a mini-plug. In situations like this, use a Y-splitter that separates the right channel from the left channel, allowing separate audio feeds from two different sources.

As far as microphones go, it would be ideal to use a shotgun mic on a boom, held over the subject's head just outside the frame (remember that sound tends to rise), or pointed at the subject's mouth from off camera. These microphones should pick up the interview very well. Also effective would be a lavalier microphone, clipped six to eight inches below the subject's mouth, with the wire running up the person's shirt out of view of the camera.

Lacking either one of the above microphones, you should at the very least have a detachable shotgun microphone. This microphone is directional, meaning that it will pick up whatever it is pointed at, as long as the subject is within a few feet. Good audio can make or break a video piece, so making sure that your audio is well-recorded in the first place will lead to a higher-quality result.

Figure 8.07 When shooting an interview, audio can be gathered either with a lapel microphone or by suspending a microphone from a boom pole above the subject. (Photo by Ethan Backer)

Pre-Interview Checklist

When composing the interview, did I . . .
1. Frame the subject so that he/she is looking into the empty part of the frame?
2. Frame the subject using the rule of thirds?
3. Vary focal lengths for both wide and tight camera angles?
4. Use a clean, orderly background?

When mic'ing the subject for the interview, did I . . .
1. Use two audio sources, both an on-camera shotgun mic and a lavalier mic? or
2. Use a shotgun mic directly over the head of the subject or six to eight inches from his/her mouth and off camera? or
3. Just use a wired lavalier mic on the subject's chest, six to eight inches from his/her mouth?

Before I started the interview, did I . . .
1. Turn off all cell phones?
2. Put on over-the-ear headphones?
3. Test audio levels to be between −12db and −6db?
4. Make sure the location is not noisy (free of animal noises, car noises, air conditioners)?

Interviewing a Person

It is important when going into an interview situation that you've done your homework ahead of time. Often, doing a phone interview prior to the shoot can provide a good idea of what questions to ask while the subject is on camera. Evelio Contreras, a video producer for CNN Digital, uses pre-interviews to outline his story:

> I pre-interview folks over the phone and type down what they are saying, and know what they will say about things before I even go out there. This gives me a general outline of what I know I will get. Having said that, if the story goes in a different direction, I'll do that too when I'm out shooting. But I want to have a baseline story that I know I can tell.

In narrative-driven pieces, the interview will play a major role in helping to tell the story. It may in fact drive the story forward. Since there is no reporter track in an interview, make sure to get the subject to say everything needed for the story to make sense. One way to do this is to have your subjects repeat each question you ask as part of their answers, so that no loose ends are left hanging and every one of their statements has context. It also keeps your own voice out of the video.

If interviewing a chef, for example, imagine asking a question like, "When did you first realize you wanted to become a chef?" This could yield a response like, "When I was little," which would not be very useful in the edit. Make sure to ask open-ended questions that will elicit more than a yes-or-no answer. A more usable response, and the best kind to elicit from a subject, would be, "I first knew that I wanted to be a chef when I was very young." Another way to make the final edit easier is to have your subjects list the steps they took to get where they are, doing what they do . . . such as becoming a chef. This will provide a wealth of background material. Ask them to go through the process of a recipe, which would provide sound bites to use as needed. If the topic is hard to understand, don't be afraid to ask the subject to explain it in a way that makes sense—and to re-explain it until it's clear.

Conducting an on-camera interview is not an easy task. You can't be an introvert when trying to get someone to speak freely. Be prepared with good questions that will generate interesting and useful responses. You need to formulate questions beforehand that will propel your story forward, and unlock people's memories, experiences, and opinions.

"People always answer your questions in three parts," said Bob Dotson, the veteran broadcast reporter and author. "They give you the answer [to the question] they think you asked, and then they explain their answer, and if you just wait a little bit, people get really nervous about silence."

Dotson emphasized that this silence can be a very effective tool in interviews. "What's the one thing we do in media?" he asked. "We are so fast that we never really wait for silence. We have another question to ask. I let the silence build a little bit, and that's where the guy goes, 'That's when I killed my wife,'" Dotson said laughingly. "Because what you are doing is forcing them . . . the silence forces them to focus on the point you want to make."

Transcribe Interviews

All interviews should be transcribed, noting the timecodes of specific quotes that are important to the story. (*Timecode* is a signal in a video recording that identifies the hour, minute, second, and frame of any point in the recording by means of an eight-digit code, e.g. 01:23:45:01.) Also, note whether there is any visual emotion in the interview footage itself, and what it is. Emotion is an important force to capture, and it plays an important part in the pitch, tone, and development of a story. Other factors that should be specifically noted are when the subject uses their hands while speaking or does anything that is outside the norm, such as wiping away a tear. While transcribing, always carefully note the timecode for the *in points* and *out points*, or the start and end points of all quotes.

There is software for the Macintosh, called Transcriva, that helps make this process easier, letting the user listen to the video clip play back while transcribing it in the same software. While playing a video clip, every time "enter" is pressed the timecode of a sound bite is noted. In long, interview-driven narratives in particular, transcribing interviews is a must. It is an essential part of organizing clips that can later be reordered into an accompanying audio track that will tell the story along with the visuals.

After an interview has been transcribed, the clips can be moved around with their timecodes in a word processing program. The interview can even be printed, cut up with scissors, and placed into an order that tells the story. There is also a piece of software called Scrivener for both Mac and PC that accepts exported files from Transcriva. Making each line a separate quote, quotes can be dragged and dropped into an order that makes sense while leaving the timecode intact. It's sort of a digital version of the scissor technique. Some nonlinear editors (NLEs) have transcription software built in, though its reliability can be questionable. Or, for an extra cost, clips can be uploaded to a service that will transcribe interviews and send them back as documents. Whatever method is used, the important part is to have a firm grip on exactly what you have before the actual editing process begins. The result will be a better video.

Another way of organizing clips combined with transcriptions is to cut and paste the transcription into the name of each individual clip in the NLE's bin that the transcription corresponds with. This will make it easy to assemble a narrative in your timeline.

Nonfiction: Shoot to Edit

In nonfiction, shooting to edit is particularly challenging. You must be thinking about what might need to be shot to tell the story, and to track what has been shot, all in the process of shooting more. This thought process happens "in the moment," as the scene is playing out in front of you. It is important in nonfiction journalism not to alter the scene or action in any way. Just be prepared, with camera in hand, alert and able to respond in the best way possible to an unfolding, unpredictable situation. The goal, of course, is to shoot the images that will tell the story best.

To speed up the post-production process, particularly while shooting a press conference or sporting event, write down the timecodes of various sound bites, topics, or moments in the action. This provides a ready index to all footage, and makes it easier to return to the sound bites and moments that will tell the story most effectively.

Determine Story Structure

While shooting, the one, overarching question you should keep on asking is, "What is my story?" Subordinate to that, but no less important, are some other questions: "How am I going to turn this into a three- to five-minute film? What structure will make this most coherent for the viewer?"

The first step on the path to answering these questions is figuring out who the main character is going to be. Sometimes this has already been determined, especially if the assignment came from a news producer or newspaper editor.

What Is your Story Commitment?

Having a basic, solid knowledge of what a story is going to be makes it much more likely that everything you do will serve the purpose of telling that story. It helps in developing a thread that will keep the story moving forward.

Every time the "record" button is pushed, it needs to be for a definite reason. There isn't time to waste on anything that will not propel the story forward, and viewers of the final piece will probably not have the time or patience for it either.

One way to stay on track is to always be thinking in terms of A-roll and B-roll. The *A-roll* is the interview track, which will convey the facts and hard information of the story. The *B-roll* is the scene and the visual interaction of the subjects, which will flesh out the film on the screen. Keep this framework in mind while shooting, and it will help you get everything you need. This is especially helpful in a news environment, where speed and efficiency are essential to meeting daily deadlines.

At the NPPA News Video Workshop, held yearly in Norman, OK, attendees repeatedly hear a mantra: "What is your commitment?" This refers to the focus of a story.

Think about a circus. It's a massive show with lots and lots of potential stories and an infinite number of interesting shots. Without a main character to tell the story you're after, much time and effort can be wasted shooting every interesting thing that passes in front of the camera. Digital media are pretty inexpensive, true, so you won't be wasting any of that old-fashioned film, but the more footage is shot, the more there will be to log, and edit, and keep track of. The story can get lost in all the confusion, and perhaps any sense of purpose as well. So always focus like a laser on what the story is. If while shooting a story about a clown you run into the lion tamer, think back to your commitment. Does the lion tamer have a place in the story? If not, don't raise the camera.

"A commitment means that you are not going to just throw the pictures up, and however they land, to cover the voice-over, they are going to work," said Sharon Levy Freed, a Denver-based videojournalist and trainer who ran the NPPA News Video workshop for ten years. "Your commitment means you have a definite target and destination that you want your story to go to," she emphasized.

So, before starting a story, take a few minutes to nail down what exactly your commitment will be. With this done, you can begin to shoot and be reasonably confident about everything eventually falling into place.

"The reporter is actively pulling the viewer along by the hand," said Mike Schuh, a reporter with WJZ Channel 13 in Baltimore, MD, adding that at "other times they are just describing somebody else's journey—plot, character, and quest—the quest is the journey. Most TV news stories fail because they don't have the journey." Schuh went on to say that the "reveal" of a surprise is the key to a good story. Newspaper writing tends to put the reveal at the top of the story, or lead, giving the kernel of the news story and the most important facts first, but in video storytelling the surprise is often best kept for later in the narrative.

Find a Lead Character

Finding a central character can sometimes be easy, sometimes quite difficult. Think about what makes a good character. Find someone who is interesting, someone who has a great story to tell—and to show.

Remember that this is nonfiction, in-the-moment storytelling. Shots will need to be captured as actual events occur. Think of that uncle you have, who is a heck of a lot funnier than your parents. That uncle is the kind of person who could be at the center of a story. Look for characters who jump out to the viewer and demand attention. But that isn't all that you need to look for.

Strive to find an engaging character, for whom something is happening with unfolding action. There should some sort of a struggle, a challenge for the character, much like the classic "hero's journey"—the hero that we care about, who is presented with a challenge—that we discussed in Chapter 2. When a character has been identified, do a preliminary interview with the camera off. Get to know the character as a person rather than as a subject. Becoming spontaneously interested in a topic or person is an acquired skill, as is the art of conversation (simply listening attentively is a large part of it), and this is a great time to become better at it. Be empathetic to this human being's issues, problems, and desires, just as you would like someone to be with yours. People can usually sense apathy, but if they feel warmth and interest they will invite you deeper into their lives. Befriend them, and not just as you would hang out with casual friends on a daily basis. Win their trust.

Developing Characters

Characters are nothing less than the people who tell the story, and engage the viewer. It is the characters for whom the audience will root, and connect with, and follow through to the end of the story, and remember in the future.

Events, experiences, and time will change characters, and the storyteller must be constantly on the lookout for transformational moments and statements. For example, think about a nonfiction story about a preacher couple who drive around the country in an eighteen-wheeler, spreading their religion to people at truck stops. Presumably these preachers will be outgoing, driven people, with strong personalities and certain goals and expectations for their mission. While following them around on their journey, you'll hopefully witness them meeting new people and having a variety of experiences, and you will be capturing these moments. The people they meet and the triumphs and defeats they experience will help to tell the story. So while shooting, be constantly aware of *what* you are shooting. Will this moment, or statement, stand up as a plot point on an arc? Is the situation currently in front of the lens something that propels the story forward?

Throughout a story, as the viewer is guided along the story arc, the characters must develop and grow. This is how nonfiction or "real life" is, no matter how subtle or long-term the changes might be.

Framing the Story

It cannot be said enough times that careful planning precedes productive shooting. There is nothing worse than starting to shoot a story without any idea as to how it will be put together at the editing station—to do this is to ask for big problems and big frustration later on. Staying aware, while shooting, of the types of shots needed (and obtainable) should be number one on your list.

There are many different formulas for shooting nonfiction footage, but it's a good general practice to get tight, super-tight, medium, and wide shots, as well as an interview, for any assignment. This will generally provide enough content to put together a coherent video for a news producer or a professor.

Log Your Footage

Upon returning from an assignment, the first task is to log the footage that has been shot. The best and most efficient method for this is to write down every shot on a piece of paper, or in your editing software, marking each clip individually with in and out points. Most software programs have this functionality built in, which can greatly speed up the process. It simply allows each shot to be quickly located when it is needed during the edit. Go through each and every clip and name it, adding a meta tagging structure that will make it even easier to find. (See "Organizing the Edit" in Chapter 6 to review this process.)

Much video editing software now has extensive databasing capability, which also helps to keep clips easily accessible. Remember that along with knowing what a clip is about, you also need to know its visual and audio content. While logging footage, note the natural sounds, sound bites, and/or quotes in each clip. As discussed earlier in this chapter, natural sounds can be an important part of a piece, making viewers feel as if they are "there." Quotes and sound bites are vital for making a point, adding authenticity to characters, and moving the story along.

Mike Schuh, the reporter with WJZ Channel 13 in Baltimore, MD, strives to be a meticulous logger for B-roll. "I pore over the video and the sound. A bird chirp, horn honk, or a door slam only last half a second, but it could be exactly what you need to reinforce or transition to or from a story element," said Schuh, who says he does the same during his interviews. "When I find a bite I like, I fully write it down. By knowing the first and last things they say, I can better tailor the words or sounds I use immediately before and after that SOT [sound on tape]. By doing that, I use fewer words."

Draw the Story Arc and Determine Plot Points

With a story commitment and character all lined up, you should start to have the reassuring sense that a story is definitely going to happen. Now is the time to draw out a story arc. The most important part of this process is to determine a beginning, a middle, and an end. Are there sound bites that tell the story? What and where is the conflict? Is it strong enough to propel the story forward, keeping viewers involved? "A good story has a surprise or hook," said Sharon Levy Freed, the Denver-based videojournalist. "Something like a punchline in a joke, which . . . makes it unique enough to tell."

Returning to the example of a circus, if the story is about a clown, what makes this clown unique? What makes this clown interesting enough to spend time editing a story about him? Maybe he is the latest in a long line of clowns that dates back three generations. Maybe he used to be a corporate attorney. Maybe he survived cancer. Look for the hook; seek out the surprise. Wait for the perfect moment, after just the right amount of preparation, to spring it on the viewer. "The good stories are the ones that you go, 'Wow, oh my gosh, I can't believe that happened. Really?'" said Freed. "Stories that go away from the obvious and surprise the viewer with something they don't expect."

Once a rough, basic structure is in place, it is possible to move forward with editing the piece together. Be aware that the current structure is merely a "wireframe" or guide for the story, and that during editing things may change. Things might pop up in an interview that you didn't see before, and this is good. The important thing is to stay committed to the original story. If the course changes in a major way halfway through, there may not be the visuals or sound bites to sustain the new direction.

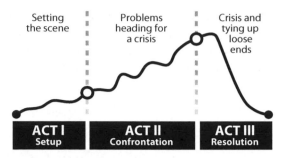

Figure 8.08 It's always important to have a basic structure in mind when working on a video story. (Illustration by Chris OBrion)

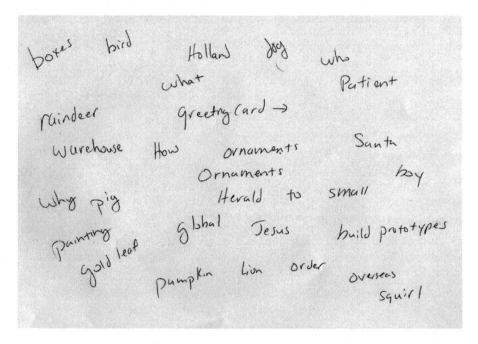

Figure 8.09 A "tag cloud" of keywords, ideas, and common themes can help to focus a story. (Seth Gitner)

Understanding the story itself is the most important piece of the puzzle. But you also need to understand how to critique your own work. Ask again and again: What's the story? What elements are needed to tell that story? Which of the ways of organizing those elements best serves the story? What absolutely cannot be done without?

It can be hard to figure out the best structure for a story. There may be thirty minutes of footage that needs to be stripped down into a ninety-second film. For a narrative-driven piece without voice-over, all of the interview will need to be captured on tape. One way to go about narrowing the focus is to use colored pens and highlighters, as former CNN photojournalist Bethany Swain, a lecturer of broadcast journalism and multimedia at the University of Maryland, does with her students. "What do you remember from the interview?" Swain asks. "What was the most important stuff that you found? What was the most compelling? Ask what the facts are. What do you remember? What really stands out? I'll write down what I am hearing." Swain said she then draws out each of the themes in a tag-cloud diagram, highlighting and underlining the topics to narrow the focus of the themes that emerge.

MEET THE PRO

Lisa Fenn, Freelance Producer, ESPN's *Outside the Lines* and *SportsCenter*, Bristol, CT

An Edward R. Murrow Award winner and feature producer with ESPN for thirteen years, during which time she earned six Emmy Awards, Lisa Fenn reported on major league sports, interviewing every big name in the game. A graduate of Cornell University, she continues to produce sports stories

Figure 8.10 Lisa Fenn, freelance producer, ESPN's *Outside the Lines* and *SportsCenter*, Bristol, CT, with Dartanyon Crockett and Leroy Sutton. (Courtesy of Lisa Fenn)

and write about the redemptive power of love. She now lives in Boston with her husband and two children.

Before becoming a freelance producer, Lisa Fenn reported human interest features for ESPN's *SportsCenter* and their magazine-style show *Outside the Lines*. As a producer, she is responsible for initial contact with the subject and for all the logistics associated with a story, from assembling camera crews to interviewing subjects, to actually writing the stories. She also directs camera crews as to what they need to shoot. "What I love about producing is the depth of the relationship that is forged with a subject, because it continues long after an interview is done," Fenn said.

When shooting has been completed, Fenn transcribes the footage, lays out the story structure, and works with the reporter assigned to the story to write the script. "It is the producer's job to provide [the reporter] with the first attempt at the outline and the structure," she explained:

> I go through all the tapes, and I start laying out all the best moments and sound bites to tell the story. I lay out the outline—"these are our best moments, this needs to be in here." . . . I have gut feelings when it affects me. When I watch something and it affects me, then I know I can trust that it's going to affect other people. . . . If I watch something and I don't have a visceral reaction to it, then I can trust it's probably not what I want to use in a piece.

(Continued . . .)

(... continued)

In 2009 Fenn worked on a story called "Carry On," about two friends who were on the Lincoln-West High School wrestling team in Cleveland, OH. It was a project into which she was drawn deeply because of the characters being covered. The idea for the story came through her father, who saw a photograph of the two wrestlers, both disabled, in his local, Cleveland newspaper and passed it along to her. Leroy Sutton, a double amputee, was riding on the back of teammate Dartanyon Crockett. "I ran into work and showed it to my manager, and told him, 'If we are going to do this story we have to do it today,'" Fenn recalled. She said her manager responded by asking what the specifics were, because *Outside the Lines* had already done many disabled-athlete pieces. She knew very few. When he asked what her gut feeling was about the story, she said it was good. "I don't know what this story is, but I know I've never seen a photo like that before," Fenn recalled saying.

"He said, 'Alright, have a good trip to Cleveland,'" remembered Fenn. "I went right to the airport from there, which never happens. We always put a lot of pre-planning into choosing our stories, so that was quite rare." A short time later Fenn was at a wrestling tournament in Cleveland with a camera crew to begin the story.

Fenn's sense that the story was going to be good proved even more correct than she had expected. The key to the story was that Leroy Sutton had been hit by a train at the age of eleven and had both his legs amputated. His best friend, Dartanyon Crockett, also his wrestling partner, was blind and homeless. "It's not like they were the greatest wrestlers and we had this amazing wrestling story," Fenn said. "It had to be something else." The pairing of the students—their friendship—is what made the story so powerful, Fenn explained:

> The sight of Dartanyon carrying Leroy—I had never seen anything like it. It was an arresting image, watching them getting around. I knew that at that tournament, like me, everyone in the gym was looking at them out of the corner of their eye, realizing "I shouldn't be staring," or looking away. . . .

Fenn said that it was initially challenging for Leroy in particular to trust her and share his struggles:

> I just wanted to get to know them. I spent the week with Dartanyon, doing his classes, and then at night I would go to Leroy's house and watch in silence for four nights while he played video games, just waiting to see if he would say anything.

Fenn followed Leroy and Dartanyon through their daily lives for five months, growing the bond and allowing the friendship to unfold organically on camera.

(Continued . . .)

(*. . . continued*)

The story was finally told through both the writing and the visuals, said Fenn:

> There are very few times in television that you are able to surprise a viewer, because they are inundated with so much content and so much formulaic television that there's very few things people aren't expecting. And in this case we were able to do it.

Fenn described how the story waited to reveal to viewers that Dartanyon was blind. Another surprise for viewers was when Leroy walked across the stage during graduation, wearing prosthetic legs. "You weren't expecting it. Those were two important attempts within our structure that we tried to pull off, and it worked," Fenn said.

The overarching theme of the story is friendship. "You have to be very clear in the focus, otherwise it loses its power," explained Fenn, who worked on the piece with ESPN reporter Tom Rinaldi. Rinaldi provided poignant voice tracks, she said, about "the wrestler with no legs being carried by the one who can't see."

For part of the video Fenn was able to use wrestling footage licensed from the local Cleveland newspaper. She also hired a still photographer to shoot portraits of the youths, to be used in the piece. The portraits ended up serving as chapter markers, sectioning the story into distinct scenes. "Thirteen minutes can be hypnotic, even with a strong storyline, and I wanted to break that up somehow," Fenn said. "We use still photos a lot in our features, but they are usually to cover voice-overs that don't have video. . . . In this case, I wanted to find a way to break up the length."

Fenn spent a great deal of time with both of the boys. At one point she drove Leroy home from practice and noticed that he did not have a ramp to get into his home, only stairs. She offered to carry his wheelchair up, but Leroy said he could handle it. He then lifted the chair over his head and put it in his house. Fenn described the moment:

> When I saw it, it wasn't a moment of elation. More a moment of, "How is this happening? Who is letting this happen to this kid? Where is the ramp? Where are the people to help him? Does anyone see what is going on here?" It was more of a moment of, "I gotta fix this."

Fenn continues to be involved in Leroy's and Dartanyon's lives, having started a trust for them and helping them find their way in life. Dartanyon went on to earn a Bronze Medal in Judo in the 2012 Paralympic games in London. Leroy has since had a child and graduated from college with a degree in video game design. "I keep in touch with a lot of my feature subjects," said Fenn. "Those relationships are the most fulfilling element of my job. If all I did was make forgettable cable television, I don't know if it would fulfill me. The relationships are what I love, they are key."

Note: This story can be viewed on the ESPN website: http://bit.ly/carryon-espn

Writing a Video Story for Broadcast on TV and Digital Platforms

When newspapers first got into video storytelling, there was a push for narrator-less video, in which subjects always told the story and there was no voice-over. Part of the reason for this was that newspaper staffers had never done voice-over; they didn't get into print journalism because they wanted to be in video. Now, however, in a world moving more toward video and audio, particularly on the web, adding one's voice to a piece is becoming as normal in newspaper work as it has always been in television. In the digital realm, journalists should have an idea of how to appear on camera, how to voice a story, and how to report a live shot.

Broadcast writing is a different undertaking than writing a fiction script. First of all, this is not writing in a designed reality. Everything being written is real or observed. It is fact.

Broadcast scripts can be written in different ways. There are broadcast *story packages*, which are self-contained stories where a reporter covers a specific story and weaves a voice track over visuals and sound bites. There are also *VOs*, or voice-overs, in which the anchor reads a script over visuals. "You've got to craft it in such a way so that the viewer stays engaged. Not every story is a plane crash or presidential scandal," said John Carlin, a news anchor for WSLS News Channel 10 in Roanoke, VA. "You have to find the most interesting parts of a story and assemble it in a way that you would lead the viewer down the path," said Carlin, who added that he often uses the technique of saying something interesting enough to raise a question in the viewer's mind, and then answering that question. The script for the story will be driven by the elements of the story: the facts that are present and the video that can be shown.

Bob Papper, in his *Broadcast News Writing Stylebook*, defines this method of storytelling as "story logic." He writes:

> As reporters, every statement we hear leads us, or should lead us, to the next logical question. We want answers to all of the who, what, when, where, why and how questions. But we don't ask those questions at random—each one has its place. The same is true when we're writing the story for the audience. As we go along, logical questions come up in the minds of the audience. If each succeeding line in our story answers the next logical question in the minds of the audience, we have achieved story logic. (74)

For example, imagine covering a car accident on the highway. The lead sentence must be worded in such a manner as to indicate that something unusual—that is, news—happened on the highway today. The first question in a person's mind from that statement is "what happened?" Answer that question by telling the viewer what happened: "There was a four-car accident and two people are critically injured." The next bit of information would include the types of cars or the names of the injured. This way you are giving out more information related to the initial statement of what happened on the highway. "You are raising questions and you are answering those questions in logical order—and really the most important or urgent question next—and then deciding how to put the pieces together," Carlin said.

Again, an important rule of writing for broadcast—and for much storytelling—is "Show, don't tell." Do not state the visually obvious in a voice-over, when the action itself is all the viewer needs to stay engaged. Unnecessary telling can be intrusive and distracting. Remember that visuals tell a story in themselves, and that words should just assist. As the Denver-based videojournalist Sharon Levy Freed put it,

> I always think writing is like writing the mood. I don't want you to write a picture that says the green grass made the sky look even bluer, because people see that in your video. You can say . . . it smelled like fresh-cut grass so much that even the sky looked more like summer. . . . Things that appeal, whether it is to the sense of smell or something aesthetic. You want the writing to supplement and complement the images.

Basic Broadcast News Writing

Most people have been writing stories and papers since they were in grade school. By the time they get to college, they have hopefully mastered at least the form of academic writing. Writing a news story is different, however, from writing a twenty-page research paper in Chicago style, especially if it is a news story for broadcast. The tone and style are different, and the words must coordinate with the powerful element of visuals. Newspaper reporters often have difficulty when they first start writing for video, because it is a whole different way of thinking.

"The majority of broadcast leads—90 percent, plus—are soft leads. Start with a sentence that draws viewers' attention," said Suzanne Lysak, a broadcast digital journalism professor at the S.I. Newhouse School of Public Communications. "Broadcast leads should be the latest development. [They] could also be the 'what's next' angle, if [the] story happened several hours ago. A hard lead is saved for breaking news."

When presenting a video story for broadcast, there's a big chance that your voice will help tell the story. Speaking into a microphone for use on camera is essentially performing for an audience. During a *stand-up*, in which a reporter looks into the camera and reports, that reporter needs to feel comfortable and look that way too. The presence and delivery of the content needs to be strong, for that is what the audience needs and expects.

The writing should have a kind of strength, too. It needs to be brief, concise, and conversational. Nobody wants to hear a newspaper story being read over video clips. That's not the way people actually talk. It needs to feel as if you are telling a story, which is "illustrated" with observations, statements, and other sound bites from the actual people involved.

Broadcast Story Types

LIVE SHOT

A reporter is live on the scene, be it a house fire, a crime scene, or outside a courtroom. The backdrop or setting—or on an ongoing story that is being reported from the field—plays better than being in the studio.

PACKAGE

A self-contained story that consists of sound bites, natural sound, and a voice track. Often this is a piece that is reported in the field and then edited and cut together as a standalone story.

VO

Voice-over is read by an anchor on air, paired with video that was captured in the field. For example, if a photographer were to capture only B-roll from a scene, with no interviews, the anchor would be able to show what happened and tell the story, but not take it much further.

VO/SOT

Voice over is paired with sound on tape. An anchor reads a script as a voice-over, leading up to a sound bite played on the air.

Scripting Basics for Broadcast News

Broadcast scripts are in a two-column format, with production cues and directions in the left column and the talent cues in the right. For some stories, the anchor reads the voice-over (VO), and then pauses when sound on tape (SOT)—sound bites—are played. The anchor may also read a short introduction to a reporter package or a live shot. The role of the news anchor is "to get the viewer to stay through your thirty minutes," said Carlin, the WSLS news anchor. "No matter what story you are talking about, you have a mandate to make it interesting."

Use everyday language and short sentences. Remember, the script is meant to be read aloud, in a limited span of time, so be as direct and sparing with words as possible. The copy itself is written in upper and lower case, and each paragraph is one or two short sentences. The duration of each piece of SOT should be noted in both columns, as broadcast news is based on time length, every show and story having a certain amount of allotted time. Broadcast time is notated in timecode, which takes the form of 00:00:00:00

(hour: minute: second: frame) at thirty frames per second. For example, 01:23:45:29 indicates a shot happened at one hour, twenty-three minutes, forty-five seconds, and twenty-nine frames.

Basic Broadcast Story Package Formula

The following is an example of a tried-and-true "formula" for a broadcast journalistic package using the building blocks of natural sound, voice tracks, and sound on tape. It is taken from a handout by Simon Perez, an assistant professor of broadcast digital journalism at the S.I. Newhouse School of Public Communications at Syracuse University.

1. **Nat Sound** – take the viewer to the scene
2. **Track** – set the scene
3. **SOT** – connect the viewer emotionally to the story
4. **Track** – more information
5. **Nat Sound** – transition to a new idea or place
6. **Track** – more information
7. **SOT** – last chance to impact the viewer
8. **Track** – wrap it up, sense of fulfillment

One reason that broadcast journalists tend to follow a formula is that they are usually driven by deadlines, and do not have time to experiment on every piece. The formulas work, so news organizations stick to them. "You need to be able to shoot a package in as little as half an hour, get visuals done quickly, and have to write it within a half an hour," said Lysak, the professor of broadcast journalism.

Broadcast journalists should be making a mental outline of their story as they shoot it. Once again, it is the "shoot to edit" principle. A broadcast journalist can't shoot an hour-long interview and then pick through the footage trying to find the best quotes. "For man-on-the-street type of stuff I always end [the conversation] with the sound bite that I am going to use," said Mark Carlson, a one-man-band videojournalist for the Associated Press based in Brussels, Belgium:

> I don't ask five, six more questions. I don't prolong the experience. I stop and say, "Awesome, thanks for talking to me." Once I have gotten my two or three that I know I am going to use, I cut it off there.

Make sure to choose sound bites that keep the story moving. Don't pick sound bites that just repeat the copy in your tracks. Sound bites should not be used for basic facts of a story; that kind of information is better suited for reporter voice tracks. Use sound bites to reveal the human aspect of a story, and to add flow and context overall.

For Carlson, creating a broadcast story is like planning a trip:

> When I look at the basic formula . . . [it is] like you have a car and you go on a road trip. The first question you ask is, "Where are you going?" You need to figure out the destination, figure out "Do I have enough fuel to get there?" If you don't know your destination, you are never going to complete a story. You are going to have a bunch of elements that don't make sense.

So essentially, by taking each piece of reporting and plugging it into the formula like a puzzle piece, you can build a successful package. The first scene introduces the people; the last scene concludes it. When the story is over, "People want to know the story is over," said Carlson. "They know that they've been taught something or that they've learned something."

But doesn't using formulas mean always producing essentially the same piece, over and over again, but with different content? Not really. That won't happen, because each person interviewed will be different, and each situation will be different, and these differences will create different rhythms, different moods, and their own, unique identities.

In Carlson's case, he knows that he will produce a video that is one minute and thirty seconds long:

> If you go dancing, you don't dance hip-hop style at a waltz. When the story is based on the video that I gather, if the video is fast-paced action, then the writing is going to pick up speed. If there is a lot of natural sound that explains the environment, then I am going to write fewer words and allow the natural sound to speak for me, so I don't have to say the words. . . .
>
> Sometimes each track is one sentence long—one or two words, maybe two sentences long. Anything more than that, then you are doing radio, in my opinion. So I stick to those basic things. They guide me.

Broadcast pieces are a puzzle, Carlson concluded, and each hole in the puzzle requires a suitable piece to fill it.

Along with always striving to tell stories that are meaningful to the audience, try as well to keep things fresh and not mundane or day-to-day, even if putting together news stories is your daily occupation. Strive to make at least one part of each package as memorable as possible, be it the writing, the visuals, or the sound. Don't just report the news. The audience needs to understand why they are watching this story. Tell a story that communicates a level of emotion and insight that goes beyond the formulaic.

Writing a TV Script to Be Read Aloud

In Suzanne Lysak's course "News in a Multimedia World," she emphasizes that the rules of broadcast scriptwriting are meant to ensure clarity and understanding, such as giving an attribution before a fact or quote ("Basics"). Thus we would write, "Police say the fire was intentionally set," instead of "The fire was set intentionally, according to police." Similarly, people's titles are always given before their names. We would cite "Airbus engineer Sarah Smith" instead of "Sarah Smith, an engineer with Airbus."

Other rules are followed simply because the news story you are writing will need to be read out loud by someone. For example, write out numbers whenever possible. When giving the number of people who attended a university basketball game between two rivals, do not write, "A record 35,446 people attended the game." Instead, write, "A record thirty-five thousand four hundred and forty-six people attended." Make things as easy as you can for the anchor, who may not have had the chance to review the script before reading it cold on air.

When writing copy leading into an SOT, don't repeat what is in the SOT. Also, write a script in the active voice, not the passive: "A bystander reported the fire," not "the fire was reported by a bystander."

If something is mentioned in the script, always be aware of whether the viewer needs to be seeing it at the same time. Strive to make the script match the visuals at all times. But again, do not simply describe exactly what the viewer is seeing on the screen. Visuals speak for themselves.

In the case of facts and figures, such as unemployment numbers that are lower than last year's, use a graphic to show the numbers on the screen at the same time that the viewer is hearing them. This helps the viewer to process the information.

Finding Your Broadcast Voice

Television and radio broadcasters both talk about the need to be conversational, and not contrived, when speaking on air. "It takes a while to find your voice, and what sounds right on the radio, and where to inflect," said freelancer Sam Eaton, who does both video and audio storytelling. "When I was first starting out, I would drive around listening to NPR on the radio, and I would imitate their reporters as I was driving—kind of crazy-looking processes."

Radio storytelling is a slightly different challenge, in that sounds must deliver the nonverbal content—sounds that very often are chosen for the visual images they conjure up. "We really like the idea that the listener comes up with their own image," said freelance radio producer and radio teacher Rob Rosenthal (2013). "You create your own image, like when reading a book. It makes you a co-author."

Verbal delivery of a story can make or break the storytelling. It can be terribly boring, or so over-the-top that it turns listeners off. Balance the need for performance with the need to sound conversational. It should "sound very natural, like you are talking to a friend," Eaton explained. "Radio is one of the most natural and intimate mediums, like you are having a close conversation and telling somebody about a really interesting story. It is harder than it really sounds to pull that off."

Self-consciousness can also become a major issue. Just as people joke about having "a perfect face for radio," it's easy to think that print journalism is a refuge for those who don't have the strong, distinctive voice of a broadcaster. Get over that thought. Whether you are studying print or broadcast, it's a multimedia world. Jump in before you fall in, or before you are pushed.

There's also a misconception in radio that the quality of a voice is the only thing listeners hear. As Dave Cohen, a former television broadcaster for the New York Yankees baseball team, explained:

> If you actually look at a lot of people on TV, you . . . come to the realization that their voices are not anything special. It's basically a lot of how they tell the story. . . . They do it by using colorful language that creates some kind of image in your mind that may accompany the picture, or they let the picture speak for itself and not detract from the images you are seeing. And they may enhance what you are seeing by not repeating the obvious.

Cohen is no longer in sports broadcasting, but he still acts in movies and television shows, does voice acting, and serves as a voice coach. Whether his clients are an over-the-air broadcaster or a teenager making a speech for the first time, he helps them get over the very common fear of performing vocally:

> You've got to get people comfortable in telling the story, I always say. Hey, you just saw an accident around the corner. And then you come around the corner and you run into your best friend. How would you tell that story? "Oh my goodness, you should have seen what just happened." You have to be really direct, and have some kind of emotion and entertainment value to your storytelling. Giving a speech or broadcast is really storytelling.

Figure 8.11 Dave Cohen, a former television broadcaster for the New York Yankees baseball team. (Courtesy of Dave Cohen)

Cohen went on to explain that there is a big difference between writing a story for a newspaper and writing a piece for broadcast:

> I tell people, You don't write for public speaking or broadcast in sentences. . . . The very first thing I tell anybody is that you cannot write a newspaper sentence and then present it like the spoken language. If you sat down and tried to read the *New York Times* out loud, it would never in a million years come off sounding as natural as somebody speaking.

Voice inflection and pauses have specific purposes, he explained:

> In print you can italicize, you can bold, you can underline, you can put in quotations, you can do all of these different things in the way of looks, but you have to use your voice to do all of that. Whether you are changing your pitch, your tone, your volume, your phrasing, your pausing, before or after, you have to do it with your voice.

When novices find themselves pausing, they think, "'Oh my God my mind is blank the audience is gonna think I am an idiot,'" added Cohen. "Effective broadcasters learn how to pause so that they let what they are about to say stand alone. They . . . give the listener a chance to clear out what they've heard, and realize that what's coming up has special importance."

 ### Exercise: Pick Apart a Broadcast Piece

Look online for a video news story posted by a local television station. While watching the video, or immediately after, answer the following:

1. What is one of the sound bites from the piece? Give the actual words.
2. What actualities do you hear?
3. What was a visual that was very effective, engaging, or poignant?

Covering a News Assignment

While reporting a story, be thinking constantly about the kinds of SOT being gathered. In news-driven storytelling, there is almost always a deadline to hit. Television airs multiple newscasts throughout the day, so be sure to "shoot to edit" and get everything that will be needed as you go. While gathering SOT, be thinking about who you are interviewing, and whether they have any sort of expertise on the topic at hand. Seek out differing perspectives and opinions. When talking to a person about a particular issue, such as a developer who is at a meeting to try to change an area's zoning to build a shopping center, seek out another person who lives near the proposed site who might be present at the meeting, and who might have an opinion on the matter. The opinion could be passionate, to the point of the person becoming emotional as he or she talks about it. Emotion makes for strong visuals and SOT.

Along with striving for quality interviews, make sure as well to put viewers at the scene of the event being covered. At a fire scene, try to get the sound of the fire, water hitting the fire, the shouts of the firefighters, the sounds of fire trucks or police scanner traffic.

Natural sound can also help to transition viewers from one place to another, spacing out a story and letting it breathe. Imagine covering the mayor's press conference about a new factory that's coming to the area. Along with attending the press conference and getting it on tape, also make sure to tell a story. This will involve some planning. It might mean doing some work well before the press conference, going out into the community where the factory is scheduled to be built, capturing the scene, and talking to residents.

The goal is to get a real person on tape who is actually living the story at hand. This may require research, phone calls, and e-mails. You are seeking people who live in the area, or who perhaps run a business or other concern, and who may be concerned about the impact of construction and eventual traffic. They will need to be asked about their specific concerns, and how much they support or oppose the factory. Do they feel that their concerns are being listened to? What outcome to the whole situation would they like to see, or what scenario do they most fear?

Viewers will also need to be "brought to the scene" with some visuals: some shots of the proposed site, perhaps with cars or people going by, a nearby landmark with a pan over to the site—anything that visually gets viewers to the location being discussed.

Depending on the kind of business that it will be (and there can be a big difference in local reactions between a candle factory and, say, an asphalt plant), look for someone who has been unemployed for some time, who might be excited to work at the new factory. They might be looking at a new job. This sound bite could put a very human face and voice on the project.

Everything in the story up to this point is leading up to the mayor's big announcement. You have the choice to go to the press conference or not, depending on a number of factors. Sometimes press conferences actually break news; sometimes they are pretty standard and dull, presenting facts readily available somewhere else. One good reason to cover press conferences, however, is what might come out in the question-and-answer session at the end.

It might be possible to pull the mayor aside for some questions that might elicit interesting sound bites—bites that are better for broadcast than anything from the press conference. Then again, there might be only official statements, which tend to turn viewers off. "Don't build stories that are simply official sound bites," Suzanne Lysak said. "Those are hard to relate to as a viewer. Give me a real person—human, people impact—and that will be a more engaging story."

Finally, on a more day-to-day note, always make sure to make deadline. Whether producing a video for broadcast or for a newspaper website, there will be a deadline. Don't break it. Video takes time to export and edit. Make sure to factor the export time into the total time available for the project. Leave a little bit of wiggle room for emergency situations.

A18 DEWITT DRONE TRIAL-VO   Duration: 0'18"

Anchor:1/shot   {***CIARRA***}

THE TRIAL AGAINST THE PROTESTORS

OF REAPER DRONES AT THE HANCOCK

AIR BASE WILL RESUME IN DEWITT TOWN

COURT.

TAKE VO

<mos>Two-person Lower Third\Dewitt Town Court\Drone Trial   {***VO***}
Continues\\\</mos>

16 PROTESTORS WERE ARRESTED AND

CHARGED WITH DISORDERLY CONDUCT

AND TRESSPASSING AT THE HANCOCK AIR

BASE BACK IN OCTOBER.

THE TRIAL CONTINUES THIS EVENING

WITH THE PROSECUTION WRAPPING UP

ITS CASE AND THE DEFENSE TAKING THE

STAND.

THE TRIAL MAY CONTINUE INTO

TOMORROW IF A DECISION IS NOT

REACHED.

Printed:1/29/2014 11:12   *Page 1*

Figure 8.12 An example of a script made for a television broadcast. (Courtesy of Suzanne Lysak)

Exercise: Storyboard a Broadcast Piece

You are assigned to do a story about new parking meters in the city. Before going out to actually shoot, get a handle on what visuals it will be possible to get.

1. Write down the visuals possible for a story like this.
2. Write down the natural, ambient sounds that could be obtained to help tell the story.
3. Write down a few questions to ask a parking enforcement officer. What kinds of sound bites are you looking for?
4. What other people would you interview to help round out this story?

Video Journalism Tips for a Better Story

- Look for central characters.
- Remember that broadcast journalism is primarily a visual medium.
- Look for "moments."
- Think about the types of shots and reporting that will go together. If the reporter track will mention specific visuals, make sure to shoot those visuals.
- Look for action and reaction when shooting.
- Make sure to place the wireless microphone in any place where it can get good audio. When using a lavalier microphone, clip it six to eight inches below the subject's mouth, with the wire running up the person's shirt and out of view of the camera.
- Think "story structure" when you are shooting and interviewing, and always shoot to edit.
- What will the surprise be, and how will you prepare viewers for it?
- Don't get stuck on the original plan for a story. Stories can change, and you must be open to it.
- Always make deadline.
- In journalism the stories you tell are always about others, not yourself. Treat people with respect. However tense or inflamed a situation might be, if you are respectful you will have nothing to worry about.
- Practice makes perfect. The more stories you work on, the better you get. Don't think that the first video you do is going to be broadcast-worthy. You are learning. Try and try again.
- Always listen. Try not to step on your subject's words during the interview. You could be talking over a great sound bite.
- Pay attention to natural sound.
- Visuals are a big part of the story. Write only what the camera cannot see.
- Write simply—try not to overdo it.
- Care for every story you do. If you put care into a story, viewers will know it and care too.

Newspaper Journalism's Use of Video Outside of Print

For the past several years newspaper journalism has been going through a change. No longer are writers only writers and still photographers only still photographers. There is a need for everyone in a newsroom to learn how to tell stories visually using video.

Wes Pope, a former newspaper photographer who produced video and multimedia at the *Chicago Tribune* and the *Rocky Mountain News*, now teaches multimedia photojournalism at the University of Oregon in Portland. "Filmmakers are pretty far ahead of attempts to do video at newspapers, which are just starting to understand video," Pope says. "Filmmakers have been doing it for 100 years."

Chuck Fadely is a videojournalist for *Newsday* in Long Island, NY. He tackled the challenge of learning video head-on, embracing the opportunity to change, and is now a visual storyteller on two platforms. Prior to *Newsday*, Fadely worked for the *Miami Herald* as both a still photographer and a videojournalist.

Video for newspapers is finally coming of age—many papers are figuring out workflows that allow them to produce content that is consistent in quality and quantity. "At *Newsday* we have three shooters and we have three full-time video editors. We shoot and then hand our stuff off to the editors; someone else edits the video," said Fadely. "The *Newsday* system is to shoot multiple assignments in one day and then hand them off to someone else so that I don't have to spend the next twenty hours editing. This is a great thing."

Fadely said he makes sure to shoot both interview and B-roll, and then he gives the editors a list of ways things might go together. "I leave it up to the editors to assemble," he said.

"Video is being shot everywhere," Fadely pointed out:

> No matter where you go or what form of communication video has become, it is an important part of literacy. It is a universal skill everyone should have, and it is important. We can try to wall people off, but I think we should let everybody have a shot at it.

At the *Milwaukee Journal Sentinel*, Mike De Sisti has gone from being a still photographer to being a multimedia journalist. "I am continually trying to evolve myself as a storyteller to keep up with the technology," said De Sisti, who has been using an iPhone to upload video to the newspaper's website. De Sisti knows that what he is doing is not the greatest way to tell a story, but

> when things need to be updated quickly . . . we have an app on the phone that records live video . . . Sixty-second clips go right to the website . . . when people are hungry for content [i.e. Green Bay Packers-related material] . . . my understanding is that for those situations they want fast clips—vignettes of what the day is like.

One project De Sisti undertook was a ninety-mile drive to Chicago before a Packers game, stopping at various predetermined places along the route and uploading small vignettes to the site. "If I am going to do it, I will have fun doing it, so that people can enjoy the pieces," he said:

> When the Packers played the Bears for the playoff game, I knew because it was the Packers I didn't need to produce the most polished video. Because it has the Packers in it, I could have videotaped my shoe and still had 200 clicks with iPhone footage. With that understanding, I was able to produce a greater number of videos, generating more views, rather than spending all my time working on one video. . . .

De Sisti knows what assignments need to be turned around quickly:

> It just has to do with being able to use the tool that's right for the story. . . . We definitely beat TV if the mayor has a press event. I will set up my iPhone to record his statement and upload it right away with my iPhone app . . . That is another thing: If you can see and hear the mayor, and the video is not shaky, people don't care . . . They want to hear what he said. You can do that with an iPhone.

Tom Kennedy is a multimedia consultant and former managing editor for multimedia at washingtonpost.com, and a former director of photography at the National Geographic Society. Kennedy was one of the first people to bring video to the newspaper world, and he had a vision for the future of visual storytelling on the web:

> I was really concerned about the diminishing role for photojournalism in print. I believed the landscape of the web offered more opportunity for revival, because it would allow for fuller expression of narrative storytelling. I wanted to see much more experimentation with the "subject-driven narrative," where the stories were told visually and aurally through close, extended observations of the subjects and the documenting of the most important situations in their life.

As newspaper culture adapts to a digital distribution system, everyone who works in a newsroom is being asked to become a visual journalist. Like most newspapers, the Newark, New Jersey–based *Star-Ledger* began its video efforts with video that was purely natural sound, but lately it's been using a voice track to help carry the story. John O'Boyle, a former staff photographer with the newspaper, explained: "With a regular one-and-a-half to two-minute video, we may do a voice intro or maybe a tiny bridge to move from one character to another."

Like many newspapers, the *Star-Ledger* shied away from using a reporter's voice as a track when it started doing videos. "I think people when they first start in the industry . . . are used to being a fly on the wall, never really getting involved with voicing. It's new to us. As newspaper video matures, it'll happen more," said O'Boyle, who worked on a multi-part video called *Chain of Life*:

> The voicing was to bridge from one scene to another, to tie up loose facts, or add something to be inserted. I think using voice has made our videos much more complete and informative, by using it in a minimal way. If you narrate the whole thing, something is wrong.

Newspapers are perfectly positioned to tell stories that are rich with content and go beyond the printed page. The need for video, even though newspapers are adopting video for their own economic survival, does not mean that the storytelling should be any less than what readers receive online or in print.

On-Camera Reporting

Going on camera is no longer just a television-news thing to do. Newspapers around the world are having their reporters record themselves on camera to introduce stories and explain content. As Steve Elfers of *USA TODAY* explained:

> We had a breaking-news reporter covering the [George] Zimmerman trial in Florida. After that day's trial she would do a stand-up. She mic'd herself up; we essentially only saw her for five seconds and used her audio track over footage from the trial feed.

The reporter then uploaded her footage to the newspaper via an FTP site, he said.

Elfers says that all the newspaper's breaking-news reporters are multimedia-capable, and all have gone on camera to cover stories in this way:

> If you take a snapshot of our newsroom, the work is gravitating to two pockets of video production. One is long-form, watchdog documentary, and the other is daily stuff. For our dailies, we explore how fast and how good can we make something if we only spend an hour or hour and a half on it.

Elfers said that *USA TODAY* is interested in people who "are comfortable stepping into something that they are still learning. We've got a number of young hosts, who were reporters first, now learning how to produce shows." As he was quick to add,

> Your competitor, at a minimum, is a blogger with a cell phone. Can you do everything you need to be able to do, or are they going to beat you to market with a story because you don't have the tech skills?

The Stand-Up

There will be times when there are no visuals, but something will still need to be on the screen while information is delivered. This is where the stand-up comes in. It's classroom show-and-tell all over again.

Stand-ups are very common, but they're more than reporters just getting in front of a camera and talking. "As much as they are parodied, stand-ups do actually play a role," said broadcast professor Suzanne Lysak. "They are an important part of storytelling, if done in the right way."

The options for a stand-up may seem limited, but keep on striving to make the story as engaging as possible. Avoid just standing in front of the camera. Be creative and try to do something that breaks the mold a little.

Baltimore reporter Mike Schuh said he tries to produce stand-ups that are out of the ordinary. "Stand-ups are always [meant] to propel the story forward, to illustrate and to cover an area of a story which you may be lacking visually," he said. "If you are doing a stand-up successfully, you should be demonstrating something or moving around to show people things about your story or its setting." Schuh said he tries as much as possible not to just stand frozen with his microphone in front of the camera. He calls these shots "Statue of Liberty" or "postage stamp" shots, where the reporter is positioned in front of a backdrop that is supposed to signify something in the story.

As for how long a stand-up should be, he said he aims for seven to fifteen seconds. "You never have to talk on camera that long," said Schuh:

> If you do three sentences on camera, that is probably a lot. That is going on about twenty seconds. That is way too long for a stand-up, unless it is complex and demonstrative. Then you already have a pattern and a pathway to follow; you are simply knocking over the dominoes from one to the next. . . . You already set up a scenario and are fulfilling it.

Figure 8.13 Mike Schuh is a television reporter for WJZ Eyewitness News in Baltimore, MD. (Courtesy of Mike Schuh)

Schuh said that he sticks to facts when writing a voice-over track—for example, how long someone has lived at a given location, people's names, information about the location or person, all gathered off camera. "I don't need any of that stuff on tape," he said.

Schuh agreed that natural sound is also key to making a good video story, and said that he tries as much as possible to use a wireless microphone. "I never use a stick mic other than for a podium shot or as an emergency, or when the boss wants to show the logo of the station or entity," he said.

Exercise: Shooting a Stand-Up

Indoor Stand-Up

Shoot a stand-up shot in a lobby of a building on campus.

1. Put the lens at its widest setting to incorporate a background element.
2. Shoot a second stand-up as a close-up, zooming in with the lens to eliminate or "clean up" the background. This should be shot from a different position than the first stand-up.

Outdoor Stand-Up and Interview

Shoot an outside stand-up with a campus building behind the reporter. Shoot one person on the street, interviewing him or her for a sound bite. Ask people anything, such as how they feel about reporters approaching them on the street.

1. Use the building as the background. Make sure you can see the *whole* building.
2. Find a subject on the street and shoot a close-up (head and shoulders only) interview for a sound bite where the background is not a distraction. The question will be determined in class.

Make Sure to Do the Following

1. *Level the tripod*
2. *Set the white balance*
3. *Focus*
4. *Check audio*
5. *Compose the shot*

Use the Following Script

This is what you will say during each standup:

"For Joe College News, reporting outside/inside [*your location*], I'm [*your name*]."

Connecting with People

Mike Schuh says he has no problem coming up to people out of the blue and talking to them for a story. For example, if he is doing a spot news story on a house fire, he needs information from possible witnesses and reactions to what is going on. He says he will go up to a person and say:

> Hi, my name is Mike Schuh. I work for Channel 13. Wow, this is something. We're doing a story on this. Do you mind if I put a microphone on you while we both stand here and check this out?

By not using a stick microphone and just making it a conversation, he says, obstacles that could make the person feel uncomfortable are removed. By just talking to someone normally, he is able to get natural reactions. "You never do an interview. You have a conversation," he said.

For some people, talking to strangers is no easy task. It takes willingness to step out of your comfort zone, along with being pretty sure of yourself and capable of making small talk easily. Sometimes people are not open to chatting. In those cases, Schuh says, "It's not personal. They don't look at me and say, 'I hate Mike Schuh.' They look at me as a reporter." Schuh said that if someone turns him down, he moves on to the next person:

> I dip my pan back in the stream. Do that often enough, you'll find gold. You are out there prospecting. Sometimes you get dust, and sometimes you get the pan knocked out of your hand. But if you don't try, you'll never get anything.

Good video stories rely on good visuals and great moments. These moments can help further a story by bringing viewers in and connecting them with what is human and emotional, by showing a person on a level that only video moments can. "My goal is to use as few words as possible, and make sure that I am letting the pictures carry their own weight," said Schuh.

Schuh emphasized the importance of creating a memorable visual story:

> Great television news stories must have great visuals, or must have supporting visuals to lead you down the path. . . . Your job is to just set up the punchline, set up the surprises, set up the reveals, and let the character knock 'em down. That will make a memorable story. Because the bottom line is, all we are trying to produce is something that is memorable.

 Exercise: Vox Pops

Find three people that you do not know personally. They must be in different settings and situations. Think about police officers, pizza shop owners, trash collectors, college presidents, roadies for bands, mall Santas—the possibilities are endless. Conduct a ninety-second on-camera interview with each.

You may record only ninety seconds per interview, and you must turn in all ninety seconds of each interview.

Once you have found each subject, prepare your interview questions. Before shooting, conduct a quick, preliminary, off-microphone interview. Determine whether to continue with this person or look for a new subject. If you decide to continue, ask your first question before you begin recording and have your subject repeat the question back to you after you start recording.

Be prepared with a follow-up question (or questions), which you may ask on tape. Remember, you have only ninety seconds. You'll need to make sure that the interviews you do are interesting and have substance.

This exercise should expand your comfort zone, and you'll get to meet some new people.

Mobile News Gathering

In 2012, as a videojournalist at the *Star Tribune* in Minneapolis, MN, McKenna Ewen had to cover the flooding in Duluth. Upon arrival in a flooded area, he first shot breaking-news footage using his iPhone and an OWLE handheld video rig. He saved the footage to the online file-sharing service Dropbox, where a producer back at the paper was able to retrieve it, edit it, and upload it to the *Star Tribune* website site as quickly as possible.

Once Ewen had gotten his first footage back to the office, he began looking for character-driven narratives to help tell the story of the flood. "Then I pulled out my [Canon] 5d to shoot a story," he said. "I'd shoot for a few, then use my iPhone and shoot some more, and continue to update [the Dropbox] . . . the numbers paid off."

At radio station WTOP in Washington, D.C., reporter Neal Augenstein has turned to doing all of his reporting using only an iPhone:

> There's curiosity when I show up for an interview and all I've got is my phone in my pocket. If I was offered an interview with the president of the United States, I am not sure that I would walk in there with just my iPhone, but for the most part, covering news, it's really revolutionized my workflow.

Augenstein said he puts his iPhone to multiple uses, including recording audio and video, updating social media, writing web stories, editing audio and video packages, and sending content back to the station.

"Every reporter has that walk of shame, when they go and cover something and realize that after they thought they had the interview, that they had nothing," said Augenstein, who said there has been only one occasion when he realized that he got a phone call in the middle of an event and did not record what he thought he did. After that incident, he wrote a tutorial on his blog so that other people could avoid the same painful situation. Augenstein blogs about many of his experiences reporting with the iPhone on his website, iphonereporting.com:

> I include a how-to on things you need to do to lock your iPhone in the "on" recording position—you press the on/off button after you start recording. You press that and your screen goes black. You think you've turned your phone off, but actually the iPhone is continuing to record in the background.

Augenstein knows that his job as a radio-only reporter is in the past, and that he now works for a digital news organization, producing multiplatform content:

> The iPhone is just a tool to help me do my work faster. Reporters can't just be radio reporters anymore. The person has to do video and write for the website, has to do social media. But the nice thing about the iPhone is that it allows you to do them all simultaneously—tweet and write out the story, all on the phone.

The iPhone in particular offers such capabilities as an 8 megapixel image and support for various attachments that bring it up near the level of some small video cameras. But limitations remain. If you're shooting with your iPhone, for example, and need to make a phone call while you shoot, you'd better have another phone on hand.

At the *Philadelphia Inquirer*, Michael Boren is a cops beat reporter. He often will record a stand-up on the scene of breaking news, edit the resulting video right on his iPhone, using iMovie, and then upload it to the newspaper's website. "A lot of times with breaking news, I do not have a photographer with me, so I just ask a cop or a firefighter or somebody else to hold the camera," said Boren, who took a video storytelling class in college, where he learned how to shoot video and edit with Final Cut Pro. "Just the ability to not have to upload everything on the computer and all that . . . saved me hours and hours of time. It's pretty amazing you can do all that with a phone now."

With the rise of digital platforms, Michel du Cille, the former assistant managing editor for photography at the *Washington Post*, sees a change in the way photographs are reported in journalism nowadays:

> From a newspaper point of view, because of the Internet, because of big changes in digital, because of economics—things have changed. . . . We are accepting sometimes a lower bar, especially for web. We accept a lower bar for Instagram; we accept a lower bar for get-on-the-scene, take-a-quick-iPhone-picture-and-get-it-out-there-because-it's-gotta-get-out-there facts.

Figure 8.14 Newspaper reporters can often be seen using iPhones to report the news for digital-based products. (Photo by Jamie Germano, *The Democrat and Chronicle*)

Du Cille added that photographers now don't have time in breaking news situations to look for and capture that perfect moment. When the photographer gets on scene, "In the first three or four minutes you just have to take a picture, and it doesn't matter what's in that picture, you just send it."

Social Media

When newspapers first started providing content online, they merely posted the same content that was being printed in the paper—the informational equivalent of "shovelware." Newspapers have since moved to providing online-specific content, including multimedia. The web offers many opportunities through social media to provide content by news reporters that has not been shown to the public through other means. "There's certainly an added incentive, when you go into the digital world, to not just rehash what you've done on television," said Bob Dotson from NBC's *Today Show*:

> It's sort of like an old farmer's tale: A farmer never threw anything away—the hooves were made into glue and the corn husks became something. It's the same way with our storytelling. You go out to do something for one medium, but you always get a lot of stuff that maybe doesn't fit, or maybe you won't have time for, or isn't part of the storyline, but also is kind of interesting.

This is the material that can be adapted for and shared on social media.

At TODAY.com, producers look for moments from the show, and from the news in general, that might appeal to the social media audience. As Carissa Ray, supervising multimedia producer for TODAY.com, explained:

> We really encourage our producers to think of how their content can play on digital platforms. If there's a great quote or moment that happened during an interview, if they have footage that is really awesome, and there's not a place for it in their edit or it feels somewhat tangential to the main point of their package, there may well be a place for that material on digital.

Ray also stresses that it's important for broadcast producers to not just think of the web as a place to put content that didn't merit inclusion in their broadcast package. She says she wants content that has a certain amount of value, and which audiences on separate platforms might really have an interest in and would want to share with others.

Short Documentary Films Online

No longer is filmmaking solely about getting your work seen in a theater. The web can be a very effective method of distribution for documentary films, with the potential for attracting millions of viewers. The website Vimeo offers a great platform for all kinds of films, which can be viewed in high quality and are served to users with lots of bandwidth and all the capabilities for a seamless experience. The site also offers curated videos; the staff goes through Vimeo's submitted offerings and designates "Staff Picks," which helps to bring exceptional content to the top for wider viewership.

"At this point in time I would rather my video get a Vimeo Staff Pick than get accepted to a second-tier film festival," said Jared Levy, a Brooklyn, NY-based documentary filmmaker who shoots both documentaries intended for the web and branded content for advertisers, "because one is going to generate e-mails from potential clients, and the other is going to be a laurel that I put up that looks good but doesn't generate things for me, usually."

One of the projects Levy worked on was *story(us)*, commissioned by the Future of Storytelling conference, which became a Vimeo Staff Pick. "It was edited out of a living room, and we hatched ideas on local runs in the park," said Levy. "I think that's the new world we are living in: taking projects that traditionally do not go to smaller outfits, because we are more nimble." The movie was a collaboration among Levy, who served as director of photography, and two others: a creative director, Jason Oppliger, and a director, Michael Marantz.

The Web Series and Online Channels

Beginning in August of 2013, the *Washington Post* published a sports video series called *First and 17*. Presented in an episodic format, the project was shot by Brad Horn, a videojournalist at the newspaper. Horn recounted the genesis of the project:

> We went to the rivals.com rankings, and we looked at those recruiting services. We looked for local kids, until we found Da'Shawn Hand, who was number one in two different rankings. We were like, "Oh man, he is number one," so we went down and met with him.

Horn then pitched a story on Da'Shawn to his editor. Horn explained that Hand was the top high school football recruit in the country and also happened to live in the Washington, D.C. area, about an hour from the newspaper. Horn's pitch included how he wanted to immerse himself in Da'Shawn's life and essentially do a video documentary about him. After being pitched several times, the project was given a green light to begin production.

The way the *Washington Post* decided to run the project was different from the ways that most long-term journalism projects with video are presented, which is usually in chapters run as a series at the end of the shooting and reporting process. With *First and 17*, the *Post* ran a video every week throughout the football season. The episode would launch a week after it was filmed, giving the video editing team some time to work on building out a story structure without trying to crank it out immediately after a Friday night game for a Saturday or Sunday rollout on the website. The series was essentially run one week behind real life.

 First and 17: story and video by Brad Horn; executive producer Jonathan Forsythe

To watch the web series: http://www.washingtonpost.com/sf/firstand17/

Figure 8.15 Brad Horn is a videojournalist for the *Washington Post*. (Photo by Andrew Maclean)

Figure 8.16 Mediastorm is a film production and interactive design studio based in Brooklyn, NY. (Courtesy of Mediastorm)

At MediaStorm, a multimedia production agency in Brooklyn, NY, Brian Storm is the executive producer. "I look for projects that are universal, timeless. Stories that move you, that make you want to do something about the issue. Of course, we are looking for visual sophistication, but story is what really matters to us," said Storm, who presents his company's films on their website, mediastorm.com. "We feel it's critical to pay for the work we are publishing, so more great work can be done in the future. We also share any revenue we generate in syndication fifty-fifty, back with the artist." Several of MediaStorm's pieces are offered on a pay-per-view basis, through a system built into mediastorm.com. A feature presentation called *Rite of Passage*, for example, by Maggie Steber, is viewable for a $2.99 fee.

Documentary film director Sean Dunne published his first film on the web in 2009, when "everyone in the world wasn't making short documentaries," he remembered. There wasn't any obvious path to follow, he said, so he just threw his first film up on Vimeo, a video sharing website. Then, "it kind of took on a life of its own. Once the film went viral I got a little bit of attention [for] that film," said Dunne, who now has a sizable following on Facebook and Vimeo. Dunne's first film, the seven-and-a-half minute *The Archive*, was successful after being distributed purely online. "I built up a little bit of an audience. It was really all on Vimeo," said Dunne. "The audience kind of found me and spread it around. That's where I felt the most loyal people were."

Dunne has since produced a feature-length film, *Oxyana*, on Vimeo that cost a lot more money to produce than his short documentaries. To pay for it, Dunne held a campaign on the Kickstarter website to round up investors. To repay investors, the video is offered for a rental fee of $3.99 and a purchase price of $7.99. Vimeo is therefore not just a place to get your work seen, but a

Figure 8.17 A frame grab from documentary filmmaker Sean Dunne's film *Oxyana*. (Courtesy of Sean Dunne)

place where filmmakers can monetize their films online and be paid for their creative work. Nonfiction narratives are slowly coming of age online as more and more people are attracted to this kind of service.

Ethical Considerations in Journalism

It cannot be understated that to be true to what we do as journalists, we must abide by basic rules to win and maintain the trust of viewers and readers. It is important to have an understanding of journalism ethics prior to starting to cover news, be it with a pen or a camera.

This chapter has been about capturing visual images as they happen, in the moment. That is an important concept. As has been stated before, in journalism it is important for the person recording what is happening not to manipulate the reality of that content in any way. To set up, dramatize, recreate, or fake events without telling the viewer is forbidden.

In certain situations a scene can be changed—in a profile piece, for example, one can place a subject in a chosen spot or in a certain kind of lighting to improve the image. In news situations, however, never manipulate a scene or change what is already happening into what you want it to be, or think it should be, or even what might make better viewing. The temptation to do this can be strong. Good, genuine stories can be hard to find, and deadlines put people under a lot of pressure to deliver something—even something fake. For example, if you are doing a story on a "busy" tattoo parlor, and when you go there no one is getting a tattoo, don't have a friend receive one, or get one yourself, just to generate some content. Nine times out of ten, if you just wait long enough, or make the effort to come back, you'll get the needed shot. It is the journalist's job to capture what is in front of the camera, not to create it.

Truth Telling

When it comes to doing journalistic video, a concept to keep in mind at all times is that of the *truth*. You are telling the truth. You are showing the truth. Journalism does not recreate events. For example, imagine covering this news event at a local elementary school: The longtime choral teacher is retiring after her final concert. One possible, emotional visual that could come out of the event would be the children presenting a bouquet of flowers to the teacher at the end of the concert, up on stage. If you are not in the right place at the right time to capture this moment, you are out of luck. It is not okay to get everyone into their places and recreate the moment, and then record it as if it were the real moment. Essentially, you missed it.

Another thing that is strictly off-limits is recording an interview and then editing it to make the audio track sound as if the person said something he or she did not say. It is acceptable to edit the imperfections out of a video; there is nothing wrong with cutting out drops in audio or camera clicks or background noises. The final audio should be pristine and free of aberrations. At the same time, it is vital to keep the audio truthful to the scene in which it was recorded. Always aim for high production quality, but never at the expense of ethical values—at least in journalism. When working on an advertising or marketing video—for a company trying to gain funding through Kickstarter, for instance—it is possible to be in nonfiction situations where adjustments and recreations are acceptable. There will be no assumption by the audience that what they are seeing is the whole truth and nothing but the truth. Using that same video for a journalistic piece, however, would require careful examination of anything that was done to enhance production quality. Are you trying to change or hide anything that "doesn't fit," or fabricate something that does? Watch out.

At times you will record a subject who uses a lot of vocal filler noises: ums and ahs. Minimizing these in the audio track is usually a matter of personal judgment. Think of writing an article for a newspaper: Would you include these noises when quoting the person? Probably not. If you are interviewing a person with a speech problem, whose vocal noises are simply part of who they are, think twice about how to edit the piece. Sometimes, ums and ahs are the result of a lot of furious thinking or hesitancy on the part of the speaker, which can be revealing. Sometimes the person is merely nervous. Be careful not to let the second look like the first. Again, it is a matter of fairness and careful judgment.

Editing in a timeline has already been discussed in Chapter 6. It is possible to take clips recorded at the start of a shoot and put them at the end of a finished piece. In nonlinear editing, things do not have to happen in the final product in the order that they were shot. The final product, though, must be a story. An interviewee's quotes must be presented in context, with a lot of care that their meaning is not altered, misinterpreted, or misused to make a better story. At worst this can lead to a libel lawsuit, in which someone sues over damage to his or her reputation. At the very least it can do great—or even fatal—damage to your own reputation and career.

Journalists must be accurate, correct, and complete with the information that they are providing. Providing information that is not correct, or omitting some essential fact (for example, one official highly praises another, and you leave out the fact that they were once business partners), puts your journalistic credibility on the line. A journalist is the source of information for a community, and cannot be seen as having any greater interest or agenda that might taint that information. Inaccuracy can even happen through sloppiness or by accident. One way to ensure that it does not is to have other people—preferably experienced people—watch your video or look over your photos before they are published.

These days, when publishing a video on YouTube is as simple as clicking the upload button, it is even more crucial to know what should be broadcast to the world. Having a professor or some other experienced editor go over your work prior to publishing is a very important safety measure. They might not always seem like it, but editors are your friends. They ask questions about a project, point out facts that should be checked or check them outright, and generally serve as a critical test audience who will fix mistakes before they become public—and often unfixable. It's not that they distrust you or want to hurt your feelings. They just want to protect you and make sure your work makes the intended impression. Even editors need editors. If the boss goes out and does a video, someone needs to criticize that work to make sure all of the proper checks and balances have been followed. The organization's credibility is at stake.

All Sides of a Story

It is very important to present all sides of a story. If two candidates are competing for a political office, it is a necessity to give equal time and coverage to both. This isn't just a matter of ethics; it is one of credibility as well. It is also vital to be objective about whatever you are covering. Everyone has personal views on politics, religion, and a host of other subjects, but the journalist's job in the field is to present all sides of an issue and the real nature of every conflict and debate. A camera does not have political views. It looks at everything in an equal light. A journalist should do the same, both in choosing which stories to cover and in the actual execution of interviews and story presentation.

Leave personal views at home, or at least in the car. It is not the journalist's place to disapprove or mock, and neither is it the journalist's place to be an enthusiastic, uncritical advocate of certain issues, political causes, political parties, or politicians themselves. This is called *propaganda*, and it makes the journalist a tool of others. When covering anything from a presidential campaign to a local, public hearing that generates a heated discussion, get both sides of the conversation, both for and against, and never assume there is a "right" and a "wrong" side.

Being seen as unbiased and fair is one of a journalist's greatest assets. In other words, it is one of your greatest powers. Viewers respect it, and so do the people being covered. Once it is lost, it is extremely hard to recover.

Digital Manipulation of Photographs

The digital revolution in photography makes images very malleable—they can be altered drastically in ways that can be hard to detect. When taking photographs for a newspaper or other media outlet, never manipulate an image to change its content. Once again, it is the job of the journalist to present what was in front of the lens, not to manufacture it.

The motivation does not matter. It is not permissible even to digitally remove something from the background of an image because it is distracting. It was the photographer's job to "control the background" to begin with, before taking the picture.

Also off-limits are filters that change a photo's colors and lighting. Mobile phones have apps that make it quicker and easier than ever to manipulate the content of an image. Do not use filters and color adjustments that alter light or any other quality of an image to make it look different than it did when it was shot, although it is permissible to do so for the purpose of improving clarity. As a photojournalist or videojournalist, it is important to show things as they really are or were, unadulterated.

Getting Permission to Film

In journalism, it is generally not necessary to obtain written permission from a subject before filming them. "The reason why people get releases for most things is that there is going to be either an entertainment aspect to it or a commercial aspect. Journalism is not commercial in a traditional sense," said Roy Gutterman, a communications law professor at the S.I. Newhouse School of Public Communications at Syracuse University:

> I have read a lot of cases on invasion of privacy where plaintiffs have objected to journalists using their images in magazines or newspapers or even TV news, and the plaintiffs often argue, "Well, these are businesses that make money." But journalism is not a traditional business, so you do not need a release to do traditional journalism.

In the entertainment film and documentary world, however, getting releases is standard. The safest and easiest way to go about this is to ask a subject at the start of filming to give an "on air" audio-visual talent release, right into the camera. This way there is documentation that your subject knew they were being filmed, and consented to it. But, if there is the opportunity, have a subject sign a talent release form.

EXAMPLE OF A TALENT RELEASE

Date:_____

I, _____, hereby grant my consent regarding my being filmed for a documentary by _____. I hereby grant to _____ and any successors, assigns and licensees, the perpetual right to use as desired all still and moving images and sound recordings which have been made of me for exhibition, distribution, promotion, or any other desired application in perpetuity.

Signature _____

Name (Print) _____

Home Address _____

Telephone number _____

Email Address _____

Witness (can be photographer) _____

SPECIFIC CODES OF JOURNALISTIC ETHICS

There are adopted ethics policies by which most photojournalists abide. This policy appears in the section that follows.

The National Press Photographers Association Statement of Principle

As adopted in 1991 by the NPPA Board of Directors

In the early days of the electronic revolution that swept through our profession, it was evident that digital photography would be very beneficial but at the same time posed a real threat to the integrity of our images. NPPA adopted this Statement of Principle to affirm unequivocally our commitment to honesty and accuracy in this new environment. It is a strong admonition aimed directly at the practice of digital manipulation but also sums up the NPPA Code of Ethics in a matter of a few sentences.

As journalists we believe the guiding principle of our profession is accuracy; therefore, we believe it is wrong to alter the content of a photograph in any way that deceives the public.

As photojournalists, we have the responsibility to document society and to preserve its images as a matter of historical record. It is clear that the emerging electronic technologies provide new challenges to the integrity of photographic images . . . in light of this, we the National Press Photographers Association, reaffirm the basis of our ethics: Accurate representation is the benchmark of our profession. We believe photojournalistic guidelines for fair and accurate reporting should be the criteria for judging what may be done electronically to a photograph. Altering the editorial content . . . is a breach of the ethical standards recognized by the NPPA.

(Continued . . .)

(...continued)

NPPA Code of Ethics

Preamble

The National Press Photographers Association, a professional society that promotes the highest standards in visual journalism, acknowledges concern for every person's need both to be fully informed about public events and to be recognized as part of the world in which we live.

Visual journalists operate as trustees of the public. Our primary role is to report visually on the significant events and varied viewpoints in our common world. Our primary goal is the faithful and comprehensive depiction of the subject at hand. As visual journalists, we have the responsibility to document society and to preserve its history through images.

Photographic and video images can reveal great truths, expose wrongdoing and neglect, inspire hope and understanding and connect people around the globe through the language of visual understanding. Photographs can also cause great harm if they are callously intrusive or are manipulated.

This code is intended to promote the highest quality in all forms of visual journalism and to strengthen public confidence in the profession. It is also meant to serve as an educational tool both for those who practice and for those who appreciate photojournalism. To that end, the National Press Photographers Association sets forth the following.

Code of Ethics

Visual journalists and those who manage visual news productions are accountable for upholding the following standards in their daily work:

1. Be accurate and comprehensive in the representation of subjects.
2. Resist being manipulated by staged photo opportunities.
3. Be complete and provide context when photographing or recording subjects. Avoid stereotyping individuals and groups. Recognize and work to avoid presenting one's own biases in the work.
4. Treat all subjects with respect and dignity. Give special consideration to vulnerable subjects and compassion to victims of crime or tragedy. Intrude on private moments of grief only when the public has an overriding and justifiable need to see.
5. While photographing subjects do not intentionally contribute to, alter, or seek to alter or influence events.
6. Editing should maintain the integrity of the photographic images' content and context. Do not manipulate images or add or alter sound in any way that can mislead viewers or misrepresent subjects.
7. Do not pay sources or subjects or reward them materially for information or participation.
8. Do not accept gifts, favors, or compensation from those who might seek to influence coverage.
9. Do not intentionally sabotage the efforts of other journalists.

(Continued...)

(... *continued*)

Ideally, visual journalists should:

1. Strive to ensure that the public's business is conducted in public. Defend the rights of access for all journalists.
2. Think proactively, as a student of psychology, sociology, politics and art to develop a unique vision and presentation. Work with a voracious appetite for current events and contemporary visual media.
3. Strive for total and unrestricted access to subjects, recommend alternatives to shallow or rushed opportunities, seek a diversity of viewpoints, and work to show unpopular or unnoticed points of view.
4. Avoid political, civic and business involvements or other employment that compromise or give the appearance of compromising one's own journalistic independence.
5. Strive to be unobtrusive and humble in dealing with subjects.
6. Respect the integrity of the photographic moment.
7. Strive by example and influence to maintain the spirit and high standards expressed in this code. When confronted with situations in which the proper action is not clear, seek the counsel of those who exhibit the highest standards of the profession. Visual journalists should continuously study their craft and the ethics that guide it.

Chapter Summary

Nonfiction visual storytelling is the communication of real situations, events, and people to the world. The goal is to show real life, as it is happening. Whether working for a newspaper, a television station, a website, or on your own as a documentary filmmaker, the nonfiction visual storyteller needs to deliver a story with a beginning, a middle, and an end. Even when simply reporting the facts while on scene at a breaking news event, the way information is delivered to the audience is going to take the form of a story.

Nonfiction storytelling is challenging in ways that fiction is not. Stories must be discovered rather than being made up, and the storyteller must deal with many real people and many real deadlines. There are methods for cultivating nonfiction stories, however, and tried-and-true formulas for arranging them and presenting them to the public. Main characters must be identified, story arcs plotted out (even if very quickly and simply), issues researched, scripts written, and technical issues dealt with.

Whether using a high-end camera or a mobile device, always think about how the story you tell will affect the audience. All television reporters will say that they want their stories to be memorable for the viewer, while sticking to the ethical principle of telling only the truth, and showing only genuine situations that are captured as they occur. The goal of creating memorable work goes all the way back to the early planning stages of a project, and is rooted in making an early commitment to a story that will shape everything done with it, including interviews, shooting, and editing.

You are the eyes and ears of all your viewers while you pursue nonfiction visual storytelling. People will learn from and be informed by your work. You, in turn, will experience a wide variety of people, witness the full range of emotions, and more than likely have some unforgettable experiences.

Review Questions

1. What is the difference between news-driven, profile-driven, and character-driven visual storytelling?
2. Describe three ways to find new story ideas.
3. In an interview, how should the subject be framed within the viewfinder?
4. In the ABDCE story wireframing paradigm, what does the "D" stand for? What is its purpose?
5. What is a "reporter sandwich"?
6. Given the choice between recording in a noisy environment with a good background, or in a quiet environment with a bland background, which would you choose? Why?
7. Why is it important to transcribe an interview in a video? When transcribing, to what part of the transcription should you pay the most attention?
8. When reading aloud for broadcast, is it more important to be conversational, or to have the right kind of voice?
9. What are the rules for doing a stand-up?
10. When taking photographs for a media organization, what are some things you should never do?

Exercises: "Everyday Hero" Character-Driven Story

Good video has a theme and a story. It is usually character-driven; someone is doing something for a reason. Make sure that the reason is compelling enough to justify the time spent telling his or her story.

"Story Pitch": Part 1

In 200 words or less, give a succinct summary of a story idea about a person who would be deemed an "everyday hero"—someone who has an interesting story that needs to be told.

Video Story: Part 2

Contact the person from Part 1 whom you deem most appropriate to serve as the face of your story, and tell his or her story in video. Think about the beginning, middle, and end, and about how best to tell the story.

Remember that the story is not about a subject, but about a person and his or her individual story within your overall story. It's best to focus the story as much as possible. Be sure to stay with a true and accurate representation.

Be sure that the person you choose will allow you to return to shoot more than once.

Produce a two- to three-minute video story about the "hero" you found.

Key Terms

Actualities – "Nat" sound or ambient sound, which paints the background for the listener in an audio track.

Beat reporter – A reporter who covers specific areas, giving them expertise in a certain topic.

Commitment – A story's reason to be; the single sentence that describes its essence.

Data-driven stories – Stories that arise from information, often involving graphics.

Digital-first – An approach in which news is first presented on a digital platform rather than on the more traditional platforms of television or print.

Drama – Tension resulting from someone not getting what they want.

Lead room – The area of the frame into which an interview subject should be looking, rather than straight into the camera.

Live shot – This is where a reporter is live on scene, and the backdrop or setting is a major part of an unfolding story.

Logging footage – The act of taking notes of video footage that has been shot.

Meta tagging – Keywording footage so that it can easily be found later.

News producer – The role in broadcast news that arranges and organizes a particular newscast or show.

News reporter – In broadcast news, the person who goes out and does field reporting about topics of relevance to an audience.

Package – A self-contained story that consists of sound bites, natural sound, and a voice track. Often this is a piece reported in the field then edited and cut together as a standalone story.

Profile-driven stories – A way to introduce an audience to an interesting and/ or influential person. These can be of individuals or leaders of communities, but they can also be stories about places or businesses, or question-and-answer reports that give insight into specific topics.

Qualitative data – Observed data that you collect yourself.

Quantitative data – Hard numbers gathered from a source or from research.

Raw video clip – Video filmed on a news scene and broadcast without any editing.

Reporter sandwich – Interview setup in which the main light is placed on one side of the reporter and the camera on the other.

Reporter track – The narration of a video by a reporter that explains what is happening.

SOT – Sound On Tape is audio that is recorded on a news scene, or ambient audio that includes sound bites that relate to a news story.

Stand-up – When a news reporter stands in front of a camera and talks into it and to the audience.

Track – A narration track that weaves in and out of SOTs to tell a story.

VO or Voice-Over – Voice-over read by an anchor on air, paired with video captured in the field.

VO/SOT – Voice-over that is paired with sound on tape. An anchor reads a script as a voice-over, leading up to a sound bite played on the air.

Sources

Alten, Stanley R., and Douglas Quin. *Audio in Media*. Boston, MA: Wadsworth/ Cengage Learning, 2014.

Andrews, Nancy. Conversation with author, April 24, 2013.

Augenstein, Neal. Conversation with author, November 5, 2013.

Ballon, Rachel Friedman. *Blueprint for Screenwriting: A Complete Writer's Guide to Story Structure and Character Development*. Rev. ed. Mahwah, NJ: Lawrence Erlbaum Associates, 2005.

Bledsoe, Greg. Conversation with author, October 31, 2013.

Boren, Michael. Conversation with author, November 22, 2013.

Carlin, John. Conversation with author, November 22, 2013.

Carlson, Mark. Conversation with author, November 5, 2013.

Carlson, Mark. "Video Journalist Tips." 47th Annual NPPA News Video Workshop, March 2007.

Chittum, Matt. Conversation with author, November 5, 2013.

Clutters, Robin. Conversation with author, November 5, 2013.

Cohen, Dave. Conversation with author, November 4, 2013.

Contreras, Evelio. Conversation with author, June 5, 2014.

De Sisti, Mike. Conversation with author, March 24, 2011.

Dotson, Bob. Conversation with author, November 1, 2013.

du Cille, Michel. Conversation with author, December 3, 2013.

Dunne, Sean. Conversation with author, November 19, 2013.

Eaton, Sam. Conversation with author, October 22, 2013.

Elfers, Steve. Conversation with author, October 23, 2013.

Ewen, McKenna. Conversation with author, June 22, 2012.

Fadely, Chuck. Conversation with author, July 19, 2013.

Fenn, Lisa. Conversation with author, November 2, 2013.

Freed, Sharon Levy. Conversation with author, October 23, 2013.

Gutterman, Roy. Conversation with author, June 23, 2014.

Hooker, Stephen. "Audio: Giving Texture to Your Pictures." 47th Annual NPPA News Video Workshop, March 2007.

Horn, Brad. Conversation with author, January 21, 2014.

Hoyt, C.J. Conversation with author, November 21, 2013.

Hubbard, Stephanie. Conversation with author, November 19, 2013.

Jensen, Scott. Conversation with author, October 29, 2013.

Jones, Barbara. Conversation with author, January 22, 2014.

Kennedy, Tom. Conversation with author, March 12, 2010.

Kenon, Danese. Conversation with author, November 21, 2013.

Lamott, Anne. *Bird by Bird: Some Instructions on Writing and Life.* 1st Anchor Books ed. New York: Anchor Books, 1995.

Levy, Jared. Conversation with author, November 11, 2013.

Lysak, Suzanne. "Basics of Broadcast News Writing." Unpublished handout. S.I. Newhouse School of Public Communications, Syracuse University, June 5, 2012.

Lysak, Suzanne. Conversation with author, November 4, 2013.

Maclean, Andrew. Conversation with author, October 23, 2013.

Maierson, Eric. Conversation with author, December 21, 2013.

McManus, W. Keith. Conversation with author, February 16, 2009.

Meltzer, Josh. Conversation with author, June 9, 2014.

Miller, Jonathan. Conversation with author, October 30, 2013.

National Press Photographers Association. "NPPA Code of Ethics." Accessed November 20, 2013. https://nppa.org/code_of_ethics.

National Press Photographers Association. "NPPA Statement of Principle." Accessed November 20, 2013. https://nppa.org/node/5167.

Noble, William. *Writing Dramatic Nonfiction.* Forest Dale, VT: P.S. Eriksson, 2000.

O'Boyle, John. Conversation with author, July 10, 2008.

Papper, Robert A. *Broadcast News Writing Stylebook.* Boston: Allyn and Bacon, 1995.

Perez, Simon. "Writing for Video." Unpublished handout. S.I. Newhouse School of Public Communications, Syracuse University, n.d.

Pope, Wes. Conversation with author, January 2011.

Ray, Carissa. Conversation with author, October 29, 2013.

Redell, Bob. Conversation with author, November 25, 2013.

Rosenthal, Rob. Conversation with author, April 7, 2009.

Rosenthal, Rob. Conversation with author, November 5, 2013.

Schuh, Mike. Conversation with author, October 28, 2013.

Storm, Brian. Conversation with author, July 14, 2009.

Storm, Brian. "Gathering Audio: Tips and Tricks from the MediaStorm Workflow." White Paper. MediaStorm, March 2005. Accessed May 28, 2009. http://mediastorm.com/sites/default/files/pdf/MediaStorm_Gathering_Audio.pdf.

Storm, Brian. Gathering Audio, Tips and Tricks from the MediaStorm Workflow. White Paper, May 28, 2009. http://mediastorm.com/sites/default/files/pdf/MediaStorm_Gathering_Audio.pdf.

Strong, Bruce. "Storytelling Basics." Lecture at the NPPA Multimedia Immersion Workshop, S.I. Newhouse School of Public Communications, May 13, 2014.

Swain, Bethany. Conversation with author, October 31, 2013.

Waite, Matt. Conversation with author, October 8, 2013.

Weiss, Joe. Conversation with author, March 11, 2011.

Young, Alison. Conversation with author, October 29, 2013.

Yurman, Will. "Introduction to Audio for Photographers." Accessed March 16, 2015. http://blogs.umass.edu/dvandal/files/2009/09/Sound20091.pdf.

9 MULTIMEDIA STORYTELLING IN STRATEGIC COMMUNICATIONS

What Makes an Effective Strategy to Push a Brand Visually on Multiple Platforms?

In this chapter you will learn

- Storytelling strategies for brand marketing
- Options for multimedia press releases
- Social media messaging strategies
- Social media content strategies
- Aspects and types of persuasive storytelling for commercials and PSAs
- The basics of creating commercials and PSAs
- How to develop digital content strategies

Introduction

In the case of entertainment and journalism, one is serving an audience that has generally shown up expecting something. They are watching and listening because they have a desire to be entertained, or a desire to find out what's happening in the world or in their city. You are dealing with a willing group of watchers.

Strategic communications has a different dynamic. Commercials, public service announcements, social advocacy, and public-relations campaigns all reach out to an audience that is not necessarily receptive, or even paying attention. Each strives to elicit some kind of action, whether it is buying a product, subscribing to an idea, or donating time or money. Essentially, they are salesmanship. They are pitches. They are out to change people who do not necessarily want to be changed, or even spoken to. This makes strategic communications more of an uphill climb than entertainment or journalism, even though it is often the very thing that steers an audience toward entertaining or journalistic content to begin with.

This is why advertisements and other calls to action are so often dressed up as entertainment, or as journalism. It is also why the most effective ads are those that use these forms to turn an unwilling or disengaged audience into one that actually wants to watch the ad again, *or tell a friend about it*.

Social media therefore have a huge role to play in strategic communications, as we will see while we explore this form of storytelling.

The News Hole

While news reporters are mainly interested in uncovering their own stories, it doesn't always happen that way. Many times journalists rely on press releases to get something into print or on the air. Newspapers are now serving multiple platforms; just providing news in print is no longer the bread and butter that it once was. Producing content for digital platforms on the Internet is quickly becoming an important way to push messages. As print advertising declines, the news hole in print publications is shrinking, so the ability to get the stories covered has diminished.

Not only are print news holes shrinking, but the number of journalists covering specific beats is shrinking, too, which places more of the burden on those who remain. This affords PR professionals new opportunities to assist journalists in getting their jobs done, and provides a promising avenue to getting stories covered and disseminated to the world. PR professionals need to adapt to these changing conditions the same way that journalists are having to change their own job descriptions.

Storytelling in Strategic Communications

Thaler Pekar, the CEO of Thaler Pekar & Partners, a firm specializing in organizational narrative and communication, had this to say about storytelling in today's multiplatform environment:

> I think a lot of people are talking about story but don't understand what it is. It has become a buzzword. . . . I believe a story is something very distinct. It is seeing something happen to someone or something. There is a beginning, a middle, and an end. It could be a person or a product; it could be a community.

Messages come in all shapes and sizes. Whether they are relating profiles about people within companies or issue-based narratives, communications professionals are eager to get their messages out. "People are zapped with ads like billboards, ads in grocery stores. Messages are everywhere. It's the same voice as before, but now there are more channels to be touched," said Tracy Rock, vice president and account director at the Publicis Kaplan Thaler advertising agency in New York City. "Advertising messaging is not a sacred place anymore," she added. "Bathrooms, TV—ads are everywhere. On napkins. The media has changed. There is a stronger influence."

"If you look at really good videos that brands are making and that people are making, even ones that are six seconds, there is a proposition in the story," said Bill Winchester, executive vice president and chief creative officer at Lindsay, Stone, and Briggs, an advertising agency based in Madison, WI:

> Storytelling has a beginning, middle, and end, and often a moral. But even if you're doing a recipe video—for instance, how to make a grilled cheese sandwich and here is the result—that would have a beginning, middle, and an end. That's the way people expect stories to go.

Julie Murphy, vice president of public relations for Sage Communications in the Washington, D.C. area, said storytelling has always been a critical component of effective PR. Today, she said,

> We are inundated with information, and the best way to break through the clutter is through effective stories, anecdotes, validators, and proof points. The customer case study is the original form of storytelling. It also validates the messages aimed at key stakeholders. For example, if a reporter is writing an article on a company, customer stories will help to paint a colorful picture and bring the key messages to life.

Brand Marketing through Advertising and Public Relations

The ability to push a brand through the marketplace is a kind of strategic communications. You have a particular brand, and that brand needs to be marketed. The brand needs as many eyes on it as possible, and it needs to be presented in a way that influences consumers to engage with it. The ability to market that brand can be separated into two different spheres: public relations and advertising. Anything that is paid for is advertising; anything that is not paid for is public relations.

"PR to me is a hybrid approach . . . pushing key messages through, using a variety of different channels," said Murphy. "People get their information from many different channels. Repetition and air cover is important."

In the age of the Internet, many corporations are hiring both ad agencies and public relations firms to specifically use the web and other forms of social media to push their messages electronically, turning largely away from legacy media such as print newspapers. With social media, the lines between the two campaigns can be blurred. "I put social media under PR, because it's about driving good content and thought leadership," Murphy said. "It's about positioning for credibility and expertise. And, most importantly, it's about being authentic. Nobody wants to be directly sold to on social media. It's about starting a conversation."

Just because there is a new platform out, like Vine or Instagram, does not mean that all brands must be on it. Some companies want to strategically locate their brand on a platform with a plan. Ken Saji, vice president and editorial director for Viacom's integrated marketing creative group, The Shop, explained his company's approach:

> Our focus is not to just be on the platforms to be on them, but to be there because our consumers are there, because we can leverage these platforms to tell a good part of that story. We don't necessarily want to be there just to be there.

Saji is responsible for directing and developing creative executions for integrated marketing campaigns that run across Viacom's music and entertainment groups. As he explained, stories are the key to pushing a brand:

> Brands are entities that not only have cultural relevance, but personal relevance—knowing what your brand stands for, and then clearly defining your brand as not just a product or a collection of products, but as an emotional connection and an experience. . . . You most effectively tell what your brand is by telling a story. Stories connect with people on a very visceral level. We've always told stories. Stories create an emotional resonance, and stories really are the most effective ways of getting your message across.

Communications Strategies

Successful communications strategies depend on professionals' ability to adapt to a changing communications landscape. Innovation and agility are requirements in today's marketplace.

Messages do not stay at the front of people's minds purely through press releases or advertising. If you have a product message that you need to get out to the world, it is crucial to ensure that the message has a long life. It takes persistence to pitch ideas constantly and to keep them relevant.

Many strategies are possible for brand management. Messages that come directly from the creators of a brand are likely to be more one-sided in advertising or public relations than ones that go through a third party such as news reporters, whose job it is to be unbiased and to ensure immediacy, impact, universal appeal, and their own credibility.

Multimedia Press Releases

The press release of the future is not a faxed document sent to newsrooms across the country. Instead, it is a campaign that includes multimedia elements such as photos, video, and other shareable content. This multimedia must be accessible on multiple platforms.

Visuals are powerful. Often stories in newspapers that are accompanied by strong images can trump another story's placement in the daily print edition of a newspaper, as far as readership is concerned. Magazine publishers all know that cover art is a major selling point for a magazine on the newsstand. Being able to understand what makes a good visual story has become imperative for all journalists and public relations professionals. Holding an event or earning media coverage by providing the opportunity for good visuals is becoming a very important part of public relations.

"Content that has a raft of multimedia elements accompanying it, a video and some images, audio and downloadable whatever, absolutely generates more visibility—significantly more than just a plain-text press release," said Sarah Skerik, vice president of content marketing for PR Newswire/MultiVu in Chicago. Skerik went on to explain that mentions of a brand in digital media also trigger outcomes that are measurable and long-lasting: An online article mentioning a brand and linking to its website becomes a catalyst for social conversation. Search engines mine social data for signals, which influences search rank, which in turn drives brand visibility.

When circulating press releases, PR professionals must answer the need to provide digital assets such as images, videos, and infographics, in addition to text-only materials with links that can help reporters research specific items as well as share them with editors, colleagues, and readers. According to a 2012 PR Newswire analysis of its press release data, press releases that include "multimedia assets garner significantly more visibility than text-only releases—up to 9.7 times more."

Multimedia news releases are becoming part of the normal framework of how a brand promotes itself in the PR realm. The standard offerings from a brand include downloadable video, audio files, photos, graphics, and written copy that can be used by media outlets in broadcasts, digital storytelling, and print media. Brands themselves are distributing their own content. Companies should not worry about having all of these types of content, but should think more about where their audience is located.

"We are seeing more companies pull more resources into their own brand journalism and content marketing efforts and [develop] more owned media," said Skerik. "When you are hearing the catch phrase 'every brand is a publisher,' what that really means is every brand is a media outlet, in a sense that they are fully equipped to tell a story."

As Skerik went on to explain, "The one trend we see is brands packaging stories and providing an array of elements for media," adding that she uses the term "media" loosely, linking it to social media, bloggers, or enthusiasts who grab items and share them on Facebook. "You could argue that many brands are starting to do the journalists' jobs . . . a more complete presentation of the content that is more journalistic," she said.

Skerik also notes something she calls the "social proof" effect, in which the brand has assets that are developed into a social media campaign, the campaign grabs the public's attention, and as a result the traditional media then report what has happened on social media.

Although the financial model of traditional media might not be doing as well as it used to, Skerik notes that traditional media outlets still have the influence that brands want and need to be successful. Still, the readership of traditional print newspapers is shrinking yearly, and the space available for press releases in their pages is contracting year by year, and Skerik believes that digital is the right place to be focusing. If she has the option of getting a brand in either the print edition of the *New York Times* or its digital edition, Skerik says that she would go with the "digital version unequivocally, all day long, every day of the week."

A 2011 analysis compiled and compared data from more than 10,000 press releases and 200 multimedia press releases from a four-week period on PRnewswire.com. The study found that building multimedia into a press release increases the visibility of the message. In fact, the research found that the more multimedia was used, the more views the news release received, on average.

According to the research, as reported by Skerik,

> The data revealed that multimedia content is more broadly distributed—because each element of a multimedia release is distributed separately, and can attract its own audience—in social networks, and on search engines. Videos, for example, are distributed to more than 70 video-specific portals.

In addition, multimedia content increases the amount of time an audience spends on a particular news item. A multimedia piece can hold audience

Figure 9.01 A screenshot of a multimedia press release from PRnewswire.com

interest for more than twice as long as text press releases. According to PR Newswire and reported by Skerik, text press releases last for 9.4 days on average while multimedia press releases can last up to 20 days, greatly extending the lifespan of the message.

Corporate Storytelling through Video

Tom Mason is a co-owner of New York City–based Redglass Pictures, a production company that specializes in short narrative films for the web:

> I think part of our pitch in any meeting with a persuasive communication project, whether it be advertising, marketing, or public relations, is that if you are doing a video you should be doing it to make an emotional connection with somebody. . . . That is the thing that our medium does better than any other one.

Mason and his partner Sarah Klein, who is also a co-director, founded Redglass Pictures as a platform for producing documentaries, web shorts, and mixed media content. They have produced shorts for the *New York Times*, *Newsweek*, The Daily Beast, and *The Atlantic*.

One piece they did for *The Atlantic* was a story about an exterminator that combined animated graphics with video storytelling. The exterminator talks about a little-known effect of Hurricane Sandy, which hit New York City and the New Jersey coast in 2012. The mouse population in New York City was displaced, creating an urgent need for pest control. The piece is more than a profile of an exterminator; it's a story. "These are sort of calling cards on some level, marketing for us, stuff that we do well and that we like to do," said Mason, whose goal is to have Redglass' short-documentary work picked up on social media. Mason said the company gets a lot of corporate marketing and nonprofit work by word of mouth through social media, with potential clients saying, "Hey, I saw this thing you did and I'd like to do something similar and let's talk."

Redglass Pictures does some corporate storytelling videos—videos where agencies are looking for this production company to help push their message online through video—in addition to documentary storytelling video. "We're applying the same storytelling principles, vision, approach, and filmmaking techniques to a message that somebody is trying to get out there and communicating it effectively through video," Mason explained.

Mason believes that on the web, short films do better than long videos:

> Three- to five-minute pieces is sort of the magic length for what works online. People will sit in a theater for two or three hours and won't have a problem with that, but the expectations change dramatically when you are in front of your computer.

Figure 9.02 A framegrab from *Of Mice and Man,* a film published by *The Atlantic* and produced by Redglass pictures. (Framegrab courtesy of Redglass Pictures)

He added that their videos are meant to be shared through social media such as Twitter or Facebook.

Redglass' work is not void of story just because it is shorter. "We strive to make it feel like it is all the best meat. No portion of our stuff is wasting your time, nor does it give a chance for the mind to wander or click off of it," he said.

Mason has told companies that a website might work better than making a video. "Make a video if you've got maybe three big-picture ideas that you want to get across really effectively, in a way that sticks, and in a way that you are making an emotional case for them," he said. "It torpedoes a film or video project when somebody says, 'Here are twenty bullet points to get across.'"

 Watch the video, *Of Mice and Man*: http://vimeo.com/68866096

Advocacy through Visual Storytelling

Spreading an organization's message is an essential part of working at a non-profit entity. Everything you do is part of the overall mission of telling the story, and doing so from the point of view of that particular organization. Whether the message is conveyed in words or through visuals, the end result must be a positive portrayal of the organization and what it does. Many nongovernmental organizations have adopted using photographs and video as ways to push their messages online through YouTube and social media.

Greenpeace

"Since its inception in 1971, Greenpeace has put visual storytelling at the front of its campaigns and actions," said Greenpeace photo editor Bob Meyers, who assigns photographers to cover Greenpeace events in the United States. Prior to working for Greenpeace, he served as a photo editor with the Associated Press. "I tell stories to call attention to a problem—that are persuasive, to encourage an action, to recruit members, and build a movement," he said.

Employing skills gained with the AP, Meyers serves Greenpeace by helping to document the organization's efforts and by coming up with ideas to spread its message. "It's sometimes like advertising photography," he said:

> To create a visual message by controlling the scene, we tell them [activists], "line up this way," or "move over here." Deciding where to put people and tell them what to do is not journalism. . . . We want to tell stories to our supporters. When you are carrying a box of 50,000 signatures to the White House, it makes sense to make it more visual. So I work with the campaign teams and suggest ways to create costumes to make it more theatrical, and bring more visual elements, to get pictures that do not need captions.

Meyers also shoots a lot of journalistic-style images, which are not manipulated and do convey the truth of a scene or occurrence. In these cases, he says,

> We are very zealous about our integrity. We don't doctor our photos, we don't put people in and take them out, we don't add smoke to the pictures of coal-fired smokestacks. . . . Greenpeace would never put out a picture of whales being killed ten years ago and say that this whale just died because of Fukushima radiation.

Greenpeace also shoots video for posting on YouTube, and for distribution to news stations. Melissa Thompson, a senior video producer for the organization, described what that can be like:

> One of the most rewarding experiences for me was when we did an action at Mount Rushmore. We hung a massive banner off of the front of Mount Rushmore; I got the footage from the shooters, then uploaded it, then my mom called and said, "Turn on the TV," and it was on *The Rachel Maddow Show*. And within a day we had 75,000 hits on the video of that action. There is nothing like that feeling of, "Oh my God, I just did something that actually had an impact." It is very, very rewarding. It is great when there's a whole bunch of YouTube hits, especially if those YouTube hits translate into people signing a petition or going to an event or taking an action.

Figure 9.03 Greenpeace relies on visual storytelling to help push their mission and goals. (Photo by Mitch Wenkus / Greenpeace)

Open Society Foundations

Another organization that uses visual storytelling to represent its programs is the Open Society Foundations (OSF), started by international investor and philanthropist George Soros in 1984. "It's not really public relations. It's advocacy. We are documenting stories that bring to light these issues, as opposed to promoting the foundations' brand to the world," said Lauren Frohne, a multimedia producer for the organization.

Prior to working for OSF, Frohne was a videojournalist for the *Boston Globe*. "Our projects address the issues, real problems, with personal stories, and try to communicate what is likely to make change. It [is] more about philosophy than it is brand," said Frohne, who characterized what Open Society produces as "advocacy documentary."

As part of an initiative on the torturous nature of health care in Ukraine, Cambodia, and Namibia, OSF hired filmmaker Scott Anger, a former director of video at the *Los Angeles Times*, and Bob Sacha, a still-photographer-turned-filmmaker who has been published in *National Geographic*, to shoot a trio of short films for a new campaign to stop torture in health care. The three pieces they filmed, *They Took My Choice Away*, *50 Milligrams Is Not Enough*, and *Violence Is Not the Solution*, were originally published on the website stoptortureinhealthcare.org. This site is no longer active, but these films are still available at opensocietyfoundations.org. As its page for the

"Stop Torture in Health Care Trailer" states: "Marginalized people worldwide encounter abuse and torture in the name of health care and treatment. The Campaign to Stop Torture in Health Care is helping them stand up to demand their human rights."

As Anger pointed out, "One of the issues with storytelling for newspaper journalism, is you produce work for a general audience. Through OSF, it's for a specific outreach to specific groups to educate people in these countries." Sacha added that they adhere to the same journalistic ethics when doing an OSF story:

> It's the same thing with a different mission, though not different. . . . We enter with the intention of being journalists. The contract with OSF involved truthful journalistic storytelling, to not create anything. The piece could have been done for any news [organization]. Our ethics never waver, and they cannot waver. I am always going to be a journalist, to always tell stories truthfully and unmanipulated. It's the core of who I am; that is something that speaks to the strength of OSF. It's journalism to push initiatives. . . .
>
> We were hired as journalists to tell stories as journalists. They did not tell us what it was supposed to be. We told the stories based on the characters we found. . . . If the world becomes a better place, if we can ease the suffering and save a life, is that a bad thing?

Frohne's job is to find photographers and video storytellers and hire them to shoot these types of stories, she said, since "photography offers a glimpse into people's lives and can connect you in a more personal way with issues and stories you are far removed from."

To Watch *They Took My Choice* **Away**: http://www.opensociety foundations.org/videos/they-took-my-choice-away

To Watch *50 Milligrams Is Not Enough*: http://www.opensociety foundations.org/videos/50-milligrams-not-enough

To Watch *Violence Is Not the Solution*: http://www.opensociety foundations.org/videos/violence-not-solution

---

American Society for the Prevention
of Cruelty to Animals

Organizations are constantly seeking new opportunities to get their messages out online. The American Society for the Prevention of Cruelty to Animals is using video to show the kinds of programs they support and to reveal what the organization does on a daily basis. "Some video is in-house video,

Figure 9.04 Open Society Foundations has hired video storytellers including Bob Sacha (left) and Scott Anger (right) to produce content specific to its mission. (Photo by Pamela Chen/Open Society Foundations)

departmental, like our neuter operations. No specific character; more of a 'this is what we do' profile; nothing dramatic," said Salvador Pantoja, a video producer for the ASPCA who is also doing a lot of storytelling work for the organization. "I'm mostly doing advocacy documentary. It's a mixture of feature stories in short format, nothing over five minutes."

Pantoja created a video about the effects of dogfighting, showing the transformation a dog went through as it moved from the dogfighting ring to being adopted by a family. He was able to interview the family after they had adopted, and was able to pair that footage with video taken during an ASPCA raid. The piece has been watched over 130,000 times on YouTube.

"A lot of the videos I produce as a motive to fundraise, not as public service announcements," said Pantoja, adding that their better-known public service announcements, narrated by musicians, are not filmed by Pantoja but by outside vendors. These spots show people on phones and portraits of animals, all edited to narration with the hope of generating compassion for the animals—and financial support.

"What I am producing is advocacy films," said Pantoja. "I am usually just trying to tell amazing stories. . . . Stories resonate with people—the transformation of the animal in need, and what happens after the rescue when they are rehabilitated and adopted." And, as he added, "it helps to have cute animals in my videos. People love cats and dogs on YouTube."

Figure 9.05 Salvador Pantoja, a video producer for the American Society for the Prevention of Cruelty to Animals. (ASPCA)

MEET THE PRO

Bob Pickard, Asia-Pacific CEO, Huntsworth, Singapore

Bob Pickard is responsible for growing Hunts-worth brands Grayling, Huntsworth Health, and Citigate in the Asia-Pacific region. Pick-ard's last role, between January 2010 and January 2013, was Asia-Pacific CEO of Burson-Marsteller, a public relations and communi-cations firm, and he previously was president of North Asia for Edelman, the world's largest public relations firm, leading its Korea and Japan operations. He first came to Asia after a twelve-year public relations career in North America, joining Edelman as managing director for Korea in 2002 and opening the firm's Tokyo office three years later.

Figure 9.06 Bob Pickard, Asia-Pacific CEO of Hunts-worth, Singapore.

Pickard has extensive experience serving clients in sectors including auto-motive, energy, financial services, health care, resources, technology, and transportation. He has a long history of involvement in sustainability issues and has significant expertise in social media communications and the rise of

(Continued. . .)

(. . . *continued*)

Asia in the public relations industry. He was named Agency Head of the Year at the Asia-Pacific PR awards in 2012.

Bob Pickard believes that all good public relations campaigns are based on storytelling. "The story is the most important thing," he said. A company needs to tell stories to its target audience,

> so that those people will do and think what we want them to do or think, know of the company, feel favorable toward its brand, recommend its products to others, invest in the stock, make positive comments online, or want to work there.

Pickard said he is seeing a change in the ways that public relations professionals use newspapers, compared to how they did in the past. He said that the norm in PR was that "through the relationship with a journalist you could 'earn' editorial media coverage." But as newspapers reduce the number of journalists available to cover press events, they are creating "challenges and opportunities for our society. . . . I grew up in a PR industry where you had to persuade a journalist to cover your story. The resulting coverage would provide a professional satisfaction that is becoming rare."

The reasons that many organizations go through traditional media companies are grounded in editorial standards. Traditional media organizations place a premium on being known as credible, unbiased sources of information. When information comes to the customer through a public relations agency, on the other hand, the content can be perceived as one-sided.

"With not as many journalists out there, journalists are overtaxed and there is not enough time to think about stories," Pickard explained. This creates the opportunity "for companies to tell their own stories, not just through journalists, but by creating editorial content for their own audiences."

These days, PR professionals can hand journalists a completely new type of press release: one complete with video, links, and a story that is ready to roll. The job of the PR professional now is to persuade the audience not just through the printed word but also through multimedia elements built around storytelling. As Pickard wrote in an August 2013 post on his blog, bobpickard.com,

> These days we also need to know how to think like the media producer in programming content for scrolling social media streams, while thinking like the researcher in applying an advanced mastery of analytics to campaign planning and accountability for results.

With the Internet enabling anyone to push content out through blogging and social media campaigns, "There are valid concerns about accuracy,"

(Continued . . .)

(. . . *continued*)

said Pickard. "I do think that the decline of standards-based journalism is a problem. . . . People trust the credibility of that source."

Of the importance of infographics, Pickard says,

> Where data meets design is the "sweet spot" for digital storytelling. Information overload means we must tell complex stories in a simple yet compelling way, in the blink of an eye, and thus the rise of infographics is one of the most transformative trends in PR at the moment.

Pickard said he believes the story is at the heart of public relations campaigns, and that "Every tactic of communication should advance the plot." If a new product is being launched by a particular company, it is the role of the public relations agency to figure out how to announce it via a new story. "Every single plan is based on a story arc," he said.

Bob Pickard's Tips For Getting Going With A Corporate Message

- Companies cannot act like things.
- They must have feelings and personality.
- They must be consistent with design and personality.
- They must have a sentient presence through storytelling.

Corporate Social Media Efforts

Corporations are beginning to form their own newsroom-like ventures to disseminate information, making their own information graphics to help push their brands and products, and hiring people with journalism backgrounds to help them do both these things.

Digital Content Strategy in Sports

Website content strategies are essential to running a successful messaging campaign. In the National Football League, each football team has its own team of digital content producers running the team website. "We are an extension of PR, to a certain extent, but from a football side of things there are different opinions of what our role should be," said Jay Adams, digital content manager for the Atlanta Falcons and a former newspaper sports reporter. "You are trying to find that balance that is going to help make people happy. . . . If we feel like it jeopardizes our advantage as a team, we do not want it out on the website."

Though the Falcons might be playing other teams on game days, the team website is not competing against other team websites online, according to

Figure 9.07 Jay Adams, digital content manager for the Atlanta Falcons. (Photo courtesy of Jay Adams)

Adams. "We're more competing with local media for eyeballs than other team websites," he explained.

Adams said that when he first came to the organization, they were trying to cover the team as a newspaper would, with longer-form stories. Since then he has changed the content strategy to one that is more short-form. "We can provide access that nobody else can," he said.

From his vantage point running the website, he is able to provide Falcons fans with behind-the-scenes content that would otherwise be difficult to see. On game day Adams can be found on the field pre-game, tweeting about activities there, or in the locker room, chatting with the staffers who get equipment ready for the players.

"On game day my number-one initiative is to interact with fans on Twitter, tweeting game information—in some cases what just happened on a recent play—to give fans a look at game day through my eyes," said Adams, whose personal Twitter account, @falconsjadams, has over 15,000 followers. "I am tweeting with people through the game. I sit next to our PR team. I am getting info as soon as it comes in," he said.

The official Twitter account @Atlanta_Falcons has 259,885 followers, while the team's official Facebook page has over 1 million likes. "The day I got here in 2010, we had 76,000 likes on Facebook. We've been number one in Facebook growth for the entire league. That's a huge credit to my social media coordinator and her tireless work," Adams said.

The number-one category of content on the Atlanta Falcons website, incidentally, is the team's cheerleaders. There are not only photographs but also videos of the women doing things like a swimsuit shoot. These items get more traffic than any other content on the site.

The site has been redesigned almost every year since Adams got there, and he is constantly trying to figure out new ways to highlight the short-form content that his team produces for the site and to figure out ways to integrate social platforms with the site in interactive ways. Adams summed up this goal with a question: "What can we bring to the home page that makes [it] easier for fans to share our content on their social platforms?"

A man of many talents who wears many hats, Adams doesn't just manage the digital media. He is also an on-camera personality for the team, running podcasts and hosting video commentary.

Adams sees the Falcons' digital content strategy as constant, ongoing, and still developing. "We are constantly trying to contribute to the conversation in social. It is really a twenty-four hour, seven-day-a-week, 365-day-a-year industry, so that's what we've got to be," he said. He said he is as busy in the off-season as he is when games are being played every week during the season. "We have different stages once we get to the off-season. You are recapping your entire season, then you move on to the NFL combine, the draft, mini-camps, and training camp," he said.

"You always heard major league baseball is America's pastime, but the NFL is trying to become America's passion," Adams added.

Digital Content Strategy in Corporate PR

Jeordan Legon was a journalist before getting into the public relations side of storytelling. Once a bureau chief for the *San Jose Mercury News*, Legon had also worked for CNN and AOL, as well as serving as a product manager at Yahoo, before moving into public relations at Chevron. "I was interested in telling stories in a more engaging way," he said. "I took a leap of faith from Yahoo to Chevron. I did not want to sugarcoat, just try to tell the story as genuinely as possible."

At Chevron, which is a multinational energy corporation, his job was to bring more journalism-style pieces to the company's website, "not puff pieces." Legon also introduced more video to the site, along with bringing a treasure trove of digital insight from the other places that he worked, including Yahoo, CNN, and AOL.

At Chevron, Legon tried to engage the audience as much as possible by adding photo slide shows and other visual and interactive elements to the company site. He was also able to get the company to change the way they shot their video:

> By being more journalistic, avoiding jargon, avoiding video from the past and talking-head videos—by showing people in their environments, taking people from the office to the outside, from on-campus to a refinery or field, showing people in their environment beyond the office—this [kept it from] feeling like a corporate video. . . . It gave an authenticity or veracity that it had not had before.

Legon currently lives in Switzerland and works for Novartis, a pharmaceuticals company, where he is global head of digital communications and social media. In that role he is responsible for the company's Internet standards, ensuring that its websites have a consistent look throughout the world and applying the brand's standards to the digital realm.

"It is important that we have people who understand digital and are passionate about it," Legon explained:

> We need to raise awareness for our target audience. Patients, doctors, and career seekers should know that we care about science and diseases, not just selling a product or positioning the brand in a favorable way. We raise awareness on social media, and on roche.com we need to be at the center of the conversation, get users to share our information.

Digital Content Strategy in University PR

At the web communications office at Virginia Tech, John Jackson has been at the forefront of social media for the university since 2008, growing the school Facebook page from zero to over 129,000 followers. Jackson tries to get the university on as many channels as possible, including Instagram, Google Plus, LinkedIn, Vine, and Pinterest. If the audience is there, he says, he is going to get Virginia Tech there.

"In a lot of ways I am doing storytelling, but I am being a bit more heavy on the promotion side of it. We are still writing stories and doing video pieces," Jackson said.

On Instagram, Jackson posts photos taken by the university photography staff and also from the archive. "It gives our fans an opportunity to reminisce. . . . Anything related to football does really well," he said. "The whole idea is to improve engagement and make people aware that this is going on, on campus."

Jackson plans out what he will post, when he will post it, and to which channels prior to actually doing it. "If we post something to Twitter in the morning, we won't post it to Facebook until that afternoon in order to improve engagement. We try not to drop it all at once," he explained.

Jackson is a former online editor for *The Roanoke Times* and roanoke. com, and even though he works for the communications department of a large university, he remains a journalist at heart:

> If there is a touchy decision or if there is an unpopular topic from the university, it will run as news. We will report whatever runs in our daily e-mail, but we may be choosy on the channels that we want to publish it to. We may not want to post to Twitter or Facebook, just given the discussion that might occur as a result of it.

Jackson knows his role as part of the public relations arm for the university, and he tells his team:

> Remember, you are a voice for the university, whether you think it or not. Keep it professional. Always keep in mind that people will look at you and determine you to be some sort of official voice of the university.

Figure 9.08 John Jackson, director, web communications at Virginia Tech. (Photo courtesy of John Jackson)

MEET THE PRO
Dan Sloan, Editor-in-Chief, Nissan Global Media Center, Yokohama, Japan

Dan Sloan is a frequent commentator on Japanese corporations and marketing for professional organizations and academic groups. He is the author of Playing to Win: Nintendo and the Video Game Industry's Greatest Comeback. *Before jumping into the corporate public relations realm, he was a correspondent with over fifteen years' experience reporting, editing, and managing television and text bureaus, including broadcast reporting for Reuters, CCTV, CNN, CNBC, the BBC, and a variety of other global television and radio outlets. He is the past president of the Foreign Correspondents' Club of Japan and an adjunct professor of global media studies at Komazawa University. He is now leading the development and management of Nissan's first dedicated global news center, established to create multimedia content and social networking sites for a wide variety of marketing and communication channels.*

Figure 9.09 Dan Sloan, editor-in-chief, Nissan Global Media Center, Yokohama, Japan. (Photo courtesy of Dan Sloan)

Some companies have come up with their own content strategies, and some even have their own in-house video teams, such as Nissan, who

(Continued . . .)

(. . . *continued*)

hired former Reuters reporter Dan Sloan to head up a social media shop built on the twenty-four-hour news cycle. This team can react and respond via social media to Nissan's stream of brand-related content on the social networks. The Nissan media team is composed of former newswire, magazine, and television journalists who are able to talk about more than just Nissan; they can talk about the automobile industry as a whole.

"I call it do-it-yourself brand narrative, or journalism, or whatever, to come in and tell compelling content with text, video, pictures," said Sloan.

Based in Yokohama, Japan, Sloan speaks fluent Japanese and has lived in the country for over twenty years. In 2012 he made a leap of faith from the journalism world into working for a corporate auto giant, starting up a news operation for Nissan. The company had decided it was time to push its messages out online and via social media.

Sloan's job is to help raise the brand image of the automaker. "They felt that they had lots of great stories, and while they could pay for advertising, they wanted an internal team to make content that would go externally and internally," he said. "Enough funds were made available to get a team started and to build a broadcast studio, and that's what we've done."

He was able to set up what eventually became the Global Media Center for Nissan, also called *koto-zukuri*, which is a phrase coined by Nissan chief operating officer Toshiyuki Shiga "to complement *mono-zukuri* (making things)—the usual business of manufacturers, in this case making brand stories," Sloan said.

The idea of the Global Media Center from the start was to hire ex-journalists with an eye for news. When PR professionals send out press releases, generally they are trying to grab the attention of a journalist covering a beat. By hiring journalists, they gained access to the journalistic thought process and production standards. Sloan explained the origin of the Center:

> They wanted a higher "so-what bar." Sometimes what corporate public relations are very content with may not seem very interesting to journalists, but that often results in . . . ideas or stories that go nowhere, because no one acts upon them or sees them as new stories.

Sloan sees the venture itself as similar to a startup, in which people come in with no guarantee of success or vision of where they want to be. He calls it "building the airplane as he flies it."

Part of Sloan's strategy is to understand the online space. Where there is a need to produce content for short attention spans, you need something visual with words. Sloan wants to produce content that users want to share and share again:

> What we discovered in the era of social media is that really, in the old era, corporate space advertisers would use traditional media and they would have traditional media clients. But now, in the social

(*Continued . . .*)

(. . . *continued*)

media era, truly corporate content can go directly through distribution via social media, and the individuals, consumers, and fans will do the work of the people who are in the marketing and communications departments.

Sloan also has to understand where his audience is and what forms of social media they are using. "Twitter has been less of a factor for us than YouTube and Facebook, to some degree," he said. "Good pictures or good video can go viral in no time at all."

Sloan said his team is producing a story a day with a lot of dependence on the metrics available from YouTube. He is very particular about the types of stories that his team tells. He does not want lofty messaging that speaks too highly about the company. "We need to be a little more brand-agnostic and innovative to grab their attention and tell the story in a different way," he explained.

Since they began posting videos to YouTube less than three years ago, the Media Center has recorded nearly 20 million views, resulting in 31.8 million minutes of measurable viewing time. The Global Media Team knows that video storytelling is an important part of what they do, especially with YouTube analytics being a major way that they tune their messages and get them out.

"This is a very helpful kind of intelligence, because it leads to decisions on where you want to put resources next," Sloan said. The team does everything from video stories to coverage of auto shows to "intelligence" shows about what is going on in the industry, along with studio work.

Sloan explained the similarities and differences between corporate and journalistic stories:

> If you are working for a brand you cannot have a lack of bias. There is bias. You will protect the brand. . . . I call what we do "storytelling," because sometimes it more closely reflects traditional journalism and sometimes it is very similar to an extended commercial, but not hopefully with the feeling of an infomercial. If I had to clarify it as anything, it is infotainment—something that is interesting enough to keep your attention.

Sloan said he thinks entities like the Nissan Global Media Center could be the wave of the future for corporate America:

> You could spend $200,000 to $500,000 on a series of commercials, or a lesser amount to hire a few people to make content for you with no extra costs to implement. . . . It's a no-brainer. Sometimes people ask what's the difference between what we make and a commercial. I usually say theirs is shorter and it usually costs more.

Figure 9.10 A frame grab from one of Nissan's videos that was posted to YouTube. (Photo courtesy of Nissan)

Persuasive Storytelling for Nonprofits

To have the ability to move an audience to take action—to motivate them to do willingly what you ask of them—is to be persuasive. Combine this with storytelling and multimedia, and the result is persuasive multimedia storytelling. Many nonprofits and corporations are making such storytelling part of their communications strategies for just this purpose: to inspire their followers to take action.

The website charitywater.org uses video to show how monetary donations are used to help people in places that lack water. "Video is a great way to tell your story," said Beth Kanter, co-author of *Measuring the Networked Nonprofit: Using Data to Change the World*:

> I think the mistake that some nonprofits make is that they put their dinner videos [a term for 60-minute videos covering organizational history] on the front of the site. You need to think, how can you tell the story of your organization or the story of the campaign or the call to action—whatever it is you want to put in your video—how can you do it [quickly] and effectively?

What Is a Nonprofit Organization?

Who benefits from an organization itself? Who stands to reap the rewards, or profits? Is it owners and shareholders, or the public at large? If it is the public at large, then the organization might well be a nonprofit. Examples of nonprofits are trade organizations, social clubs, governmental groups, some political groups, and charities. Often the groups exist for the purpose of serving others.

Determining the Audience

A large part of persuasive storytelling for the nonprofit sector is determining the audience. If a large number of people can be targeted on a particular issue, assets and ideas need to be developed that can grab their interest, get past any resistance, and motivate them to action. Say, for example, a certain percentage of the audience buys water in plastic bottles, and the goal of a campaign is to stop this practice and replace it with the purchase of water in reusable, metal containers. You will need to catch the attention of the plastic-bottle buyers, make them see the error of their ways in a manner that is not annoying or antagonizing, connect with them emotionally, and present your client's needs as the best possible solution or course of action. This will involve careful assessment of people's attitudes and daily lives, as well as your client's needs, and how the audience can best be persuaded to change their behavior or give their time and/or money to the organization. First, however, one has to understand who the audience is and what they value the most.

An important part of all this is being able to think like the audience. "One of the most valuable skills in the advertising business is the ability to imagine lives unlike your own," said Kevin O'Neill, a former advertising executive who is a professor of practice at the S.I. Newhouse School of Public Communications in Syracuse, NY, teaching advertising. "To be able to imagine other folks, with other problems, with other aspirations, with other values—it's one of the things that make the business so interesting," O'Neill added.

If the target audience uses a product other than the one you're pushing, the end goal is to get these people to start using your product instead. In consumer advertising, success is usually easy to measure. "There is no measurement on earth for advertising like the cash register," O'Neill said.

Nonprofits and Social Media

Now nonprofits are using the Internet and social media to get their messages heard. By using social media, many organizations have been able to drive traffic and donations to their organizations.

Beth Kanter feels it is important for a nonprofit to be connected on different social media channels:

> People . . . want to understand what their money is going to do. What is the end result of their donation? Is it going to save lives? Is it going to help a cat get adopted? Save the environment? In today's connected world, a lot of nonprofits are used to our fathers being the donors. The

profile of the older donor, who looked at the organization as the brand—they wrote checks for twenty-five dollars every year and renewed year after year. The younger donors want to be a part of the organization, and they have more of a marketplace mentality. They are interested more in the cause of a specific organization.

There is a difference between fundraising and social media marketing. Just because a tweet is sent out or a post made to Facebook does not mean that money for a cause will come rolling in. The vital part of the equation is to use social media as a way to connect with the community, and then to get support from the people who believe in the cause.

Storytelling and Social Responsibility

When working on a social media campaign for a nonprofit, it's important to think about telling stories with every Facebook post and every tweet. Amanda Lehner, digital strategist and producer at HelpsGood, a marketing agency focused on social good, defines storytelling this way:

> When we say story, we look for people. How are they impacted by the issue? Survivor stories are really great testimonials . . . profiles on people. How has that nonprofit made an impact on somebody? . . . If I am trying to help someone get out of poverty, I want to try and tell the story of someone that was at poverty level or overcame it and is now thriving.

One example of a social-issues initiative is "One for One," in which the company Tom's Shoes will help a person in need for every pair of shoes or eyewear someone purchases. In addition, the company has a social media team that posts images and stories of people using their products, as well as a stories blog called "Inspiration" (http://www.toms.com/stories/category/inspiration/). One of the posts asked users to help raise awareness of visual impairment and global blindness on World Sight Day by wearing sunglasses indoors. Under the hashtag #BESHADY, "lomographers" (people who use toy or low-quality cameras to shoot stylized images) were asked to shoot inspirational photographs. "Throw on some shades indoors or show us what #BESHADY means to you," the campaign announced. Images submitted in the first two weeks of the contest were displayed in the flagship Tom's Shoes location in Venice, CA.

Lehner said that many nonprofits stick to formal messaging strategies on social media. Lehner said she likes to "fun it up" and make social media campaigns "human."

"If you were at a party and you were just rattling off your on-point messages the entire time, people would run from you. You have to be a well-rounded person on social, with many interests," said Lehner, who also runs the social media strategy for an environmental group. "When I write for them, I think about someone who is down-to-earth, loves nature, and is environmentally conscious."

Lehner said it is important to think about the personality of the brand, its mission and the community: "At a party you would want to be yourself, but also fit in. We look at a community, we see what they are like and match their tone and personality while staying true to the brand."

HelpsGood also works with the Ad Council, which we'll discuss in the next section, to be the voice of Smokey Bear on social media. In late June of 2013, when several hotshot firefighters were killed battling a wildfire in Arizona, people were calling on Smokey to mourn with them. "We had to be there and say things that were very timely and appropriate," Lehner related. "The community was very thankful. We shared an image of Smokey with his hat off and crying with forest animals surrounding him in Arizona. That image alone got over a million views on Smokey Bear's Facebook page."

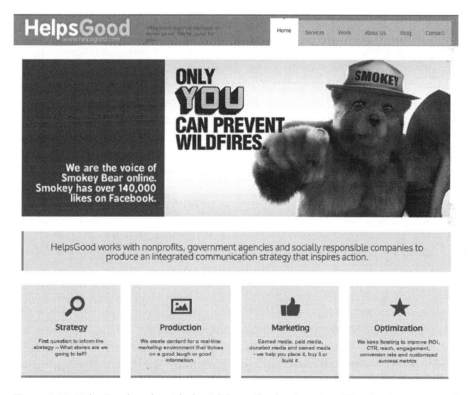

Figure 9.11 HelpsGood works with the Ad Council to be the voice of Smokey Bear on social media. (Screengrab courtesy of HelpsGood)

Exercise: Partner Messaging

Before they launch a campaign, social media agencies may do something called *partner messaging*. This is the practice of wrangling all of the influencers and partners they can, in order to make a big impact. The object is to get everybody to tweet and post the same thing on the same day.

1. Identify a popular cause, or choose one of the following:

    - Aging-related problems
    - At-risk youth
    - LGBT equality and support
    - Cancer prevention
    - Climate change

2. Search out the Twitter names of ten of the top influencers for your chosen cause.

3. Develop a set of social media messages that you feel are appropriate to be sent out to that specific community.

Advertising That Serves the Public Interest

Nonprofits and federal agencies have access to free public service announcements to help get their messages out. Until relatively recently, public service announcements were primarily television and print ads. In today's digital age, the Ad Council is using a multiplatform strategy to get their clients' messages out to the public.

Since 1947 the Ad Council has been working to provide assistance to various nonprofit groups. They take between five and ten requests per year out of the hundreds they receive, based on certain criteria. The campaign has to be based on the themes of education, family and community, or health and safety. In addition, each organization has to meet these requirements, as their website states (adcouncil.org):

- The issue should be of sufficient seriousness and public importance to warrant donations of space and time by the media.
- The issue must offer a solution through an individual action.
- The effort must be national in scope, so that the message has relevance to media audiences in communities throughout the nation.
- The effort should be such that advertising can help achieve its objectives and those objectives can be measured.
- The issue must be noncommercial, nondenominational, nonpartisan, and not be designated to influence legislation.

Advertising agencies work with the Ad Council on a pro bono basis, and the council works in a three-way partnership with the client and the advertising agency. "We get over $1.5 billion donated for time and space for Ad Council campaigns across the board annually," said Ellyn Fisher, vice president of public relations and social media for the council.

One component of the Ad Council's multiplatform strategy is bringing social media agencies into the process. "Social media provide an opportunity for us to have a daily dialogue and ongoing engagement with our target audience," said Fisher. Prior to digital and social, agencies would create campaigns and then push them to the media, but the response would be slower and more slowly reported. Now the Ad Council can make Facebook pages and Twitter accounts for their clients and have daily, sustainable inter-actions. The Smokey Bear campaign, for example, has over 175,000 people active and engaged in its Facebook presence.

In addition to social media campaigns, the Ad Council works to provide clients with video, also called public service announcements. This public service advertising is defined on the Ad Council website FAQ as "advertising that serves the public interest." The council is looking to raise public aware-ness of social issues in an effort to change attitudes and behavior, and to stimulate social change.

Much of the time, these PSAs provide opportunities for advertising agencies to stretch their wings. They get to be more creative than when working with large, well-known brands that are trying to cultivate a specific image. The videos produced are typically fifteen, thirty, or forty-five seconds in length, and are intended to be used as free ad spots on television. Many of these videos are also placed online, which offers the opportunity to take them a little further. "The beauty of online video and other social media strategies is that we can do something a lot more in-depth and longer," said Fisher. "It's exciting and incredibly gratifying in our [social media] group. We get to see the direct impact of the ads and the messages that we are putting out there." Since much of her work in social media is up-to-the-minute, she said:

> You can see the dialogue and see and hear the impact directly and immediately—how they are being touched, moved, and inspired by the campaign. . . . You can see on Facebook somebody saying, "Thank you so much for that men's health campaign; I actually made my dad go to the doctor and get a cholesterol test."
>
> There are all kinds of ways to tell stories, from websites and social media to print advertising, press releases, and videos in the form of public service announcements.

The history of PSAs dates back to World War II, when the War Advertising Council coined the saying, "Loose Lips Sink Ships." Many ads were made as a public service, warning Americans that if they revealed information about what was happening stateside, even in casual settings, that informa-tion could find its way to the ears of enemy spies and harm the war effort.

PSAs have since taken on many other forms and causes. They are the most common strategy used by nonprofits to tell their stories and help to build brand awareness. Long common on television and radio, they have now joined the migration to Internet sites like YouTube, thereby gaining the ability to be played repeatedly, saved, and shared, and to reach huge new audiences beyond those of legacy media.

Characteristics of a Public Service Announcement

- Must have a public service message
- Created to raise brand awareness
- Created by a nonprofit organization
- Goal of increasing contributions
- Goal of increasing awareness (What does the Red Cross do?)
- Goal of changing behavior (smoking, drunk driving, drug abuse)
- Created to increase exposure (radio, TV, web, movies)

Things to Think about before Launching a Public Service Campaign

1. Typically a PSA done as a television spot runs thirty seconds.
2. The message should rally around and reflect the nonprofit's vision statement.
3. It should do this by harnessing the power of storytelling.
4. Define your audience; make sure to target the people most likely to support your cause.
5. Think about a multiplatform approach, with video being the first goal and social media and other platforms supporting the video message. Remember that online, a video spot can have a virtually unlimited lifespan.
6. Think about how your PSA will play into your overall communications strategy, including multimedia press releases and the like.

Stories as a Call to Action

A story gives a special, animating force to a PSA. Anyone can put an actor or a list of bullet points in front of a camera to describe the importance of clean water, the dangers of using tobacco, the plight of mistreated animals, or the dangers of abusing drugs, but a story will do more. It will hook viewers and get them interested in something that is unfolding on their screen, even if they do not have the slightest idea what the purpose of the story is. They will continue to watch simply because their curiosity has been aroused, and they want to know what is going to happen.

A PSA by Charity Water (charitywater.org), a group whose stated goal is nothing less than "to bring clean and safe drinking water to every person in the world," begins with people in a modern, urban environment—beginning with a pretty mom and her children—carrying yellow plastic jugs. It's a mysterious sight. Immediately we want to know why, and where they are going. We keep watching. It turns out all these people are carrying their jugs to a city pond, and filling them there. The narrative question grows stronger: Why is this happening? Finally we see the young mother serving the cloudy, brown water to her children at the kitchen table, even as they sit in a clean, modern apartment with a laptop nearby. Then the message appears, delivering the twist and putting the whole story into context: "Imagine drinking this." No mere statement of facts could have such an engaging, literally gut-level impact. Because the viewer, by now, really is imagining "drinking this." The story has perfectly smoothed the way for the message, getting around the viewers' resistance by catching their interest, and has even slipped a memorable icon of the PSA campaign into the viewer's mind: the yellow plastic jug.

A 2007 spot from The Truth smoking-cessation campaign grabs the viewer with another odd urban sight: two cowboys riding along through big-city traffic. They dismount in the middle of the street, set up camp, and start singing a song with guitar accompaniment. The song is, "You Don't Always Die from Tobacco," and the cowboy vocalist is using an electronic larynx to sing. He removes it to reveal a surgical hole in his neck, standing the image of the rugged, cigarette-smoking Marlboro Man on its head. All the while a crowd has gathered to watch with increasing shock and horror, just as the viewers of the television spot are watching, pulled in by their curiosity about two cowpokes riding through traffic.

A final example shows that a PSA story doesn't need to be long. A viewer sees a hot frying pan, sizzling with oil. A voice-over says, "This is drugs." An egg is cracked and dropped into the pan with a loud sputtering, and immediately congeals into white bubbles. The voice reads, "This is your brain on drugs." End of story. An otherwise appetizing image is combined with startling sound and words to created a vivid image with a whole different context. It is an unexpected, fifteen-second allegorical story about drug abuse.

The power of these short stories—particularly the last two—has been proven by their effect on American culture. Most people have heard of them. They rose to prominence chiefly through television, but it isn't hard to see how perfectly they are suited—as quick-hit stories that elicit a strong viewer reaction—to being spread like wildfire through social media.

PSAs and Social Media

The nonprofit that wants to get people to believe in what the nonprofit does—ideally to the point of altering their own behavior and/or donating their hard-earned money—faces some steep challenges. This is an opportunity to reach an audience, but what does the nonprofit's product have to offer that audience?

A nonprofit can offer its PSA viewers and listeners the power to be a part of something, to help effect changes, to enlist others as ambassadors or influencers of change. What you as a PSA producer need to do is to persuade viewers to become convinced and passionate about a cause—passionate enough to work for your client unpaid or help build up their bank account. You need to make the audience loyal and personally involved.

This is where the power of social media like Facebook and Twitter really comes into its own. You are now able to reach people on a personal, essentially first-name basis, and to do so in a way that all their connections, in turn, will be able to see—also on a personal basis. As you start pushing messages, marketing your product or service or message, you can build on your fan base as they share your ideas and messages. Not only are you talking to the audience personally, but they are talking to you, and to each other in your presence. Even more excitingly, you will have instant feedback and metrics on your growing following as the "likes" pile up, the tweets are retweeted, the followers sign on, and videos and messages are shared. Your client can go from blindly putting out a message and hoping for the best to having an active conversation with a growing user base. Any public service campaign must now be multiplatform; to let the powers of social media go unused would be almost unthinkable.

It is still storytelling, however—connecting emotionally with your audience through both words and visuals—that starts the social media ball rolling.

YouTube Nonprofit Program

Nonprofits that use YouTube to spread their video messages can get access to special analytics programs that help track the spread and viewing of videos. They can also get access to specific functionality that allows a "call to action" overlay feature, allowing the poster to include a short headline, ad text, a destination URL, and to upload an optional image that will then be tracked. There are also fundraising tools. To start the program, YouTube launched a campaign for Charity Water (of the yellow-jug ad), also placing the campaign on the front page of the youtube.com website, and within one day of launch the site had helped raise $10,000 from users (Kincaid, 2013).

YouTube also has a function called Google Wallet, which allows donations to be made straight from the YouTube page that is playing the video.

 To Watch: http://www.youtube.com/nonprofits

YouTube Tips for Storytelling Success with Nonprofits

The following tips are taken from YouTube's "Playbook for Good."

Create a standard call to action video that conveys a clear message about your organization:

- Be concise and catchy, especially in the first few moments of the video.

- Acknowledge the audience and offer a clear call to action for support (share video, subscribe, get involved, spread the word, donate, etc.).
- Create conversation and dialogue about your work. Ask questions and solicit responses from viewers.
- Be sure to select the right person or subject to tell your story. Consider tapping a YouTube personality to be your spokesperson.

MEET THE PRO

Larry Swiader, Executive Director of Bedsider.org, Washington, D.C.

Larry Swiader spent his career studying the intersection of technology, media, and education, and how they can better people's lives. As senior director of digital media at the National Campaign to Prevent Teen and Unplanned Pregnancy, he leads the Bedsider program, an initiative that makes use of new media to change the reproductive health behaviors of young adults in the United States. For ten years before that, he used technology as a

Figure 9.12 Larry Swiader, executive director of bedsider.org, Washington, DC. (Photo courtesy of Larry Swiader)

tool to teach about the history of the Holocaust and to motivate people to act to end contemporary genocide. In his second home of Athens, Greece, he has consulted on various projects for clients including the Athens Metro and museums of Greek history.

"We want to be to birth control what Google is to search," says Larry Swiader of his role in bedsider.org, a campaign to prevent teen and unplanned pregnancy. At Bedsider, Swiader had the opportunity to build both the brand and the website from scratch. It's not enough trying to figure out what the structure of the organization's website should be. A big part of the process is developing a content strategy.

Bedsider was formed after the National Campaign to Prevent Teen and Unplanned Pregnancy did research into why people ages eighteen to twenty-nine were not using birth control correctly. He was tasked not just with building a website around this mission, but also with developing a content strategy for it. The goal of the organization is to reduce unplanned pregnancy by 20 percent by the year 2020.

"Bedsider is not a website that people are going to visit every day of the week," Swiader says. "People don't need that much information about birth control. They need it when they need it, yet it is important for our brand to keep it in front of them."

One way of doing this is through social media; the organization uses Instagram to push its messages visually, sometimes taking content directly

(Continued . . .)

(. . . *continued*)

from the site and distributing it on Instagram. "We thought with our own photography and visual design we could do well by taking really great pictures and giving them away," said Swiader, who has an art director and team that have a hand in creating content. "We share our photography all of the time; we know that has become an important part of getting the word out."

When deciding what the website would be about and what content to cover, Swiader did a lot of research, including interviewing members of the target audience—people eighteen and older.

"Because women are in charge of most of the methods of birth control, we spoke with a lot of women," he said. Swiader concentrated on a human-centered design process, testing website users and what they understood and knew about the topic. The process was geared toward fully understanding users' needs and desires, not just those of the organization. "We interviewed people at the extremes of behavior in their own settings," he recounted. "We went into their homes and asked them how they protected themselves when they had sex—what forms of birth control they used." Swiader said interviewees would get up from the interview and proceed to their bedsides and physically show what they used.

Swiader wanted to make sure that the brand related to the users themselves: "We don't use the word 'contraceptives'; we use 'birth control' when we talk to them. We don't talk to them the way doctors talk to them."

A big part of Bedsider's content strategy is real stories from real people as video testimonials. The videos feature the target audience talking about their own use of birth control. To find these people, the organization used the online classified ad site Craigslist. Swiader explained the reasons for this approach:

> We know that one of the barriers has to do with self-efficacy. Seeing one of your peers talk about their experience and getting their feedback is critical to your own experience to get the method that is right for you. . . . We have found that once you get people starting to talk about this issue, if they feel like they are in a safe place, they'll go anywhere. . . . That tells us something.

The site was then built with a complete brand-building strategy. "We came up with a color palette and have a complete brand book," Swiader said. "It is my job, as guardian of the brand, to articulate what the brand is trying to achieve and then let my partners achieve it."

Something else that Bedsider does is partner with the Ad Council to make public service announcements that can be used on television. "For a lot of people this is still a taboo topic, but it hasn't been all that difficult," Swiader said.

"Ninety-nine percent of the women in the United States have used birth control some time in their life. It's not controversial—everybody uses it—we just need to give the majority some voice," Swiader said.

Figure 9.13 Bedsider.org is a website devoted to preventing teen and unplanned pregnancy. (Screenshots courtesy of Bedsider.org)

Before the Story Comes the Goal

Advertising is everywhere, from product placement in movies to television, billboards, the web, print ads, restaurant menus, and even racing cars. Everything from large corporations to mom-and-pop stores advertise products and services that they need to sell to turn a profit. Whether you are marketing a bar of soap or a movie, a news outlet or a point of view, the whole idea is to get people to buy it, watch it, read it, or adopt it. This takes persuasive communication, of which stories are a very effective form. But first it takes a clear understanding of just exactly what your product is.

In the realm of public service announcements, knowing the product leads naturally to being able to say something specific about it that is noticeable and memorable. These days, this means achieving the priceless, almost magical potential for being enthusiastically shared on the web and through social media.

In other words, before producing a PSA there needs to be a vision and a mission. Much like developing a logline for a film, you need to design a vision statement and a tagline that will define the campaign. A vision state-ment should include the desired end result of the campaign. A tagline, on the other hand, is a public face for a campaign. It can be funny, or serious, or wise, or surprising (and ideally all of these things), but its chief duty is to deliver a short brand message that resonates with an audience. Note though that there is a difference between a slogan and a tagline. In the book *Integrated Marketing Communication*, author Robyn Blakeman explains, "A slogan deals with the company or corporate philosophy, and a tagline defines the campaign or ad philosophy" (56).

Developing a Tagline

For any writer—whether a journalist, a screenwriter, an advertising copy-writer, or even a college student—the hardest thing is getting started. This roadblock goes away with the realization that good ideas are needed for good writing, and that you need to spend time staring at the wall and gen-erating those ideas before starting the actual writing of the prose. Generating ideas takes effort, though—a lot of effort.

"Stop trying to be 'creative' and focus on being interesting to the target audience, which is a very different assignment," said Kevin O'Neill, who in the early 1990s coined the tagline for Hanes underwear: "Just Wait'll We Get Our Hanes on You."

When collaborating as part of a team, just brainstorming can be a difficult process. Sometimes that's because people start out overthinking a process or an idea. "It's a progressive process of working through things, identifying things that had a kind of glint to them—that interest you—then developing them and building on those," O'Neill said.

Kevin O'Neill's Tips for Generating Taglines

- Start by getting it straight: Just write in plain, boring English what the brand's benefit is.
- Don't get fancy, don't get creative; just write it with nouns and verbs.
- Put that on a table in front of you, so you know exactly what the com-munication objective is.
- Feel free to use a simple free-association technique: Ask yourself eve-rything you know about the advertising problem in front of you and write it all down. For example, if faced with the task of writing about recycling water bottles, write down absolutely everything you know about bottled water: thirst, users, occasions of use, water sources, plastic—everything.
- Take those images, words, and phrases and find the ones that feel the "richest" and separate them from the rest.
- Using the ones you picked, repeat the process, whittling down to the ideas that work best.

Examples of Vision Statements

The following are taken from "30 Example Vision Statements" on the website topnonprofits.com. The website also mentions some things to notice about this list:

- The best vision statements are inspirational, clear, memorable, and concise.
- The average statement length for all organizations on the list is 14.56 words (excluding brand references).

1. Oxfam: A just world without poverty
2. Feeding America: A hunger-free America
3. Human Rights Campaign: Equality for everyone
4. National Multiple Sclerosis Society: A World Free of MS
5. Alzheimer's Association: Our vision is a world without Alzheimer's
6. Habitat for Humanity: A world where everyone has a decent place to live
7. Oceana seeks to make our oceans as rich, healthy and abundant as they once were
8. Make-A-Wish: Our vision is that people everywhere will share the power of a wish
9. San Diego Zoo: To become a world leader at connecting people to wildlife and conservation
10. The Nature Conservancy: Our vision is to leave a sustainable world for future generations

Examples of Taglines

Eric Swartz, on his website Taglineguru.com, uses the following criteria to compile his list of the 100 Most Influential U.S. Taglines Since 1948:

- **Longevity:** Have they endured the test of time?
- **Equity:** Have they become synonymous with a company or product?
- **Portability and Memorability:** Have they exercised an influence on our culture, media, and language?
- **Originality:** Have they broken new ground in the advertising industry?

And here is the very top of Swartz's list:

1. Got milk? (1993) California Milk Processor Board
2. Don't leave home without it. (1975) American Express
3. Just do it. (1988) Nike
4. Where's the beef? (1984) Wendy's
5. You're in good hands with Allstate. (1956) Allstate Insurance

6.   Think different. (1998) Apple Computer
7.   We try harder. (1962) Avis
8.   Tastes great, less filling. (1974) Miller Lite
9.   Melts in your mouth, not in your hands. (1954) M&M Candies
10. Takes a licking and keeps on ticking. (1956) Timex

The Agency Process

The idea for a commercial or PSA starts at the advertising agency level, where ideas are hatched and then pitched to the client. If the ideas are approved by the client, the art director for the account then reaches out to, say, three production companies that have the capability and skill set to produce the idea that the client approved. The art director would seek out directors at these companies whose capabilities they know, or whose portfolios they have seen and been impressed by. The agency will have already created its own initial storyboards of the project, sometimes done as drawings or a collage of ideas.

"The personality of the director must jive with the client and . . . the brand storytelling," said Hillary Cutter, who owns and runs a New York City–based production company called Cutter Productions, specializing in commercial productions. "The skills must match the goals of the brand that they are launching. The hard part is getting the invitation to bid, and then, obviously, landing the job. It's extremely competitive," she said.

Cutter explained the process of shaping an idea:

> The agency, their training is in advertising, not in film production. They sometimes come up with ideas that are not executable from a production standpoint. Sometimes we rewrite the scripts for them or rework the idea so that it can become a real mini-movie, not just a big idea on paper that is just impossible to execute.

So while scripts are usually written within the advertising agency itself, it is the job of the production company to execute the script and make it come to life in video as a commercial or PSA.

Cutter said that advertising agencies call on her production company specifically for the directors themselves—they call on individual directors to come up with specific treatments. Essentially she has her staff submit estimated costs and a director's treatment as part of their bid package. "My production team's job in the bid process is to write an itemized budget proposal," she explained. The agency then picks the vendor/production company it likes best and that seems to have the most to offer. "Usually it is a triple-bid scenario," said Cutter. "A client invites several companies to have a conversation about a project. When an agency invites a company to bid, they give all three bidders a spec sheet so the bids are evenly competitive," she recounted, adding that "making a bid for a job feels like the NCAA basketball tournament."

Director's Treatment

When directors shoot a television commercial or PSA, they take their story-telling skills and ideas for filmmaking and translate them into the advertising world. It is the director who steers the transformation of the project into filmed reality, and the specific plan for this is known as a *director's treatment*. Whether it is for a thirty-second television commercial or PSA, or a longer pre-roll advertisement that will play immediately before a video that a web user has selected, a director's treatment is similar to a *writer's treatment* (see Chapter 7). Like a writer's treatment a director's treatment is a sales presentation, only it pitches the director's ideas for how a spot will be realized on film with music, actors, cinematography, and effects—in short, how the piece will be shot. It is the director's vision, populated with many technical details about location, soundtrack, lighting, and wardrobe, among other things.

A director's treatment can take many different forms: a written document, or a series of still photos in printed or .pdf form. Chandler Kauffman is a director for Cutter Productions, and he writes treatments that are paired with visuals and designed in page layout software. Kauffman said that he will often use images from other shoots or images taken on his own to illustrate his treatments. "The words are sort of a stand-in for sound, in a way, and the pictures are a stand-in for the visuals," said Kauffman:

> It is almost like a love letter to these people, in the most cynical way. I can describe it that way because you are trying to win them over, and you also need to make them feel good about the idea they have.

Kauffman explained that after an initial conference call with a representative from the advertising agency—"usually with the agency producer and the key creatives on the concept," he said—he will work with the ideas that were presented and formally draw up a treatment that can hopefully win the bid. He said the treatment acts "like an essay on what you would do in this project—what you would do to extrapolate on their idea and make it better, throw in original ideas, and give them a sense of your creative vision of it." It is a delicate game he needs to play with the agency, he explained, because if his idea is too far off he may not be awarded the job. If he is too vague, the agency may have nothing to get its teeth into and move on. The director wants to get the job, naturally, so he or she will strive to come across as clearly and compellingly as possible.

One thing the treatment should make sure to address is storytelling. As before, and as always, this will need to be a story with a beginning, a middle, and an end. It may be tough to impose the time-tested three-act structure described in Chapter 2 on a video that will last a mere thirty seconds, the common length for television commercials and PSAs. But it can be done—and it has been done for decades.

"You want to generate something in there—maybe not a full-on conflict—to intrigue people," Kauffman said:

It's a different kind of structure. In a lot of ways it's more along the ways of a scene in a film or TV show. . . . There is usually a resolution in a commercial. Usually it is "Buy this thing." It's a question and an answer.

Try not to think of a treatment as a chore or an assignment. Think of it as a well-articulated plan for what will happen on the shoot. This will help to solidify exactly what will be in the commercial in advance, so that during actual shooting there will be time for other important things, like working with actors.

What Does a Treatment Consist Of?

1. **Title page**
   Make sure to include the client's name and the name of the production company. Remember that in the real world the client will be looking at several of these proposals. You do not want yours to get lost in the shuffle.

2. **Concept**
   Write a few paragraphs on what you plan to do for the brand. Make sure to explain how your vision meshes with what they are trying to achieve. Make it lively, confident, and conversational. Other proposals are waiting, and yours needs to push all others to the background. It is time to grab the spotlight. You have formulated a good angle, and this is the time to sell it, not just to the agency, but to every member of the spot's ultimate audience. You might even try speaking directly to that hypothetical audience.

3. **The visual story**
   This is the verbiage that explains in detail what you plan to do with the commercial. Walk the client through the whole thing, from shot to shot. It can be done visually, using pictures or video that you have downloaded or created yourself. This is your opportunity to show your visual capabilities, and that you are fully ready and able to turn your concept into a viewable product. The client should feel as if the piece has already been created, and that they are free to assess and respond to it: "We start out the commercial with a wide shot of the store. We cut to a medium shot of the owner and a customer, then a dolly shot moves through the store . . . " and so on. By the time the client is getting curious about the technical and casting needs to shoot, you are waiting with them, having anticipated everything the client will ask about and need.

4. **Notes**
   Any agency will have its own ideas about how a commercial or PSA should be executed. The agency will not have the expertise or hands-on experience that you may have as director—that's the reason you got hired—so this is where you carefully and constructively explain

what you have cut from their plans and why, and what could be done in its place. Remember that the client wants a well-executed commercial, but they signed off on an idea as presented by the advertising agency. Depending on the circumstances, it might well be you and the skills you bring to the table that make everything successful.

After a director's treatment gets a green light, the director's vision can start to be brought to life. For Kauffman, this means making a shot list and then going out on location with his director of photography to shoot stills, with models standing in for actors, and setting up the planned shots and angles in the real world. These photographs will then act as a storyboard according to which the commercial will be shot. "It at least provides a road map, and

Figure 9.14 An example of a director's treatment for a television commercial. (Photos by Sam Dean)

other times you shoot exactly what you did in your boards," said Kauffman. In any case, you need to be ready for changes, he added:

> Things always change on set to some extent due to any number of factors, including the usual controlled chaos of production, the cast, changes to the creative since we scouted, the agency/client changing things on set, etc. The key is to roll with the punches and balance the original intent with the changing variables.

Exercise: Director's Treatment

Develop a director's treatment for a television commercial that will sell a local media outlet, either a newspaper or a television station. Make sure you describe the technical details of how you will bring the story to life on video or film. Include as many details as you can about how the film will look, sound, and feel.

Feel free to use Creative Commons images from the Internet to help describe what you plan to do for the client.

Think about what the media outlet has to offer its viewers, from multiplatform capabilities to news that cannot be found elsewhere.

A good way to create the treatment—which also should be able to serve as a bid presentation—is to make slides in a program like Apple Keynote or Microsoft PowerPoint. If you make the treatment a visual presentation, you might be able to get your message across more compellingly and completely.

Genres and Story Types of Commercials and PSAs

Persuasive video spots, whether they are commercials or PSAs, come in several different types and structures. Whether the objective is selling a product or raising awareness and inspiring action, there are tried-and-true storytelling options to follow, combine, mimic, and generally adapt to your concept.

Comedy

Good comedy is a tough thing to pull off, but when it works its power is enormous. Everyone loves to laugh, and since making people laugh bestows a unique kind of power, people have always loved *sharing* the things that make them laugh with others. Hence the power of the joke, which predated electronic social media considerably. Now that the age of social media is here, this power to share has increased a thousandfold. It is the jokes and funny videos and pictures that get sent around more than anything else.

Comedy always involves a story, and there is always a punch line or a big twist. Take the commercial for the 2012 Volkswagen Passat. It features a little boy dressed in a Darth Vader costume, going around the house and trying (unsuccessfully) to use "The Force" on everything from the washing machine and dryer to his sister's dolls. So we have a main character, instantly in the dramatic situation of having an intense desire that can never be realized. But then his dad comes home, in his wisely chosen Volkswagen Passat. The boy goes outside to the car and takes a shot at using The Force on it. Little does he know that his father, watching from inside the house, is holding the remote starter and is about to throw the big twist into the story. The car starts up! The boy stands there amazed in his oversized Vader costume, and the viewer is left laughing at the boy's amazement, the father's cleverness, and the way this automobile has fit so perfectly into family life.

 To Watch: http://bit.ly/1EwmKZO

Real People

This more serious form of commercial presents people in the real world, giving the audience a chance to meet someone new who is involved with something that they care about, and to whom they can become emotionally connected. This kind of spot is all about authenticity and credibility. This is no comic character or smooth-talking salesman; it's just a normal person, telling what she knows, what happened to her, or what she can do. "Real" people working for real companies tell how they can help you the same as they helped someone else. Imagine a commercial for a community college, in which students carrying books and backpacks stop to talk to the camera about what they are studying, and how soon they will be taking their skills into a new job. Another example is a commercial for Deloitte called "Real People Real Results," which shows certified public accountants who helped companies save money or turn their business around.

 To Watch: http://bit.ly/1Ewne21

Presentation

This tends to be a news-oriented format, in which important facts are reported to the viewer. It is often a "stand-up," with a reporter-like person standing in front of a business or activity, "reporting" the script. The viewer knows it isn't the news but is so strongly conditioned to listen to the words of on-the-scene reporters that the message still gets through. Sometimes the "reporter" is merely a well-put-together person, such as a serious, attractive woman walking down the hall of a hospital, talking about a new drug. This format does well when you don't have much else to work with, or what is being pitched is a service or a store at a particular location.

For example, a commercial for William Mattar, a lawyer in Syracuse, NY, features, attractive, well-dressed people repeating a slogan: "Hurt in a Car, Call William Mattar," against a slide show of wrecked automobiles and urgent, newscast-sounding music. He even has a catchy phone number: 444-4444. Another example is the excited car salesman who is trying to get you down to the lot to buy a car. An example of this, also in Syracuse, NY, is Billy Fuccillo Sr. of Fucillo Nissan. Fucillo's slogan is "It's Huge," with "huge" spoken as two syllables.

To Watch "Hurt in a Car": http://bit.ly/hurtinacar
To Watch "It's Huge": http://bit.ly/itshugeusedcars

Slice of Life

This genre shows normal people doing normal things, giving viewers "real" situations and everyday moments they can relate to. One example of this is a commercial for Tide laundry detergent, in which a grandmother talks about her grandson's sensitive skin and how she uses the detergent on his blanket. This is while we are being shown scenes of the grandson dragging his "blanky" along the ground and pouring an ice cream sundae onto it, a gentle suggestion that this is a piece of laundry that needs to get washed a lot.

To Watch: http://bit.ly/1EwnJJu

Testimonial

This is a form in which someone relates his or her experience with a certain product or service, vouching for it and convincing us that it would be good for us as well. The more famous that someone is, either locally or nationally, the better.

In small-market cities where a college football or basketball coach is considered a "star," he or she can be seen on television speaking for everything from charities to backyard landscapers. In Southwest Virginia, Virginia Tech football coach Frank Beamer recommends gutter guards, a certain convenience store with good coffee, and other businesses. In Syracuse, NY, head basketball coach Jim Boeheim urges the audience to

> Do me a favor and stop by Landmasters Showroom . . . and check out their selection of home and landscape products. Their service is as good as their products, and I should know—I have a Landmasters deck and landscape at my house.

The commercial shows Boeheim in front of a stone wall, then shifts to a montage of different landscapes the company has built.

 To Watch: http://bit.ly/1tJFLSk

Choddy

This is a specific type of public service announcement that cuts in and out of interviews with different people. Sometimes the characters finish each other's sentences. Often each character will read the same script in its entirety, and the takes will be cut up and mixed together so that the "characters" change while the message comes through intact.

This technique was made famous after the election of President Barack Obama, when several famous sports figures, actors, and musicians, including Will.i.am, got together to make a commercial congratulating him. Called "Yes We Can," the piece consists of different people reciting portions of one of Obama's speeches during the 2008 presidential campaign. The YouTube version has well over 24 million views. *Choddy*, which is not an industry-wide term or something that can be found in the dictionary, was coined by the advertising agency Door Number 3 to try to put the brakes on the use of this style. The website http://stopthechoddy.org collects choddys submitted by users, along with offering a spoof that picks apart the technique.

 To Watch the Obama choddy: http://bit.ly/obamachoddy

Motion Graphic

Motion graphics are often used online to sell products or services. They can be made in a variety of graphics programs, such as Adobe After Effects, Apple Motion, or any number of 3D animation packages, or done in media that appear more traditional, such as sketches, paint, or stop-motion animation. These pieces often have voice-over and grab viewers with their interesting styles, colors, animation, and imagery. One example is a video that won the 2011 DoGooder Award at the Nonprofit Video Awards, which are presented by YouTube. Produced by the Post Carbon Institute (http://www.postcarbon.org/), it features a real human hand illustrating the history of fossil-fuel use, leading up to a modern-day predicament. The video is called *300 Years of FOSSIL FUELS in 300 Seconds.*

 To Watch: http://bit.ly/1sG5L1v

Demonstration

This genre shows the viewer a person demonstrating a product, service, or process. It could be someone pushing around a vacuum, a pickup truck hauling rocks or pulling train cars, or the all-too-familiar kitchen utensil ads for various knives or chopping gadgets. Seeing something in action can be a powerful motivator to acquire one for yourself. A video for the As Seen On TV device called the Slap Chop shows the device being used to easily dice, chop, and mince everything from vegetables and fruits to hard-boiled eggs. The announcer, Vince, tells viewers that they will be "in a great mood all day because they will be slapping their troubles away."

 To Watch: http://bit.ly/1GQV45Q

Audio Slide Show

In this form, a product or idea is described through still photographs shot specifically for the advertisement or through already-existing images. An example could be the commercial "God Made a Farmer," first shown during the 2013 Super Bowl. It is a collection of still images of farmers, with the ultimate goal of selling Dodge trucks, although the advertisement was also part of a campaign to raise funds for Future Farmers of America. For every view on its website, Chrysler would donate one dollar, up to one million views. At this book's time of writing, the views are approaching seventeen million.

 To Watch: http://bit.ly/1xPgA4R

Visuals First

This style depends on visuals to tell the story. Another Chrysler commercial depends on urban street scenes to paint a portrait of a town that built cars: Detroit, also called "the Motor City." The commercial includes snippets that show the hard-working city and its inhabitants. Toward the end of the commercial, a beat by rap star and Detroit native Eminem ramps up as a car is revealed. At the end, the viewer is surprised to see Eminem himself get out of the car and walk into a theater.

 To Watch: http://bit.ly/1xPgGtk

Music First

This kind of advertisement is based on the music. "Have Yourself a Merry Little Christmas," played by Cat Power, is the piece of music that defines a 2013 ad for Apple iOS devices. The advertisement pushes heavily toward capturing intimate family moments with your phone. As the understated music plays, a boy appears to be preoccupied with his phone during a holiday family get-together. He seems isolated and even appears to be getting scolded for his behavior, but at the end he is revealed to have been putting together a short movie of his family and relatives, of funny and touching moments, which he shows them on Christmas morning. The music is the binder that holds the scenes together.

 To Watch: http://bit.ly/1116Qd5

MEET THE PRO

Jason Wertheimer, Director of Interactive Production at DDB, San Francisco Bay Area, CA

Jason Wertheimer is director of interactive production at DDB California, a full-service advertising agency. He has over fifteen years of experience developing interactive and cross-channel marketing programs. He has worked with clients including Clorox, Chevron, Citrix, General Motors, Procter & Gamble, Kraft, Disney, Allstate, Pfizer, Qualcomm, Google, Stubhub, Birdseye Foods, Dell, and Blue Shield of California. He specializes in translating creative ideas into initiatives that engage with consumers across all media. Although he is a producer at his core, Wertheimer's role spans many disciplines, including user experience, creative media integration, interactive production, digital marketing strategy, analytics, concept development, design, and technology. He earned a bachelor's degree from the University of Pennsylvania, and he currently lives in San Francisco. When not working in advertising, he is a glassblower, photographer, and cyclist.

Figure 9.15 Jason Wertheimer, director of interactive production at DDB. (Photo by Michael Winokur)

"Things are definitely blurred; all of the ad agencies right now are repositioning. The agency is really summed up in the phrase 'twenty-first century storytelling'—storytelling through brands," said Jason Wertheimer. As an example of this process he told the story of DDB's successful multiplatform campaign for Fresh Step cat litter:

> At DDB, we were challenged with developing a "seeding" campaign for Fresh Step cat litter for our client, Clorox, to launch ahead of the TV ads that would strengthen the effectiveness of our TV ads once they did launch. Any great brand story starts with an insight and an idea about how to engage our target audience with this insight. In the case of Fresh Step, we needed to develop a story around a product that, in most cases, people don't want to think much about at all: kitty litter.
>
> Instead of just telling people why our product was better, we began by understanding the relationship between an owner and their cat. People care more about their cats than they do their cat's litter. What we found is that owners are captivated by the intelligence of their furry friends.
>
> Our concept for the campaign was based on the idea that smart cats deserve a smart litter, and Fresh Step is the smart litter that your smart cat deserves. . . . Everybody loves to think their cat is smart. . . . But it takes more than just a brand insight to tell a twenty-first-century story. We needed to understand how to best connect our creative with our target consumer.

(Continued . . .)

(*. . . continued*)

The whole zeitgeist around cats on the Internet is obviously tre-mendous, which gave us a terrific venue for this positioning. We did some research, and met with some folks from Tumblr, a popular blog-ging service that had recently been acquired by Yahoo! We found that 67 percent of Tumblr users own at least one pet, and that Tumblr reaches over 17.2 million pet owners, comprising over 2.4 million daily unique users.

We created a Tumblr blog called "The Smartest Cats in the Universe." The blog for the brand belongs to a fictitious person named "Dan," who has unusually smart cats who use DJ turntables and ride remote-controlled cars when "Dan" is not home. DDB also created picture memes and animated gifs and posted them on the Tumblr blog, all of which helped to promote the "smart" kitty litter. [This is] positioning.

The Tumblr blog is a great example of where it is much more about the story you are telling than it is about the production value per se . . . assets are easily made in Photoshop or a meme-maker online. It costs very little to make those, other than licensing the images—it's relatively easy to create that content. . . .

A blog alone does not, however, constitute a twenty-first-century brand story. A true brand story is cross-channel, so our approach was to leverage the best that each medium has to offer. The Tumblr blog launched first, followed by social seeding of video content and paid Tumblr promotion of our blog, and, finally, the launch of online display advertising and our paid TV spots.

Additionally, a twenty-first-century brand story is not just a one-way conversation. The Tumblr blog encouraged consumers to submit their own "smart cat" content and truly participate in this conversation. Some of these submissions were republished back to the blog, thus enabling our consumers to actually become the voice of the brand, which con-tributed to the authenticity of the effort.

Our unbranded "seeding" video has over 200,000 views [http://bit.ly/1xPgVEJ], most of which were accumulated before the TV spot even launched. One thirty-second television commercial now has over 448,000 views on YouTube [http://bit.ly/1116Yt4], and the other over 424,000 [http://bit.ly/1xzADGf]. The Fresh Step website says, "See what smart cats are doing when you're not looking. Our cat DJs here know how to scratch on the decks in Fresh Step's latest commercial. That's why smart cats also want to use smart cat litter to do their business."

The purpose of the seeding efforts for the campaign was to get people to go to the Tumblr site and become involved with the brand in a fun way, forming a connection among smart cats, smart litter, and Internet culture. They would then be much more inclined to purchase Fresh Step litter for their own cat at home.

Chapter Summary

Technology has changed the way consumers behave and interact with brands, from Nissan to Greenpeace to wire services such as PR Newswire. The news media are being pushed aside by companies and nonprofits that are looking to make their own news and push their own brands digitally. New forms of storytelling continue to gain traction.

Websites are now the faces of corporations, and social media are now the connector to the audience. The way that messages are being disseminated through social media has changed both public relations and advertising. Brands are now seeing the possibilities that come with being their own media outlets and pushing out their own messages, rather than constantly trying to tap into the news media's influence on consumers, with varying degrees of success.

The messaging streams for paid and unpaid content have led to the integration of advertising and public relations. It is now almost unheard-of for a company not to have a presence on the Internet. Nonprofits now use social media to seek out volunteers and donors, and to attract and interact with new audiences.

Video now serves as a form of communication outside the television platform as well as inside it. New platforms such as YouTube are major players in this realm. Not only can a public service announcement be produced for airing on television, it can now also be deployed on nonprofit websites and shared through social media, adding enormously to any group's ability to get its messages seen and heard.

In order to reach and connect with consumers on a granular level, groups and companies must increasingly embrace visual storytelling. Through video, photographs, and well-designed websites, multimedia storytelling continues to occupy a larger and larger place in society and culture.

 Review Questions

1. Name some elements of the press release of the future. What multimedia forms and elements can be used to grab the attention of an audience on multiple platforms?
2. What is one way to track how well an advertising campaign has taken hold with consumers?
3. In what ways do the goals of strategic communications differ from those of entertainment and journalism?
4. Give some examples of digital content strategy. What are some new and innovative ways to build an audience on a digital platform?
5. What is a nonprofit organization, and what are some ways that nonprofits utilize advertising to get their messages out?
6. What should be included in a director's treatment for a television advertisement?

7. Name a video commercial story type and provide an example of it that is viewable on YouTube.

Exercise: Build a Digital Strategic Campaign

For the following exercises, use one of the following fictitious groups as your client:

1. Waste Not Want Not
2. No More Bottled Water
3. Diverse Community International
4. Let's Go Hunting
5. Support Local Business
6. Teens for Personal Responsibility

Assume a nonprofit company has hired your team to create a campaign of public service announcements that will persuade people to change their behavior. Your team will agree on a campaign concept that will produce a thirty-second video showcasing the client's mission.

1. Develop a mission statement and a tagline for the nonprofit.
2. Develop a director's treatment that outlines a PSA video and that includes a storyboard.
3. Develop a digital media content strategy for your client that includes a social media campaign to promote your film and the organization. Formulate possible tweets and Facebook posts that could mobilize people for your cause.
4. Draw a wireframe for a digital application or website that will display the video, and that has the capability of developing an online audience for the client.

Key Terms

Analytics – The practice of tracking users' visits to websites and their interactions on social media.

Ad Council – A nonprofit organization that produces, distributes, and promotes public service announcements on behalf of various sponsors.

Advertising – The creation of persuasive content aimed at compelling consumers to purchase a product or service.

Brand – A specific identity, which can include a logo, design, idea, and description, that separates one product from another.

Digital content strategy – Planning and development of content specific to a digital platform.

Director's treatment – Pitches the director's ideas for how a story will be realized on film with music, actors, cinematography, and effects—in short, how the film will be shot.

Infographic – A picture that illustrates trends and patterns of data to explore and explain it.

Koto-zukuri – Japanese phrase coined by Nissan chief operating officer Toshiyuki Shiga, to mean "making brand stories."

Legacy media – Media operations, such as broadcast, newspapers, and radio, that existed before the advent of the Internet.

Mood board – A collection of images, textures, colors, and typography that establishes the style and "feel" for a graphic project.

Multimedia press release – A package of information that is heavy on video, images, audio, and downloadable content, which supplants the plain text press release.

Nonprofit – An organization in which no owner benefits financially from how the organization does financially.

Public relations – Distribution and management of information for a company, cause, or other group.

Public service announcement (PSA) – A "commercial" that does not sell a product but rather promotes a cause or calls for action.

Social media – Internet-based digital messaging or networking platforms that connect users.

Tagline – A short, catchy statement that delivers a brand message that will resonate with an audience.

Vision statement – A declaration of an organization's purpose and means for achieving it.

Sources

Ad Council. "Frequently Asked Questions." Accessed September 25, 2013. http://www.adcouncil.org/About-Us/Frequently-Asked-Questions#What%E2%80%99s%20the history of the Ad Council?

Adams, Jay. Conversation with author, September 19, 2013.

Anger, Scott. Conversation with author, April 20, 2011.

Blakeman, Robyn. *Integrated Marketing Communication: Creative Strategy from Idea to Implementation*. Lanham, MD: Rowman & Littlefield, 2007.

Cutter, Hillary. Conversation with author, August 22, 2013.

Fisher, Ellyn. Conversation with author, September 20, 2013.

Frohne, Lauren. Conversation with author, September 5, 2013.

Jackson, John. Conversation with author, September 12, 2013.

Kanter, Beth. Conversation with author, August 28, 2013.

Kauffman, Chandler. Conversation with author, December 3, 2013.

Kincaid, Jason. "Special YouTube Ads Earn Nonprofit $10,000 In A Single Day." *TechCrunch*. Accessed December 27, 2013. http://techcrunch.com/2009/03/27/special-youtube-ads-earn-nonprofit-10000-in-a-single-day/.

Legon, Jeordan. Conversation with author, August 28, 2013.

Lehner, Amanda. Conversation with author, September 26, 2013.

Mason, Tom. Conversation with author, September 13, 2013.

Meyers, Bob. Conversation with author, September 6, 2013.

Murphy, Julie. Conversation with author, September 5, 2013.

O'Neill, Kevin. Conversation with author, December 28, 2013.

Open Society Foundation. "Stop Torture in Health Care Trailer." With explanatory text. Accessed March 15, 2015. http://www.opensocietyfoundations.org/videos/stop-torture-health-care-trailer.

Pantoja, Salvador. Conversation with author, September 5, 2013.

Pekar, Thaler. Conversation with author, September 13, 2013.

Pickard, Bob. Conversation with author, September 11, 2013.

Pickard, Bob. "The Rise of the Digital Storyteller." Accessed August 26, 2013. http://bobpickard.com/the-rise-of-the-digital-storyteller/.

PR Newswire. "Multimedia Content Drives Nearly 10 Times More Visibility than Text." PR Newswire Study. Accessed November 16, 2012. http://www.multivu.com/players/English/59124-pr-newswire-visual-pr/.

Rock, Tracy. Conversation with author, September 8, 2013.

Sacha, Bob. Conversation with author, April 23, 2011.

Saji, Ken. Conversation with author, September 18, 2013.

Skerik, Sarah. Conversation with author, September 30, 2013.

Skerik, Sarah. "Multimedia Content Drives Better Press Release Results." *Beyond PR*. Accessed October 10, 2012. http://blog.prnewswire.com/2011/05/02/multimedia-content-drives-better-press-release-results/.

Sloan, Dan. Conversation with author, September 3, 2013.

Swartz, Eric. "The 100 Most Influential U.S. Taglines Since 1948." Slogan and Jingle Survey. TaglineGuru.com. Accessed March 15, 2015. http://www.taglineguru.com/survey05.html.

Swiader, Larry. Conversation with author, September 10, 2013.

Thompson, Melissa. Conversation with author, September 24, 2013.

Toms.com. "TOMS Stories: Inspiration." Accessed February 8, 2014. http://www.toms.com/stories/category/inspiration/.

Top Nonprofits. "30 Example Vision Statements." Accessed October 10, 2012. http://topnonprofits.com/examples/vision-statements/.

Wertheimer, Jason. Conversation with author, December 30, 2013.

Winchester, Bill. Conversation with author, September 6, 2013.

YouTube. "YouTube: Playbook for Good." Accessed December 27, 2013. http://www.youtube.com/nonprofits.

INDEX

Made in the USA
Middletown, DE
29 December 2021

57274119R00239